D1824159

Intersections

Intersections:
Applied Linguistics as a Meeting Place

Edited by

Elke Stracke

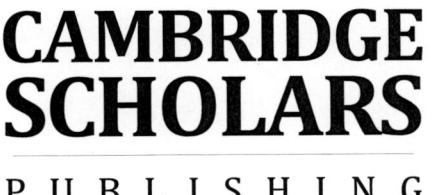

CAMBRIDGE
SCHOLARS
PUBLISHING

Intersections: Applied Linguistics as a Meeting Place,
Edited by Elke Stracke

This book first published 2014

Cambridge Scholars Publishing

12 Back Chapman Street, Newcastle upon Tyne, NE6 2XX, UK

British Library Cataloguing in Publication Data
A catalogue record for this book is available from the British Library

ISBN (10): 1-4438-6654-7, ISBN (13): 978-1-4438-6654-5

TABLE OF CONTENTS

Part III

LIST OF ILLUSTRATIONS

LIST OF TABLES

FOREWORD

TERRENCE G. WILEY

As noted in the introduction to this collection, there have been a broad range of definitions offered of applied linguistics. According to Wilkins (1999), one of the earliest published uses of "applied linguistics" can be traced to a 1931 publication by Lockhart titled *Word Economy: An Essay in Applied Linguistics*. Grabe (2002) suggests that a realistic history of the field can be marked with the publication of the journal *Language Learning: A Journal of Applied Linguistics* in 1948. In the early years, as Grabe notes, there was a tendency to see the field as an application of insights from structural and functional linguistics to second language teaching.

Wilkins (1999) notes that the relationship of applied linguistics to other disciplines is often as applied linguistics "in" another discipline. So it may be construed as a sub-discipline within others, although it is not uncommon to construe applied linguistics as having its own sub-fields. Wilkins (1999) contends that it is evident that "the term 'applied linguistics' is too broad in its potential application to be interpreted literally" (p. 7). So he places emphasis on applied linguistics *in* language teaching and learning as the domain where the field has "generated the greatest body of research and publication" (p. 6). Even so, as Grabe observes, since the 1980s—if not much earlier—applied linguistics had expanded well beyond the domains of teaching and learning to encompass "language assessment, language policy and planning, language use in professional settings, translation, lexicography, multilingualism, language and technology, and corpus linguistics" (p. 4). This list has expanded to include a wide range of systemic analyses and discourse studies, as well as foci dealing with linguistic accommodation, discrimination and language rights in a wide variety of societal contexts. Add to these new emphases on critical postcolonial and postmodern studies and those related to language identity and language as performance. Even with this expansion, applied linguistics has tended to be grounded in situated, contextualized, real-world, problems-based foci even as it is concerned with theorizing.

The metaphors of "intersections" and a "meeting place" chosen for the contributions of this volume are fitting therefore to underscore "the role of applied linguistics as a mediating discipline and applied linguists as mediators" (Grabe 2002, p. 9). The organization of this volume highlights applied linguistics as a mediating discipline as it intersects with other disciplines and its own internal sub-disciplines and specializations.

The contributions in Part I, dealing with workplace interaction, medical contexts involving cross-cultural mediation and translation, understanding the contextualization of humor in doctor-patient interactions, and appropriate approaches to the cross-examination of children in legal settings illustrate the power of applied linguistic analysis in real-world daily interactions. These contexts are often sites where language and cultural differences require special sensitivity among interlocutors.

The contributions in Part II illustrate the importance of bringing the expertise of applied linguists to a variety of educational contexts involving not only the learning of languages but the increasing importance of language as a skill for teaching and learning subject matter.

The contributions in Part III highlight the significance of applied linguistic work in the domains of documenting endangered languages and protecting the rights of language minorities. They demonstrate the importance of intersecting applied linguistics with advocacy. The breadth of the contributions of this volume is both multicultural and transnational in scope. The volume as a whole extends the boundaries of the field while providing spaces for mediating within it and between other disciplines.

Terrence G. Wiley
Center for Applied Linguistics
Washington, D.C.

References

Grabe, W. 2002, "Applied linguistics an emerging discipline for the twenty-first century", *The Oxford Handbook of Applied Linguistics*, Oxford, U.K.: Oxford University Press, pp. 3-12

Wilkins, D.A. 1999, "Applied linguistics", *Concise Encyclopedia of Educational Linguistics*, Amsterdam: Elsevier, pp. 6-17

ACKNOWLEDGEMENTS

Over the time of preparing this volume I have been encouraged and helped by many people. First and foremost, I would like to thank all contributors to this volume for answering my call for chapters and submitting their excellent proposals and manuscripts. Special thanks go to Terry Wiley for making time to write the Foreword to this book. I would also like to thank those colleagues whose work I could not include in this volume for submitting their proposals as well as the reviewers whose valuable feedback unquestionably improved the overall quality of the book.

I have been very fortunate to have the professional assistance of Meredith Thatcher, who took care of the project management and all the editorial work that such a volume requires before it can be submitted to the publisher. My warm thanks go to her for her generous support over the time that we have been working on this volume together. My thanks also go to Cambridge Scholars Publishing for agreeing to publish this book.

Preparation of this manuscript was facilitated by the financial assistance that the Applied Linguistics Association of Australia (ALAA) and the Faculty of Arts and Design, University of Canberra, provided me with and for which I am grateful. Without their support this book might not have come to fruition.

I sincerely hope that the chapters in this book will make a contribution to the ever-expanding field of Applied Linguistics. For me, editing this book has been a rewarding learning experience; my understanding of applied linguistics has certainly grown through my engagement with the ideas presented by the authors in this volume. I now hope to share this experience with a larger audience.

Elke Stracke
University of Canberra
Canberra

APPLIED LINGUISTICS AS A MEETING PLACE: AN INTRODUCTION

ELKE STRACKE

Applied linguistics is an interdisciplinary field and often described as hard to define. Traditionally, applied linguistics focused on language teaching. Today, it attracts researchers and practitioners who are concerned with the numerous practical applications of language studies. This book makes a contribution to its developing and expanding scope through understanding applied linguistics as a *meeting place*. It presents 16 papers[1] by key researchers working in various countries around the globe. The volume focuses on the many junctions within applied linguistics and its intersections with other disciplines and areas of practice as diverse as *Education, Indigenous Issues, Language Development, Literacy,* and *Social Interaction*. Applied linguistics also has connections with broader areas such as the *Arts, Law, Medicine and Health, Society, Politics and Policy,* and *Technology*.

Like all metaphors, thinking in images allows us to develop our own images and stories around the idea of the *meeting place*. My own understanding of the term is intimately linked with the popular understanding of the name of the capital of Australia, Canberra. Canberra's name is often thought to mean *meeting place*, derived from the Aboriginal word Kamberra, reminding us that Australia's capital is located on the lands of the indigenous Ngunnawal people.[2] Even though this meaning is most likely academically unsustainable (Koch 2009) it has become generally accepted, perhaps because the federal parliament resides in Canberra. The *meeting place* emphasizes Canberra's role as the capital where people from Australia and the world gather, connect, share and

---

[1] All chapters in this volume are original studies, appearing in print for the first time. The authors presented earlier versions of their papers at the 2nd Combined Conference of the Applied Linguistics Associations of Australia and New Zealand in Canberra in December 2011 before they submitted them as chapter proposals for this book. All proposals and manuscripts went through a rigorous double-blind peer-review process.
[2] See www.visitcanberra.com.au/Visitor-Info/Facts

develop ideas. So the idea of using this popular understanding of Canberra as a *meeting place* transpired quite naturally when developing the conference theme, *Applied Linguistics as a Meeting Place*, for the 2nd Combined Conference of the Applied Linguistics Associations of Australia and New Zealand in Canberra in December 2011, as the main goals for the conference were to focus on the intersections between applied linguistics and other disciplines and areas of practice. This book brings together 16 outstanding pieces of work from this conference.

A brief overview of this book

The 16 chapters in this book are grouped within three broader areas. Part I has chapters that focus on the intersections between applied linguistics and a variety of workplaces or public spheres in multicultural and multilingual contexts. All studies in this section are concerned with enhancing the communication between members of these various workplaces and communities and show how applied linguistics can contribute to such an improvement.

Janet Holmes' chapter (Chapter 1) presents a study that analyzes the attitudes of New Zealanders towards skilled migrants with overall positive results, namely consistently positive attitudes to skilled migrants in New Zealand workplaces. This chapter shows how applied linguists can work with the community to reflect on how to better accept diversity in the slow advance towards a multicultural society. In a world that is increasingly multicultural, such work is critical. Louisa Willoughby, Simon Musgrave, Marisa Cordella, and Julie Bradshaw (Chapter 2) examine bilingual medical consultations in suburban hospitals in Melbourne, Australia. Their study shows the need to carefully research multiparty medical consultations (patient, family member, doctor, interpreter) to ensure that the multiple voices get heard and effective communication takes place so that the health and wellbeing of the patient are assured. Suzanne Eggins (Chapter 3) also examines hospital discourse in the Australian context. She argues that applied linguistics research into humor can help improve the communication and interaction between clinicians and patients. Her research shows how patients initiate humor as an appeal to clinicians to speak to them in a more inclusive everyday mode of interaction. Applied linguists play an important role in understanding and improving the discourse needed to empower patients in talk about their health. Kirsten Hanna (Chapter 4) looks at the intersection of law, linguistics and psychology in the cross-examination of child witnesses, drawing on evidence from New Zealand courtrooms and other adversarial systems. She convincingly argues that applied linguists can, and indeed must, help improve the courts' interactions with child witnesses for fair cross-examination of children and other vulnerable witnesses. In the last chapter in this part of the book (Chapter 5) Farzana Gounder presents the intersection of linguistics with media studies, history and narrative analysis through the careful analysis of a public Fiji-Indian radio commemoration of Indian indenture. Yet again, the role of applied linguistics is seen in its potential to help us understand how discourses work and shape us, ultimately constructing identity and society.

While Part I of the book focuses on the intersections between applied linguistics and a variety of workplaces or public spheres in multicultural and multilingual settings by reporting on studies conducted in such contexts, the chapters in Part II report on research conducted in educational contexts. All chapters emphasize the role that applied linguists play in the various educational contexts (from early childhood education to tertiary education) studied. Chapter 6 provides a useful transition into this group of papers, with its focus on the intersection of higher education and the workplace. Stephen Moore and Hui Ling Xu are concerned with the communication needs of international undergraduate accounting students in Australia, who are often not adequately prepared for the accounting workplace. Based on their study in a university accounting program, they suggest ways to improve these students' communicative skills needed in the accounting workplace. Angela Ardington (Chapter 7) focuses on the communication needs of undergraduate engineering students in Australia from her perspective as an academic language and learning practitioner who works at the intersection of applied linguistics, sociocultural theories of learning, and discourse studies. She convincingly argues for a pedagogical shift towards the integration of academic literacy in the core curriculum of these students, with the ultimate goal of making their learning experiences more valuable.

The following four chapters (Chapter 8 to Chapter 11) focus more explicitly on the traditional priority area of applied linguistics, language teaching, and its connections with the development of academic literacy and proficiency in various educational contexts. Hiroyuki Nemoto (Chapter 8) is concerned with the development of L2 literacy through the examination of the role of online intercultural activities. Integrating the perspective of Learning Management Theory he shows how, in an email exchange project, learners of English in Japan and learners of Japanese in Australia become socialized into L2 academic literacy through various language management actions triggered by identity transformation. In Chapter 9 Carol Hayes and Yuki Itani-Adams develop the theme of identity formation through an eLearning project (the Japanese Digital Storytelling Project) that they conducted with learners of Japanese at an Australian university. This project gives learners opportunities to express themselves and calls for a more holistic view of communication in language education. Wan-lun Lee (Chapter 10) argues for the integration of literature and cooperative learning in university English language education in Taiwan and provides rich evidence of students' perceptions of the benefits of such integration. The following chapter by Rosalie Grant, Rita MacDonald, Aek Phakiti and H. Gary Cook (Chapter 11) discusses the interesting intersection of English language teaching and mathematics. The authors show how cross-disciplinary collaboration between applied linguists and mathematics educators can provide English language learners in U.S. elementary and high school classrooms with essential practice to improve their writing when articulating mathematical problems, so contributing to students' academic mathematics achievement. The following two chapters (Chapter 12 and Chapter 13) examine the links between applied linguistics and language education among Aboriginal people in Australia. In Chapter 12, Liz Ellis brings together applied linguistics and early childhood education and argues compellingly for a better understanding of Aboriginal ways of talking and of effective preschool pedagogies for young indigenous learners in Australian preschools. The recognition of Aboriginal English as a valid variety— along with Standard Australian English—plays an important role in improving outcomes for these students. Ian Malcolm (Chapter 13) continues the discussion of Aboriginal students' use of Aboriginal English and Standard Australian English through an integration of cultural linguistics. Cultural schema theory is presented as a powerful tool to make the educational setting for Aboriginal students more culturally inclusive, so overcoming unacceptable hierarchies of languages and cultures.

The chapters in Part III discuss important issues around language documentation, policy, and language rights that lie in the public domain and at the heart of all language communities. In Chapter 14 Denise Angelo and Sophia McIntosh carefully examine Australian Census language data and find disturbing data inaccuracy. Their chapter focuses on the data about languages spoken by Aboriginal and Torres Strait Islander people in Queensland, Australia, and shows that language data is not always accurately collected and disseminated. Through their case studies they show the important contribution that applied linguists can make to communities and governments through community-based and academic research. In Chapter 15 Karen Lillie discusses language policy and language rights for language minority students in Arizona. Her analysis of

U.S. legal history and the events in Arizona shows the detrimental effect that language policy can have on English language learners, and serves to remind applied linguists—and indeed all disciplines—to protect and support language rights so that future language minority students receive an equal education, regardless of their first language. The last chapter in this volume (Chapter 16) further underlines the important role that applied linguists play in shaping educational policy and curriculum. Molly Townes O'Brien and Peter Bailey show how indigenous children in the world are often deprived of their sense of cultural identity and value. For the Australian context they argue that some statutory protection of the right to bilingual education will be required to secure an appropriate education for children who speak indigenous languages.

As seen from this brief overview, this volume's contributors write from a variety of perspectives and use various methodological approaches in their exploration of the contributions of applied linguistics across disciplines and areas of practice. I am pleased to present this book that shows how these researchers understand the influence of applied linguistics in the world. Naturally, this book cannot cover all disciplines and areas of practice that applied linguistics intersects with. I hope that it inspires researchers and practitioners to explore more and new intersections of applied linguistics so as to allow the understanding of applied linguistics as a *meeting place* to further mature.

References

Koch, H. 2009, "The methodology of reconstructing Indigenous placenames: Australian Capital Territory and southeastern New South Wales". In H. Koch and L. Hercus, eds, *Aboriginal Placenames: Naming and re-naming the Australian landscape*, ANU: E Press and Aboriginal History Incorporated, pp. 115–74

PART I

CHAPTER ONE

JOINING A NEW COMMUNITY
OF WORKPLACE PRACTICE:
INFERRING ATTITUDES FROM DISCOURSE

JANET HOLMES

Keywords: attitudes to migrants, workplace discourse, discourse analysis, intercultural communication

Abstract

Over the last few decades, New Zealanders have increasingly perceived their country as a relatively diverse and multicultural society. Yet people migrating to New Zealand often find that their experiences do not always live up to this rhetoric. Drawing on a theoretical model developed to analyze workplace discourse in its wider sociocultural context (Holmes, Marra & Vine 2011), this paper examines research evidence of the attitudes of New Zealanders towards skilled migrants as they enter the professional New Zealand workforce. The concepts of "new racism" (Barker 1981; van Dijk 2000), and "benevolent racism" (Lipinoga 2008, p. 47; Villenas 2002) are critically examined and rejected as inapplicable. While majority group norms and values underlie much of the advice given to skilled migrants, the discourse analysis provides evidence of "benevolent patronage" rather than harmful prejudice. The paper concludes with reflections on ways in which applied linguists can work with members of the wider workplace community to identify and research such areas of mutual concern, presenting research which is paradigmatically "applied linguistics applied" (Roberts 2003; Sarangi 2002).

Introduction

Over the last few decades, New Zealanders have increasingly perceived their country as a relatively diverse and multicultural society. New migrants often find, however, that their experiences do not always live up to this rhetoric. Responses to their attempts to learn English, to find work, and to demonstrate that they have something to offer in their new work environments sometimes suggest that they are perceived through a lens of cultural and linguistic deficiency.

Research on attitudes to migrants in England and the United States has introduced the concepts of "new racism" (Ansell 1997; Barker 1981; Hanson-Easey & Augoustinos 2010) and "benevolent racism" (Lipinoga 2008, p. 47; Villenas 2001) to describe covertly negative or overtly patronizing attitudes to newcomers to a country. Such attitudes can act as severe impediments in the newcomers' attempts to gain respect and recognition for their knowledge and skills in their new workplaces. These concepts provide a useful basis for evaluating evidence of attitudes to migrants in spoken workplace interaction. Talk at work is multifunctional and provides a wealth of information, not only about the transactional requirements of the job, but also about the relationships between participants (Holmes & Stubbe 2003), including subtle and not-so-subtle indications of attitudes. Every time we speak we convey our perception of the relationship between ourselves and our addressees, and provide clues about our attitudes. Making use of data from authentic spoken workplace interactions, this paper examines talk at work, and especially advice-giving, for evidence of the attitudes of New Zealanders to skilled migrants in New Zealand workplaces.

The first section of the paper outlines the broad theoretical framework and concepts used in the analysis. The methodology used to collect the data is then described, followed by the analysis of this data. The final section discusses the implications of the analysis and considers what host society speakers can learn from the opportunity to interact with professionals from different countries and cultures.

Theoretical framework and analytical concepts

In every society, people operate within institutional and social constraints that influence their talk in each context. We construct our social relationships and social identities within the limits of culturally available, sense-making frameworks or "discourses" (Ehrlich 2008, p. 160). In other words, our talk is constrained by the parameters of broad societal norms and "inherited structures" of belief, power, opportunity, and so on (Cameron 2009, p. 15). We have developed a theoretical model to analyze workplace discourse in its wider sociocultural context. This model suggests (Holmes, Marra & Vine 2011) that these social constraints operate at a number of different levels, from the encompassing societal or institutional level to the specific levels of the Community of Practice (CoP) or workplace team (cf. Hecht, Warren, Jung & Krieger 2005; Wodak 2008) and face-to-face interaction. [1] In the analysis of attitudes, this model highlights the hegemonic impact of majority group interactional norms, such as English as the normal, expected language of workplace interaction, egalitarianism as a value that inhibits self-promotion, and New Zealand-born Pākehā as the experts on matters of sociocultural interaction.

Cross-cutting these potential components is the influence of Māori discourse norms. Material from our database suggests these norms are relevant, taken-for-granted, background norms for many New Zealand interactions. For instance, most New Zealanders are aware that Māori discourse rules for appropriate interaction differ from those of the majority Pākehā group. The difference is especially noticeable in formal greetings, which tend to be elaborated by Māori but minimized by Pākehā (Holmes & Marra 2011a; Holmes, Marra & Vine 2012). Yet most relevant for the analysis below is that Pākehā and Māori do share the view that self-promotion is culturally unacceptable, though the roots of this value are different in each culture. Among Pākehā, egalitarianism is based on a belief that social standing should depend on achievement and not on birth, and that achievement is appropriately assessed by somebody else, not by the individual concerned (Lipson 1948, p. 8). Consequently, Pākehā New Zealanders do not comfortably tolerate explicit demonstrations of power, or boasting, and people often seek ways to reduce status differences and to emphasize equality with their colleagues. For Māori, avoidance of self-promotion is not based in a philosophy of egalitarianism but rather in the priority of the group over the individual, and the perception of a leader as a servant of the group. Māori leaders are expected to demonstrate concern for others and to avoid focusing on their own attributes. [2]

Overall, then, given this range of relevant sociocultural components, the model we have developed provides a useful macro-level background framework for critically examining how different norms, values, and positionings are conveyed, sometimes explicitly, and sometimes less consciously, at the micro-level in face-to-face workplace interaction.

The concept of "new racism" (Ansell 1997, Barker 1981, Hanson-Easey & Augoustinos 2010, van Dijk 2002) provides a further useful analytical tool to examine attitudes to migrants in the workplace. Overt racism is typically easy to identify, institutionally proscribed, and socially unacceptable in New Zealand as in most other Western democracies.

---

[1] See Holmes, Marra and Vine (2011) for a detailed discussion of this model and how it can be applied in New Zealand workplaces.
[2] See Holmes, Marra and Vine (2011) and Metge (1995) for further discussion.

However, as van Dijk (2002) points out, institutional and social intolerance of explicit racism has driven racism underground to manifest itself more covertly as "hidden racism," "xenoracism" (Del-Teso-Craviotto 2009) or "new racism" in contexts where racism is no longer tolerated. New racism refers to cultural and symbolic discrimination where "a politics of difference is used to claim legitimacy for dominant cultural practices" that result in subtle injustices (Tilbury & Colic-Peisker 2006).

This less blatant form of prejudice, "distant, cool and indirect" (Zick, Pettigrew & Wagner 2008, p. 240), has been identified and validated by the West (Blommaert & Verschueren 1998; Condor, Figgou, Abell, Gibson & Stevenson 2006; Foster 2009; Santa Ana 1999), and infiltrates many mundane settings without attracting comment. In particular, it often serves as a subtle and invidious means of discriminating against immigrants (De Fina & King 2011). For example, by drawing attention to cultural and national differences it constructs migrant workers as a threat. This is subtle, covert racism, expressed and experienced in everyday discriminatory practices (such as workplace talk) which reinforce stereotypes and prejudices. Identifying such indirect prejudice means examining everyday interaction for evidence of opinions that betray covertly negative attitudes and imply potentially racist ideologies. Clearly it is important in a study of attitudes to migrants to be alert to the possibility of such subtle prejudice and discrimination.

The third component in our analytical toolkit derives from House's (2005, p. 21) framework for analyzing intercultural interaction. Her model provides five potentially universal dimensions for analyzing cross-cultural differences:

1. degree of directness
2. degree of explicitness
3. the degree to which communication is oriented towards self rather than other-oriented
4. the degree to which communication is oriented towards content rather than the addressees
5. the extent to which the discourse is characterized by verbal routines as opposed to unplanned formulations.

This framework provides a useful guide for considering the ways that different interactional norms are negotiated in intercultural workplace interaction, and for identifying potential sources of misunderstanding. The analysis below focuses on the different ways that advice is given in workplace interaction. In the context of this study of attitudes to migrants, the dimensions of degrees of directness and degrees of explicitness proved particularly useful when analyzing advice-giving between migrants and their mentors.

Methodology and dataset

The data used to analyze attitudes towards migrants in New Zealand workplaces was collected as part of the research of the Wellington Language in the Workplace Project (LWP). The LWP team has been recording and analyzing workplace interactions since 1996. Most of this data has come from white-collar environments, including government departments and large and small corporations (see Holmes & Stubbe 2003).[3] In total our 2-million word database comprises more than 2,000 interactions, involving around 700 participants from more than 30 workplaces. The interactions range from brief telephone conversations to lengthy strategy meetings. In the last four years we have also collected data involving intercultural interaction in the workplace between New Zealanders and migrants from professional backgrounds.

The workplace interactions analyzed below were collected by volunteers in a 12-week communications skills course with an internship component. The course is one of a number of courses offered in New Zealand cities to professionals who do not speak English as their first language, and who have found it hard to find suitable employment. All the participants have relevant expertise in their chosen profession, but do not know about or have experience with New Zealand culture. Because of employer attitudes, this lack of knowledge and experience tends to limit the participants' opportunities for employment. The participants include accountants, lawyers, judges, doctors, financial analysts, and engineers. They come from a range of countries, including China, Germany, India, Japan, Malaysia, and Russia. After five weeks of intensive classroom teaching and learning, focused on developing awareness of sociopragmatic aspects of communication in the New Zealand workplace, the participants spend six weeks in supported internships in a New Zealand organization matched to their area of interest.

The 12 volunteers (5 women and 7 men) who agreed, with their workplace mentors and colleagues, to record their everyday workplace interactions during their internships came from a wide range of professional backgrounds and countries. Using the standard methodology of the LWP team, the volunteers carried small devices that recorded their normal workplace interactions for the first two weeks and last two weeks

---

[3] See the project website www.victoria.ac.nz/lals/lwp for more information.

of their internship. They were in control of what was recorded, and they provided a range of material from one-to-one sessions with their mentors to morning tea and social interactions with a wide array of workplace colleagues. These recordings and recordings between New Zealanders from the wider LWP database selected for comparison purposes provided the data used in the analysis below.

Analysis of data

Giving advice has some similarities with giving directives. [4] While directives are attempts to get someone to do something, usually for the benefit of the speaker, advice is more specifically other-oriented, with the addressee's welfare as its distinguishing characteristic. Bach and Harnish (1979, p. 49) define advice as follows: "what the speaker expresses is not the desire that H [hearer] do a certain action but the belief that doing it is a good idea, that it is in H's interest." The addressee is not obliged to comply, but it is generally regarded as in their best interests to do so (Vine 2004; Koester 2006). Given the situation of the skilled migrants during their internship, it is not surprising that they were the target of a good deal of advice from their mentors. Much of this advice was intended to help them work well with their colleagues and fit into the workplace. This relationally oriented advice was the focus of the analysis, that is, advice oriented to how the new workers should manage their workplace relationships.

Direct and explicit advice about interactional norms

The most obvious feature of the interactions between the skilled migrants and their mentors was the remarkable directness of the advice given at every level, from general advice about New Zealand sociocultural norms to more specific advice about how to fit into a particular CoP. Of course, this is not very surprising since the role of the mentors was precisely to provide such guidance to their mentees, and they frequently did so very clearly and firmly. In a number of interactions, the mentors explicitly described "the way New Zealanders talk" for the benefit of the skilled migrant.

---

[4] This section draws on Vine, Holmes and Marra (2012).

Example 1

[Transcription conventions are at the end of this chapter.]

> *Context*: Henry is a Chinese accountant. Simon, Henry's workplace mentor, gives him advice about New Zealand ways of interacting.
> 1. it doesn't work that way in New Zealand...
> 2. I know that you've a diff- different culture
> 3. a different you know language
> 4. so people will be more understanding
> 5. they will be more understanding um
> 6. but you need to say things with energy
> 7. that's a New Zealand thing very much
> 8. that we like en- energy we like enthusiasm
> 9. we like keen people...
> 10. when you want to say something
> 11. you have to say it with a bit of energy ...
> 12. really, really important that when you speak to people
> 13. that you get your voice level up

Simon here first acknowledges that Henry's cultural background and language are different, but then explicitly asserts the need for him to conform to New Zealand norms by saying things with *energy* (lines 6, 8 and 11) and *enthusiasm* (line 8). These features of interaction are presented as generalizations about national norms, which Simon clearly feels qualified to present.

In the context of assessing attitudes to skilled migrants, it is important to note that Simon does not assume that Henry lacks linguistic proficiency, but rather assesses Henry's reticence as a cultural phenomenon. Even so, when compared with ways that New Zealand born speakers are addressed, this excerpt illustrates a number of features in our data that characterize talk to skilled migrants, such as repetition (lines 4, 5, 6, 8 and 11), the use of syntactically simple clauses with parallel structures: e.g. *we like energy, we like enthusiasm, we like keen people* (lines 8 and 9), and paraphrase: e.g. *say it with a bit of energy, get your voice level up* (lines 11 and 13). There is little mitigation or hedging; the clauses are simple and direct and there is no evidence of negotiation.

The specific message that Simon conveys here is a common theme in our data: skilled migrants from Asia are regularly encouraged to speak up, to speak louder and more confidently. The content, directness and explicitness of this advice contrast with advice-giving sequences between native-speaking New Zealanders where such features were never the focus of advice, and repetition was rare (see Vine 2004; Holmes 2005). A similar pattern was observable in advice focused more specifically on the norms of a particular CoP.

Example 2

> *Context*: Helena is a Chinese accountant from Hong Kong. Trish, her workplace mentor, is giving advice about the norms of this particular workplace.
> 1. the way WE react to people (3)
> 2. WE help people that come and ask us questions +
> 3. we help the ones that talk the loudest (laughing) ...
> 4. if you were gonna [going to] start prioritizing things
> 5. it's a whole (lot easier to)
> 6. get rid of the loudest one first

Again the message is characterized by repetition and paraphrase, with syntax that involves relatively simple structures: *we help...we help...* (lines 2 and 3). The repeated pronoun *we* (lines 1, 2 and 3), stressed in lines 1 and 2, emphasizes that repetition and paraphrase are being presented as the local CoP norms: drawing attention to yourself by asking questions and talking loudly is a strategy that is recognized as effective in this CoP.

Similarly, in example 3, Leo gives Isaac advice about how to behave socially in their CoP.

Example 3[5]

> *Context*: Isaac is a Chinese accountant. Leo, his workplace mentor, is giving advice about the norms of their particular workplace.
> 1. try and integrate yourself more with everyone
> 2. ... but also the learning is
> 3. to sit with people at lunch time
> 4. and learn the language and listen to the jokes
> 5. and the and participate so sometimes ...
> 6. for your development I think
> 7. you need to work harder at that ...
> 8. ... just listen to people ...
> 9. and participate ...
> 10. so you get more confident ...

---

[5] This example is discussed from a different perspective in Vine, Holmes and Marra (2012).

Leo is encouraging Isaac to join in more with social interaction in the workplace, so that he gets more practice and becomes more confident in speaking English. This is very direct language characterized by explicit imperatives such as *integrate yourself, sit with people, learn ..., listen..., participate....you need to...; just listen...*(lines 1, 3, 4, 5, 7, 8 and 9). Again there is a significant amount of repetition (lines 5 and 9, and lines 4 and 8) and paraphrase. Yet again it is worth noting that this kind of advice from interactions between New Zealanders is completely absent in our data. Perhaps it seems too face-threatening to comment on a person's social competence and suggest they behave differently.

In summary, the advice that mentors gave the skilled migrants about how to behave appropriately when interacting in New Zealand workplaces was typically direct, relatively unattenuated and repeated. Also it was reinforced, often with elaboration over an extended session of interaction. The remarkable feature of this advice was the degree of explicitness compared to how our larger database showed advice was typically conveyed between New Zealanders. We analyzed comparable mentoring situations between managers and subordinates, where the manager provided advice to the mentee. The analysis clearly showed that advice about practices that needed changing was typically hedged and often negotiated or phrased as a suggestion for consideration (see Holmes 2005), especially if it related to managing relationships with other colleagues.

Indirect advice about New Zealand interactional norms

Another perspective on this type of information was provided by comments on how the skilled migrants' behavior differed from the behavior of New Zealanders. Often in such cases, while the surface message was clear and explicit, and related to behavior to be avoided, there was an underlying message that required some inferencing on the part of the intern. One such case involved a skilled migrant from Russia whose workplace interactions were characterized by a significant amount of self-promotional talk—something discouraged in New Zealand society. Yet his mentor focused instead on an aspect of the migrant's interactional style as he perhaps found discussing the style easier or more comfortable.

Example 4

> *Context*: Andrei is an events manager. Emma, his workplace mentor, is giving advice about his interactional style.
> 1.   about um communication style

2.   um you're quite clear in what you say
3.   and your English is very good
4.   and you seem to understand pe- perfectly well
5.   so I have absolutely no issue with that
6.   but um the only thing I'd say is that
7.   um you can be very direct
8.   you need to think constantly about
9.   how can I just tone it down a bit
10. do you know what I mean?

The feedback consistently given to Andrei is that his style is too direct. Again the mentor starts with positive feedback about Andrei's English proficiency before raising the issue of directness.

There are two interesting points to note. First, Andrei is told not that New Zealand colleagues experience his style as too direct, but rather *you can be very direct* (line 7), and then *you need to think constantly* about how you can *just tone it down a bit* (lines 8 and 9). In other words, New Zealand norms are taken for granted and the possibility that Andrei's colleagues might react differently or be more tolerant is not considered. Second, our analyses of the recordings of Andrei's interactions in his workplace show that another underlying cultural issue exists that none of his mentors or colleagues mention. This cultural issue is Andrei's tendency to talk explicitly about his high status and standing in his former occupation in Russia at every opportunity. Example 5 is one example from a number of instances.[6]

Example 5

> *Context*: As stated, Andrei is an events manager. Camille is his manager. They are discussing the parameters of Andrei's job in the organization. [XXX] is used to protect the identity of the organization where Andrei works.
> 1.   And: I er [clears throat] I was involved in the same
> 2.   similar to the similar similar work back in Russia
> 3.   Cam: oh right
> 4.   And: er but for international er financial er institutions
> 5.   like international monetary fund //and the World\ Bank
> 6.   Cam: oh wow\\
> 7.   And: and the European Bank for Construction and Development
> 8.   Cam: oh

---

[6] A longer section, which includes this excerpt and the related issue, is discussed in more detail in Holmes and Riddiford (2010), and is analyzed from a different perspective in Holmes and Marra (2011b).

9.	And:	and for our ( ) of ch- chairman and deputy chairman
10.		and deputy director of some of the departments
11.		were [XXX] departments not just [XXX] /but\\
12.	Cam:	//mm\
13.	And:	[XXX] and then financial [XXX]
14.	Cam:	right yes
15.	And:	banking supervision and accounting
16.	Cam:	that's quite big work
17.	And:	yes //really big\ the whole um
18.	Cam:	/yeah\\
19.	And:	I was a team leader
20.	Cam:	mm
21.	And:	and five people reported to me ++
22.		and I w- and I coordinated the (role) for the first deputy
23.		chairwomen missus [NAME] she was right hand
24.		of chairman of the European bank bank of Europe
25.	Cam:	oh
26.	And:	chair govern Reserve Bank
27.	Cam:	oh okay one of my brothers is going to Moscow next week

Andrei begins appropriately here by linking what he wants to say to the current context in which his responsibilities are being outlined. In lines 1 and 2, Andrei indicates that he has relevant previous experience. He then goes on to describe his previous position in considerable detail. In a typical interaction between New Zealanders, the information in the first two lines would almost certainly be considered enough. Most New Zealanders tend to play down expertise; it would be unusual to hear someone elaborate their experience in Andrei's level of detail. Andrei mentions the banks he has worked for (lines 4, 5 and 7) and lists the important people he has worked for (lines 9 and 10). He then provides a detailed account of his role as a team leader of five people (lines 19 and 21), and finally his role working for an important woman—the right hand to the chairman of the bank of Europe (lines 22, 23, 24, and 26).

Camille's responses show that she finds this elaborated, explicit professional identity construction somewhat excessive. Her responses become progressively less encouraging until, finally, she takes over firmly *oh okay* (line 27) and changes the topic. Considerately, she selects a social topic that Andrei can likely contribute to: *one of my brothers is going to Moscow next week* (line 27).

Research with Russian immigrants in Israel (Zaldman & Drory 2001) and research on Russian requests (Larina 2008; Ogiermann 2009) suggests that the amount and level of detail Andrei supplies about his experience and competence would be perfectly appropriate in a Russian context. A

Russian employee might see as important, emphasize, and manage how they are viewed by those higher up in the workplace. This explanation is consistent with Andrei's subsequent behavior in this workplace. He is confident and assertive and continues to inform people about his extensive and significant professional experience throughout his internship. To a New Zealander, Andrei's claims about the importance of his role and status are needlessly detailed. Andrei is too "bald on record" and, from the perspective of New Zealand interactional norms, his talk in this excerpt could be classified as inappropriately "blowing one's own trumpet," boasting or "skiting." Yet nobody tells him. As example 4 illustrates, even the most explicit feedback Andrei receives comments on his "directness" rather than on his self-promoting discourse. Again this indicates that New Zealanders are willing to give advice about such features of talk as appropriate volume, the need to speak with confidence, and not being too direct; but comments on self-presentation are less forthcoming where deep-rooted values such as egalitarianism are involved.

Though most advice given to the skilled migrants was clear and explicit, in some areas the messages were less direct. Even though the mentor's role sanctioned comment on behavior which was likely to be regarded negatively through the eyes of most New Zealanders, some aspects of behavior were clearly regarded as too sensitive for explicit comment. When deep-seated sociocultural values are involved, it seems that New Zealanders consider transgressive behavior as not a matter for discussion. This reaction precludes the possibility of discussion, negotiation of understanding, and adaptation to alternative norms—a point discussed further in the next section.

This section ends with some examples of positive feedback provided to the skilled migrant interns. Our data shows abundant evidence of New Zealanders appreciating the skills of the migrants and being interested in their professional and cultural experiences. When analyzing the full range of data from all 12 interns, Nicky Riddiford (forthcoming) identified six indications of positive feedback.

- Giving praise and expressing appreciation
- Expressing understanding of challenges
- Giving constructive feedback
- Being supportive
- Showing interest in mentor's family, country of origin etc
- Evidence of assumptions about competence in (i) language; (ii) cultural awareness; and (iii) professional area/expertise.

Examples 6 and 7 illustrate these points.

Example 6

> *Context*: Isaac is a Chinese accountant. Leo, his workplace mentor, is
> providing feedback on his writing.
> 1. Leo: you've done very well..
> 2.   that's very good no ...
> 3.   that sentence you had there that was perfect...
> 4.   that's really good
> 5.   that last sentence was just beautiful

Leo compliments Isaac fulsomely on his writing, repeating and emphasizing how impressed he is with it. This is one typical example of many such instances of positive feedback. In example 7, Chris responds positively to Ava's rather direct criticism of the organization's accounting system.

Example 7

> *Context*: Ava is a Chinese accountant. Chris is her manager. Ava makes
> some critical comments about the accounting system used in the
> organization and Chris responds.
> 1. Ava: if er if they're overdue that mean um
> 2.   firstly that mean probably user don't want to use it
> 3.   and not update correctly and er timely
> 4.   and another reason if the this other system is not er
> 5.   the interface is not quite er friendly
> 6. Chris: mm
> 7. Ava: and er also some function a functionality cannot meet the users
>   requirement
> 8.   so they think always it's a waste of time waste my time
> 9.   or probably they will think they don't want to use it ....
> 10. Chris: yeah no this looks excellent
> 11.   and um I mean y- you- you do raise
> 12.   some um very valid valid points there

It is noticeable that although Ava has been very direct and made some very critical remarks about the inadequacies of the system, Chris's response is positive and appreciative. There is no hint of defensiveness and he provides a high evaluation of her work. This is promising evidence of the willingness of some mentors to accept alternative interactional norms in workplace interaction.

Overall, then, the analysis provides a picture of New Zealand mentors who are keen to help the skilled migrants settle into the New Zealand workplace context and to adapt to New Zealand ways of behaving and interacting at work. The direct and the indirect messages are identical: the skilled migrant must adapt to New Zealand interactional norms which are presented as clear-cut, unvarying and non-negotiable. It is important to note in this context that our analysis of mentors' feedback indicates very positive attitudes to the skilled migrants.

The analysis also suggests that the direct advice from mentors about the importance of conforming to New Zealand norms did not stem from ignorance or lack of interest in the different cultural and linguistic background of the skilled migrants. Indeed there was evidence that the New Zealand mentors were interested in cross-cultural differences, and in some cases were aware of culturally different interactional norms (for example, see Simon's comments in example 1).

Even so, the data does not provide possible ways to negotiate alternative ways to interact. Also the data does not provide evidence of the interns' New Zealand colleagues accepting a different way of interacting at work. Even when the skilled migrants offered cultural explanations for why their behavior differed from New Zealand norms, and for which they were being implicitly criticized, the possibility of countenancing alternative interactional norms was not considered. These issues are explored further in the discussion below.

Discussion

The analysis of interactions between mentors and interns suggests that the New Zealand mentors orient strongly to normative New Zealand models in providing advice to newcomers. Advice about speaking confidently and loudly is provided very explicitly. Ways of doing things in a specific organizations and CoP are presented as the interactional norms to which the skilled migrants are expected to conform. More implicit norms are also identifiable in the interactions analyzed, though these less direct messages require skillful reading of subtle clues, as illustrated in Camille's responses to Andrei's self-promoting discourse. Overall, the New Zealand colleagues of the skilled migrants seem to overlook the fact that every workplace has diversity in how New Zealand born speakers behave and interact with each other. Not everyone speaks up in meetings and not everyone speaks loudly, though these are the models presented to the interns. Most of us tolerate significant diversity, but when this interacts with the status of new migrants it seems our tolerance buttons are muted.

Given the compelling evidence of generally positive attitudes towards the interns and the skills and experience they bring to the organizations where they have been placed, this muting is apparently unconscious; the resulting advice is certainly well-meaning.

We return to a pivotal question raised at the start of this chapter. Is there evidence of "new racism" in the interactions between skilled migrants and their New Zealand colleagues? The short answer is "no." It is true that "majority group" ways of doing things are presented as the norm, and majority group values can be discerned in the underlying responses to the discourse of the skilled migrants. Yet no evidence exists of discriminatory practices or harmful prejudice, or of the construction of migrant workers as a threat, as in the data from England and the United States discussed in this chapter's Introduction. Rather, the responses of workplace colleagues to the interns and their work are encouraging, admiring and consistently positive.

Turning to the less corrosive concept of "benevolent racism" (Lipinoga 2008; Villenas 2001), it is worth considering whether this has any relevance to the analysis of the relationship between the skilled migrants and their New Zealand colleagues. Lipinoga (2008, p. 47) defines "benevolent racism" as "a welcoming attitude to newcomers that frames them through a deficit lens that highlights what they lack rather than their strengths and resources." It is clear that the motivations underlying benevolent racism are generally positive; but they can also be regarded as patronizing. Citing Urciuoli (1996), Villenas argues that "the line between viewing people with 'needs' and viewing people with 'deficits' can be very thin" (2002, p. 22). Such attitudes, however positively based, reflect a power differential and clearly constrain the perception of newcomers' abilities.

Our analyses indicate that it is almost impossible to determine whether positively motivated feedback about culturally based interactional differences provides evidence of a deficit perspective or not. It is clear that many of the mentors are very well-informed about the sources of the skilled migrants' interactional behavior where it differs from New Zealand norms. It is evident also that their motives are consistently affirmative; they are anxious to help the interns learn about the New Zealand way of doing things to improve their chances of permanent employment. Direct advice and constructive feedback are clearly based in a well-intentioned desire to help the interns integrate smoothly into New Zealand workplaces. This behavior cannot be appropriately labeled "racism"; indeed, there is every indication that it is motivated by positive intentions.

Importantly, similar attitudes were evident in advice directed to young native-speaking New Zealanders working in an apprentice role (Holmes & Woodhams, forthcoming). We might call this "benevolent patronage" since, while an unavoidable power differential exists, there is clearly no racial component. Yet the analysis does raise the important issue of how we can progress from what appear to be assimilationist motivations towards skilled migrants to attitudes that are more accepting of culturally different ways of doing things.

One source of insight here is the long and sometimes painful experiences of New Zealanders in developing a relatively bicultural society. While many people would argue that Pākehā and Māori are still far from equal in many spheres, it is also true that as a result of living alongside Māori for almost two centuries, many Pākehā New Zealanders have learned much about respecting alternative values and different interactional norms (Metge 1995, 2010).

Our recent research in Māori workplaces describes what we, as researchers, learned by working alongside Māori during the research experience. That research documented some of the culturally different ways of doing things that characterize workplaces committed to Māori values and objectives (Holmes, Marra & Vine 2011). For example, the research shows a tolerance for and appreciation of alternative ways of opening and closing meetings, for indirect ways of expressing criticism, and for the use of self-deprecating humor to avoid self-promotion by Pākehā and Māori leaders. This perhaps suggests a way forward to which applied linguists can contribute.

Conclusion

The analysis in this chapter has illustrated consistently positive attitudes to the skilled migrants we recorded in New Zealand workplaces. There is no evidence of either "new" or "benevolent" racism in the attitudes of their New Zealand colleagues, though some interactions have features of "benevolent patronage." Most importantly, the analysis suggests that there is room for greater acceptance of alternative ways of interacting, and for encouraging new migrants to discuss interactional norms that differ between their home culture and their new workplaces. These norms are typically taken for granted and assumed as shared knowledge: in many contexts they are not a topic for reflection or comment.

Yet, through opportunities for contact with Māori culture and interacting with Māori people in Māori contexts, many New Zealanders have developed an awareness of the potential damage incurred through culturally ethnocentric values, attitudes and behaviors. This augurs well for the possibility of extending this learning to newcomers from different cultural backgrounds.

While interactional style, like good manners, is not generally a focus of comment, applied linguistic research, practicing "applied linguistics applied" (Roberts 2003; Sarangi 2002), and working on "real world" issues identified in collaboration with "real world" partners (Bygate 2004, p. 18), can provide a basis for giving it legitimate attention, and so raise awareness of the potential gains from developing more accepting attitudes to alternative ways of doing things. Awareness that speaking quietly is a sign of respect in some cultures, or that identifying one's strengths is considered important in constructing a professional identity in others, can be useful first steps to accepting diversity in the slow advance towards a multicultural society. This chapter has demonstrated one way in which applied linguists can play a role in facilitating progress along this important road.

Transcription Conventions

Examples have been edited to protect the anonymity of the contributing organizations and all names used in extracts are pseudonyms. Minimal feedback and overlaps are sometimes edited out for ease of reading where the features are irrelevant to the point being made. Line divisions are intended to support understanding and typically represent sense unit boundaries. The main conventions used are outlined below:

[laughs]	Paralinguistic features and editorial information are in square brackets
: :	Colons indicate start/finish
+	Pause of up to one second
(3)	3-second pause
... //......\ ... ... /.......\\ ...	Simultaneous speech
( )	Unclear utterance
(hello)	Transcriber's best guess at an unclear utterance
-	Utterance cut off
...	Section of transcript omitted

Note

I would like to first thank the noble volunteers who collected data in various New Zealand workplaces. I also gratefully acknowledge the contribution of Meredith Marra, Bernadette Vine, and Nicky Riddiford, members of the Language in the Workplace team, as well as the research assistants who transcribed material used in this paper. I would also like to thank Andy Gibson and Sharon Marsden for their help with the references.

References

Ansell, A.E. 1997, *New Right New Racism: Race and Reaction in the United States and Britain*, New York: New York University Press

Bach, K. and R.M. Harnish. 1979, *Linguistic Communication and Speech Acts*, Cambridge, MA: MIT Press

Barker, M. 1981, *The New Racism*, London: Junction Books

Blommaert, J. and J. Verschueren. 1998, *Debating Diversity: Analysing the Discourse of Tolerance*, London: Routledge

Bygate, M. 2004, "Some current trends in applied linguistics: Towards a generic view". In S.M. Gass and S. Makoni, eds. *World Applied Linguistics (AILA Review 17)*, Amsterdam: John Benjamins, pp. 6–22

Cameron, D. 2009, "Theoretical Issues for the Study of Gender and Spoken Interaction". In P. Pichler and E.M. Eppler, eds. *Gender and Spoken Interaction*, London: Palgrave Macmillan, pp. 1–17

Condor, S., L. Figgou, J. Abell, S. Gibson and C. Stevenson. 2006, "They're not racist . . . ": Prejudice Denial, Mitigation and Suppression in Dialogue, *British Journal of Social Psychology* 45: 441–62

De Fina, A. and K.A. King. 2011, "Language Problems or Language Conflict: Narratives of Immigrant Women's Experience in the US", *Discourse Studies* 13: 163–88

Del-Teso-Craviotto, M. 2009, "Racism and Xenophobia in Immigrants' Discourse: the Case of Argentines in Spain", *Discourse and Society* 20: 571–92

Ehrlich, S. 2008, "Sexual Assault Trials, Discursive Identities and Institutional Change". In R. Dolón and J. Todolí, eds, *Analysing Identities in Discourse*, Amsterdam: John Benjamins, pp. 159–77

Foster, J.D. 2009, "Defending Whiteness Indirectly: a Synthetic Approach to Race Discourse Analysis", *Discourse and Society* 20: 685–703

Hanson-Easey, S. and M. Augoustinos. 2010, "Out of Africa: Accounting for refugee policy and the language of causal attribution", *Discourse and Society* 21: 295–323

Hecht, M.L., J.R. Warren, E. Jung and J.L. Krieger. 2005, "A Communication Theory of Identity: Development, Theoretical Perspective, and Future Directions". In W.B. Gudykunst, ed, *Theorizing about Intercultural Communication*, Thousand Oaks: Sage, pp. 257–78

Holmes, J. 2005, "Leadership Talk: how do Leaders 'do Mentoring', and is Gender Relevant?" *Journal of Pragmatics* 37: 1779–80

Holmes, J. and M. Marra. 2011a, "Relativity Rules: Politic Talk in Ethnicised Workplaces". In B.L. Davies, M. Haugh and A.J. Merrison, eds, *Situated Politeness*, London: Continuum, pp. 27–52

—. 2011b, "Harnessing Storytelling as a Sociopragmatic Skill: Applying Narrative Research to Workplace English Courses", *TESOL Quarterly* 45: 510–34

Holmes, J., M. Marra and B. Vine. 2011, *Leadership, Ethnicity and Discourse*, Oxford: Oxford University Press

—. 2012, "Politeness and Impoliteness in New Zealand English Workplace Discourse", *Journal of Pragmatics* 44: 1063–76

Holmes, J. and M. Stubbe. 2003, *Power and Politeness in the Workplace. A Sociolinguistic Analysis of Talk at Work*, London: Pearson Education

Holmes, J. and N. Riddiford. 2010, "Professional and Personal Identity at Work: Achieving a Synthesis through Intercultural Workplace Talk", *Journal of Intercultural Communication* 22. http://www.immi.se/jicc/index.php/jicc/article/view/177

Holmes, J. and J. Woodhams, forthcoming, "Building Interaction: the Role of Talk in Joining a Community of Practice". To appear in *Discourse and Communication*

House, J. 2005, "Politeness in Germany: Politeness in Germany?" In L. Hickey and M. Stewart, eds, *Politeness in Europe*, Bristol: Multilingual Matters, pp.13–28

Koester, A. 2006, *Investigating Workplace Discourse*, New York: Routledge

Larina, T. 2008, "Directness, Imposition and Politeness in English and Russian", *Cambridge ESOL Research Notes* 33: 33–38

Lipinoga, S. 2008, "Benevolent Racism in an Adult Educator's Talk", *Working Papers in Educational Linguistics* 23: 47–73

Lipson, L. 1948, *The Politics of Equality: New Zealand's Adventures in Democracy*, Chicago: University of Chicago Press

Metge, J. 1995, *New Growth from Old: the Whanau in the Modern World*, Wellington: Victoria University Press

—. 2010, *Tuamaka*, Auckland, Auckland University Press

Ogiermann, E. 2009, "Politeness and In-directness Across Cultures: a Comparison of English, German, Polish and Russian Requests", *Journal of Politeness Research* 5: 189–216

Riddiford, N. 2013, "Talking to Builders and the Elderly: Using Authentic Data to Develop Resources for ESOL Learners", 3rd Combined ALANZ & ALAA Conference, Victoria University of Wellington, New Zealand, 27–29 November 2013

Roberts, C. 2003, "Applied Linguistics Applied". In S. Sarangi and T. van Leeuwen, eds, *Applied Linguistics and Communities of Practice*. London: Continuum, pp. 132–49

Santa Ana, O. 1999, "'Like an Animal I was Treated': Anti-immigrant Metaphor in US public Discourse", *Discourse and Society* 10: 191–224

Sarangi, S. 2002, "Discourse Practitioners as a Community of Interprofessional Practice: some Insights from Health Communication Research". In C.N. Candlin, ed, *Research and Practice in Professional Discourse*, Hong Kong: City University of Hong Kong Press, pp. 95–135

Tilbury, F. and V. Colic-Peisker. 2006, "Deflecting Responsibility in Employer Talk about Race Discrimination", *Discourse and Society* 17: 651–76

van Dijk, T.A. 2000, "New(s) Racism: a Discourse Analytical Approach". In S. Cottle, ed, *Ethnic Minorities and the Media*, Buckingham, U.K.: Open University Press, pp. 33–49

—. 2002, "Discourse and Racism". In D.T. Goldberg and J. Solomos, eds, *A Companion to Racial and Ethnic Studies*, Malden, Mass.; Oxford: Blackwell, pp. 145–60

Villenas, S. 2001, "Latina mothers and Small Town Racisms: Creating Narratives of Dignity and Moral Education in North Carolina", *Anthropology and Education Quarterly* 31: 3–28

—. 2002, "Reinventing Educación in New Latino Communities: Pedagogies of Change and Continuity in North Carolina". In S. Wortham, E.G. Murillo, and E.T. Hamann, eds, *Education in the New Latino Diaspora: Policy and the Politics of Identity*, Connecticut: Greenwood Publishing Group, pp. 17–35

Vine, B. 2004, *Getting Things Done at Work: the Discourse of Power in Workplace Interaction*, Amsterdam: John Benjamins

Vine, B., J. Holmes and M. Marra. 2012, "Mentoring Migrants: Facilitating the Transition to the New Zealand Workplace". In M. Locher and H. Limburg, eds, *Advice in Discourse. Studies in Discourse Series*, Amsterdam: John Benjamins, pp. 145–65

Wodak, R. 2008, "Controversial Issues in Feminist Critical Discourse Analysis". In K. Harrington, L. Litosseliti, H. Sauntson and J. Sunderland, eds, *Gender and Language Research Methodologies*, London: Palgrave, pp. 193–210

Zaldman, N. and A. Drory. 2001, "Upward Impression Management in the Workplace: Cross-cultural Analysis", *International Journal of Intercultural Relations* 25: 671–90

Zick, A., T.F. Pettigrew and U. Wagner. 2008, "Ethnic Prejudice and Discrimination in Europe", *Journal of Social Issues* 64: 233–51

Chapter Two

Being Heard: The Role of Family Members in Bilingual Medical Consultations

Louisa Willoughby, Simon Musgrave, Marisa Cordella and Julie Bradshaw

Keywords: bilingual medical discourse, family members in medical consultations, interpreted medical discourse

Abstract

In medical consultations, patients with limited English may seek the support of interpreters, and may also bring family members to assist them. This transforms the archetypal doctor–patient dyad into a multiparty interaction in which others may speak for the patient: the patient's attempts to present their symptoms and concerns are filtered through the representations of others, trained and untrained. Four medical consultations with older Italian-Australian patients are examined to identify how the interaction is managed between doctors, patients, family members and interpreters (where present). The family members vary in the roles they play in establishing the medical facts and supporting or challenging the patient's claims, creating a more complex discourse for doctor and interpreter to negotiate.

Introduction

Research on the role of family members who accompany patients to medical consultations has shown that the companions may contribute in a range of ways to how the interaction is accomplished. When the patients are members of linguistic minorities with limited command of the dominant language they need additional support to communicate effectively. In the past family members often played this role, but an interpreter service is available to speakers for a wide range of languages in Australia. This chapter explores the interaction of four older Italian-speaking patients in Australian medical consultations, and the contributions of their accompanying family members. In three cases an interpreter is present, while in the fourth the doctor is able to communicate in Italian. We focus on the particular issues that arise when companions contribute to bilingual consultations. They have the potential to support, elaborate or contest the patient's account.

The interpreter's role is to accurately represent the ratified participants' first language (L1) utterances in a second language (L2). The status of family members as ratified participants is sometimes problematic, as we explore in this chapter. Our data comes from recorded scheduled hospital outpatient clinics consultations at two Melbourne hospitals. The consultations in our collection were mostly interpreted, but in one case the physician was bilingual. This analysis explores the companions' attempts to get their views on record, a topic not investigated in the context of bilingual discourse. In doing so, we bring together insights from studies of medical discourse and from the interpreter training literature. In this meeting place of research approaches, we are able to address a language problem arising from migration and language contact.

Multiparty medical discourse

Three-party or four-party medical discourse shares many of the properties of medical discourse in general. Research on two-party doctor–patient communication has focused on the asymmetrical relationship that emerges in the medical visits due to the different levels and types of expert knowledge that participants bring to the events (Candlin & Candlin 2002; Candlin 2002; Sarangi & Clarke 2002). Professional medical knowledge, lay medical knowledge and personal knowledge are exchanged through the sequential organization of turns, with participants differing in participation and control in the medical consultation (Ainsworth-Vaughn 1998; Fisher 1991; Mishler 1984; Todd 1993).

More recent work has studied triadic medical consultations, in which a companion or family member is added to the doctor–patient dyad. This work has mainly centered on pediatrics and geriatrics (Adelman, Greene, & Charon 1987; Beisecker 1989; Coupland & Coupland 2000; see also Tates & Meeuwesen 2001 for a review). But it has been noted that there is still a tendency for the speech of a companion (including a family member) to be excluded from any discourse analysis of the medical consultation (Aronsson & Rundström 1988; Ishikawa et al. 2005; Tannen & Wallat 1983), presumably because they are not seen as ratified participants (cf. Goffman 1978).

Research that acknowledges the presence of companions shows that they may play a variety of roles within the medical consultation. Adelman, Greene and Charon (1987) identified three stances taken by the family member or companion: the *patient advocate*, who is an activist for or extender of the patient, or a mediator for both doctor and patient; the *passive observer* who is disengaged from the exchange; or the *antagonist* who undermines the patient or acts opportunistically. Street and Gordon (2008) found that the companion's involvement is often that of a watchdog or affected stakeholder who monitors the interaction and interjects questions, opinions, and concerns when they feel certain issues need to be addressed (2008, p. 249). We may infer on the basis of the Adelman et al. work (cited above) that this interjection may show a stance as advocate or antagonist and, as discussed below, this may be locally constructed in the discourse.

Recent studies have extended the focus from the roles that participants play to the nature of the discourse constructed. In particular, the focus has extended to the co-construction that accompanying family members engage in, and so to the vital information that is exchanged (Cordella 2011a, 2011b; Gordon, Street, Sharf & Souchek 2006; Lienard et al. 2008). Yet this influence is not always positive, with Tsai (2007) finding that the family member's contributions often interrupted and limited the patient's provision of information. A patient's satisfaction with their companion's contributions may depend on the patient's expectations of their companion's role. Hasselkus (1994, p. 291) observes that, with elderly patients, the presence of a family member tends to marginalize the patient and trigger assumptions about dependency. She notes that

> an inexplicable tendency for the physician and caregiver to address each other instead of the patient was often still present. [...] The patient's sphere of influence shrinks and, hence, his or her power or control in the situation is also diminished. (Hasselkus 1994, p. 304)

In the studies described above, all participants share a common language. The present study explores additional issues that can arise when not all parties in the interaction are proficient in English and need to draw on the language skills of others.

Bilingual medical discourse with interpreters

In Australia, the Government provides free access to interpreters for patients in medical settings and these professional interpreters are governed by a code of ethics[1] set up by the National Accreditation Authority for Translators and Interpreters (NAATI). This creates a quite different context for medical interpreting than that found in much of the world, where interpreters are frequently untrained and do not follow a code of ethics (Hale 2007, pp. 44–45).

The role of the interpreter is to provide the language and cultural resources that facilitate communication between the doctor and the patient (Angelelli 2004; Gray, Stanley, Stubbe & Hilder 2011; Major, Napier & Stubbe 2012; Wadensjö 1998). The presence of the interpreter may change the dynamics of the interaction as they have the power to decide what value to assign to contributions from a patient (and their family members). Within the literature on interpreting there is some debate about how best to instantiate this role. Advocates of direct interpreting (e.g. Hale 2007; Tebble 1999) argue that the interpreter's role is best fulfilled by neutrally and accurately interpreting all turns between doctor and patient. Under this approach the onus lies on other parties in the interaction to repair any miscommunication. This stands in contrast to a mediated approach to interpreting (e.g. Angelelli 2004; Bolden 2000), where the interpreter takes a proactive role in managing the conversation and information required. This role may include paraphrasing the doctor's words into layman's terms, editing the patient's response for perceived relevance or providing additional information about procedures that they feel the doctor does not explain clearly (cf. Angelelli 2004, chapter 6).

Issues around interpreting style become particularly relevant in medical interactions where a family member is present. The family member adds an extra party for the interpreter to attend to, and one who may speak simultaneously with other parties. They may also have different levels of proficiency in the heritage language and in English from those of the patient. So the interpreter must continually make a range of judgment calls about the extent to which the family member is a ratified participant (Goffman 1978) at that point in the conversation between the doctor and the patient. The status is therefore locally constructed and is the basis for the interpreter's decision about whether and how to interpret family member contributions in the heritage language (in this case Italian) into English for the doctor. The status is also the basis for whether to interpret English utterances from the patient or family member into Italian in case their relative did not understand what was said. These complexities have not been investigated in the research literature on either medical discourse or interpreter engagement.

---

[1] http://www.naati.com.au/PDF/Booklets/Ethics_Booklet.pdf

Ageing immigrants and their language needs

The current study focuses on older Italian speakers living in Melbourne, capital of the state of Victoria, Australia. Australia has a substantial Italian-speaking population, and Italian is the most widely spoken language in Victoria other than English. The 2011 Census found Victoria has just under 125,000 Italian speakers, many of whom are ageing. While 14 percent of Victorians as a whole are aged 65 and above, the proportion of Italian speakers in this age group is much higher, at 40 percent, because of the shift to English of subsequent generations. Analysis from the 2011 Census also shows that Italian speakers in the group aged 65 and above are much more likely than those in the younger age groups to report speaking English not well or not at all (34 percent as opposed to 4 percent). While the post-war migrants generally developed English skills that allowed them to function well in day-to-day life in Australia, many may not have the skills to negotiate a complex medical encounter in English. In addition, the frequency and complexity of health issues they experience increases as they age.

Older Italian speakers in Melbourne generally arrived from rural communities in regional Italy, often with limited formal education. This means many of them speak dialects quite different from standard Italian. Previous research with focus group members reported that "elderly Italian people who have functioned effectively in English or standard Italian are now reverting to the Italian dialects of their youth, and are having increasing trouble with standard Italian" (Bradshaw, Deumert & Burridge 2008, p. 112). Italian interpreters in Australia are accredited based on their skills in standard Italian. This means they may have varying facility in the dialects that elderly clients speak, potentially leading to miscommunication. The data analyzed here showed little evidence of dialect use, but frequent switches to English may reflect a patient's attempts to compensate for gaps in standard Italian.[2] Older Italian speakers in Australia bring to the patient role in interpreted medical consultations varied (and sometimes partial) repertoires of Italian dialect, standard Italian and English. This allows them to interact directly with the doctor and bypass support from an interpreter.

---

[2] We are indebted to a conference participant for this observation.

Methodology

The data considered in this chapter is drawn from four recordings of multiparty, bilingual medical consultations, conducted in English and Italian. One consultation involved a bilingual doctor, while in the other three consultations an interpreter was present. Interpreter A is female; interpreter B is male. The bilingual doctor was born in Australia from Italian parents. He does not have the language proficiency of a native speaker, but is sufficiently proficient to get his points across to the patient and family member. All of the patients are aged over 70, and each is accompanied by a family member.

The interactions took place in outpatient clinics in two public hospitals in the southeastern suburbs of Melbourne. Hospital 1 is a specialist rehabilitation and aged care facility. Hospital 2 is a large, general hospital. Details of the four consultations are summarized in Table 2-1.

Table 2-1: The participants

Patient pseudonym	Gender	Family Member	Hospital	Clinic Specialist	Interpreter
Anna	f.	Daughter	1	Neurologist	-
Bruno	m.	Wife	2	ENT	A
Francesco	m.	Daughter	2	Vascular surgeon	B
Gia	f.	Husband	2	Endocrinologist	B

The consultations all provided ongoing care for chronic conditions. The patient we have called "Anna" was attending the clinic for assessment of the effect of medication intended to improve her mobility.

"Bruno" suffers from Osler's Disease, which causes frequent hemorrhaging from his nose and the roof of his mouth. "Francesco" was attending a check-up following major heart surgery and "Gia" is a diabetic attending for regular monitoring of her condition. As all patients were attending for the monitoring of a "known problem" (cf. Heritage & Robinson 2006, p. 50), they bring a certain level of lay medical expertise to the consultation. There is no evidence from the recordings that the respective specialist or interpreter had previously worked with the patient.

Ethics approval was sought from and granted by both the Monash Human Research Ethics Committee and the hospitals' ethics committee. After all parties had given consent for the recording, each participant was provided with an individual radio microphone. The consultation was recorded on equipment in a room next to the consultation room. Four individual mono tracks and a stereo mix were recorded. Although the stereo mix was the main source for transcription, the individual microphone tracks were referred to often to clarify overlapping speech segments and to pick up back-channeling and self-directed speech. The annotation tool ELAN[3] was used to enter the transcription as time-aligned annotations keyed to the main audio file. Transcriptions were done using the Du Bois system (see Du Bois, Schuetze-Coburn, Cumming & Paolino 1993). Initial transcription was done by either a fluent bilingual, who was also a NAATI accredited interpreter, or by a competent second language speaker of Italian. A second bilingual speaker checked the transcriptions and translations of Italian. The discourse was then analyzed using a discourse analysis approach that encompasses conversational analysis and interactional sociolinguistics. Conversational analysis focuses on the local organization of talk, attributing meaning to utterances solely on the basis of interlocutor response, without recourse to knowledge of external social factors (cf. Sacks, Schegloff & Jefferson 1974). Interactional sociolinguistics provides knowledge of the turns at hand while interpreting them through a sociocultural lens. This adds to the turn-by-turn analysis, by incorporating Gumperz's (1982a, 1982b) "socio-cultural background knowledge" and Goffman's (1967, 1981, 1983) "interactional framework" as a way to understand the institutional alignments and social identities represented in the discourse. Recurrent patterns were identified and described in the data, with a focus on the local organization of talk and negotiation of meaning, with typical examples forming the basis of the data presented in this chapter.

Roles of family members in bilingual consultations

This chapter focuses on the contribution of family members to medical consultations. We note though that most conversations in the consultations were between the doctor and patient, often mediated by an interpreter. The following extract from Francesco's consultation is typical of this pattern. In our extracts we have used **bold** to represent what was actually said, while the non-bold lines are the English glosses of Italian utterances. Square brackets [ ] in adjacent lines indicate overlapping speech, curly brackets { } indicate transcriber comments, and asterisks * * indicate audible speech that cannot be interpreted. The participants are represented as D (doctor), I (interpreter), P (patient) and F (family member).

---

[3] http://tla.mpi.nl/tools/tla-tools/elan/

Extract 1

1	D:	**h-h-how's he been going with the walking around**

2   I: **camminare/come ti senti a camminare in giro::: muoverti**
are you walking/ how do you feel walking around:::moving around

3   P: **oh:::c-ca-cammino cammino abbastanza (H) pero dopo::: mi deb- er mi debbo anche fermare**
oh ::: I w-wa-walk walk enough (H) but after:::I hav- er I have to stop too

4   P: **perchè (H) eh poi mi sento un pochettino stanco certe volte le gambe poi sono un po- you know (H) mm:::**
because (H) er then I get a little bit tired sometimes my legs you know are a bit – you know (H) mm:::

5   I: **I do I do walk quite a bit but then after a while I have to stop because I [feel ti:::red [(2)] I feel tired and::: it affects my legs also**

6   D: **good   hmm**

In this extract the patient first provides information in line 3 of his level of mobility, which he elaborates in line 4. The interpreter renders this information into English in line 5. The doctor's response of "good" in line 6 signals that this is an appropriate level of progress for the patient to have made, and that the answer was informative enough for him to end that line of questioning.

In our collection of recorded remarks, when family members contributed comments they often did so as simultaneous talk with the patient's own response. These answers were often to questions where the doctor was checking that he[4] had understood earlier talk correctly, as in the Extract 2 below with Anna, her daughter and an Italian-speaking doctor.

Extract 2

1   D: **puo' escere dal letto, [andare e ritorna].**
but (.) but (.) she can get out of bed, go and come back

2   P: **[sì sì sì sì]**
[yes yes yes yes]

3   F: **[sì sì]**
[yes yes]

---

[4] All doctors in this study were men.

In such instances the family member's contribution does not directly add new information to the conversation, but does serve to confirm and reinforce the patient's assessment. In cases where the fact-checking exercise requires a more extended answer, we also see examples of the patient and their family member co-constructing an account, as Bruno and his wife do in Extract 3.[5]

Extract 3

1	D:	so the most recent one here on our records was april 11 .. one month ago
2	I:	*recio* il più recente e qui in aprile the most recent is the one in April
3	F:	[in aprile] in April
4	I:	[in due mille] undici .. un mese fa in 2011, a month ago
5	F:	sì sì yes yes
6	I:	Yes
7	D:	yeah .. then you were in Hillside
8	D:	is that right [Hillside hospital and then you got then transferred to the ICU here] in Midtown
9	P:	[yeah Hillside <unclear>yes yes]
10	F:	{backchannels}
11	D:	Ok
12	P:	but this is not the first time is another time was the [same] thing
13	F:	[yes]
14	P:	there's from last year I think or two years ago .. I was in intensive care ... the same
15	F:	Yeah

---

[5] The names for hospitals used in these examples are pseudonyms.

Bruno's wife makes frequent use of back-channeling and quick confirmations (such as "yes") to support the flow of the discourse—a style that Tannen (1994, p. 63) has labeled "high-involvement." This style means Bruno's wife sometimes gains the floor to answer routine questions addressed to Bruno, as in line 3 of this extract where she first echoes the doctor's interpreted ("in aprile") before answering the question in Italian in line 5. Yet, in response to the doctor's next question (line 8), Bruno takes the floor and responds directly in English (lines 9–14), pre-empting the interpreter and his wife. As Bruno responds his wife continues to provide short back-channel responses in English, reinforcing the correctness of the account and coincidently demonstrating her ability to follow this dialogue in English.

The degree to which English is used in Extract 3 raises an important issue for interpreters. Before starting to collect data, we assumed that patients who requested an interpreter would have little or no knowledge of English. But it became clear in all the consultations that they had acquired considerable English ability in their 50 or so years in Australia. Their accompanying family members also all brought at least some English proficiency to the consultation, though this varied from a strong preference on the part of Bruno's wife to use Italian in the consultation, to the native-like fluency in English from Francesco's daughter. So interpreters in these consultations needed to make judgment calls throughout the consultation about which stretches of English dialogue to interpret and which to leave alone. Our data showed that when the patient or family member spoke in English, the interpreters did not interpret this speech into Italian. The many possible reasons for this include an assumption that the patient and family member will have roughly equal levels of English, a desire to save time by avoiding repetition, or a view of their only role being to mediate communication between the doctor and the patient.

Another issue that arises from the asymmetrical English knowledge our participants bring to the discourse is that comments of family members in Italian may be lost in the interactional moment. When family members speak Italian they are generally interpreted (cf. lines 5 and 6 in Extract 3), but when the patient and family member compete to be heard the family member's comments may get marginalized. This happened at several points, and it meant that potentially important clarifying information was lost. This is shown in Extract 4, where Bruno is answering in Italian the doctor's question about how often he has laser treatment (a question which does not get an answer).

Extract 4

1	P:	**e allor- non ho mai sofferto dopo laser** ah well I have never suffered after the laser
2	P:	**sto bene tre o quattro settimane .. tre settimane ... Sometimes** I'm ok for three or four weeks .. three weeks .. sometimes
3	F:	**prima era un pocchettino più a lungo** at first it lasted a little bit longer
4	I:	**look I've never suffered with the [laser .. I] I go ahead maybe** **three weeks and**
5	P:	**[and the other one]**
6	I:	**then=**
7	P:	**=and then go back and ... the same before**
8	D:	**mhmm...OK**

As Bruno vacillates on the point of whether the effects of the surgery last for three or four weeks in line 2, his wife latches on to his turn to add (in Italian, line 3) that the treatment was more effective initially. At the end of the wife's utterance, the interpreter is able to regain the floor and begin to interpret what Bruno said (line 4). She conveys Bruno's first statement about not suffering "after the laser" and the effective duration of three weeks (line 4), but is interrupted by Bruno speaking English (line 7) before she can add the wife's contribution. The conversation then moves on in English. This extract suggests that interpreters in multiparty interactions may find it harder to hold the floor and interpret all contributions than those who simply mediate between doctor and patient.

In Extract 4, Bruno's wife is seeking to provide additional information about the patient's condition that she believes may be relevant to the diagnosis and treatment plan. This behavior can be interpreted as playing the watchdog role (Street & Gordon 2008) or the patient advocate role (Adelman, Green & Charon 1987). Yet her ability to act effectively in these roles is undermined by her reliance on the interpreter to place her utterances on record. This stands in contrast to the other three family members in our study, who use more extended English on occasion as a way of ensuring that the doctor receives their clarification message. For example, in Extract 5 Gia and the interpreter are negotiating a convoluted answer to the doctor's question, when her husband interjects in English (line 8).

Extract 5

1	D:	**mm hmm**
		and are you seeing the cardiologist

2   P: **yeah .. yes**

3   I: ***cai* al cardiologo**
           you go to the cardiologist

4   P: **Yes**
           sono andata:
           I went

5   I: **ti controla lui**
           he checked you

6   P: **yeah**
           sono andata: .. con settimana fa

7   I: **I went .. weeks ago**

8   F: ***twice a time***

9   P: **e per *mu mi cecca* pace maker**
           and for a check up of the pacemaker

10   I: **quanto .. due settimane**
           when .. two weeks

11   P: **due settimane**
           two weeks

12   I: **two weeks ago I went for a check up   for a pacemaker check up**

13   D: Ok

In this extract we see an example of a mediated interpreting approach (Angelelli 2004), where the interpreter seeks additional information from the patient before interpreting her response back to the doctor. Rather than accept Gia's answer in English in line 2 as sufficient for the doctor, in lines 3 to 5 the interpreter uses his own questions to clarify Gia's understanding before interpreting the message at line 7. At this point, Gia's husband interjects with the comment "*twice a time*." It is not immediately clear whether this comment is supposed to mean that Gia has been to the cardiologist twice, or to answer how many weeks ago the visit was (since the pause in line 6 suggests Gia is searching for this information). So in line 10 the interpreter gives Gia a candidate understanding of the husband's contribution and, having received confirmation, interprets the history back to the doctor. In this instance then, Gia's husband can be said to be using English to ensure that information is put on record and not lost to the moment. His contribution does not solve the interactional trouble in itself, but it is enough to steer the conversation and help the interpreter and Gia to co-construct a narrative for the doctor.

Unlike the spouses, the daughters who accompanied their parents were highly fluent speakers of English and so could contribute more fully to the discourse in English. Both showed facility in Italian as well; however, Francesco's daughter showed a strong preference for responding in English, while Anna's daughter spoke Italian at almost all points in the conversation. Extract 6 shows a rare occasion where Anna's daughter starts her response in English, but even here she quickly self-corrects to Italian and repeats much of what she first said in English (line 8).

Extract 6

1	D:	**ma c'ha disturbo con la vista Lei** but do you have problems with your eyesight
2	P:	**no non c'è disturbo con la vista** no no there isn't any problem with my sight
3	D:	**no così non c'ha cataract er ..[glaucoma]** no like this, no cataracts er glaucoma
4	F:	**[actually she] does have cataracts (.) [yeah and she's got glaucoma as well yeah]**
5	D:	**[(.) glaucoma (1) oh (..) so (.) ok (.) ok (..) yeah]**
6	F:	**so she's taking um she's she's**
7	P:	**ce l'hai la medicina là** do you have the medicine there?
8	F:	**yeah, yeah c'ha prende la medicina per glaucoma per la pressione pressure in the eyes** yeah, yeah taking the medicine for glaucoma to control the blood pressure in her eye

In response to the doctor's question about her eyesight, Anna provides a negative statement "no no there isn't any problem with my sight." Even so, the doctor persists, adding "... no cataracts er glaucoma" (line 3). The patient's daughter uses a pre-disclosure of information token ("actually") to answer the doctor. This shows that the information to be disclosed differs from the patient's answer. When refuting the patient's claim the daughter has codeswitched to English. She does so possibly to soften the "face threat" (Brown & Levinson 1987) implied by her utterance, which challenges the veracity of her mother's previous assertion. In line 8, the daughter corrects her earlier use of English and reproduces the information she has shared with the doctor in Italian, presumably because she wants to ensure that her mother remains fully included in the conversation. Yet Anna's comment in line 7 ("do you have the medicine there?") suggests that she has in fact been following the conversation in English just fine, and is assuming her daughter is stumbling because she can't remember the name of the glaucoma medicine. So the "yeah, yeah" at the start of line 8 can be seen to index recognition of the glaucoma medicine her mother takes, while concomitantly signaling absence of attending to her mother's request.

In Extract 6 Anna's daughter is acting as a health advisor with the full knowledge and blessing of her mother. However, not all interjections by family members were welcomed. Gia in particular objected on several occasions to her husband's input, such as the scolding she gives in Extract 7 as she is explaining a change to her insulin dose.

Extract 7

1	D:	**how long**
2	I:	**da quanto tempo che .. prendi trenta** how long have you been taking thirty
3	P:	**e da: più di una .. due settimane** for more than one .. two weeks
4	I:	**a couple of weeks**
5	F:	**cause before <inaudible> before was very high <inaudible>**
6	P:	**just wait because I'm talking—you be quiet**

While Hasselkus (1994) has commented that the presence of a family member may lead to the doctor talking about the patient to the family member rather than addressing the patient directly, this rarely occurred in our data. As has been clear in the seven extracts shown above, doctors overwhelmingly addressed patients directly and patients had no trouble getting their comments on record. Indeed as Extract 4 and Extract 7 show, family members sometimes had their comments marginalized or deemed illegitimate in these interactions. One extended sequence in our data did show the doctor talking to the family member rather than the patient. This happened in response to a question in English from Francesco's daughter. Interestingly, although Francesco and the interpreter were both present, the interpreter chose to leave this discussion uninterpreted.

Extract 8

1	F:	um (1) can- sor-can I just quickly ask something as well/
2	D:	yeah
3	F:	since he's had this (..) um operation he's become::: (.) i dunno sometimes he seems a bit depressed/ and he gets very emotional like he cri:::es like (.) you know like he'll be talking to someone and he'll get very emotional
4	D:	hm
5	F:	is that normal with a big surgery [like that]/
6	D:	[oh it's a..]e-e-everyone sort of deals with having cos it's a massive life event and th- then they worry about the <XX> everyone sort of talks to you about not making it through the operation and so you know we-we-you you've got yourself sort of emotionally geed up tha-you you're about to have something huge done and everyone sort of deals with that differently
7	F:	{back channelling}
8	D:	some people sort of shrug it off some people get really fixated on it an- oh it always is i-i-it s-sounds like e-everything's sort of going going very well for him but ah but everyone sort of deals with sorta
9	F:	yeah .. it's just yeah he gets very depressed
10	D:	it's it's a high stress situation so everyone deals with that sort of stress a little bit differently ah but I mean from him it should be good er er to to know that I mean that today we'l-after we'll have a good look at him make sure everything IS going WELL for him to know that everything is going very well from our point of view normally sort of makes people feel a bit better as well
11	FM:	Ok

Extract 8 reveals the preference for English of Francesco's daughter, but there appears to be more going on here. The intervention is potentially "face threatening" for Francesco. He may not acknowledge his depression or be willing to discuss his mental state with the doctor. If so, using

English may be a partial attempt to save his "positive face" (Brown & Levinson 1987), as we also suggested for a similar language change in Extract 6. On one hand, the interpreter's lack of engagement may show sensitivity to the patient's "face," while potentially being complicit in his exclusion and disempowerment. On the other hand, interpreters may see interpreting for non-ratified participants or rendering into Italian their client's English contributions as outside their brief. Without interviewing the interpreter, it is not possible to disentangle these facets. It is clear that more research is needed in this area.

A second question raised by Extract 8 is: How do we determine what stance is being taken? In Adelman et al.'s terms (1987), is Francesco's daughter his advocate or his antagonist? She may see her intervention as in her father's interests, but is she acting on his behalf? The complex power issues raised by Extract 8 need to be explored in further research.

The potential difference between a patient's agenda and the agenda of his family member is demonstrated in Extract 9, in which Bruno's wife tries to persuade him to use Italian and he ignores her.

Extract 9

1	D:	**and what's the biggest operation that we've done for you**
2	P:	**Yes**
3	I:	**quale e la più grossa operazione o interventi che hanno fa** what is the biggest operation or procedure that they have done
4	P:	**now.. me was a three**
5	F:	**yeah**
6	P:	**if I remember that's one**
7	F:	**dillo in italiano [così lo] spiega meglio** say it in Italian so she can explain it better
8	I:	**mmhmm say it in Italian so that she can explain it**
9	P:	**one is uhh the skin**
10	F:	**yeah**
11	P:	**no (1s) the fir- . the first probably is .. make a mistake**

Bruno's wife is placing him as in need of interpreter support, presumably because of his limited English skills, while Bruno rejects this ascription and engages in English directly with the doctor. In demonstrating his confidence in his English abilities, Bruno is also showing how highly he values that direct connection. Bruno's stance is empowering, if potentially less effective communicatively.

Conclusion

We began this study with the assumption that the patient and their companion (such as a family member) would use Italian only in the medical consultations and that the interpreter would be the only bilingual participant. Our "pre-view" (Bell 2011) was of an archetypal patient narrative in Italian, delivered in English by the interpreter. Yet, as the data shows, what happens in reality is a much messier mix of language proficiencies and practices. Not only did we have a bilingual doctor consulting in Italian without the need for an interpreter, but the patients and family members showed varying degrees of facility in English and Italian and manipulated their code choice to achieve a variety of ends. Patients and family members often used English as a way of ensuring that important information got on record. English was also used to save time when patients were able to answer a doctor's question directly without waiting for it to be interpreted into Italian. The rapport function of communicating directly with the doctor (rather than via an interpreter) should also not be overlooked. It is one reason that low-English proficiency patients often report higher satisfaction when seeing a doctor who speaks their first language than when using a professional interpreter (cf. Ngo-Metzger et al. 2007).

The family members in these consultations perform a number of roles. They support, remind, and sometimes speak for and about the patient. This changes the dynamic of a traditional doctor–patient exchange and can provide a challenge for interpreters, particularly when a mix of language is used. In community settings in Australia, interpreters often meet patients with some facility in English and so will have developed a range of strategies for judging when to interpret an utterance into the client's L1 and when (if ever) to leave material untranslated. Yet the complexities of multiparty interactions mean that interpreters must also make decisions about who to interpret and which contributions to prioritize.

For adherents of direct interpreting (Hale 2007; Tebble 1999), the question of who or what to interpret should be self-evident—every utterance will be interpreted verbatim. This style has much to commend it, as it helps to bring the patient back in to potentially exclusionary discourse between family members and doctors (as in Extract 8). Yet it also comes at some cost. Most obviously, interpreters may be accused of prolonging the consultation unnecessarily if they interpret information that appears to have been understood already. If all parties are not aware when the consultation starts that *all* utterances will be interpreted, they may face anger from family members if those members interpret some discourse as a private aside between them and the doctor (in English) or them and the patient (in Italian). But perhaps the biggest issue is that the fast pace and frequent occurrence of overlap in multiparty medical discourse means that interpreters will have to intervene heavily in the discourse to manage turn-taking, and ensure parties speak one at a time, if they are to interpret all utterances. The time pressures of medical consultations and the power difference between the doctor and the interpreter can make this hard to enforce. Interpreters who wish to take this strategy would doubtless benefit from more extensive training. Interpreters who prefer a mediated approach or who do not want to interrupt the flow of discourse between parties who appear to understand each other can also benefit from training and reflection on how to manage the multiple voices present in a multiparty medical consultation.

The evidence presented in this chapter shows that family members frequently play an important "health advisor" role, supplementing and correcting information provided by the patient and raising concerns that the patient may otherwise have forgotten to mention. These contributions should be interpreted whenever possible. Considering that time is always a concern in medical exchanges, we may suggest that the interpreter focuses on any information that could help the medical practitioner in assessing the health and wellbeing of the patient regardless of who is delivering the information. In cases when the patient and family members speak in a common language, the interpreter may need to identify whether some sensitive and private information is being exchanged between them and use this as a basis for selecting what they interpret.

Acknowledgements

Our profuse thanks go to the patients, family members, doctors and interpreters, to Ana Cek and the staff of the outpatient clinics, and to two anonymous reviewers whose suggestions have assisted us greatly.

References

Adelman, R.D., M.G. Greene and R. Charon. 1987, "The physician-elderly patient-companion triad in the medical encounter: The development of a conceptual framework and research agenda", *The Gerontologist* 27(6): 729–34. doi:10.1093/geront/27.6.729

Ainsworth-Vaughn, N. 1998, *Claiming Power in Doctor-Patient Talk*, New York: Oxford University Press

Angelelli, C.V. 2004, *Medical Interpreting and Cross-Cultural Communication*, Cambridge; New York: Cambridge University Press

Aronsson, K. and B. Rundström. 1988, "Child discourse and parental control in pediatric consultations". *Text* 8: 159–89. doi:0.1515/text.1.1988.8.3.159

Beisecker, A.E. 1989, "The influence of a companion on the doctor-elderly patient interaction", *Health Communication* 1(1): 55–70. doi:10.1207/s15327027hc0101_7

Bell, A. 2011, "Re-constructing Babel: Discourse analysis, hermeneutics and the Interpretive Arc". *Discourse Studies* 13(5): 519–68. doi:10.1177/1461445611412699

Bolden, G.B. 2000, "Toward understanding practices of medical interpreting: Interpreters' involvement in history taking", *Discourse Studies* 2(4): 387–419. doi:10.1177/1461445600002004001

Bradshaw, J., A. Deumert and K. Burridge. 2008, *Victoria's Languages: Gateway to the World*, VITS Language Link: http://www.vits.com.au/resources

Brown, P. and S.C. Levinson. 1987, *Politeness: Some Universals in Language Usage*, Cambridge; New York: Cambridge University Press

Candlin, C.N., and S. Candlin. 2002, "Discourse, expertise, and the management of risk in health care settings", *Research on Language and Social Interaction* 35(2): 115–37. doi:10.1207/S15327973RLSI3502_1

Candlin, S. 2002, Taking risks: An indicator of expertise? *Research on Language and Social Interaction* 35(2): 173–93. doi:10.1207/S15327973RLSI3502_3

Cordella, M. 2011a, "A triangle that may work well: Looking through the angles of a three-way exchange in cancer medical encounters", *Discourse & Communication* 5(4): 337–53. doi:10.1177/1750481311418100

—. 2011b, "Enfrentándose al cáncer en compañía: el rol del familiar en la consulta", *Discurso & Sociedad* 5(3): 469–91

Coupland, N. and J. Coupland. 2000, "Relational frames and pronominal address/reference: The discourse of geriatric medical triads". In S. Sarangi and M. Coulthard, eds, *Discourse and social life*, London: Pearson, pp. 207–29

Du Bois, J.W., S. Schuetze-Coburn, S. Cumming and D. Paolino. 1993, "Outline of discourse transcription". In J. Edwards and M. Lampert, eds, *Talking Data: Transcription and Coding in Discourse Research*, Hillsdale, N.J.: Lawrence Erlbaum, pp. 45–89

Fisher, S. 1991, "A discourse of the social: medical talk/power talk/oppositional talk?" *Discourse & Society* 2(2): 157–82. doi:10.1177/0957926591002002002

Goffman, E. 1967, *Interaction Ritual : Essays in Face-to-face Behavior*, Chicago: Aldine.

—. 1978, "Response cries", *Language* 54(4): 787–815. doi:10.2307/413235

—. 1981, *Forms of Talk*, Philadelphia: University of Pennsylvania Press

—. 1983, "The interaction order: American Sociological Association, 1982 presidential address", *American Sociological Review* 48(1): 1–17

Gordon, H.S., R.L. Street, B.F. Sharf and J. Souchek. 2006, "Racial differences in doctors' information-giving and patients' participation", *Cancer* 107(6): 1313–20. doi:10.1002/cncr.22122

Gray, B., J. Stanley, M. Stubbe and J. Hilder. 2011, "Communication difficulties with limited English proficiency patients: Clinician perceptions of clinical risk and patterns of use of interpreters", *Journal of the New Zealand Medical Association* 124(1342): 23–36

Gumperz, J.J. 1982a, *Discourse Strategies*, Cambridge: Cambridge University Press

—. ed. 1982b, *Language and Social Identity*, Cambridge; New York: Cambridge University Press

Hale, S.B. 2007, *Community Interpreting*, Basingstoke; New York: Palgrave Macmillan

Hasselkus, B.R. 1994, "Three-track care: Older patient, family member, and physician in the medical visit", *Journal of Aging Studies* 8(3): 291–307. doi:10.1016/0890-4065(94)90005-1

Heritage, J. and J.D. Robinson. 2006, "Accounting for the visit: giving reasons for seeking medical advice". In J. Heritage and D.W. Maynard, eds, *Communication in Medical Care: Interaction Between Primary Care Physicians and Patients*, Cambridge, U.K.; New York: Cambridge University Press, pp. 48–85

Ishikawa, H., H. Hashimoto, D.L. Roter, Y. Yamazaki, T. Takayama and E. Yano. 2005, "Patient contribution to the medical dialogue and perceived patient-centeredness", *Journal of General Internal Medicine* 20(10): 906–10. doi:10.1111/j.1525-1497.2005.0200.x

Lienard, A., I. Merckaert, Y. Libert, N. Delvaux, S. Marchal, J. Boniver, A-M Etienne, J. Klastersky, C. Reynaert, P. Scalliet, J-L Slachmuylder and D. Razavi. 2008, "Factors that influence cancer patients' and relatives' anxiety following a three-person medical consultation: Impact of a communication skills training program for physicians", *Psycho-Oncology* 17(5): 488–96. doi:10.1002/pon.1262

Major, G., J. Napier and M. Stubbe. 2012, "'What happens truly, not textbook!': Using authentic interactions in discourse training for healthcare interpreters". In L. Swabey and K. Malcolm, eds. *In Our Hands: Educating Healthcare Interpreters*, Washington, D. C.: Gallaudet University Press, pp. 27–53

Mishler, E.G. 1984, *The Discourse of Medicine: Dialectics of Medical Interviews*, Norwood NJ: Ablex

Ngo-Metzger, Q., D.H. Sorkin, R.S. Phillips, S. Greenfield, M.P. Massagli, B. Clarridge and S.H. Kaplan. 2007, "Providing high-quality care for limited English proficient patients: The importance of language concordance and interpreter use", *Journal of General Internal Medicine* 22(Suppl 2): 324–30. doi:10.1007/s11606-007-0340-z

Sacks, H., E.A. Schegloff and G. Jefferson. 1974, "A simplest systematics for the organization of turn-taking for conversation", *Language* 50(4): 696–735. doi:10.2307/412243

Sarangi, S. and A. Clarke, A. 2002, "Zones of expertise and the management of uncertainty in genetics risk communication", *Research on Language & Social Interaction* 35(2): 139–71. doi:10.1207/S15327973RLSI3502_2

Street, R.L. and H.S. Gordon. 2008, "Companion participation in cancer consultations", *Psycho-Oncology* 17(3): 244–51. doi:10.1002/pon.1225

Tannen, D. 1994, *Gender and Discourse*, New York: Oxford University Press

Tannen, D. and C. Wallat. 1993, "Doctor/mother/child communication: Linguistic analysis of a pediatric interaction". In S. Fisher and A.D. Todd, eds, *The Social Organization of Doctor–patient Communication*, Norwood, N.J.: Ablex Publishing Group, pp. 31–48

Tates, K. and L. Meeuwesen. 2001, "Doctor–parent–child communication. A (re)view of the literature", *Social Science & Medicine* 52(6): 839–51. doi:10.1016/S0277-9536(00)00193-3

Tebble, H. 1999, "The tenor of consultant physicians: Implications for medical interpreting", *The Translator* 5(2): 179–200. doi:10.1080/13556509.1999.10799040

Todd, A.D. 1993, "A diagnosis of doctor–patient discourse in the prescription of contraception". In A.D. Todd and S. Fisher, eds, *The Social Organization of Doctor-patient Communication*, Norwood NJ: Ablex Publishing Group, pp. 183–212

Tsai, M. 2007, "Who gets to talk? An alternative framework evaluating companion effects in geriatric triads", *Communication & Medicine* 4(1): 37–49. doi:10.1515/CAM.2007.005

Wadensjö, C. 1998, *Interpreting in Interaction*, London: Longman

CHAPTER THREE

HOSPITAL HUMOR: PATIENT-INITIATED HUMOR AS RESISTANCE TO CLINICAL DISCOURSE

SUZANNE EGGINS

Keywords: humor, healthcare communication, critical linguistics, stigma

Abstract

While hospitals might not seem very funny places, naturally occurring interactions reveal that patients and clinicians laugh and joke with each other even as they go about the serious business of suffering and caring. This humor occurs against a background of evidence that miscommunication in hospitals poses a significant threat to patient safety and satisfaction (Arora et al. 2005; Garling 2008; Haig et al. 2006). Health communication research suggests that many clinicians fail to build empathy with patients, do not give patients space to tell their story and often exclude patients from discussions about their care (Slade et al. 2011). While ethnographically-based research has indicated that humor among clinicians functions to enforce hierarchies and establish solidarity, there is little critical discourse-based research into patient-initiated humor with clinicians in hospital settings. In this chapter I apply concepts from interactional sociology and critical linguistics to argue that patient-initiated humor allows patients to intervene in and resist the clinical discourse that risks stigmatizing, excluding and disempowering them. I suggest that critical applied linguistic research into humor can help us support clinicians to rethink what it might mean to interact with patients as "co-producers" of their healthcare.

Introduction

Contemporary healthcare debates are dominated by the interconnected drives to improve patient safety and to achieve the cultural shift from "a passive view of patients as undiscriminating recipients of care defined by others" to an emerging view of patients as active partners and "co-producers" in their healthcare (Iedema et al. 2008, p. 105). Australian and international evidence has demonstrated that miscommunication in hospitals poses a significant threat to patient safety and satisfaction (Arora et al. 2005; Garling 2008; Haig et al. 2006). Empirical evidence suggests that patient involvement improves clinical outcomes (Haynes, McKibbon & Kanani 1996; Kravitz & Melnikow 2001; Wong et al. 2008). Yet research suggests that many clinicians fail to build empathy with patients, do not give patients space to tell their story and often exclude patients from discussions about their care (Slade et al. 2011). While hospitals might not seem very funny places, naturally occurring interactions reveal that patients and clinicians laugh and joke with each other with surprising frequency. This chapter uses critical sociological and linguistic approaches to explore what patients are doing when they initiate humorous exchanges with their clinicians. I ask whether clinicians are managing these humorous moments in ways that build empathy and recognize the patient's democratic right to be included as active partners in their healthcare.

Data and methodology

During fieldwork for a national study of how doctors and nurses hand over information about patients in public hospitals (ECCHo[1], see Eggins & Slade forthcoming), I was struck by how frequently patients introduced humor into their interactions with clinicians. To investigate this, I drew on data from the ECCHo study and from Slade et al.'s (2011) study of communication between clinicians and patients in an emergency department (ED).

Both qualitative studies combine detailed ethnographic observation, interviews with clinicians, audio and some video recording of naturally occurring interactions, and discourse analysis. From the ECCHo and ED corpora, I established a data subset, based on the quality of the audio and transcribed data and on the availability of observation notes or my own presence as observer. The subset consisted of transcripts of:

1. interactions between six patients and their clinicians, from triage to discharge from the ED (for each patient, interactions were spread over several hours)

---

[1] ECCHo—Effective Clinical Communication in Handover—is a three-year health communication research project directed by Diana Slade, University of Technology Sydney, 2011–2014.

2. 18 handover events where outgoing nurses handed over information
    about patients to the incoming nursing team at the patient's bedside.
    (each handover event lasted about 20 minutes and involved the
    handover of multiple patients).

Participants in the subset included male and female nurses, paramedics,
doctors and patients, and ranged in age from mid-twenties to mid-sixties,
with most participants of Anglo-Australian background.

To identify moments of demonstrated humor or when humor was most
likely intended, I used the following recognized signals of entry into what
Goffman (1974) has called the "play mode" and Hymes (1974) refers to as
"humorous key:"

- laughter (by initiator or responders)
- change of pace, volume, intonation, stress
- facial expression or physical posture
- hyperbole or other verbal content that could not 'be taken seriously' in
  the textual context.

As examples throughout this chapter demonstrate, spontaneous humor in
naturally occurring interactions is created collaboratively through dialogic
negotiation. For this reason, interactive sequences (technically, exchanges,
see Eggins & Slade 2004)—rather than isolated sentences—are taken as
the unit of humor analysis.

Initial observations and research questions

An initial review of the data subset confirmed my anecdotal observations
of the comparative frequency of patient-initiated humor. I identified only
nine exchanges during which clinicians initiated humor with patients,
against about 80 exchanges during which patients initiated humor with
clinicians. To contextualize further discussion, I begin with two examples.
In Text 1, a male ED paramedic in his forties is about to take blood from
Dulcie, a 62-year-old Anglo-Australian woman who presented to the ED
with difficulty breathing. The paramedic is an Anglo-Australian male, in
his early thirties.

Text 1 "Dulcie" [Communication in Emergency Departments project data]

Paramedic: *[preparing to take a blood sample from the patient]* So it
                stings a bit to have this one done.

Patient: Yeah.

Paramedic: Okay?

Patient: Well I hope you can get it because when I usually have
                blood tests, I'm like a cow that won't give milk.

Paramedic: Oh, you're not are you?

Patient: *[laughs]* I just wish you all the best, mate.

Paramedic: *[chuckles]* May the force be with me, hey?

Patient: Yeah, I've always been like that.

Text 2—"Edna"—occurs during a 1pm nursing shift handover. The
outgoing nurse—an Anglo-Australian woman in her thirties—has just
finished working the morning shift and is handing over her patients to the
four nurses on the afternoon shift. Since January 2012 this hospital has
required that nurses do these shift handovers at the patient's bedside (see
Eggins & Slade, in preparation, for discussion of the communication
challenges of bedside handovers). Here the outgoing nurse is handing over
an Anglo-Australian patient in her seventies.

Text 2 "Edna" [ECCHo project data]

Outgoing Nurse:	*[handing over to the four incoming shift nurses, the outgoing nurse stands with her back to the patient, who is in bed]*
	Here we have um Edna Locks with her cellulitis as well as the left leg. Um general diet that she's tolerating well. QID obs are good. She's afebrile. All other obs are good. She's on oral ABs. Ah mobilizes with a wheelie walker and stand-by assistance. Set-up assistance in the shower this morning. One point five fluid restriction. Fluid balance chart. Um she's for a Geri's review[2] as well. Um family meeting which she had this morning um.
Patient:	*[lightly, cheerfully]* The only thing I can't eat is tomatoes. That's why I'm in the hospital.
Receiving nurses:	*[all laugh]*
Outgoing Nurse:	Um no plan from that family meeting.
Patient:	I'm to go to another ward sooner or later.
Outgoing Nurse:	Ward B most likely. OK, she's all good, just waiting a Geri's review and a plan where she's going when she goes home. And then we go to ... *[moves to next patient]*

Examples of patient-initiated humor raised three main research questions that this chapter addresses:

1. Why do patients initiate light-hearted, humorous exchanges with clinicians?
2. What types of humor do patients initiate with clinicians?
3. Why is it that clinicians sometimes respond in a light-hearted way to patients' humor (e.g. Dulcie), while others make no response at all to patients' humorous contributions (e.g. Edna)?

As the following brief literature review makes clear, published research offers limited insights into patient-initiated humor.

---

[2] The Geriatric medical team will review the patient.

Literature review

Research into humor from philosophical, psychological and literary perspectives has suggested that humor arises where there is incongruity of some kind (Bateson 1973; Bergson 1950; Freud 1905; Koestler 1964). Within linguistics, Brown and Levinson's (1987) account of "face" proposed that joking is a strategy to minimize the threat to positive face, to which sociolinguistic studies added the crucial distinction between "joke telling" and "conversational" (i.e. spontaneous) humor (e.g. Boxer & Cortes-Conde 1997; Kotthoff 1996; Norrick 1993). Research from conversation analysis approaches drew attention to laughter and its association with "troubles talk" (Jefferson 1984). More linguistic orientations suggest humor makes both serious and non-serious meanings, available simultaneously (Mulkay 1988).

Critical sociological accounts suggest that humor functions to expose social differences and conflicts. Douglas suggests that joking only arises when the social structure itself involves a "joke" of some kind (Douglas 1975, p. 98). Drawing on Douglas as well as critical linguistics (Kress 1985) and critical discourse analysis (Fairclough 1995) to explain humor in casual conversation, Eggins and Slade suggest humor can usefully be interpreted as incongruous polysemy that simultaneously draws attention to and manages social tensions, predominantly around power relations (Eggins & Slade 1997/2004).

Empirical sociological and linguistic research identified the workplace as a site where spontaneous humor plays a critical role, especially in creating group cohesion, communicating in-group/out-group boundaries and managing "upwards" (e.g. Fine & De Soucey 2005; Lynch 2010; Roth & Vivona 2010; Roy 1960; Tracy et al. 2006). Studies like those of Holmes (2000) on the context-bound nature of workplace humor and its often complex relationship to power indicated that politeness interpretations of humor that deploy the concept of "face" need significant contextualization and refinement.

Perhaps because of the significant practical and ethical challenges of collecting data, empirical studies of humor in hospitals are both methodologically and theoretically limited. Methodologically, research is dominated by self-reporting, questionnaires and interview studies. Patenaude and Hamelin Brabant's 2006 literature review of humor in nurse–patient relationships lists only one study in the 15 identified–Mallett and A'Hern (1996)–that recorded authentic interactions.

Theoretically, early interpretations of hospital humor focused on the potentially therapeutic value of humor to ease anxiety (Madden 1986;

Robinson 1977). Although Mallett and A'Hern (1996) video-recorded natural communication between nurses and five haemodialysis patients, they offered a similarly limited interpretation of humor as "improving the relationship" between nurse and patient and helping them deal with difficult situations.

More critical ethnographic research includes Coser's (1959, 1960) early study of a private psychiatric hospital. Coser highlighted humor's role in expressing power relations, noting that humor operated along downward hierarchical lines, and suggested humor made it possible for nurses to switch quickly between "friendly" and "professional" modes of interaction.

Yoels and Clair's (1995) symbolic interactionist study observed humor among and across clinician and patient groups in an outpatient clinic. Yoels and Clair found that junior doctors shared "in-group" humor about their workload, mentoring and social characteristics of patients. Between senior and junior doctors, Yoels and Clair found support for Coser's claim of the "downward" flow of humor, with consulting physicians teasing junior residents. And when the residents joked with the nurse manager Yoels and Clair suggest the humor reflects the tensions around status and institutional power. I discuss the similarities and differences between Yoels and Clair's findings and humor among clinicians in the ED and clinical handover project in Eggins (in preparation).

On humor initiated by doctors with patients Yoels and Clair claim this "most clearly reflects the dual effects of humor as both integrating and differentiating" (p. 49). Again, they suggest clinician–patient humor may "blur status lines" by emphasizing commonalities between patients and clinicians. Clinicians also used humor to mitigate their intrusions into patients' personal life, although patients sometimes misunderstood clinician-initiated humor. Unfortunately, Yoels and Clair present no observations of humor initiated by patients, implying that humor is initiated only by clinicians. This conflicts with the evidence of the data I have studied.

Monrouxe and Rees (2010) take a conversation analysis approach to bedside teaching encounters—hospital medical events at which the senior consultant, one or more junior doctors and patients are present. Monrouxe, Rees and Bradley (2009) show how patients are constructed as "passive objects" in these encounters. Rees and Monrouxe (2010) focus on the power relations enacted by clinicians through laughter—how consultants' teasing of their students can be met by resistance. However, the researchers note—but do not elaborate on—"numerous examples" where they say patients "subvert the power asymmetry momentarily through asking playful questions" (Rees & Monrouxe 2010, p. 3393).

Symbolic interactionists Waskul and van der Riet (2002) present extracts from interviews with patients in palliative care who are dying of disfiguring cancers. The researchers draw on Goffman's (1963) account of "stigma" to theorize patients' expressions of violation, alienation and powerlessness. Waskul and van der Riet identify two "corrective measures" that patients employ to deal with their "abject" bodies: (1) to objectify the abjection so as to distance themselves from it; and (2) to employ humor, to make it a subject they can laugh about or at least "take somewhat more lightly" (p. 501).

While these approaches to hospital humor provide useful starting points, to theorize and describe adequately the humor in my data I found I needed a closer integration of sociological and linguistic concepts. The following section draws on Goffman's (1963) notion of "stigma" and Kress's (1985) Foucault-influenced critical linguistic identification of institutional discourses to theorize a critical discourse-based approach to spontaneous humor in patient–clinician data.

Theorizing patient–clinician humor as a response to stigmatized identity

Like Yoels and Clair (1995) and other critical ethnographically-based research (e.g. Strauss et al. 1985/1997; Slade et al. forthcoming), my own fieldwork suggests several tensions or "jokes" in the social structure of public hospitals. The most striking aspect is that patients must cede agency over their bodies to a class of objective "professionals." In relinquishing autonomy patients are expected to repress their personal attitude and emotions, and to bear their illness and its associated indignities and institutional intrusions with patient stoicism.

This loss of agency and autonomy is so central to what it means to become a hospital patient that, as Waskul and van der Riet (2002) suggest, it invites theorization in terms of Goffman's (1963) discussion of normative role identity and "stigmatized" identity. For Goffman, a "stigma" refers to any characteristic, known or knowable, about an individual that sets that individual apart from identity norms for the culture. I suggest we can theorize that patients use humor with clinicians to manage the extreme social shock of finding themselves in the "stigmatized" role of hospital patient.

Patients are "stigmatized" because they violate the social norm of the physically healthy and mentally competent individual capable of exercising autonomy and agency, a norm that is implicit in all areas of social life—from architecture to employment, transportation, clothing, advertising and civic duties. Wearing pyjamas and being in bed both overtly "discredit" and radically disempower patients. Once hospitalized, you no longer manage your own body. Your private, offstage life becomes a public, onstage life, controlled by what Goffman refers to as "normals," and observed by normals and by others as stigmatized as you. Patients—not staff—have limited visual and no auditory privacy, even when undressing or performing bodily functions.

As Goffman points out (1963, p. 13), interaction is the critical place for negotiating relationships between stigmatized and normal individuals, constituting "one of the primal scenes of sociology." Goffman and others have noted that stigmatized people typically carry the burden of "emotion work," which includes managing their stigma in interactions (e.g. Cahill & Eggleston 1994; Goffman 1963; Strauss et al. 1985/1997; Waskul & van der Riet 2002). Yet neither Goffman nor others have traced this management work in examples of actual interactions.

To do so, we need to recognize that patients must manage their stigma in a context where the clinical discourse is dominant. The term "discourse" is used here in the critical linguistic sense defined by Kress, drawing on Foucault, where discourses are

> systematically-organized sets of statements which give expression to the meanings and values of an institution … A discourse provides a set of possible statements about a given area, and organizes and gives structure to the manner in which a particular topic, object, process is to be talked about in that it provides descriptions, rules, permissions and prohibitions of social and individual actions. (Kress 1985, p. 7)

Discourses are expressed through patterned linguistic choices. We can recognize a discourse when we identify a cluster of linguistic features that characterize a relatively stable way of speaking within a particular institutional domain of knowledge or sphere of action.

Clinical discourse is the expression of the "professional," expert, institutional world of medical care. Its meanings and values stand in opposition to those of everyday discourse, for which we might consider casual conversation to be "the unmarked register." Table 3-1 lists some of the main oppositions between these discourses. These oppositions are realized linguistically through patterns in discourse, grammar, lexis, and phonology. For example, the contrast between technical/vernacular is largely realized through vocabulary choices. Objective/subjective is expressed through grammatical patterns such as pronominal choice. The concise/expansive contrast is realized through ellipsis and clause combining relations, and also in topic choice. Contrasts are also expressed through the sources of intertextual references and embedded registers. For example, clinical discourse is a restricted discourse that does not often "borrow" other texts, while everyday discourse frequently incorporates popular culture references and intertexts, as discussion of textual examples will demonstrate.

If we look again at Text 2 "Edna," we can see the nurse using this clinical discourse in her first turn. Her speech is characterized by the objectification of Edna as body parts and attributes. Syntactically the nurse's speech is elliptical, in the third person and impersonal. The vocabulary is technical. The discourse is restricted in topics and in grammatical choices, with heavy use of verbs of being and having rather than verbs of material action.

Table 3-1: Contrasting "clinical" and "everyday" discourses

Contrasting discourses	
Clinical	**Everyday**
Scientific	Commonsense
Objective	Subjective
3rd	1st person
Factual	Attitudinal
Public	Private
Technical	Vernacular
Impersonal	Personal
Distant	Intimate
Formal	Colloquial
Serious	Humorous
Restricted	Open
Concise/Elliptical	Expansive/Redundant
Restrained	Exaggerated
Polite	Coarse
Monotextual	Intertextual (especially popular cultural intertexts)

Clinical discourse is dominant in the hospital context, particularly in clinician-initiated encounters with patients. Yet in his study of patients with chronic disease, Frank suggests that the objectification and passifization of you-as-body-parts that characterizes clinical discourse may contribute to you becoming "a spectator to your own drama" (Frank 1991).

Re-registration: humorous resistance to clinical discourse

So how can patients manage the stigmatized role that clinical discourse accords them in interactions? The data suggest that patients may comply or resist. If compliant, patients may accept their stigmatized role and speak only when spoken to, speak about their body as an object and restrict their contributions to clinical discourse. This last requirement is of course highly constraining, as only patients with long-term serious or chronic illnesses and multiple previous hospital admissions are likely to be able to "speak" clinical discourse to any extent.

Patients have strong motivations to comply with their relative exclusion from clinical discourse—fear of offending clinical staff and so incurring less-than-optimum treatment are obvious drivers. Text 3 "Andrew" (a 53-year-old Anglo-Australian) shows the patient's acceptance of his passive role *and* his realization that his humorous remark could be interpreted as subversive.

Text 3 "Andrew" [ECCHo project data]

Outgoing Nurse: *[standing at the foot of the patient's bed and addressing the incoming team of nurses]* His blood pressure was a little bit low this morning, so we have encouraged some fluids and it has come up a little bit now. So he was musing a 2 but now he's only musing a 1. And he has been up sitting out of bed for meals which—he is going to be getting up and sitting out of bed for meals. He's tolerating his diet. He transfers times one onto the commode. And Andrew has declined the rehab and TTCP. He just wants to um discharge home with social work input. So we are encouraging him to get up and do everything. Didn't quite get to the shower but he's been up and the bed's all been changed and everything's been done. And he's—when his sister comes in today he'd like to get hold of a wheelchair to go for a walk with his sister in the wheelchair. Is that right, Andrew?

Patient:	It'd be right if you said so!
Incoming Nurses:	*[laughter]*
Outgoing Nurse:	OK.
Patient:	I don't mean that to be sarcastic.
Outgoing Nurse:	No. That's alright. Now remember, drinking lots.
Patient:	Yeah.
Outgoing Nurse:	Lots of fluids.

The alternative to complying with the role positioning clinical discourse offers is to resist. As a patient you may assert your subjectivity and agency and speak out of turn, speak about yourself as a sentient, emotional subject, and use everyday discourse.

It is here, I argue, that humor comes in. Humor is a resource that allows patients to subvert the "patient" role without alienating their professional caregivers. In the previous example Andrew gets away with his comment "It'd be right if you said so!" because it is said light-heartedly and, he quickly asserts, is not meant to be sarcastic. Humor allows Andrew to both say and not say what is going on in the situation: that the clinical staff determines his present and future actions.

The principal humorous technique that patients draw on to resist the positioning of clinical discourse is what I call "re-registration." Re-registration occurs when one or more participants shift from clinical to everyday discourse during interaction. For example, when Edna in Text 2 intervenes with "The only thing I can't eat is tomatoes," her contribution is incongruous because it offers first person, anecdotal, informal, non-technical, private information that is, from the clinical discourse point of view, irrelevant.

In this account, humor through re-registration represents the patient's insistent attempts to reclaim personal identity and agency and so resist the stigmatizing force of "patienthood." This means that humor is inherently subversive: it signals a resistance (however mild) to the dominant discourse and the power relations that discourse implies.

I would predict that if someone is challenging a dominant discourse, even humorously, they are likely to meet some opposition—as Andrew worries in Text 3. And indeed, this is what happens. Goffman's theory allows us to make sense of a striking but not infrequent behavior that I, other researchers and many patients have observed in hospital wards: nurses and doctors stand at a patient's bed and speak *about* the patient as if the patient was not there. And if by chance the patient tries to intervene in the interaction, some clinicians ignore them. As Goffman (1963, p. 18) predicts in his account of stigma, in interaction "normals" may act towards the stigmatized as if they were non-persons: "not present at all as someone of whom ritual notice is to be taken."

If we return to Text 2, we can see that although Edna is not invited to contribute, she does so anyway—using emphatic vernacular: "The only thing I can't eat is tomatoes." This incongruous juxtaposition of the clinical and the everyday is greeted with laughter by the receiving nurses *but not by the outgoing nurse*. The outgoing nurse refuses to let Edna disrupt her clinical discourse and all it represents for power relations. Edna is "a non-person." The laughter from the receiving nurses is neutralized as the outgoing nurse reasserts her control of the discourse.

Compare that with what happens in Text 1—"Dulcie." Here we see the patient shifting into playful everyday language with the simile "I'm like a cow that won't give milk." This elicits at least an acknowledgement from the paramedic. Dulcie then recontextualizes the encounter, invoking an everyday register of ironic "good luck" wishes, as if the paramedic were a friend who was about to take on a sporting challenge they're unlikely to succeed in. But this time the paramedic responds in kind, invoking the popular culture intertext of *Star Wars*. So here we see an example where the clinician responds empathetically, and is happy to step "out of" the clinical discourse to build rapport with the patient. It is suggestive that this example involves a paramedic rather than a nurse or doctor. Perhaps the paramedic is less institutionalized into clinical discourse than the "professionals."

It is important to stress that the argument here is a structural one. It is not a matter of individual clinicians being more or less friendly to their patients or being "too busy" to respond to the humorous contributions of those patients. At issue is the construal of patients as stigmatized through the patterns of clinical discourse that allow clinicians to ignore patients as a legitimate professional act. Clinicians are able to violate two of the taken-for-granted default conditions that participants respect in everyday interactions: (1) "do not speak about people in their presence—speak *to* them"; and (2) "if someone speaks to you, acknowledge them and respond."

I have suggested that the shift out of the clinical into the everyday discourse is the main technique in patient–clinician humor. I will now exemplify five different types of re-registration humor: (1) stigma-minimization; (2) humorous misinterpretation; (3) interposing; (4) disconfirming; and (5) sending-up.

1. Stigma-minimization

By humorously self-describing in vernacular language, often with evaluative hyperbole, patients note and accept their stigma. One of the implicit assumptions of clinical discourse is that symptoms do not matter "personally." Symptoms are talked about objectively, as temporary factual components of a de-personalized body. However, patients may resist this assumption, as in Text 4.

Text 4: "Ugly" [ECCHo project data]

Discharge Nurse:	So once the drain's out and it's been cleaned up
Patient:	Yeah.
Discharge Nurse:	it will look—at the moment you look
Patient:	*[lightly]* ugly!
Discharge Nurse:	*[chuckles]* No. I was going to say 'bloody' is ==[3]what I was going to say.
Patient:	==Yeah, that too.
Discharge Nurse:	*[laughs]* So yeah um once—well we'll get a nice dressing for going over it and then that can just stay on and we'll make sure it's waterproof.

In this example, the patient reminds the nurse that her stigma has, for her, affective or attitudinal meaning. "Ugly" is an evaluative term; "bloody," as used by the nurse, is factual. The conventional description of humor of this type as "self-deprecating" is not entirely accurate. Patients are not understating their worth out of modesty; they are acknowledging their flawed identity against conventional standards.

2. Humorous misinterpretation

By deliberately reacting to clinical questions or comments in a personal way, patients re-inject the personal into the clinical discourse. This is a common type of mild resistance by patients to the unequal power relations that clinical discourse imposes by giving the clinician sole rights to ask questions and control the interaction.

---

[3] The == symbol marks points at which another speaker begins talking (i.e. overlap).

Text 5: Examples of humorous misinterpretation

1	ED Nurse:	*[filling in a form]* Have you got any allergies to anything?
	Patient:	Only the normal one, to hospitals.
	ED Nurse:	*[said without humor]* To hospitals, right. Do you drink alcohol at all?
	Patient:	I have. [ED project data]
2	ED Nurse:	*[filling in a form]* Have you got any allergies to anything?
	ED Nurse:	Now, you don't have any large amounts of money on you, do you?
	Patient:	Oh, only a couple of million, that's all. I wish.
	ED Nurse:	You happy to hang on to that? [ED project data]
3	Discharge Nurse:	*[filling in form]* So the other day we got up to ... you ... not needing an interpreter and speaking English. And do you identify as being Aboriginal or Torres Strait Islander?
	Patient:	*[jokey tone]* Very rarely, very rarely.
	Discharge Nurse:	*[laughs]* [ECCHo project data]

As these examples show, clinicians sometimes play along with humorous misinterpretation (as in 2 and 3 in Text 5). But they can also ignore it (as in 1 in Text 5), where the patient is treated as a non-person.

3. Interposing

By inserting into clinical discourse a personal, attitudinal contribution, patients remind clinicians that they are human, sentient and present. In Text 6, we see the nurses acknowledging such an intervention:

Text 6: "Sarah" [ECCHo project data]

1	Outgoing nurse:	This is Sarah. She's come in after a fall with a fractured left arm. Er she's getting increasingly independent every day. We've also got some bruising of the right leg and whatnot. She's got those elevated and they're doing quite well.

		They're just a little bit of pain there. Increasing pain in the left arm as we're starting to move around more and more. We had a good shower today though. You're eating really well.
2	Patient:	Uh huh.
3	Outgoing nurse:	Yeah ==um we've had an x-ray.
4	Patient:	==Got my hair washed again.
5	Incoming nurse:	Good! *[chuckles]*.
6	Outgoing nurse:	*[laughs]* Yeah. We've got um we've had an x-ray today ah and the ortho team are going to review that ah either today or tomorrow and we're going to get a plan from there cause we're not sure whether we're going to use conservative management or go for surgical. That's still up in the air. But yeah we're a bit sick of the whole thing, aren't we? *[laughs]*
7	Patient:	Oh well I'm not going anywhere till it gets fixed one way or ==the other.
8	Outgoing nurse:	==No, that's right. Yes, we're just managing pain and waiting for further review and ah plans.

In turns 1 and 3 we see the nurse "being professional" in using clinical discourse. Note that the nurse uses *we* in statements where the patient (*you* or *she*) would be the logical subject (*we had a shower today*). This is a non-reciprocal style: patients cannot speak as nurses, which perhaps explains why patients can hear this falsely inclusive *we* as patronizing rather than friendly. In turn 4 the patient intervenes with the personal, irrelevant comment about her hair, its incongruity provoking humor. Both the outgoing and incoming nurses respond, and then the outgoing nurse resumes her clinical discourse. But this nurse, having already incorporated the patient's humor into the interaction, adds her own light-hearted vernacular comment at the end of turn 6, showing a willingness to build rapport with the patient.

4. Disconfirming

By expressing surprise and counter-expectation in vernacular language, patients comment humorously on how their symptoms or its management have not conformed to clinical expectations. One example is Text 7: "Weird!"

Text 7 "Weird!" [ECCHo project data]

1	Outgoing nurse:	Yeah. He's currently on the IV antibiotics. They were querying [Outpatients] however Hugh [Patient] lives out of town. Yeah, so it's not close enough so they're looking at whether he can stay, just continue the IV antibiotics. That cannula was started yesterday. No complaints of pain. Obs have been stable. He's been afebrile when we take the temperature on the tongue but the ear's a different story. They're ==higher in the ear
2	Patient:	I'm weird!
3	Some incoming nurses:	*[laugh]*
4	Outgoing nurse:	Yeah, it's really strange but
5	Patient:	It really shifts from there and there *[points to ear and tongue]*
6	Outgoing nurse:	he's been sort of 36 low grade temp to high temp the whole time.

Although the patient's humorous remark in turn 2 looks similar to a stigma-minimizing move, the difference is that, in disconcerting humor, patients are not accepting the negative implications of their illness but are almost celebrating their departure from the clinical norm.

5. Sending-up

By ironically imitating clinical discourse and its assumptions, patients draw attention to oversights and inadequacies in the treatment they've received or their unequal status in the context. One assumption of clinical discourse is that doctors meet the needs of patients in a timely fashion. Patients sometimes show they don't believe the "line" the nurses are asked to feed them.

Text 8 "Best case scenario" [ECCHo project data]

1	Discharge nurse:	And the doctor knows that you're here *[rising tone]*, OK? So I've told him that you're here. He's on rounds still at present. So but once his round's finished he's ==he'll come down.
2	Patient:	*[jokey tone]*==He's going to come straight away and fix me up.
3	Discharge nurse:	*[laughs]* We==
4	Patient:	==He's got nothing better to do.
5	Discharge nurse:	*[laughing]* Yeah, he's got NO other patients, I'm sure. So yeah so you're probably looking at about lunch time for you know ... best case scenario.

Humor in unfolding interaction

As the examples above demonstrate, spontaneous humor is created interactively: collocutor reactions influence whether a participant's contribution is interpreted as humorous and whether humor is jointly sustained or cut off. Analyzing complete interactions shows how persistent patients can be to be heard, how they often mobilize humor to do this, and how reluctant some clinicians are to depart from their clinical script. Text 9 "Jason" is from a nursing shift handover delivered by a junior nurse of non-English speaking background. The patient is an Anglo-Australian male in his fifties.

Text 9 "Jason" [ECCHo project data]

1	Outgoing Nurse:	*[standing at the foot of the patient's bed and addressing the team of four incoming nurses]* The next is Jason Masters. This is the afternoon shift, Jason.
2	Patient:	Oh how yer going? Alright? Good?
3	Incoming Nurse 1:	Good, good.
4	Outgoing Nurse:	He came in this morning I think it was about 8 o'clock.
5	Patient:	I'm under warranty. Been in five times and they haven't fixed me!

6	Outgoing Nurse:	He just came in for Doctor Crown with cellulitis and he have that history there OSA ... CKD *[struggles to pronounce what's on wardsheet]*. He's eating and drinking well. Obs are stable. I did a BS—I ask him if he diabetic but he—I do BS today and it nine point seven. The doctor will review it. Um he also have blood collected this morning for the FBC and INR. And I give him just now and the doctor is just writing a note and I don't have the chance to read it cause it happen just now.
7	Patient:	They can't find out what's wrong with me.
8	Outgoing Nurse:	==He's also on Warfarin[4] and
9	Patient:	==They've been treating me with antibiotics for ten weeks and it's not cured. So they reckon it's the wrong antibiotic.
10	Incoming Nurse 1:	Uh huh.
11	Patient:	Started off in that leg *[uncovers leg to show group]*.
12	Outgoing Nurse:	Mmm.
13	Patient:	See what I mean and now it's in this leg.
14	Incoming Nurse 1:	Mmm *[sympathetic sound]*
15	Outgoing Nurse:	That is all.
16	Patient:	And the antibiotics won't fix it. Not enough beer in them, I think.
17	Outgoing Nurse:	Anything you want to? *[glances briefly at patient]* That's it.
18	Patient:	Yeah, no, that'll do me, thank you.

In turn 5, Jason's humorous interpose "I'm under warranty" involves an intertextual allusion: the patient construes himself as an appliance that needs fixing. This receives no reaction. In turns 7, 11 and 13 he repeatedly tries to interest the nurses in his version of his story, and in turn 16 again, this time using humor. Although one incoming nurse has indicated sympathy, no-one reacts to his joke in 16 or his sending-up in turn 18.

---

[4] Drug name.

But just when it seems the outgoing nurse has finished with Jason, the nurse hesitantly asks Jason a specific question about his recent consultation with the doctors. The interaction continues:

Text 9 "Jason" (continued)

19	Outgoing Nurse:	What the ah what the doctor told you when they see you?
20	Patient:	Yeah, well they don't know! They reckon it's the wrong antibiotic. I showed 'em. I had the ones out of the bag.
21	Outgoing Nurse:	Yeah.
22	Patient:	I showed them the antibiotic. It's a big one, they say, it's the world leader and they didn't know I'd been taking it for 14 days. *[laughs]*
23	Some incoming nurse:	*[laughs]*
24	Outgoing Nurse:	And he's also ==on Warfarin.
25	Patient:	==It doesn't work. See, none of them been working.
26	Outgoing Nurse:	He's also on Warfarin 14 milligrams is charted there [...] He's mobilising independently, self-caring.
27	Patient:	I mean I'm a good bloke, aren't I?
28	All:	*[laugh]*
29	Outgoing Nurse:	Do you have Panadol[5] this morning?
30	Patient:	No, no.
31	Outgoing Nurse:	Anything I miss?
32	Patient:	No. You mention whatever you want!
33	All:	*[laugh]*
34	Incoming nurse:	Thanks, Jason.

In turn 22, the patient offers a humorously disconfirming statement: "they didn't know I'd been taking it for 14 days." Here Jason draws attention to

---

[5] Drug name.

the fact that his condition has not conformed to clinical treatment expectations. This at least gets some reaction from some of the incoming team—but not the outgoing nurse who resumes his clinical script. In turn 27 the patient interposes with the vernacular comment "I'm a good bloke, aren't I?" which is at last met with laughter from all the nurses, possibly because it is a tagged declarative. The outgoing nurse asks one more clinical question (turn 29) and invites the patient to add information (turn 31), to which the patient makes a humorous sending-up response (turn 32), reminiscent of Andrew's comment in Text 3: "It'd be right if you said so!" But, unlike Andrew, Jason does not backtrack from the humor.

Conclusion

In this chapter I have drawn on sociological and critical linguistic theory to argue that patients use humor with clinicians to manage the extreme social shock of finding themselves in the "stigmatized" role of hospital patient. Patients initiate humor largely by shifting the interaction from clinical to everyday discourse. Through this re-registration, patients create humor that subverts at least some of the values and assumptions of the patient role (as it is construed within clinical discourse) without alienating their professional caregivers.

While I've drawn on Goffman's (1963) sociological analysis of stigma, I have extended his analysis to language, developing a critical linguistic explanation of actual interactions. Fairclough (1995, p. 43) argues that critical discourse analysis must address "the question of how discourse cumulatively contributes to the reproduction of macro structures." The critical linguistic approach to theorizing humor taken here allows us to see connections between the micro-semiotic interactions at patients' bedsides and the macro-social structure of institutionalized hospital care. I have suggested that clinical discourse arises from an institutionalized view of patients as "stigmatized" and even "non-persons" against the social norm of the healthy individual. We see that the values and assumptions construed by clinical discourse contrast markedly with those construed by everyday discourse, and we see how these contribute to excluding the patient from discussions about their care. We can interpret a patient's frequent attempts to initiate humor with their clinicians as their appeal to clinicians to depart from their "professional" script and instead see and speak to patients in the more inclusive, accessible and egalitarian modes of everyday interaction.

Critical applied linguistic research into humor can help us support clinicians to rethink what it might mean to interact with patients as "co-producers" of their healthcare. Analysis of spontaneous patient–clinician humor suggests that patients want greater inclusion. It also suggests that, to achieve this, we need to challenge the ideology implicit in "professional" clinical discourse that allows patients to be excluded, objectified and disempowered in talk about their health.

References

Arora, V., J. Johnson, D. Lovinger, H. Humphrey and D. Meltzer. 2005, "Communication failures in patient sign-out and suggestions for improvement: a critical incident analysis", *Quality and Safety in Health Care* 14: 401–407

Bateson, G. 1973, *Steps to an Ecology of Mind*, London: Granada/Paladin

Bergson, H. 1950, *Le Rire: essai sur la signification du comique*, Paris: Presses Universitaires de France

Boxer, D. and F. Cortes-Conde. 1997, "From bonding to biting: Conversational joking and identity display", *Journal of Pragmatics* 27: 275–94

Brown, P. and S. Levinson. 1987, *Politeness: Some Universals in Language Usage*, Cambridge: Cambridge University Press

Cahill, S. and R. Eggleston. 1994, "Managing Emotions in Public: The Case of Wheelchair Users", *Social Psychology Quarterly* 57(4): 300–12

Coser, R. 1959, "Some Social Functions of Laughter", *Human Relations* 12: 171–82

—. 1960, "Laughter among Colleagues", *Psychiatry* 23: 81–95

Douglas, M. 1975, *Implicit Meanings*, London: Routledge and Kegan Paul

Eggins, S. In preparation, "Covering, criticising and controlling in humor among hospital doctors"

Eggins, S. and D. Slade. 1997/2004, *Analysing Casual Conversation*, London: Continuum (Reprinted 2004, London: Equinox)

—. Forthcoming, "Contrasting discourse styles and barriers to patient participation in bedside nursing handovers". To appear in *Text and Talk*

—. eds, forthcoming, *Effective Communication in Clinical Handover—Research and Practice*, To be published in 2015 by Mouton de Gruyter, Berlin

Fairclough, N. 1995, *Critical Discourse Analysis*, London: Longman

Fine, G. and M. De Soucey. 2005, "Joking cultures: Humor themes as social regulation in group life", *Humor* 18(1): 1–22

Frank, A. 1991, *At the Will of the Body: Reflections on Illness*, Boston: Houghton Mifflin

Freud, S. 1905, *Jokes and their Relation to the Unconscious*, London: Routledge and Kegan Paul

Garling P. 2008, *The Final Report of the Special Commission of Inquiry into Acute Care Services in NSW Public Hospitals*, Sydney: N.S.W. Government

Goffman, E. 1963, *Stigma: notes on the management of spoiled identity*, New York: Simon & Schuster

—. 1974, *Frame Analysis*, New York: Harper and Row

Haig, K., S. Sutton and J. Whittington. 2006, *The SBARR Technique: improves communication enhances patient safety*, Joint Commission's Perspectives on Patient Safety 5: 1–2

Haynes, R., K. McKibbon and R. Kanani. 1996, "Systematic review of randomised trials of interventions to assist patients to follow prescriptions for medications", *Lancet* Aug 10: 383–86

Holmes, J. 2000, "Politeness, power and provocation: how humor functions in the workplace", *Discourse Studies* 2(2): 159–85

Hymes, D. 1974, *Foundations in Sociolinguistics: an ethnographic approach*, Philadelphia, P.A.: University of Pennsylvania Press

Iedema, R., R. Sorensen, C. Jorm and D. Piper. 2008, "Co-producing care". In R. Sorensen and R. Iedema, eds, *Managing Clinical Processes in Health Services*, Sydney: Elsevier, pp. 105–20

Jefferson, G. 1984, "On the organization of laughter in talk about troubles". In J.M. Atkinson and J.C. Heritage, eds, *Structures of social action: Studies in conversation analysis*, Cambridge, U.K.: Cambridge University Press, pp. 346–69

Kress, G. 1985, *Linguistic Processes in Socio-cultural Practice*, Geelong: Deakin University Press

Koestler, A. 1964, *The Act of Creation*, London: Hutchinson

Kotthoff, H. 1996, "Impoliteness and conversational joking: On relational politics", *Folia Linguistica* 30(3/4): 299–327

Kravitz R. and J. Melnikow. 2001, "Engaging patients in medical decision making", *British Medical Journal* 323(7313): 584–85

Lynch, O. 2010, "Cooking with humor: In-group humor as social organization", *Humor* 23(2): 127–59

Madden, T. 1986, "Joking relationships", *Journal of the Royal College of General Practitioners* (May): 197

Mallett, J. and R. A'Hern. 1996, "Comparative distribution and use of humor within nurse–patient communication", *International Journal of Nursing Studies* 33(5): 530–50

Mulkay, M. 1988, *On Humor: Its Nature and Its Place in Modern Society*, London: Polity Press

Monrouxe, L., C. Rees and P. Bradley. 2009, "The Construction of Patients' Involvement in Hospital Bedside Teaching Encounters", *Qualitative Health Research* 19(7): 918–30

Norrick, N. 1993, *Conversational Joking: Humor in Everyday Talk*, Bloomington: Indiana University Press

Patenaude, H. and L. Hamelin Brabant. 2006, "L'Humor dans la relation infirmière–patient: une revue de la literature", *Recherche en soins infirmers* 85: 36–45

Rees, C. and L. Monrouxe. 2010, "'I should be lucky ha ha ha ha': The construction of power, identity and gender through laughter within medical workplace learning encounters", *Journal of Pragmatics* 42: 3384–99

Robinson, V. 1977, *Humor and the health professions*, (2nd edition 1990), Thorofare, N.J.: C.B. Slack Incorporated

Roth, G. and B. Vivona. 2010, "Mirth and Murder: Crime Scene Investigation as a Work Context for Examining Humor Applications", *Human Resource Development Review* 9(4): 313–32

Roy, D. 1960, "'Banana Time' Job Satisfaction and Informal Interaction", *Human Organization*, 158–68

Slade, D., M. Manidis, J. McGregor, H. Scheeres, J. Stein-Parbury, R. Dunston, E. Chandler, M. Herke and C. Matthiessen. Forthcoming, *Healthcare Communication in Hospital Emergency Departments*, Heidelberg: Springer

Strauss, A., S. Fagerhaugh, B. Suczek and C. Wiener, C. 1997, *Social Organization of Medical Work*, New Brunswick, N.J.: Transaction Publishers (originally published by University of Chicago Press, 1985)

Tracy, S., K. Myers and C. Scott. 2006, "Cracking Jokes and Crafting Selves: Sensemaking and Identity Management Among Human Service Workers", *Communication Monographs* 73 (3): 283–308

Waskul, D.D. and P. van der Riet. 2002, "The Abject Embodiment of Cancer Patients: Dignity, Selfhood and the Grotesque Body", *Symbolic Interaction* 25(4): 487–513

Wong, M.C., K.C. Yee and P. Turner. 2008, *Clinical Handover Literature Review*, eHealth Services Research Group, University of Tasmania Australia. http://www.safetyandquality.gov.au/internet/safety/publishing.nsf/Content/PriorityProgram-05

Yoels, W. and J. Clair. 1995, "Laughter in the Clinic: Humor as Social Organization", *Symbolic Interaction* 18(1): 39–58

CHAPTER FOUR

LINGUISTICS IN LAW: IMPROVING THE CROSS-EXAMINATION OF CHILD WITNESSES

KIRSTEN HANNA

Keywords: child witnesses, cross-examination, intermediaries

Abstract

Modifications to court processes over the past 20 years have improved conditions for child witnesses in many ways; yet it has been much harder to bring about significant improvements to the way children are cross-examined in adversarial trials. Criticisms of the traditional cross-examination of child witnesses include the types of questions posed, their complexity and tactics employed in the name of truth-seeking. There is growing acceptance within the legal profession that the traditional style of cross-examination is inappropriate for child witnesses. This acceptance presents new opportunities for linguists to help improve how the courts interact with child witnesses. The challenges these witnesses face cross disciplinary boundaries. Further, the defendant's right to a fair trial must be vigorously safeguarded. By bringing together the knowledge and practical experience that resides within the disciplines of law, linguistics and psychology, linguists could contribute to improving the practice of cross-examination by informing and providing training on guidelines for questioning children, acting as intermediaries, conducting and disseminating research on children's language comprehension, and contributing to interdisciplinary discussions on a best-practice model of cross-examination that is fair to children and the accused.

Introduction

So what I'm putting to you is that you've discussed this allegation with your mother prior to making it. What do you say? (Question posed to a 12-year-old witness)

Testifying in a criminal trial can be daunting for adults, let alone children.[1] Yet children are increasingly called upon to give evidence in trials. Most children testify for the prosecution as the victim of crime; some testify as bystander witnesses. Many testify about sexual assaults committed by people they know. All will be vulnerable.

Since the 1980s adversarial jurisdictions have been transforming court processes to better accommodate children, in recognition of the stressful nature of courtroom testimony and the impact this can have on children and their ability to provide best evidence. Today in New Zealand, for example, a child complainant's initial statement is often taken via a video-recorded interview conducted by a forensic interviewer—a statutory social worker or police officer with specialist training in communicating with children. If the case proceeds to trial, the videotape is usually shown at court as the child's evidence-in-chief (where the child says what happened), so the child need not repeat the story again. This is followed by cross-examination, with the child testifying from another room in the courthouse via closed-circuit television or in the courtroom with a screen between the child and the accused. The child may then be re-examined by the prosecutor. Provisions to better accommodate children are now commonplace in adversarial jurisdictions internationally. For instance, before trial, most children participate in a court education program; courts are closed to the public when complainants testify in relation to sexual assault; and children may testify with a support person. However, one longstanding problem which has resisted resolution is the way children are cross-examined. Put simply, if children are asked complicated and coercive questions about past events (often long after those events took place), the quality of their evidence can suffer and the quality of justice delivered by the courts will be compromised.

Drawing on an earlier study examining the courtroom evidence of child witnesses in New Zealand,[2] and transcript and experimental studies from other adversarial jurisdictions, this chapter starts by outlining problems with the way children are cross-examined. The chapter then appraises recent attempts to address these problems, with reference to innovations and studies done in England and Wales, Australia and

---

[1] In this chapter, "children" are defined in line with the UN Convention on the Rights of the Child (that is, as people who are less than 18 years of age).

[2] This study involved analysis of the testimony of 18 child witnesses who had testified in New Zealand criminal courts in 2008, examining the types of questions posed, their complexity, and tactics of cross-examination (Hanna, Davies, Crothers & Henderson 2012a). All examples of courtroom questioning in this chapter derive from that study.

New Zealand. The chapter ends by considering the potential role of linguists in improving questioning practices in adversarial courts, through informing innovative practices, as well as interdisciplinary approaches to developing a best-practice model of cross-examination.

The problem

...regardless of whether a witness is thought to be truthful or not, the best approach to any child witness is one which reduces the risk of contaminating their evidence through inappropriate questioning techniques. (Hanna, Davies, Henderson & Hand, 2012)

Cross-examination should be about exposing the truth by testing the evidence of a witness, although, as we shall see, its function can be rather different. The assumption in practitioner manuals on cross-examination is that the truth is robust and resistant, while lies will eventually unravel under careful questioning (Henderson 2000). However, studies over the past decades suggest that some traditional practices of cross-examination aimed at testing the evidence and unravelling lies run the risk of distorting and contaminating the evidence. Recurring criticisms of the cross-examination of children, as they relate to language, center on the types of question asked, their complexity, and the tactics of traditional cross-examination.

Question type

The types of question used to elicit evidence from children can affect the accuracy and fullness of that evidence (Powell & Snow 2007). Responses to open-ended, free-recall questions such as "Tell me about X" are more likely to be accurate than responses to other question types (Lamb, Hershkowitz, Orbach & Esplin 2008). Closed and leading questions (ones that indicate the desired response, including tagged questions) such as "He didn't do it, did he?" can be risky (Lamb & Fauchier 2001; Orbach & Lamb 2001; Walker 1999; Waterman, Blades & Spencer 2001). If the purpose of questioning is to elicit accurate, full information, open-ended questions which invite a free-recall narrative response should be maximized and riskier question types, such as closed and leading questions, avoided wherever possible.

However, cross-examination of children is characterized by closed and leading questions (Hanna, Davies, Crothers & Henderson 2012a; Powell 2005; Zajac & Cannan 2009). This follows at least in part from the perceived need to tightly control the evidence of a witness, among other things, to prevent evidence emerging that damages the lawyer's case. A series of such questions gives the lawyer narrative control, with the witness relegated to agreeing or disagreeing. The anonymized exchange below, involving a 9-year-old witness with the pseudonym Beryl, illustrates how a series of closed, leading questions allows lawyers to promote their version of events to the fact-finder.[3] The lawyer's version is that Jordan went to sleep on the couch; Chris (the accused) carried Jordan to bed; then Beryl asked Chris to carry her (Beryl) to bed. The witness denies the first and third events occurred (lines 2 and 6); and her response in line 4 is ambiguous. Regardless of the response of the witness, in lines 8 and 12, the lawyer then asserts that the witness doesn't "remember" these events happening. The rhetorical repetition of "you don't remember" in lines 8, 10, and 12 arguably creates an impression that Beryl's recall is defective, which could undermine her credibility in the eyes of the jury. A negative response to a "You don't remember [x]" question is ambiguous as "no" could mean "no, that didn't happen" or "no, I don't remember that". But the child's response here is probably irrelevant—putting the idea and casting doubt on the memory of the witness are the main aims of this approach.[4]

1	Defence:	So the first night you spoke about, Jordan went to sleep on the couch.
2	Beryl:	Not that I remember.
3	Defence:	You don't remember Chris carrying Jordan down to bed?
4	Beryl:	No.
5	Defence:	OK. Do you remember asking Chris if you could be carried to bed as well?
6	Beryl:	No, I didn't ask him that.

---

[3] Spencer (2012) points out that the practice of using cross-examination to put the accused's version of events before the fact-finder may be a relic of the early days of legal representation in felony trials when lawyers were restricted to arguing points of law and examining/cross-examining witnesses; speech-making was the responsibility of the accused. Lawyers got around this by using cross-examination to put the client's version of events before the court in the manner illustrated. These restrictions were lifted in 1836 in the United Kingdom, when counsel was permitted to make closing speeches to the fact-finder. However, "the practice of bending cross-examination to this end, once established, was permitted to continue, even though there was no longer any need for it" (p. 182).

[4] Hanna, Davies, Henderson & Crothers (2012a, p. 540).

7		[*16 utterances intervene*]
8	Defence:	So you don't remember Jordan falling asleep on the couch.
9	Beryl:	No, she was asleep with Charlie.
10	Defence:	You don't remember Chris carrying Jordan to bed.
11	Beryl:	No.
12	Defence:	You don't remember you asking Chris if he would carry you to bed.
13	Beryl:	No.
14	Defence:	Okay. Can we talk about the second time?

Cross-examination can be a lengthy test of endurance. Faced with a drawn-out barrage of leading questions, it would not be surprising if some children eventually agree with the questions posed, just to bring the ordeal to an end.

Complexity

The language of the courts is characterized by its formality: complex syntax, high-register vocabulary and legalese are the norm. Experimental studies confirm that complex language can reduce the accuracy of young children's reports of past events (Carter, Bottoms & Levine 1996). Even adolescents can be tripped up by "lawyerese" (Perry et al. 1995). Studies over many years reveal that the questions posed to children during cross-examination are often developmentally inappropriate (Davies & Seymour 1998; Hanna, Davies, Crothers & Henderson 2012a; Zajac & Cannan 2009; Zajac, Gross & Hayne 2003). In one study, nearly one in five questions posed during cross-examination contained difficult vocabulary;[5] double negatives were significantly more common during cross-examination than during evidence-in-chief and forensic interviews; and defense and prosecution lawyers used questions containing multiple forms of complexity more often than forensic interviewers (Hanna, Davies, Crothers & Henderson 2012a):

---

[5] Difficult vocabulary was defined as high-register vocabulary for which a lower register alternative is available such as "siblings" instead of "brothers and sisters"; legal jargon such as "I put it to you that…" or "Is it your evidence that…"; unnecessarily formal language such as "make available to the police"; and figurative language such as "in the spotlight."

Defence:	If he told the police that that was what he thought you wanted to do, are you saying that you don't think he could have thought that? (To a 16-year-old witness)
Defence:	And if I put it to you that nobody drank [substance], what would you say?
Child:	I don't get you.
Defence:	Well, what I'm trying to say is that it's odd that there's [substance] in the house if it was against their religion at the time to drink it. Do you understand what I'm asking you?
Child:	No. (14-year-old witness)
Defence:	After going to the church, I'll put it to you that he at no time told you not to say anything to anyone. (To a 15-year-old witness)

Children are usually told to indicate if they have not understood a question. Yet they may not always know when a question is beyond their comprehension. Some children, particularly adolescents, may be reluctant to admit it; others may be too diffident to do so. An experimental study found that participants aged 5 to 22 had more difficulty assessing whether they had understood lawyerese[6] compared to simplified questions (Perry et al. 1995). Plotnikoff and Woolfson (2009) found that fewer than half of the 111 young witnesses in their study who realized they were struggling (for example, with comprehension, the pace of questioning or being interrupted) told the court, even though most were advised they could do so. In another study, of the 8,154 questions posed to children by forensic interviewers, prosecutors and defense, children asked for clarification to 138 of the questions (Hanna, Davies, Crothers & Henderson 2012a).[7] When the young witnesses did ask for clarification, the responses from adults were not always helpful—even with the best of intentions:

---

[6] In this study, lawyerese questions contained negatives, double negatives, questions containing two parts with each part requiring a different response (such as "At the end of the video, was Sam mad [yes] or was Katie happy? [no]"), difficult vocabulary, and complex syntax (multiple subordinate clauses, including "before" and "after" temporal clauses).

[7] Zajac et al. (2003) similarly reported that in their study of courtroom transcripts children rarely sought clarification.

Defence:	But you were quite happy to go and be close to your mother in all those events including in the photo, weren't you?
Child:	Can you just say the question again?
Defence:	That you were quite happy to be content in those photos, and be quite happy, you didn't show any sign of being hostile to your mother or being upset at being close to her, were you?
Child:	Just can't think. (14-year-old witness)

Defence:	Now do you remember what day you said that the later sexual violation occurred?
Child:	Pardon?
Defence:	Do you remember what date it was or when it happened?
Child:	On the first one.
Defence:	No the second.
Judge:	Mr X, ask a question in a less confusing manner.
Defence:	Yes, Your Honour. The—
Judge:	Like this. When was the first time that you told anybody about sex abuse when you were a lot younger? (To a 15-year-old witness)

Some lawyers use complex language intentionally.[8] Others may not realize how complex or otherwise developmentally inappropriate their questions are. Interviewing a small sample of British and New Zealand lawyers in the 1990s, Henderson (2003) found that most believed there was no need to adjust their language with child witnesses of normal development over the age of 10 or 12. This is patently not the case: among other things, an adolescent's understanding of common legal terms can be wildly inaccurate, such as confusing cross-examination with a medical examination (Crawford & Bull 2006; Freshwater & Aldridge 1994). Understanding of some morphologically complex nouns and adjectives (Nippold & Sun

---

[8] As one lawyer put it, "The difference [between adult and child witnesses] is in being able to consistently communicate in a public forum ... You're looking ... to make sure they make mistakes. [...] Some counsel ... give double negatives to kids. And the kids get it wrong ... But that is a valid technique that is used by very senior counsel and very successfully" (lawyer cited in Henderson, 2002, p. 286).

2008) and of lower-frequency adverbial conjuncts such as "moreover," and "conversely" (Nippold & Shwarz 1992) is still developing during early adolescence. Comprehension of concession clauses with "although" is not complete by age 15 (Perera 1984), and acquisition of the syllogistic reasoning required to understand "if-then" relationships stretches into adulthood (Nippold 2007). There is clear potential for lawyers to unknowingly overestimate the level of a young person's comprehension. However, inculcation into the formal language of the courts may make it doubly difficult for legal professionals to recognize and shed complex language when performing in their professional arena.

Tactics of cross-examination

The declared purpose of cross-examination is to assist in the investigation of the truth by eliciting favorable information from the witness and critiquing their unfavorable evidence. In practice, however, the techniques used can go well beyond legitimate testing of the account of the witness and risk distorting the jury's impression of the evidence and the witness. Further, cross-examination is also used as an opportunity to speak to and persuade the fact-finder. Over time, practitioners of cross-examination have developed an arsenal of tactics to accomplish these various ends. Yet, as Spencer (2012, p. 182) notes, the use of these tactics to discredit the evidence of witnesses is "proper only to the extent that the cross-examination makes the witness seem less credible for good reasons rather than for bad reasons." One dubious tactic is the skip-around technique, where counsel moves unexpectedly from one topic to another in the hope of catching the witness off guard. This is illustrated (albeit clumsily) below (Hanna, Davies, Henderson & Crothers, 2012a, p. 540), where the witness had earlier testified that her alleged assailant wore ripped boxers at the time of the assault:

Defence:	Now you were aware that there were some arguments between your mother and your uncle. Is that correct?
Child:	Yes.
Defence:	Okay. There was a bit of argument over family things and over a funeral. Would that be correct?
Child:	Yes.
Defence:	You say he had ripped trousers—sorry, ripped boxers. I put it to you that he didn't have ripped boxers at all.

Child: He did. (15-year-old witness)

It is standard practice for advocacy manuals to recommend this tactic where there are suspicions that the witness has memorized their testimony. Stone suggests that it gives liars insufficient time to concoct answers, putting them off balance and leading to "inconsistencies, improbabilities, or testimony which can be contradicted by other evidence" (1995, as cited in Henderson, 2000, p. 90). Yet it seems just as possible that this tactic could put honest witnesses off balance, unfairly undermining their credibility in the eyes of the fact-finder.

Another technique is to focus on details that are peripheral to the main events. It is well known that salient information tends to be easier to remember than peripheral information (Fivush, Peterson & Schwarzmueller 2000; Reed 1996). Inconsistencies around peripheral details are normal. In contrast, advocacy manuals tend to assume "…real memories are complete in every particular and peripheral detail and inconsistencies indicate untruthfulness" (Henderson 2000, p. 89), and so questioning on peripheral details is a valid test of the reliability of a witness (p. 91). An inconsistency then becomes fertile ground for attacking the credibility of a witness and for accusations of lying. Child witnesses often cite such accusations as one of the worst aspects of their involvement with the courts (Cashmore & Trimboli 2005; Eastwood & Patton 2002; Hamlyn, Phelps, Turtle & Sattar 2004). In one cross-examination transcript the author analyzed, a child was accused of lying five times within 11 utterances by the defense lawyer (Hanna, Davies, Crothers & Henderson 2012a). Of course, where the case theory is that a witness is lying, the lawyer must address this. However, repeated accusations are likely to induce any witness—adult or child—to anger or tears, reducing their ability to gather their wits to continue with the questioning (Spencer & Flin 1993).

Addressing the problem

Some courtroom professionals struggle to accept that there are problems with the way that children are cross-examined:

> People underestimate most adults' ability to understand children's limitations in answering questions. You simply do not see unreasonable cross-examination of children. I cannot think of a single case. Criminal lawyers are generally very good with children. (U.K. barrister cited in Plotnikoff & Woolfson, 2007, p. 66)

Yet others are acutely aware that the traditional style of cross-examination is unsuitable when the witness is a child, including legal scholars such as Spencer (2012) and judges in the U.K. Supreme Court and England/Wales Court of Appeal:

> [The civil court does not] assume that an 'Old Bailey style' of cross examination is the best way of testing that evidence. It may be the best way of casting doubt upon it in the eyes of the jury but that is another matter. (*W (Children)* [2010] UKSC 12, at paragraph 27)

> [In the case of a young witness who changed her testimony under cross-examination] Most of the questions which produced the [changes in testimony], unlike many others, constituted the putting of direct suggestions with an indication of the answer: 'This happened, didn't it?' Or: 'This didn't happen, did it?' The consequence of that is … that it can be very difficult to tell whether the child is truly changing her account or simply taking the line of least resistance. (*R v. W & M* [2010] EWCA Crim 1926, at paragraph 31)

In a mock trial study involving a small, experienced group of legal professionals, seven of the eight judges and lawyers involved agreed that there are problems with the way children are cross-examined in New Zealand courts; and all eight gave examples of poor practices. These practices included the use of developmentally inappropriate language, counsel intentionally confusing children, too many issues in one question, the use of "inappropriate language for effect rather than truth-seeking" (p. 21), and the "confirm, confirm, put" style of cross-examination[9] (Davies, Hanna, Henderson & Hand 2011).

Part of the problem is that advocates in New Zealand receive no training on questioning children, either during university studies or when doing the Law Society's Litigation Skills Programme. Advocacy training on communication with vulnerable witnesses is also patchy in the United Kingdom (Plotnikoff & Woolfson 2012), but U.K. judges are trained and ticketed before hearing cases involving serious sexual assault. This includes training on communication issues. So "there cannot now be many judges who do not know what a tag question is and why it is not an acceptable means of communication with a witness" (Judge Peter Collier QC, 2012).

Some jurisdictions (or individual courts) have developed guidelines on cross-examination to help improve the questioning of children and other

---

[9] That means where counsel asks the witness to confirm a series of points; then puts an issue or challenge.

vulnerable witnesses. For example, those produced by the District Court of Western Australia include recommendations that "questions be short and simple"; that child witnesses are given enough time to answer questions; terminology is appropriate to the age or mental capacity of the witness; accusations of lying are appropriately phrased; and that legalese, mixing topics, and unduly repetitive questioning is avoided (District Court of Western Australia, 2010). The United Kingdom has produced comprehensive toolkits to help advocates question children, and other vulnerable witnesses and defendants, appropriately;[10] in 2012 the body responsible for judicial training produced official guidelines for hearing child witness cases. These guidelines recommend (among other things) that ground rules are established before trial as to how the child will be questioned; that tagged questions are avoided; and that questions are short, simple and contain one idea at a time. They also remind judges not to rely on children to indicate that they haven't understood a question.[11] Guidelines such as these could be a useful starting point for a shared understanding between the judiciary and counsel as to what is and is not an acceptable approach to questioning young or vulnerable witnesses. These guidelines must be reinforced through training to help courtroom professionals recognize, for example, when a sentence is not so simple, what types of question can be leading (such as tagged questions and declaratives), and to encourage counsel to abandon poor questioning practices.

While training judges and counsel would be beneficial, there are limitations to this approach to improving questioning practices.[12] To name just two, post-training skills slippage is a perennial problem and, even if armed with the tools to recognize problematic language, judges can be constrained in their ability to prevent it, despite a duty to do so.[13] However,

---

[10] See http://www.theadvocatesgateway.org/

[11] See http://www.judiciary.gov.uk/publications-and-reports/guidance/2012/jc-bench-checklist-young-wit-cases

[12] For a fuller discussion of the limitations of training, see Cossins (2012); Hanna, Davies, Henderson & Hand (2012); Henderson (2012).

[13] That is, judges must maintain neutrality. Comments from judges in New Zealand and the United Kingdom respectively illustrate the issue: "...the more you interrupt (even though you may need to), the more the jury are likely to think, 'Oh, this judge is imposing his or her views on the evidence as a whole and interfering with our role'" (Davies et al., 2011, p. 26); and "You can only interrupt or send the jury out so many times. If I interrupt four out of seven questions, I can't do it again ... [and even if the advocate's poor practice is brought to the attention of the head of chambers] they come back and do it in exactly the same way. Their role is to get the client off and they will" (Plotnikoff & Woolfson 2010, p. 8).

training in conjunction with other modifications to the courtroom process could make a significant impact on questioning practices.

Since 2004, intermediaries have been available in England and Wales to "enable complete, coherent and accurate communication" between the courts and eligible children and other vulnerable witnesses (Ministry of Justice 2012). The intermediary role is part time. Most are speech language therapists; all must undergo screening, training, examination, and assessment before becoming registered (Plotnikoff & Woolfson 2012).

Intermediaries can be appointed to help police interview vulnerable witnesses and/or to assist counsel question witnesses at trial. Intermediaries begin by assessing the communicative competence of each witness. This assessment is written up as a report. These reports include recommendations on how best to question the witness and other relevant matters, such as the need for communication tools and the likely attention span of each witness.[14] Depending on the results of their assessment, intermediaries often advise avoiding leading questions (or certain types, such as tagged questions). If involved at the police stage, they then brief the officer in charge on the communication needs of the witness before the officer interviews the witness. Intermediaries may also get involved in planning or conducting the police interview.

When intermediaries assist at trial, the report is discussed at a pre-trial hearing involving the trial judge, intermediary and counsel, and ground rules for questioning the witness are agreed.[15] At trial, the intermediary sits with the witness and monitors the questions that counsel asks. If a question is too hard for the witness or otherwise violates the ground rules, the intermediary alerts the judge. A common practice is for the judge to ask the lawyer to rephrase the question. If they fail to do so appropriately, then the judge may ask that the intermediary rephrase the question on counsel's behalf.[16]

---

[14] Anonymized intermediary reports that the author has sighted covered a range of communication issues, including information about the auditory memory of a witness (hence the number of key words each question should contain); the witness' comprehension of embedded phrases, passives, negatives, temporal vocabulary, and tenses; interpretation of non-literal meaning; how long the witness might need to respond to questions; the likely impact of stress on the witness to participate in questioning; and vocabulary range.

[15] The Criminal Procedure Rules require this pre-trial hearing, yet this rule is not always followed (Cooper 2012).

[16] Plotnikoff & Woolfson (2007, p. 53).

Prosecutor:	…What was the weather condition? Was it sunny, rainy, foggy, what was the situation, what was it like?
Intermediary:	What was the weather like?
Defence:	One time, the once, a different time from the second incident?
Intermediary:	How many times have you been to B's house?

If the witness has severe difficulty in communicating, the intermediary may translate for them. Importantly, intermediaries are independent and neutral officers of the court rather than expert witnesses or witness supporters (Lord Chief Justice of England and Wales 2011).

An evaluation of the intermediary scheme amply illustrated that, with few exceptions, intermediaries are highly valued by the courtroom practitioners that have worked with (Plotnikoff & Woolfson 2007). Judges, barristers and police officers have "described intermediaries as highly professional and neutral. Lawyers and judges were particularly enthusiastic about the written reports prior to trial" (Davies et al., 2011, p. 13). Initial reservations about the intrusion of a third party into the examination process often dissipate once legal professionals experience working with an intermediary: "[I] still feel that for many barristers this is their first experience of a trial with an Intermediary—but all have commented that they would use an Intermediary again" (Intermediary, as cited in Cooper, 2012, p. 10).

Judgments from the higher courts too have commented on the value and contribution of intermediaries to improving trial processes.[17] The Lord Chief Justice of England and Wales (2011, p. 16) has noted that "…their use is a step which improved the administration of justice and it has done so without a diminution in the entitlement of the defendant to a fair trial." Provision of this communication assistance has increased access to justice for some children who might otherwise have been deemed unable to testify at trial, such as preschoolers and those with autism or serious disabilities (Henderson 2010). That intermediaries are valued by courtroom professionals is testimony to their professionalism, skills, and training. Their role as neutral officers of the court is no doubt critical to their acceptance. It is also clear that, given the specialist skills that intermediaries display, some courtroom professionals are coming to recognize the limitations of their own knowledge:

---

[17] See, for example, *R v. Barker* [2010] EWCA Crim 4; *R v. Cox* [2012] EWCA Crim 549; *R v. W & M* [2010] EWCA Crim 1926.

> A defence advocate is naturally suspicious of doing anything like this
> [speaking to the intermediary before trial] in case he loses the advantage of
> surprise. As it was, I ended up being the one who was surprised—by the
> extreme difficulty the complainant had in understanding what I thought
> were the simplest questions. (barrister, as cited in Plotnikoff & Woolfson,
> 2007, p. 66)

Yet intermediaries are generally restricted to intervening on individual
questions. This makes it hard, for example, to prevent counsel from
switching abruptly between topics, a lengthy examination on peripheral
details, or repeated accusations of lying unless these points form part of
the ground rules. Even so, if counsel wants to ignore the ground rules or is
unable to follow them, intermediaries and judges can be limited in their
ability to enforce them:

> [E]ven where [registered intermediary] recommendations are accepted at
> the ground rules hearing, some advocates find it difficult or seem unwilling
> to adapt their questioning to ensure it is appropriate to the communication
> needs of the witness. (Plotnikoff & Woolfson, n.d., p. 8)

Bearing in mind these limitations with the England and Wales model, a
small study explored alternative intermediary models via mock
examinations of a "child" witness (role-played by an experienced forensic
interviewer) (Davies et al. 2011; Hanna, Davies, Henderson & Hand 2012).
Under one of the models, a speech language therapist worked with defense
counsel a few days before the mock examination to prepare questions to be
put to the child witness. At "trial" the intermediary posed the questions on
behalf of counsel, in line with best practice in interviewing children. The
questions were asked in topic-based chunks, allowing the intermediary to
consult with counsel after each topic-chunk to receive further instructions
before proceeding to the next topic. The mock examinations, observed by
other judges, prosecutors, defense lawyers, academics, and forensic
interviewers, illustrated the potential for knowledge-exchange between
language and legal professionals. The defense lawyer who worked with
the speech language therapist was positive about the process: "So the
process ... was fantastic ... just in terms of the discipline ... of sitting
down and being told you're going to be asking questions of less than
eight[18] words." "We made [questions] shorter and snappier or broke them
down. No subordinate clauses. You're not allowed to use something called
'subordinate clauses!'" The exercise also illustrated for some lawyers the

---

[18] The "child" in this case was 8 years old.

difference between their own notion of appropriate questioning and that of language specialists:

> I was impressed with [the specialists'] ability to put things into child-friendly language. I think most of us lawyers think that we can do that ... but seeing it being done by the real specialists was impressive. (defense lawyer)

Participants identified a range of potential benefits accruing from this intermediary model, as well as potential disadvantages, including significant concerns about interference with defense counsel's ability to fulfill obligations towards the client. But for some witnesses this may be the only way of ensuring they can testify effectively and get access to justice:

> Where children are very immature, or have serious communication problems, or are highly vulnerable, there is surely no sensible alternative to the use of an intermediary in the full sense of the word: not the intermediary as used in the [England/Wales] courts today, who merely intervenes when counsel's questions are beyond the child's comprehension .... But the intermediary who is given a list of issues that the other side wishes to explore, and is then allowed to ask the questions in his or her own way. (Spencer 2012, p. 190)

An interdisciplinary approach

Fiat justitia ruat caelum: Let justice be done though the heavens fall

Eliciting accurate and full testimony from children requires an understanding of the multiple factors that can impact on a child's ability to produce such evidence. A key determiner is the questions asked. Many legal professionals have a growing unease about the suitability of traditional cross-examination for questioning children. This presents new opportunities for linguists to help improve how the courts interact with child witnesses. These improvements might include informing, and contributing to training on, guidelines for examining children, such as those developed by the District Court in Western Australia and in the United Kingdom; teaching law students and contributing to professional development for barristers and judges; conducting research to increase understanding of children's communication and bringing that research to the courts' attention; and, where legislation allows[19] and the individual has the relevant expertise, acting as intermediaries. In each case, the contributions of linguists will be most valuable when they are based on a clear understanding of the roles and responsibilities of legal professionals, including the duties of defense counsel to their clients and, as one defense lawyer put it, "…what it is that under our current system lawyers are trying to achieve and why we do what we do" (Davies et al. 2011, p. 38).

Those wishing to improve questioning practices still face a model of cross-examination to which many legal professionals are wedded. Modifying the model will require advocates and judges to significantly shift their thinking. Even so, the willingness of higher courts in some jurisdictions to contemplate cross-examination absent of tradition features (such as tagged questions and repeated accusations of lying) shows that these courts are not immune to change.[20] As the Lord Chief Justice of England and Wales (2011) remarked, in the interests of trial fairness, "…we must rid ourselves of any straight jacketed conceptions of the form cross examination must invariably take."

What form a fairer cross-examination might take—fair to the accused and the witness—was the subject of considerable debate among participants in the mock trial study cited earlier. The researchers (a psychologist, a legal scholar, a speech language therapist, and a linguist) began the study with a clear idea; the responses from defense lawyers and judges gave the researchers pause for thought. The exercise highlighted the need to deconstruct cross-examination to distinguish between its form and "proper" functions, as a first step in developing a form consistent with those proper functions—one that does not exploit children and the vulnerabilities of other witnesses, while vigorously upholding the defendant's right to a fair trial. Legal professionals cannot achieve this alone, any more than linguists or psychologists can do so in isolation. Rather, the researchers concluded that it would require bringing those disciplines together in a process of mutual knowledge exchange and

---

[19] In 2011, the New Zealand Government signaled an intention to introduce intermediaries into the court process. Countries with some form of intermediary scheme include South Africa, Israel, the United States, and England/Wales (Henderson 2012).
[20] In the United Kingdom, the Criminal Bar Association, Crown Prosecution Service, Advocacy Training Council, Law Society, Bar Council and the National Society for the Prevention of Cruelty to Children) jointly funded a training video that promotes a change in the culture of cross-examination of vulnerable witnesses and defendants (www.theadvocatesgateway.org/a-question-of-practice).

exploration to ensure any new model was informed by the knowledge and practical experience residing within those disciplines.

When children were first allowed to testify from outside the courtroom 20 years ago, the innovation was so controversial that many lawyers were convinced the heavens would fall. They did not, and testimony via closed circuit television is now commonplace and unremarkable (Cossins 2012; Hanna, Davies, Crothers & Henderson 2012b). With concerted effort and pressure, perhaps in another 20 years the fair cross-examination of children and other vulnerable witnesses will be just as commonplace and unremarkable.

References

Carter, C., B.L. Bottoms and M. Levine. 1996, "Linguistic and Socioemotional Influences on the Accuracy of Children's Reports", *Law and Human Behaviour* 20(3): 335–58

Cashmore, J. and L. Trimboli. 2005, *An Evaluation of the NSW Child Sexual Assault Specialist Jurisdiction Pilot.*
http://www.lawlink.nsw.gov.au/lawlink/bocsar/ll_bocsar.nsf/vwFiles/r57.pdf/$ file/r57.pdf

Collier, Judge Peter (QC). 2012, *R v. G P and 4 Others.*
http://www.crimeline.info/case/r-v-g-p-and-4-others (December 11, 2012)

Cooper, P. 2012, *Tell Me What's Happening 3: Registered Intermediary Survey 2011*, London: City University

Cossins, A. 2012, "Cross-examining the Child Complainant: Rights, Innovations and Unfounded Fears in the Australian context". In J.R. Spencer and M.E. Lamb, eds, *Children and Cross-examination: Time to Change the Rules?* Oxford: Hart Publishing, pp. 95–112

Crawford, E. and R. Bull. 2006, "Teenagers' Difficulties with Key Words regarding the Criminal Court Process", *Psychology, Crime & Law* 12(6): 653–67

Davies, E., K. Hanna, E. Henderson and L. Hand. 2011, *Questioning Child Witnesses: Exploring the Benefits and Risks of Intermediary Models*, Auckland: Institute of Public Policy, AUT University

Davies, E. and F.W. Seymour. 1998, "Questioning Child Complainants of Sexual Abuse: Analysis of Criminal Court Transcripts in New Zealand", *Psychiatry, Psychology and Law* 5(1): 47–61

District Court of Western Australia. 2010, *Guidelines for Cross Examination of Children and Persons Suffering a Mental Disability.*
http://www.districtcourt.wa.gov.au/C/criminal_procedure_practice_directions. aspx?uid=4595-2157-0490-1544

Eastwood, C. and W. Patton. 2002, *The Experiences of Child Complainants of Sexual Abuse in the Criminal Justice System.*
http://www.criminologyresearchcouncil.gov.au/reports/eastwood.pdf

Fivush, R., C. Peterson and A. Schwarzmueller. 2000, "Questions and Answers: The Credibility of Child Witnesses in the Context of Specific Questioning Techniques". In M.L. Eisen, J.A. Quas and G.S. Goodman, eds, *Memory and Suggestibility in the Forensic Interview*, Mahwah: Laurence Erlbaum Associates, Inc.

Freshwater, K. and J. Aldridge. 1994, "The Knowledge and Fears about Court of Child Witnesses, Schoolchildren and Adults", *Child Abuse Review* 3: 183–95

Hamlyn, B., A. Phelps, J. Turtle and G. Sattar. 2004, *Are Special Measures Working? Evidence from Surveys of Vulnerable and Intimidated Witnesses.* http://www.homeoffice.gov.uk/rds/pdfs04/hors283.pdf

Hanna, K., E. Davies, C. Crothers and E. Henderson. 2012a, "Questioning Child Witnesses in New Zealand's Criminal Justice System: Is Cross-examination Fair?" *Psychiatry, Psychology & Law* 19(4): 530–46

—. 2012b, "Child Witnesses' Access to Alternative Modes of Testifying in New Zealand", *Psychiatry, Psychology & Law* 19(2): 184–97

Hanna, K., E. Davies, E. Henderson, C. Crothers and C. Rotherham. 2010, *Child Witnesses in the New Zealand Criminal Courts: A Review of Practice and Implications for Policy*, Auckland: New Zealand: Institute of Public Policy

Hanna, K., E. Davies, E. Henderson and L. Hand. 2012, "Questioning Child Witnesses: Exploring the Benefits and Risks of Intermediary Models in New Zealand", *Psychiatry, Psychology & Law* 19(4): 530–46

Henderson, E. 2000, "Cross-examination: A Critical Examination", Unpublished Ph.D thesis, Cambridge University

—. 2002, "Persuading and Controlling: The Theory of Cross-examination in Relation to Children". In H.L. Westcott, G.M. Davies and R.H.C. Bull, eds, *Children's testimony: A handbook of psychological research and forensic practice*, Chichester: John Wiley & Sons

—. 2003, "Psychological Research and Lawyers' Perceptions of Child Witnesses in Sexual Abuse Trials". In D. Carson and R. Bull, eds, *Handbook of Psychology in Legal Contexts*, 2nd ed., Chichester: Wiley

—. 2010, "Innovative Practices in Other Jurisdictions". In Hanna et al., *Child Witnesses in the New Zealand Criminal Courts: A Review of Practice and Implications for Policy*, Auckland: Institute of Public Policy, AUT University

—. 2012, "Alternative Routes: Other Accusatorial Jurisdictions on the Slow Road to Best Evidence". In J.R. Spencer and M.E. Lamb, eds, *Children and Cross-examination: Time to Change the Rules?* Oxford: Hart Publishing, pp. 43–74

Lamb, M.E. and A. Fauchier. 2001, "The Effects of Question Type on Self-contradictions by Children in the Course of Forensic Interviews", *Applied Cognitive Psychology* 15: 483–91

Lamb, M.E., I. Hershkowitz, Y. Orbach and P.W. Esplin. 2008, *Tell Me What Happened: Structured Investigative Interviews of Child Victims and Witnesses*, Chichester: John Wiley & Sons Ltd

Lord Chief Justice of England and Wales. 2011, *Vulnerable Witnesses in the Administration of Criminal Justice.* http://www.judiciary.gov.uk/media/speeches/2011/lcj-speech-vulnerable-witnesses-in-admin-criminal-justice

Ministry of Justice. 2012, *The Registered Intermediary Procedural Guidance Manual*, London: Ministry of Justice

Nippold, M.A. 2007, *Later Language Development: School-age Children, Adolescents, and Young Adults*, 3rd ed, Austin, TX: PRO-ED Inc.

Nippold, M.A. and I.E. Shwarz. 1992, "Use and Understanding of Adverbial Conjuncts: A Developmental Study of Adolescents and Young Adults", *Journal of Speech and Hearing Research* 35(1): 108–18

Nippold, M.A. and L. Sun. 2008, "Knowledge of Morphologically Complex Words: A Developmental Study of Older Children and Young Adolescents", *Language, Speech and Hearing Services in Schools* 39: 365–73

Orbach, Y. and M.E. Lamb. 2001, "The Relationship Between Within-interview Contradictions and Eliciting Interviewer Utterances", *Child Abuse & Neglect* 25: 323–33

Perera, K. 1984, *Children's Writing and Reading: Analysing Classroom Language*, Oxford: Basil Blackwell Ltd

Perry, N.W., B.D. McAuliff, P. Tam, L. Claycomb, C. Dostal and C. Flanagan. 1995, "When Lawyers Question Children: Is Justice Served?" *Law and Human Behavior* 19(6): 609–29

Plotnikoff, J. and R. Woolfson. 2007, *The Go-Between: Evaluation of Intermediary Pathfinder Projects*.
   http://www.lexiconlimited.co.uk/witness_projects.htm

—. 2009, *Measuring Up? Evaluating Implementation of Government Commitments to Young Witnesses in Criminal Proceedings*.
   http://www.nspcc.org.uk/inform/research/findings/measuring_up_wda66048.html

—. 2010, "Cross-examining Children—Testing not Trickery", *Archbold Review* 7: 7–9

—. 2012, "'Kicking and Screaming': The Slow Road to Best Evidence". In J.R. Spencer and M.E. Lamb, eds, *Children and Cross-examination: Time to Change the Rules?* Oxford: Hart Publishing, pp. 21–41

—. (n.d.), *Registered Intermediaries in Action: Messages for the CJS from the Witness Intermediary Scheme SmartSite*, London: Lexicon Ltd

Powell, M. 2005, "Improving the Reliability of Child Witness Testimony in Court: The Importance of Focusing on Question Technique", *Current Issues in Criminal Justice* 17(1): 137–43

Powell, M. and P. Snow. 2007, "Guide to Questioning Children during the Free-Narrative Phase of an Investigative Interview", *Australian Psychologist* 42(1): 57–65

R v. Barker [2010] EWCA Crim 4

R v. Cox [2012] EWCA Crim 549

R v. W & M [2010] EWCA Crim 1926

Reed, L.D. 1996, "Findings from Research on Children's Suggestibility and Implications for Conducting Child Interviews", *Child Maltreatment* 1(2): 105–20

Spencer, J.R. 2012, "Conclusions". In J.R. Spencer and M.E. Lamb, eds, *Children and Cross-examination: Time to Change the Rules?* Oxford: Hart Publishing, pp. 171–201

Spencer, J.R. and R. Flin. 1993, *The Evidence of Children: The Law and the Psychology*, 2nd ed, Oxford: Blackstone Press

W (Children) [2010] UKSC 12

Walker, A.G. 1999, *Handbook on Questioning Children: A Linguistic Perspective*, 2nd ed., Washington D.C.: ABA Centre on Children and the Law

Waterman, A.H., M. Blades and C. Spencer. 2001, "Interviewing Children and Adults: The Effect of Question Format on the Tendency to Speculate", *Applied Cognitive Psychology* 15: 521–31

Zajac, R. and P. Cannan. 2009, "Cross-examination of Sexual Assault Complainants: A Developmental Comparison", *Psychiatry, Psychology and Law* 16: S36–S54

Zajac, R., J. Gross and H. Hayne. 2003, "Asked and Answered: Questioning Children in the Courtroom", *Psychiatry, Psychology and Law* 10(1): 199–209

CHAPTER FIVE

WHO IS 'WE'?:
ANNIVERSARY NARRATIVE
AS COLLECTIVE MEMORY

FARZANA GOUNDER

Keywords: media linguistics, master narrative, identity, discourse and power, Fiji Hindi, Indian indenture

Abstract

Studies have addressed the dialogic relationship between anniversary journalism and the (re)construction of collective memory. What is missing from the discussion is a fine-grained linguistic analysis of how anniversary journalism succeeds in providing insight into the past while simultaneously maintaining relevance for the present. Through the analysis of a Fiji-Indian journalist's narrativized reconstruction of Indian indenture, which frames a commemorative radio documentary, the study asserts that journalistic anniversary narrative is a discourse of power which, through the construction of structural and thematic coherence and audience relevance, redefines collective memory and national identity. The study implements Gee's (1991) poetic framework to narrative parsing and finds that the media's presentation of anniversary news can be an agent of persuasion in promoting nationalistic identity through its emphasis on the spatial frame of the narrative, the agency of protagonists in nation building, and the links made between the positive actions of the protagonists in the past and the audience in the present.

Introduction

Applied Linguistics has a range of definitions, as reflected in this book. This chapter defines applied linguistics as a field of study that draws on the intersection of linguistics with other research fields to seek an understanding of how discourses shape who we are. To this end, the study presents the intersection of linguistics with media studies, history, and narrative analysis to address issues around language, identity, and power within a culturally constituted space.

This study is in line with research that views journalism as a *social narrative* (Bennett 2009; Carey 1988, 1989; Jacobs 1996; LaPoe & Reynolds 2013; Lule 1995; Wahl-Johgensen 2013), which journalists use to position themselves as authoritative social interpreters (Zelizer 1990, 1993) by creating an authoritative discourse around events (Edy 2001, 2006; Harro-Loit & Kõresaar 2010; Kitch 2000, 2002, 2003; Mander 1987; Twomey 2004). In this study, I take this discussion further by analyzing how journalists' narrativization of historical events in anniversary narrative reconstructs "who we are" as an internal community construct.

The study focuses on a Fiji-Indian radio announcer's reconstruction of Indian indenture, which provides the introductory framing of a radio documentary that commemorates both the introduction of Indian indenture to Fiji and the Fiji-Indian community's beginnings. The study analyzes the construction of a historical narrative in terms of its spatial and temporal organization and the attribution of agency to protagonists. The study then explores the construction of social relevance, and, by extension, national identity, through the narrative's drawn parallels between the actions of the protagonists and those of the audience in the betterment of Fiji.

Anniversary journalism and collective memory

The analysis is rooted in the theoretical notion that media is an institution of power. Its representations are not simply reflections of the society in which they are produced; rather, they are the conceptual roadmaps that construct society's very existence. Media's discourse, in other words, gives socially relevant meaning to places, events and people at different moments in time, making concrete both what we remember and also how we remember (Hall 1997, p. 19).

Anniversary journalism

Anniversary journalism is a particular genre of news that takes place around anniversaries for commemorative purposes (Edy 2001, 2006; Kitch 2000, 2002, 2003; Zelizer 1990, 1993). Anniversary journalism draws on a community's historical antecedents deemed worthy of veneration at the time. It focuses on events at a particular time in the past and, through the temporal links between salient thematic events, forms a social narrative.

Because the narrative makes use of "facts" in the form of dates, times, places and people, the narrative takes on the appearance of a historical overview of the event being commemorated, and the journalist adopts the role of a public historian. Yet anniversary journalism not only provides an insight into the events of the past; it draws on cultural knowledge in recreating the events being commemorated. This lets the audience form personal links to the past (Johnson 2008, p. 174), so making the events being commemorated worth remembering. These regularly repeated links to the past form a group's collective memory and are central to the construction of the group's identity (Harro-Loit & Kõresaar 2010, p. 325).

Anniversary narrative, collective memory

Maurice Halbwachs (1950) is credited with first discussing "collective memory." He defines it in terms of a shared social consciousness of remembering. According to Halbwachs, collective memory occurs at the group level. The individuals within a group are actively involved in the process of remembering and the private memories of individuals "have meaning only in relation to a group to which they belong" (Halbwachs 1950, p. 54). Further, a group's use of commemoration is important as, without the regular reinforcement from commemoration, individual memories fade over time. A group's commemorative practices imbue certain events, times, places and people with social symbolism, while also deliberately practicing social amnesia regarding other events, times, places and people. It is through such commemorations that the group constructs selective remembrance, which forms the collective memory handed down intergenerationally. Given the differing belief systems of groups, what is commemorated and generationally transmitted as collective memory differs across groups. Further, as the reconstruction of the past is always done in the present, both *what* and *how* events are remembered is from the perspective of what is important today. The continual reconstruction of what is forgotten, remembered, or emphasized from the group's past allows collective memory to take on the function of a social narrative.

Narratives of the past are never complete, and may also be distorted, irrational, and conflict with other narratives on similar events (cf. Edy 2001, p. 56). Edy notes that it is not the narrative's plausibility of the facts that is important; rather, it is the meaning that the community associates with these facts that gives the narrative social worth in the construction of collective memory (2001, p. 56). Because of the narrative's power to construct a group's perception of itself, journalists' reconceptualizations of the past play a significant role in the construction of a group's national culture.

Anniversary narrative, national culture

Hall defines national culture as "a discourse—a way of constructing meanings which influences and organizes both our actions and our conception of ourselves" (Hall 1992, pp. 292–93). National cultures construct national identities "by producing meanings about 'the nation' with which we can *identify*; they are contained in the stories which are told about it, memories which connect its present with its past, and images which are constructed of it" (Hall 1992, pp. 292–93). According to Hall, the discourse of national culture is made up of five elements.

1. *The narrative of the nation* is a narrative about the nation's successes and hardships, which provides a set of stories, images, places, events and rituals that allow us to feel part of the nation's experiences. The narrative gives our lives meaning beyond the mundane, connecting us to a national destiny that pre-existed and will continue to exist beyond our lifetime.
2. *Origins, continuity, tradition and timelessness* focus on the group's character being eternal and changeless, despite the varied experiences over time.
3. *The invention of tradition* or "the way we do things." While traditions may not be as old as often thought, through repetitions of their practices they take on the façade of "the way we've always done things." This implies "continuity with a suitable historical past."
4. *Foundational myth* is a set of invented traditions, such as acts of remembrance, that provide us with a narrative to make sense of the confusions, disasters, and disarray of history, and see them not as tragedies but as national triumphs. The narrative also seeks to unite a disparate group of people as a community.
5. *Pure original people or "folk"* is the symbolic notion that the origins of our group can be traced to these people.

The anniversary narrative, with its emphasis on public remembering, is a discourse of national culture. The anniversary narrative has ritualized acts of selective remembrance and creates personal links between the audience and the narrative's focus. This ensures that the narrative becomes "our" history, encompassing events beyond our lifetime. The links rely on cultural understandings of what norms and values the community identifies with. By illustrating that these same norms and values existed, exist and will continue to exist, the narrative gives a sense of permanence to the community's identity. Finally, while the anniversary narrative is about the past, it does not end in the past. It connects with today's audience and carries the narrative's triumph into the future, laying the foundational myth of the community.

The increasing number of studies on the relationship between journalistic representations and creating and/or maintaining collective memory (such as Edy 2006; Kitch 2003; Zelizer 1993) illustrates that the influence of journalism is acknowledged in shaping society's understanding of itself. This is particularly so in the case of the genre of anniversary journalism, where the narrative takes unrelated events and enchains them around a theme to provide "new" perspectives on the past, "to encourage re-examination and integration" (Edy 2006, p. 95) in light of the narrative's relevance for the present. This study adds to the discussion by analyzing how anniversary narrative uses rhetorical devices to both provide an insight into the past and stay relevant for the present. While the study does not claim that this is how all anniversary narratives use rhetorical devices, the study goes some way in drawing attention to the processes that anniversary journalism can use to reconstruct society's collective memory.

Fiji's indenture commemoration and the anniversary narrative

The narrative was produced by radio announcer Tej Ram Prem as an introduction to the documentary *Girmit Gāthā* or "Stories of indenture". The program was first broadcast in 1979 on Radio Fiji 2, which at the time was Fiji's only Hindi radio station (Usher & Leonard 1979, p. 25). *Girmit Gāthā* played at 8:30pm on Tuesday nights and focused on the life narratives of Indians who, between 1879 and 1916, had voyaged from Colonial India to Fiji. These Indians were to work mostly as indentured laborers on sugarcane plantations (cf. Ali 2004; Lal 2004a, 2004b; Naidu 2004 on Indian indenture; and Gounder 2011 on the *Girmit Gāthā* life narratives). Prem's narrative precedes the laborers' narratives on *Girmit Gāthā*. It begins by reframing the historical circumstances that brought Indians to Fiji and concludes in the present.

Part 1: Why indenture was introduced to Fiji

Strophe 1:	*Factors behind implementation*
Stanza 1:	*The beginning*
Line 1:	On 10th October 1874, Fiji's chiefs ceded the country over to Britain

Stanza 2:	*Measles epidemic*
Line 2:	In 1875, that is, one year later, an English battleship brought a measles epidemic to Fiji
Line 3:	From this epidemic the Fijian's population dropped to one third
Line 4:	And on the Europeans' plantations the number of labourers suddenly dropped significantly
Stanza 3:	*Sir Arthur Hamilton Gordon*
Line 5:	At that time Fiji's Governor Sir Arthur Hamilton Gordon had also been the Governor of Mauritius
Line 6:	That is, the Indian labourers' courage and hard work was very familiar to him
Line 7:	He also knew that the Indian labourers by contract, in other words, 'agreement' , which our forebears by the name of 'Girmit' have immortalized
Line 8:	With the use of this term, how easily they could be brought to Fiji
Strophe 2:	***Indian indenture in Fiji***
Stanza 4:	*Beginnings of indenture era*
Line 9:	To resolve the Europeans' dire situation,
Line 10:	To provide labourers on their plantations,
Line 11:	Sir Arthur Gordon gave his blessings to the indenture system, the result of which was seen in 1879 when on the ship *Leonidas*, the first Indians, who were labourers, were dropped off in Fiji
Stanza 5:	*End of indenture era*
Line 12:	The indenture era ended in 1920
Line 13:	That is, in thirty eight years, approximately sixty one thousand contract bound labourers were brought to Fiji
Line 14:	That is, after serving five years of indenture, the majority of Indians stayed back in Fiji

Part 2: The history of indenture

Strophe 3:	**Reflections**
Stanza 6:	*Negative aspects*
Line 15:	In indenture's origins where
	the torment of shame
	pain
	anguish
	tears
	illness
	and death
	is history
Stanza 7:	*Positive aspects*
Line 16:	In that same origin
	fight
	determination
	courage
	and victory
	is also part of that history

Part 3: The laborers and us

Strophe 4:	**Bridging then and now**
Stanza 8:	*Extolling the virtues of the labourers*
Line 17:	Our forebears'
	hard work
	and sacrifices
	have made Fiji fruitful
Stanza 9:	*Extolling the virtues of Fiji Indians*
Line 18:	In that same way
	their descendants too
	are today taking the country forwards
	toward development and progress

Girmit Gāthā was produced as part of the centenary events to mark Fiji's indenture beginnings. The near non-existence of photos, letters, and other memorabilia brought a realization that a historical era was slipping away and that we needed to hear from the remaining handful of laborers before it was too late. So, *Girmit Gāthā*, the collection of these laborers' oral narratives, is a crucial cornerstone to the community's cultural memory of indenture.

The community's interest in understanding what had brought their ancestors to Fiji ultimately lay in negotiating a cultural identity for Indians born in Fiji. This was a *hybrid identity* (Bhabha 1994)—a fusion of the cultures and languages of their great-grandparents' country of origin and that of the Fiji-Indians' own place of origin. So it carried a *double consciousness* (Du Bois 2009) summed up in the label "Fiji-Indian."

Yet the Fiji-Indian pan-ethnic label does not equate to homogeneity. In the 1970s, almost 100 years after the first Indian laborers arrived in Fiji, their descendants were beginning to fracture along both the sub-ethnic divide of North and South Indian, and the religious lines of Hindu and Muslim, with further schisms arising within each religion (Ali 1980, pp. 107–29; Kelly 1991).

At the same time, Fiji-Indians were becoming a prominent fixture in Fiji. This was evidenced in their increased numbers, political representation, and the establishment of Indian schools and religious institutions. Further, various landmarks were starting to bear Fiji-Indian names. So, at the time of the interviews, Fiji-Indians were able to reflect on the progress of Fiji-Indians from "unschooled" laborers to "educated" landowners. *Girmit Gāthā*'s broadcast coincided with the community's interest in its history.

The radio played a crucial role in the indenture commemoration. As Fiji's population is spread over a number of islands, using radio meant the entire community could take part in the celebrations[1] without having to be physically present at the commemorative functions (cf. Moore 2005, p. 63; Scannell 1996, p. 76).

---

[1] At the time of the narrative's first broadcast, the only forms of media in Fiji were radio and newspaper. The three newspapers had limited production and distribution. The three English newspapers (*Fiji Times, Daily Post* and *Fiji Sun*) are produced daily and the Fijian (*Nai Lalakai*) and Hindi (*Shanti Dut*) newspapers are produced weekly. These newspapers did not reach the more isolated island communities until a few days after publication. Further, few people in these communities, particularly the older generation in rural areas, could read. So the radio played an important role in maintaining the community's links within itself and with the rest of Fiji (cf. Mangubhai & Mugler 2003, pp. 370–71).

The indenture centenary was a literary event, featuring poems by prominent individuals from the community on the themes of the shameful legacy of Indian indenture, the duplicity of colonial authorities and recruiters in getting Indians to Fiji, the Indians' naivety in agreeing to become indentured, and the laborers' immense hardship at the hands of the plantation authorities. These viewpoints represented and re-presented the viewpoints of the Fiji-Indian community. In his narrative, Prem continues this discourse but reframes it in a "new" perspective around the theme "we are one," making the indenture discourse relevant for the present, and letting the listeners carry on the discussion.

Method

Given that this is a highly fluent, pre-constructed[2] narrative told over the airwaves by an experienced radio announcer, it becomes important to analyze the manner of telling. To this end, I have used a three-way translation.[3] The Fiji Hindi is on the left with a corresponding syntactic gloss and the translation is on the right. Using Jefferson's (2004) transcriptional notation, I marked for intonation (high ↑, low ↓), stress (word), acceleration (>word<), deceleration (<word>), pause (.), and inbreath (.h) on the original language.

To analyze, I implemented Gee's (1991) poetic structural approach. Gee places emphasis not only on *what* is said, but also *how* it is said. Although Gee's approach has, to my knowledge, been restricted to narratives produced or translated into English (cf. Ohlen 2003; Riessman 2008), I have applied his approach to the Fiji Hindi narrative because it is hard to closely represent prosodic features and poetic segments in a translation. The intonation pattern allows the narrative to be demarcated into poetic segments, as explained below.

Idea Unit is the smallest prosodic phrase. It contains a single focus made up of one piece of new information, signaled by pitch glide. In Prem's narrative, there is a slight pause marking the end of one Idea Unit and the start of the next. In addition, Prem uses a change in intonation to signal the end of an Idea Unit.

---

[2] Because of it being broadcast, the narrative was most probably read aloud. This would help explain the marked absence of disfluencies, such as repairs, hesitations, and false starts.

[3] See Gounder (2011, pp. 47–66) for a detailed discussion on my transcriptional approach.

To illustrate, the Idea Units have been bracketed in the following sentence:

Line 1: (das oktobar athārā so chouhatar   On 10th October 1874 Fiji's chiefs
         ↑me) (.h)

         ten October eighteen hundred
         seventy.four LOC

         (fījī ke samanto ↑ne)

         Fiji POSS lord.PL

         (↓deš ko britan ko ↓samartit ↓kar   ceded the country over to Britain
         ↓diya) (.)

         country Britain ownership do PST

The first Idea Unit ends with a higher intonation on the locative and is followed by an inbreath. Similarly, the second Idea Unit ends with a higher intonation, followed by a slight pause. The final Idea Unit, however, has a falling intonation and ends with a pause—a typical pattern that Prem uses to mark the end of his Lines.

One or more Idea Units around a central argument form a Line. Each Line consists of a new piece of information while concurrently carrying forward old information. In Line 1 above, we begin with the date (1874). This is followed by the introduction of the major characters for that timeframe (Fiji's chiefs) and what they did that year (ceded Fiji to Britain). This example illustrates that the presence of old information builds *coherence* (Linde 1993) across the narrative while the new information provides *reportability* (Labov 1997)—a reason to continue listening to the unfolding narrative. This balance between coherence and reportability not only exists within a Line but also between Lines.

A group of lines, next to each other and with similar ideas, forms a stanza. Stanzas are large argument units, with one theme and no internal change of place, time or major characters. In the transcript above, Line 1 is in a separate stanza from Lines 2–4 because the timeframe and the protagonists are different for the two stanzas. In Line 1, the event takes place in 1874, while the events in Lines 2–4 occur in 1875. Line 1 focuses on the actions of Fiji's chiefs, while Lines 2–4 are about the effect of the measles epidemic on the indigenous Fijians. The use of a pause and a marked change in intonation pattern at the start of Line 2 also signal the movement between the two themes.

The combination of stanzas, often as related pairs around a central theme, is a strophe. Strophe 1 focuses on the reasons for implementing indenture while Strophe 2 is about how indenture was applied in Fiji. The penultimate strophe (Strophe 3) presents the cultural ideologies about indenture while the final Strophe (Strophe 4) draws parallels between the actions of the laborers and that of the listeners.

Finally, the largest section (Part) is a combination of strophes to form the story as a whole. Strophe 1 and Strophe 2 belong to the same part (Part 1), as together they give an overview of Indian indenture in Fiji. Strophe 3 and Strophe 4 are in their own parts as they each have a different focus from Part 1 and from each other.

This poetic representation is a reminder that the text we are analyzing is a re-presentation of an oral narrative, and that the telling of this narrative is an interactive process between the narrator and a wider unseen audience—an important aspect for this study.

A major drawback of Gee's method of narrative parsing is that it is quite laborious to identify the start and end of lines and stanzas. This means the method is challenging to implement with longer narratives (Elliott 2005, p. 56). Yet Prem's narrative is relatively short at 2 minutes and 10 seconds. Also, because Prem's narrative lacks disfluencies and is not a multiple teller narrative I did not have to worry about these aspects (but see Elliott 2005, pp. 54–56; Mishler 1997, 1999; and Riessman 2008, pp. 93–103).

Analysis

The narrative is in three Parts. Part 1 establishes a causal relationship for implementing indenture in Fiji. Part 2 discusses the emotive connotations associated with the term "indenture." Part 3 acts as a coda by linking the actions of the protagonists to the actions of the listeners. So it emphasizes the relevance of the narrative, and the documentary, for these listeners (cf. Labov 1972 on coda). In this section, the narrative's structural and thematic coherence is analyzed first, followed by the discourse features that signal the construction of collective national memory.

Structuring narrative cohesion

Part 1

In this section of Prem's overview, a causal relationship becomes evident. I have emphasized this by using the strophe and stanza headings (for the transcript see earlier section *Fiji's indenture commemoration and the anniversary narrative* in this chapter).

Prem combines salient and habitual incidents to explain how Indians arrived in Fiji. He sees the causal chain as being triggered by two separate, yet interrelated events: the ceding of Fiji to Great Britain in 1874 and sailors from a visiting British warship introducing measles to Fiji in 1875. The two events are interrelated in that if Fiji had not been ceded to Great Britain, the warship would probably not have been in Fiji waters. Without the warship the epidemic may not have occurred, and some 60,000 Indians might have not been affected. The other salient events (for Prem's theme) are the first indenture ship arriving in Fiji in 1879 and Indian indenture being abolished in 1920. In addition to these one-off events are habitual incidents that occurred over time, such as the decline in the number of Fijians in the population and the regular shiploads of Indians arriving in Fiji.

Through temporal and thematic links (Fig. 5-1), the timeline in Prem's narrative becomes evident.

The dates impose temporality, but this is suspended by the background information on Sir Arthur Gordon provided in Stanza 3. As Gordon was the Governor-General of Mauritius from 1871 to 1874, the attributed knowledge is in analepsis and pre-dates even the first date in the narrative. We need to question why this information is placed in an otherwise chronological narrative. Mauritius was the first colony to introduce Indian indenture in 1834. Gordon, having been governor of Mauritius before becoming governor of Fiji, is attributed with first-hand knowledge of the Indian indenture system. This knowledge and his recommendation for implementing Indian indenture in Fiji lend credibility to Prem's assertion in Line 6 that Indians are hardworking and courageous.

Fig. 5-1: Causal chain for Part 1

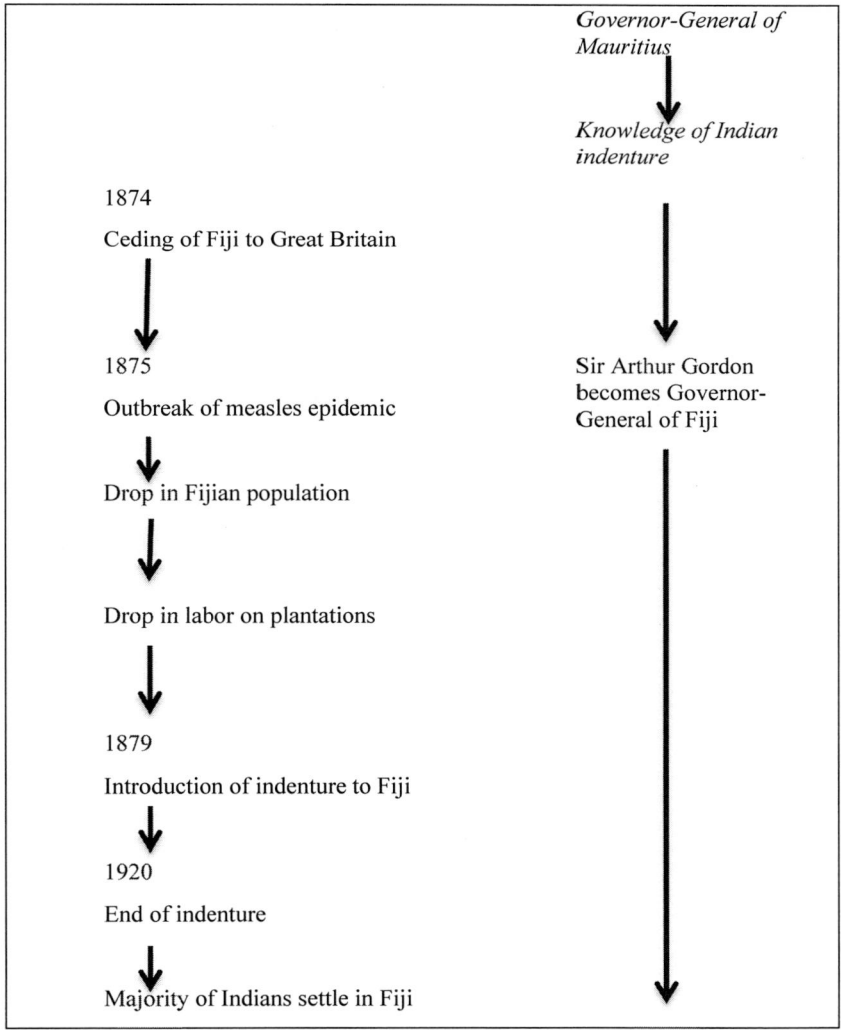

The cohesion of Part 1 is seen in its strophe structure. Stanza 2 and Stanza 3 in Strophe 1 are each devoted to a separate factor behind implementing Indian indenture. Stanza 2 focuses on the effects of the measles outbreak, while Stanza 3 focuses on the Governor-General and his actions. Strophe 2 presents the convergence of the two factors in the form of the first shipload of Indian laborers arriving in Fiji and marks the start of 38 years of indentured arrivals to Fiji.[4]

In Stanza 1 a single line sets the stage for the rest of the stanzas in Part 1. Other than Stanza 1, the final line in each stanza acts as a coda, explaining the relevance of that stanza to the theme of indenture:

Stanza 2: And on the Europeans' plantations the number of labourers suddenly dropped significantly

Stanza 3: With the use of this term [agreement], how easily they [the Indians] could be brought to Fiji

Stanza 4: Sir Arthur Gordon gave his blessings to the indenture system the result of which was seen in 1879, when on the ship *Leonidas*, the first Indians, who were labourers, were dropped off in Fiji

Stanza 5: After serving five years of indenture, the majority of Indians stayed back in Fiji

Further, as seen above, the last line in Part 1 indicates that Part 1 also serves to explain why the Fiji-Indian community was established. But elaboration on this theme is suspended until the final part (Part 3) of the narrative.

Part 2

In Part 2, the structure of the narrative changes from enchaining incidents to contrastive listing. As seen below, the items in Stanza 6 collectively depict indenture as filled with immense suffering. So the theme of Stanza 6 could be "the hardship of indenture." The list itemizes the effects of suffering this hardship, and moves from psychological to physical effects,[5] with the final item—death—marking the ultimate effect. The tone in Stanza 7 is in sharp contrast to the inagentive tone of the previous stanza. Stanza 7 portrays an image of immense achievement, with the ultimate outcome being "victory." So the stanza's theme could be "triumph over adversity."

---

[4] While indenture was not abolished until 1920, the transportation of laborers ended in 1916.

[5] In Stanza 6 *piṟā* (pain) could mean either physical or psychological pain. When considering the preceding and following words, that both refer to emotional upheavals, *piṟā* in this context is taken to mean psychological pain.

The stanzas have parallel structure, and can be likened to poetic verse. For this purpose, I have listed the two stanzas next to each other first in Fiji Hindi and then in English. As the translation cannot do justice to the strophe's structure, I analyze the stanzas in the original language.

Stanza 6	**Stanza 7**
ja↑hā girm↑it ka prayam↑bik ithi↑hās	↑wahī
where indenture POSS origin history	*REFLEX*
šram yātn↑ā	saŋ↑arš
shame torment	*battle*
pi↑↑ā	saŋ↑kalp
pain	*determination*
kleš	tir niš↑che
anguish	*courage*
ās↑u:	
tears	
bimārī	
illness	
our mout	ou vije
and death	*and victory*
kī ithihās he	ka ↑bhī ithihās he(.)
POSS history be.PROG	*POSS too history be.PROG*

in indenture's origins where	in that same origin
the torment of shame	fight
pain	determination
anguish	courage
tears	and victory
illness	
and death	
is history	is also history

As seen from the excerpt above, the pattern of the two stanzas is:

Stanza 6	**Stanza 7**
jahā girmit ka prayambik ithihās	wahī
where indenture POSS origin history	*REFLEX*
List with [negative] connotations	List with [positive] connotations
kī ithihās he	ka ↑bhī ithihās he (.)
POSS history be.PROG	*POSS too history be.PROG*

Stanza 7 continues the structure of Stanza 6. But rather than repeating the words that marked the start of Stanza 6, in Stanza 7 the anaphoric reference marker *wahī* is used to indicate the maintenance of this structure. Similarly, Stanza 7 ends with the repetition of the final units in Stanza 6, but with the insertion of *bhī*. The use of this word and the associated high intonation and stress hark back to Stanza 6. By doing so, through anaphoric reference and lexical repetition, cohesion is maintained between the two stanzas and they are also bound together (as Strophe 3) from the rest of the narrative.

Stanza 7 ends with a pause that is missing from the end of Stanza 6. This indicates the end of the verse form of Strophe 3. While Part 2 presents an image of indenture through the contrasting descriptors in the two stanzas, no mention is made of the laborers. They are the focus of Part 3, the final section of the narrative.

Part 3

As discussed above, Stanza 6 focuses on the negative aspects of indenture while Stanza 7 has a more positive outlook. When Part 2 is seen in relation to Part 3, the reason for this ordering becomes clear. The positive connotations in the final stanza of Part 2 flow into the first stanza of Part 3, so maintaining cohesion between the two Parts.

The use of parallelism and lists, both seen in Part 2, continue in Part 3. Yet unlike in Part 2, where parallelism is in terms of the structure of the stanzas, and lists contrast affective connotations associated with indenture, in Part 3 the parallelism is thematic and the aim is to show similarities between the positive actions of the laborers and those of the listeners:

Stanza 8	**Stanza 9**
	weise hī
hamāre ↑purwajo ko	*REFLEX be.PROG*
1ST.POSS forebear POSS	unko santān ↑bhī(.h)
mahin↑at masakat(.h)	*3RD.REM.POSS descendents too*
hard.work	deš ko ↑āj
unkī kurbānī ↑se(.h)	*country POSS today*
3RD.REM.POSS sacrifice LOC	pragati our vikāš kī or
jeise fījī des abād ↑huā	*improvement and progress OBJ towards*
like Fiji country fruitful	le jā rahī ↑he(.)
happen.PERF	*COP.PERF take go be.PROG*

Our forebears'	In that same way
hard work	their descendants too
and sacrifices	are today taking the country forwards
have made Fiji fruitful	toward development and progress

While Part 3 has no structural parallelism, it does show contrasts between stanzas and anaphoric references. The two stanzas can be contrasted in terms of focal characters and timeframe. In Stanza 8, Prem uses the phrase "our forebears," while Stanza 9 uses "their descendants." Also, Stanza 8 is set in the past ("have made") while Stanza 9 is moving from the present into the future ("today taking the country forwards toward"). To avoid repetition of lexical items from Stanza 8, and to indicate the similarities between the themes of both stanzas, Stanza 9 uses anaphoric reference widely. The stanza starts with "In that same way," to refer to the "hard work and sacrifices" in Stanza 8. Stanza 9 also uses the third person "their" to refer to the laborers, and "the country" to refer to Fiji. Through these contrasts and anaphoric references, the two stanzas are sequenced together.

The suspended theme of Part 1, establishing the Fiji-Indian community, is elaborated on in Part 3. This final part of the narrative makes the link between "our forebears" and "their descendants" explicit. The fact that these descendants are the current radio listeners is indicated by a shift in tense from past to present. So Part 3 acts as an overall narrative coda by explaining to the listeners how this overview is relevant for them.

Structuring collective national memory

Through the analysis of a Fiji Hindi radio commemoration of Indian indenture, the article demonstrates that the anniversary narrative fulfills Hall's (1992) five elements to be a discourse of national culture.

1. *The narrative of the nation:* The indenture anniversary narrative provides a set of stories about the laborers who, through great personal hardship, successfully helped to modernize Fiji. The anniversary narrative's act of remembrance therefore takes the personal difficulties that the laborers experienced and endured when they knowingly or unwittingly became indentured and re-casts those difficulties in a narrative about the nation's triumphant beginnings to become a leader within the South Pacific region. Further, the narrative's coda traces a seamless process of the laborers' initiation of Fiji's modernization and the current and future generations' efforts in sustaining this modernization. In doing so, the coda emphatically weaves the audience into Fiji's destiny, giving personal actions of listeners a national significance.

2. *Origins, continuity, tradition and timelessness:* To ground the narrative as a construct "about us," the coda emphasizes continuity of shared worldviews over the generations (Gadamer 1975, p. 264), bridging, through parallelism, the efforts of the laborers and those of the listeners in the betterment of Fiji.

3. *The invention of tradition:* Through the coda's links between the laborers' positive actions and that of the current (and future) audience, we have the making of tradition, ingrained in a favorable past, which, therefore, is all the more likely to continue. The attributes extolled in Part 3 are taken to be symbolic of Indian practice, inculcating cultural values and norms into what it means to be "Fiji-Indian."

4. *Foundational myth:* To create a "new" Fiji-Indian identity, the anniversary narrative, unlike academic discourses on indenture,[6] seeks to construct a narrative that unites the listeners. In the narrative, Prem mentions the laborers six times. But he does not call them *Girmitya*, the term the laborers coined to refer to themselves and which is commonly used in the Fiji-Indian community. Prem's preferred term is *Bharatye masdur* (which occurs four times—in Lines 6, 7, 11, 13), which literally means "Indian laborer." The term emphasizes the commonality of India as the laborers' place of origin, and

---

[6] For discussions on religion, see Ali (1980); on gender, see Lal (2000); and on ethnicity, see Naidu (2004).

simultaneously de-emphasizes that the laborers came from different Indian regions. On two occasions, Prem uses the term *Purwajo* meaning "forebears." The first is as part of a relative clause within the analepsis at Line 7 in Stanza 3. The second is in Stanza 8. Both times the term occurs within the set phrase "our forebears." By often repeating the first person, Prem aligns himself with the radio listeners and emphasizes his in-group membership, while also establishing the participant role of the targeted addressee (Talbot 2007, p. 52) in furthering his theme "we are one."

5. *Pure original people or "folk":* Despite the stress on common origin through the referral terms, the spatial frame of India is marked by its absence. The narrative is firmly set in Fiji, signifying a distancing from India, physically and emotionally. No mention is made of the recruitment process or even the voyage to Fiji. The first ship "materializes" in Fiji waters. The focus on Fiji and the lack of focus on India holds a cautionary note for the Fiji-Indian community of the time for the need to let go of the skirts of *Bharat Mata*, or "Mother India," and to start seeing Fiji as the foundation of Fiji-Indian history.

The anniversary narrative therefore commemorates not only Fiji's indenture beginnings but also the beginnings of the Fiji-Indian community, with the indentured laborers as the founding members of this community. By emphasizing the "shared" indenture "experiences" of "our" forebears, the narrative works to promote a "national" Fiji-Indian "culture" (Hall 1992, p. 293).

Conclusion

In this study, applied linguistics contributes to the empirically grounded approach to understanding the world we inhabit as discourse, culturally and historically held together by the threads of narrative. Of interest here are narratives that are performed in the public sphere, and how these normative discourses in turn become our textile yardsticks by which we negotiate who we are (Bamberg 2004, p. 360). The study contends that journalism's anniversary narrative reconstructs national identity. To demonstrate, this chapter used Gee's (1991) poetic approach to narrative parsing—also demonstrating the usefulness of his approach for non-English oral narratives. The chapter used narrative analysis to demonstrate that journalists link discrete temporal and spatial events into a thematic causal chain and reassign agency to characters. Through these historical "facts," produced within the context of a radio documentary, journalists re-create a coherent and authoritative narrative from their position as sanctioned social interpreters. This chapter further demonstrates that journalists appeal to an audience by using inclusive pronouns and drawing parallels between the praiseworthy actions of the protagonists and those of the audience. In so doing, the narrative maintains a place in the collective memory of the culture.

The purpose of this book is to raise awareness of the significant nuances that come to the fore through the interaction of applied linguistics with other disciplines. The analysis of media text as a discourse of power provides the ideal framework to showcase this interaction. Discussing the construction of anniversary narratives within the sociopolitical climate of the time in turn provides an opportunity to explore the complex hegemonic forces that are at play in discursively constructing national identities.

Given the study's empirical nature, which requires the study to remain grounded in the text, the study cannot provide a rigorous argument of the influence such public narratives have on the audience members' conceptualization of "who we are." Nor can the study attribute motives to Prem to explain why the narrative is constructed in this manner.

The study exemplifies how applied linguistics focuses on contextual intersections to explore how we construct and are (re)constructed through discourse. Prem uses the public sphere of the radio to draw on the community's collective memory to (re)tell the story of indenture and to (re-)present indenture as a shared history and as a convenient start of the community. In so doing, Prem's narrative demonstrates its power as a normative discourse in determining who to include in the discursive "we." But, just as Prem's narrative is one interpretation of the historical narrative of indenture, it is possible to have counter-readings of his narrative when seen from other points of intersections. By continuing this discussion through further studies, we acknowledge the multilevel web of influence that discourse has in constructing society.

References

Ali, A. 1980, *Plantation to Politics: Studies on Fiji-Indians*, Suva, Fiji: University of the South Pacific; The Fiji Times and Herald Ltd
—. 2004, *Girmit: Indian Indenture Experience in Fiji.* Suva, Fiji: Fiji Museum; Ministry of National Reconciliation and Multi-Ethnic Affairs
Bamberg, M. 2004, "Considering counter narratives". In M. Bamberg and M. Andrews, eds, *Considering counter narratives: Narrating, resisting, making sense*, Amsterdam: John Benjamins, pp. 351–71
Bennet, W.L. 2009, *News: The Politics of Illusion*, 8th ed, New York: Pearson Longman

Bhabha, H.K. 1994, *The Location of Culture*, London: Routledge

Carey, J. 1988, *Media, Myths, and Narratives: Television and the Press*, Newbury Park, CA: Sage

—. 1989, *Communication as Culture*, New York; London: Routledge

Du Bois, W.E.B. 2009, *The Souls of Black Folk*, New York: Library of America

Edy, J.A. 2001, "The Presence of the Past in Public Discourse. In R.P. Hart and B.H. Sparrow", eds, *Politics, discourse, and American society: New agendas*, Lanham, CO: Rowman & Littlefield, pp. 53–70

—. 2006, *Troubled Pasts: News and the Collective Memory of Social Unrest*, Philadelphia, PA: Temple University Press

Elliott, J. 2005, *Using Narrative in Social Research: Qualitative and Quantitative Approaches*, London: Sage

Gadamer, H.-G. 1975, *Truth and Method*, New York: Seabury Press

Gee, J.P. 1991, "A Linguistic Approach to Narrative", *Journal of Narrative and Life History* 1(1): 15–39

Gounder, F. 2011, *Indentured Identities: Resistance and Accommodation in Plantation-era Fiji*, Amsterdam: John Benjamins

Halbwachs, M. 1950, *The Collective Memory* (trans. F. Ditter & V.Y. Ditter), New York: Harper and Row

Hall, S. 1992, "The Question of Cultural Identity". In D.H. Hall and T. McGrew, eds, *Modernity and its Futures*, Cambridge: Polity Press, pp. 273–316

—. ed. 1997, *Representation: Cultural Representations and Signifying Practices*, London: Sage Publications; The Open University

Jacobs, R. 1996, "Producing the News, Producing the Crisis: Narrativity, Television and News Work", *Media, Culture and Society* 18(3): 373–97

Jefferson, G. 2004, "Glossary of Transcript Symbols with an Introduction". In G.H. Lerner, ed, *Conversation Analysis: Studies from the First Generation*, Amsterdam: John Benjamins, pp. 13–31

Johnson, V.E. 2008, *Heartland TV: Prime Time Television and the Struggle for U.S. Identity*, New York; London: New York University Press

Kelly, J.D. 1991, *A Politics of Virtue: Hinduism, Sexuality, and the Countercolonial Discourse in Fiji*, Chicago; London: The University of Chicago Press

Kitch, C. 2000, "'A News of Feeling as well as Fact': Mourning and Memorial in American Newsmagazines", *Journalism* 1(2): 171–95

—. 2002, "Anniversary Journalism, Collective Memory, and the Cultural Authority to tell the Story of the American Past", *The Journal of Popular Culture* 36(1): 44–67

—. 2003, "'Mourning in America': Ritual, Redemption, and Recovery in News Narrative after September 11", *Journalism Studies* 4(2): 213–24

Harro-Loit, H. and E. Kõresaar. 2010, "National Temporality and Journalistic Practice: Temporalising Anniversary Events in Estonian Television News", *Trames* 4: 323–41

Labov, W. 1972, *Language in the Inner City: Studies in the Black English Vernacular*, Oxford: Basil Blackwell

—. 1997, "Some Further Steps in Narrative Analysis", *Journal of Narrative and Life History* 7(1-4): 395–415

Lal, B.V. 2000, *Chalo Jahaji: On a Journey through Indenture in Fiji.* Canberra: Australian National University; Suva: Fiji Museum

—. 2004a, *Girmitiyas: The Origins of the Fiji-Indians*, 2nd ed, Canberra: Australian National University

—. 2004b, "Girmit, History, Memory". In B.V. Lal, ed, *Bittersweet: The Indo-Fijian experience*, Canberra: Pandanus Books, pp. 1–29

LaPoe, V.B. and A. Reynolds. 2013, "From Breaking News to the Traditional News Cycle: A Qualitative Analysis of How Journalists Craft Resonance Through Storytelling", *Electronic News* 7(1): 3–21

Linde, C. 1993, *Life Stories: The Creation of Coherence*, New York: Oxford University Press

Lule, J. 1995, "The rape of Mike Tyson: Race, the Press, and Symbolic Types", *Critical Studies in Mass Communication* 12: 176–95

Mander, M. 1987, "Narrative Dimensions of the News: Omniscience, Prophecy, and Morality", *Communication* 10(1): 57–71

Mangubhai, F. and F. Mugler. 2003, "The Language Situation in Fiji", *Current Issues in Language Planning* 4(3&4): 367–456

Mishler, E.G. 1999, *Storylines: Craftartists' narratives of identity*, Cambridge, MA: Harvard University Press

—. 1997, "The Interactional Construction of Narratives in Medical and Life-history Interviews". In B.L. Gunnarsson, P. Linell and B. Norbert, eds, *The Construction of Professional Discourse*, London; New York: Longman, pp. 223–44

Moore, S. 2005, *Media/theory: Thinking about Media and Communications*, London: Routledge

Naidu, V. 2004, *The Violence of Indenture in Fiji*, 2nd ed, Lautoka: Fiji Institute of Applied Studies

Ohlen, J. 2003, "Evocation of Meaning through Poetic Condensation of Narratives in Empirical Phenomenological Inquiry into Human Suffering", *Qualitative Health Research* 13: 557–66

Riessman, C.K. 2008, *Narrative Methods for the Human Sciences*, Thousand Oaks, CA: Sage

Scannell, P. 1996, *Radio, Television and Modern Life*, Oxford: Blackwell

Talbot, M. 2007, *Media Discourse: Representation and Interaction*, Edinburgh: Edinburgh University Press

Twomey, J.L. 2004, "Searching for a Legacy: The Los Angeles Times, Collective Memory and the 10th Anniversary of the 1992 LA 'Riots'", *Race, Gender & Class*: 11 (1) 75–93

Usher, L. and H. Leonard. 1979, *This is Radio Fiji: Twenty-five Years of Service 1954-1979*, Suva: Fiji Broadcasting Commission

Wahl-Johgensen, K. 2013, "Subjectivity and Story-telling in Journalism: Examining Expressions of Affect, Judgement and Appreciation in Pulitzer Prize-winning Stories", *Journalism Studies* 14(3): 305–20

Zelizer, B. 1990, "Achieving Journalistic Authority through Narrative", *Critical Studies in Mass Communication* 7(4), 366–76
—. 1993, "Journalists as Interpretive Communities", *Critical Studies in Mass Communication,* 10(3): 219–237

PART II

CHAPTER SIX

WHERE THE ACADEMY MEETS THE WORKPLACE: COMMUNICATION NEEDS OF TERTIARY-LEVEL ACCOUNTING STUDENTS

STEPHEN MOORE AND HUI LING XU

Keywords: accounting discourse, bilingual stimulated recall, accounting simulations

Abstract

While the accounting profession in Australia has long stressed the need for accountants to possess strong communication skills, these remain largely undefined, and certainly uninformed by any serious linguistic analysis. There is a considerable gap between the communication skills actually developed in accounting programs at Australian universities and those needed in the accounting workplace (see, for example, Burns & Moore 2008a; Moore & Burns 2008). This chapter reports research at the intersection of higher education and the workplace through its investigation of the communicative skills demonstrated in simulated role plays by Chinese-background undergraduate accounting students and their lecturers. Our chapter has two points of focus. First, the performances of the lecturers are analyzed for move structure and pragmatics, and used as benchmarks to judge the performances of the students, revealing considerable differences in approach and success in terms of task fulfillment. Second, the value of triangulation using a bilingual stimulated recall protocol (that is, the intersection between languages (first (L1) and second (L2)) and cultures (first (C1) and second (C2)) is explored. The results show the value of simulated role plays in developing an accountant's persona, while a self-access DVD created from the role plays highlights important pedagogical issues and implications.

Introduction

Over the past decade the accounting profession in Australia has claimed that Australia has a shortage of accountants. This situation has persisted despite favorable immigration policies allowing the entry of qualified accountants as skilled migrants (Birrell & Healey 2008), and tens of thousands of students graduating from Australian university undergraduate and postgraduate accounting programs (Cable, Dale & Day 2007). Many university graduates are from Chinese language and cultural backgrounds and they, and other overseas accounting students, face considerable difficulties in securing accounting positions despite the shortage of skilled accountants (Birrell & Rapson 2005). These graduates are not held back by their technical knowledge and skills ("hard skills") in accounting. Instead, they are held back by their communication skills (Birrell 2006) and, in particular, their ability to communicate appropriately in a variety of contexts important to professional accountants.

Despite the obvious need for the systematic development of communication skills among trainee accountants, what constitutes "good" communication skills in the profession is only articulated in vague terms by the accounting bodies. For example, the Institute of Chartered Accountants Australia (2007) has reported that "sound communication skills include the ability to listen and read effectively and comprehend what is read and heard; assimilate knowledge and understand its contexts; speak and write on a subject succinctly; [and] be open to new and different perspectives."

Indeed, the professional accounting associations in Australia have revealed a simplistic understanding of the issue by offering a pathway for non-English speaking background applicants that requires an International English Language Testing System (IELTS) score of 7 to secure employment in their profession. This demonstrates that (1) the accounting profession is conflating professional communication skills with English proficiency; and (2) the accounting profession misunderstands the usefulness of an academic IELTS test since it is only validated as a test of academic English to gain entry to study in an English-medium university.

Studies of oral communication skills of accountants in New Zealand (Gray 2010; Gray & Murray 2011) further describe the skillset valued by the accounting profession, but their data are self-reports from questionnaires and interviews instead of actual discourse in the accounting workplace. Yet Gray (2010, p. 54) does acknowledge that

> [Accounting] Educators face a difficult task, needing to acknowledge the problem of transferability [of skills], the need for graduates to gain

localized knowledge about the application of institutional and situational norms to oral communication in the workplace, and the reality that such learning can often best be undertaken during the job, in the workplace.

The aim of the research reported in this chapter is to investigate more rigorously some of the common qualities of communication skills evidenced by Chinese-background undergraduate accounting students as they perform workplace-related tasks and to compare these against performances by professional accountants. We also report on an innovative self-access DVD that was a principal output of this research project (Moore & Xu 2010). The systematic identification of areas in which the students perform poorly relative to professional accountants is a vital step for producing pedagogic materials that can directly address these needs. A range of discourse analytic tools exist that enable a linguistic analysis to better understand role play discourse. Our analysis draws from several of them, including speech act theory, cooperative principle, conversation analysis and genre analysis.

Literature review and research question

In recent years the accounting profession has been increasingly voicing the importance of communication skills as essential to the efficient functioning of the contemporary accounting workplace (Ogilvie 2006; Rumney 2006) and employers are highlighting these skills in their recruitment drives (Simister 2001; Walters 2004). Yet, the skills remain largely undefined. Applied linguists have begun to tentatively investigate the discourse of accountants, generally in terms of written communication and studies of written genres used in the accounting workplace (Forey & Nunan 2002; Ho 2006; Jones & Sin 2003). In terms of spoken communication, Stephen Moore (this paper's co-author) and Anne Burns have produced the only published studies informed by applied linguistics. The topics they have researched include investigating accountant–client interactions for power relations and turn-taking, advice initiation and termination, and communication repair (Burns & Moore 2007); patterns of questioning (Burns & Moore 2008b); and the use of a tax return form as an institutional artifact to scaffold a professional consultation (Moore & Burns 2008).

The research project reported in this chapter arose out of a concern for how a university accounting program could meet the language and communication needs of a major constituent of its undergraduate accounting program, namely Chinese-background undergraduate students. Murray (2010) notes that these students need three relevant strands of development: general English proficiency, academic literacies (spoken and written), and professional communication skills. The first two strands are generally being addressed by university accounting programs, but we find little or no evidence that the third strand is being addressed either in university programs or in the accounting profession. To our knowledge, no published accounts exist of the systematic development of communication skills among accounting students or professionals. So our general research question is to identify, using customized simulated role plays, what the qualitative differences are between the role play performances of professional accountants and accounting students of Chinese background.

Methodology

An interdisciplinary team of three academics (applied linguist, Chinese specialist, and accountant) designed the project. Our research design involved creating four role-play scenarios linked to four core second-year accounting courses (Fundamentals of Management Accounting; Organisational Planning and Control; Accounting and Information Systems; and Financial Management). We used our knowledge of each course's syllabus to design role plays that featured content (such as using costs for decision making; assessing performance management; understanding business processes; and understanding risk and return) that had been covered in the first half of the course. The role plays then took place during the mid-semester break, after the first half of the course.

We sought expressions of interest from second-year accounting students enrolled in any of the four core units, and we were able to recruit 10 students. As some of these students were taking more than one core unit, they agreed to perform role plays for more than one unit. We also arranged for one accounting lecturer (a Chartered Accountant) to participate in two role plays, while our accounting lecturer team member (a Certified Practising Accountant) also participated in two role plays. Both accountants were native speakers of English. All participants (accountants and students) played the role of "accountant" in video-recorded role plays, with a professional actor playing the role of "client." The actor was given the four scenarios several days in advance of the video recording sessions, while the other participants were given the role play scenarios approximately 24 hours in advance of the recordings (see this chapter's Appendix for a sample role play scenario). The reason for this difference was to help ensure that the client was more intimately familiar with the scenario, especially the details of their business and its needs, while the accountant was given more general information appropriate as background to an upcoming consultation.

A total of 21 role plays were recorded, 4 with accounting lecturers, 17 with accounting students, and with roughly equal numbers recorded for each of the four scenarios. The project team viewed and reviewed these various role play performances so they could become familiar with and make the initial identification of strengths and weaknesses of the performances. Two of the four scenarios were identified as being more effectively performed by the students than the other two, so a decision was made to focus only on the effective scenarios—a total of 10 student performances. (The ineffective scenarios lacked a degree of workplace authenticity as they showed students clearly misunderstood the scenario and/or the client's speech.)

We took as our starting point the "tidiest" performance by one of the accounting lecturers, and proceeded to analyze it by referring to its generic structure of moves (Hasan 1985; Moore 2006). We then performed a similar analysis with the second accounting lecturer's role play (in a different scenario) and compared the two. Then we used our findings of similarities from this comparison as benchmarks for the performances of students in the same role play scenarios. In particular, our analyses looked for examples of misunderstood illocutionary force (Austin 1962; Searle 1969); breaches of the cooperative principle (Grice 1975); preferences in adjacency pairs (Levinson 1983); and pragmatic failure (Thomas 1983). Finally, six months after the video recordings were made, but following a stimulated recall protocol, we invited the student participants to view their performances and provide a retrospective account to help us understand why they performed as they did, or said (or didn't say) certain things at certain points in their role plays. This step enabled us to achieve a "member's validation" and to ensure that the researchers' interpretation of the discourse was accurate. In respect of this last point, it is worth noting the "analyst's paradox," which relates to the activity of obtaining the insight of members so as to inform analytic practice (Sarangi 2007). In particular, what one hears, reads or sees explicitly as an analyst may not be what the participants implicitly understand is going on in their interactions.

Results and discussion

We present our results and discussion in terms of three key aspects of our research: comparing performances, retrospective stimulated recall, and a self-access pedagogical tool.

Comparing performances

Even though the two scenarios we investigated were considerably different (one was a bookshop seeking to expand its premises; the other was an IT company wishing to retain its key managerial staff), there were many generic similarities in how the accountant–client consultations unfolded. For example, there were distinct phases where the accountant was:

- mainly listening and attending to what the client was saying
- seeking to clarify information
- summarizing the key issues
- suggesting the next steps to be taken.

Even given these generic similarities we found some distinct differences between the two role play performances by the accounting lecturers; perhaps, most notably, the foregrounding of the consultation by one accountant as an opportunity to recruit a new client to his accounting firm.

By contrast, the student performances in these same two role plays (with the same actor as their client) were quite inferior overall, although within each performance there were usually passages that the students performed quite well. Interestingly, only one student reported, in the subsequent stimulated recall, that he felt he had performed well; half reported that they had performed poorly. Among our more significant findings was that students usually provided their advice to the client early in the consultation, sometimes even when they first spoke. This contrasted sharply with the professional accountants who took a cautious stance, seeking to clarify the situation and find out more about the business (e.g. "existing practices," "industry-wide practices," and "future trading goals"). Only then did they offer any advice, and always with the proviso of needing to do some background checking with colleagues "back at the office." Students also often missed the illocutionary force of utterances (Austin 1962; Searle 1969). An example of this is shown in Table 6-1, where the client was inviting the student accountant to offer their firm's services for a longer term, and the student did not respond directly through an unambiguous acceptance (the preferred response for this adjacency pair) or declining (the "dispreferred" response) (see Levinson 1983).

Table 6-1: An example of misunderstood speech acts

	Actual utterances	Illocutionary force and response
Client:	Okay, can you set...can you set this all up for us? And if so, what would it cost us to have you set this up?	[Initial offer of work]
Student:	Okay.	[Backchannel marker, rather than agreement]
Client:	That's what we're going to need to know too, so we'd need a budget from you and your costs, but would you be able to set these systems up and train our staff to use them?	[Reformulation of offer]
Student:	Okay, you mean the cost of these accounting information systems?	[Backchannel and request for clarification]
Client:	No, I mean we don't have the capacity, we don't have the ability to set this up ourselves, so...	[Side sequence: Clarification]
Student:	Oh.	
Client:	We would need an expert to come in and set up the system...and show us how to use it.	
Student:	Okay.	
Client:	Yeah, and that's where you would come in as a consultant...and obviously for a fee, so you know would you be interested in helping us that way?	[Clarification and reformulation of offer]
Student:	Yeah, you know MYOB and QuickBooks are all very easy to use and you know if you...if your company has an accounting department, that means you have some accountants now, then...	[No second pair part. Off-topic response]
Client:	Not really. That's why I'm talking to you.	[Side sequence: Clarification]
Student:	Oh really?	
	[8 turns omitted]	

| Client: | [somewhat exasperated] *I'm trying to give you a job* | [Explicit expression of illocutionary force of speech act]. |
| Student: | *Yeah, I know.* | [Confirmation of understanding of previous turn] |

Occasions such as these resulted in the client having to re-evaluate the quality of the discourse and the advice the student accountant was giving them. Another significant contrasting feature of the performances of students compared to the professional accountants was that they were sometimes "uncooperative" (Grice 1975) in the relevance of their turns to the client's turns. This is shown in the student's rather jarring off-topic response about Mind Your Own Business (MYOB) and QuickBooks in Table 6-1. Indeed, it was not uncommon for the student accountants to appear to ignore the just-completed turn of the client and start a new line of thought. Below are three further examples of such interactions.

Example 1:

Student:	*Who are your target customers?*
Client:	*...It's more your sort of middle-class, sit down have coffee type of readers...*
Student:	*Have you ever considered doing a branch instead of one single book...shop?* [Off-topic, "uncooperative" turn]

Example 2:

| Client: | *...You know you can sort of sit there and on a Saturday morning you can ... you can bring the family in if you want to and have a cup of coffee and be surrounded by books and maybe browse a little bit...I don't know if you can quantify that [ambience] in money but it's certainly good PR.* |
| Student: | *But can you count these things about what the cost [of] drivers are?* [Off-topic, "uncooperative" turn] |

Example 3:

| Client: | *And the electricity, water and sundries are pretty much the same, so that's why we get to the same bottom line.* |
| Student: | *Yeah Okay I know that, so where we use the method called SWOT, that means your strength, your weakness, your opportunities and your threats.* [Off-topic, "uncooperative" turn] |

Such practices gave the strong impression that the student was not sufficiently acknowledging the client's turns. Indeed, the client seemed to be mildly yet perceptibly irritated on several such occasions.

Retrospective stimulated recall

The retrospective interviews with the students, conducted in English and Mandarin (or, in one case, Cantonese) were very helpful in shedding light on how and why the students performed as they did. For example, and quite remarkably, we learned that no participant had previously been involved in any simulated role play (i.e. one where they keep their own identity as a person, but have to act in the role of some professional status such as a doctor, lawyer or accountant). As Jones (1995) notes, in simulations the environment is simulated but the behavior is real: "The power of a simulation arises from the reality of the communication skills, the analysis, the decision making ... [and] require[s] professional behaviour" (p. 7). Our participants' lack of experience in simulated role plays was evident in that many of them bore a "student persona" rather than an "accountant persona," with their performances seeming superficial and lacking professional credibility. Indeed, the opportunity to apply what they had learned in the core accounting unit to a practical scenario was generally not taken up, but was intended to help students handle the consultation in a more professional manner.

Many students seemed to lack a level of English proficiency that could enable them to perform the tasks well. For example, some students were confused by unfamiliar colloquial expressions used by the client, such as "make it work for us" and "put it in a nutshell." For some participants, there were notable pauses and hesitations when it came their turn to talk. Also, many used "false equivalents" (Kenny 1998) in their vocabulary choices, such as "unprofessional" to mean "incapable professionally," "benefits" to mean "profits," "physical danger" to mean "risk," "environment" to mean "situation," and "gain fame" to mean "become well known in a public relations sense." Such uses led to ambiguity in some interactions. Similarly, some students used accounting or business jargon that was not entirely appropriate to the situation (cf. Burns & Moore 2007). This created a sense of doubt about their understanding of the specific situation. (Example 3 above appears to be an unwarranted digression from what the client was focused on.) Low proficiency in English was also evident in many of the participants at times finding the Australian actor's voice hard to understand. Further, without appropriate strategies to seek clarification, the students were often apparently groping in the dark in understanding what was going on in the consultation. Interestingly, we also discovered that a Chinese cultural influence was at play when some students stated that they were reluctant to ask the client (a middle-aged man aged about 55) for clarification, because the students felt their behavior might be seen as rude or unprofessional. This is a good example of sociopragmatic failure—that is, where the values or norms from one culture are carried across in interactions in a second language context (Thomas 1983),—and such behavior is also supported in intercultural communication literature (Clyne 1994; Scollon & Scollon 2001; Young 1994). Lastly, the retrospections revealed that some participants felt nervous in the confined space of the recording studio, and this had affected their ability to perform at their best. These findings were all interesting, because they shed light on the complex variety of factors involved in performing well in the simulated role plays. They also help to explain why the student performances were generally weak when compared to the performances of the professional accountants.

As a final comment on our stimulated recall protocol, we broke with convention (Bowles 2010; Gass & Mackey 2000) by holding our interview sessions about six months after the recordings were made rather than within a day or two of the recording, as is the norm. This situation was not by design, but happened because one researcher was overseas when the initial data were collected. Rather than abandon the stimulated recall exercise, we decided to delay and then proceed with caution. We planned carefully and structured the interview to allow the students to become familiar again with the actual role play scenario (again, see Appendix). The students then viewed their recorded performance once without interruption. Finally, they provided a commentary or answered our questions about specific passages of the recordings. We were somewhat surprised at the detail the students were able to provide about their performances, despite the time lag of six months. Yet we feel satisfied that their comments were consistent with their experiences at the time of the role-play recordings. For example, they sometimes contradicted in Chinese our first interpretation of their performances based on an English use and anglo-centric perspective. So what could have been perceived as a weakness or limitation in this study (that is, the time delay between the two stimulated recall interview exercises) didn't eventuate. Although it is impossible to know if the students would have provided significantly different accounts of their performances had the interviews taken place within, say, 48 hours of the role plays, we are satisfied that the actual interviews did provide important and useful insights about their performances.

A self-access pedagogical tool

A significant output of this research project was producing a DVD to be used for pedagogical purposes for future cohorts of second-year accounting students (Moore & Xu 2010). We decided to produce a self-access DVD because we felt it was important to create a DVD that could stand on its own, without the need for a lecturer or tutor to guide the user in its use. Our DVD has three parts. Part 1 is the "tidy" accounting lecturer role play referred to above, but segmented into nine sequential sub-units. A "before viewing" point is raised and then a video clip of the segment is shown. A key point is then raised for that particular segment. This approach was repeated for each subsequent segment. The key features we highlighted were that the accountant:

- is attentive to what the client says
- determines the facts of the situation
- clarifies the client's goal(s)
- is attentive to the client's needs throughout the interaction, not only at the start
- uses phrases and fillers to change topic
- draws on their background experience and general understanding of business to provide sound advice from a professional point of view
- ensures that no key information is missing before formulating what advice to give
- refrains from giving hasty, on-the-spot advice
- ends the consultation by assuring the client about any follow-up actions.

We note that these points were not necessarily "steps" in the consultation. Rather, they were issues that we found prominent in the segmentation sequence of the particular performance in Part 1. For all nine segments, we focused on the wordings the accountant used and the body language they displayed to communicate the purpose of the various stages of the consultation.

Part 2 of the DVD shows the second accounting lecturer role play in its entirety, without pausing, but with an occasional running footer that alerts the viewer to an upcoming feature that was previously noted in Part 1. This is followed by Part 3, which shows excerpts of the student performances, again with reference to the key features covered in Parts 1 and 2. For each excerpt the viewer is asked to rate the performance as "good," "average" or "poor," and to provide reasons for their choice of rating. After a short pause, the viewer is then shown our evaluation of the excerpt and our reasons for rating it that way. Then the viewer can consider whether they were noticing the key points that we identified as contributing most to the evaluation we gave.

The accounting students with a Chinese background who viewed the DVD gave positive feedback, but the Accounting Department must decide whether or not to utilise the DVD. Certainly the students and academics who viewed the DVD can see its use as a pedagogical tool for developing the communication skills of students with a Chinese background.

To sum up our study, we found that simulated role plays are a valuable way to understand the dynamics of accountant–client interactions and relevant soft skills. Indeed, role plays are well-suited to generating "behavioral data," and so are very useful to English for Specific Purpose (ESP) and workplace English programs. We think that accounting students should be exposed to pre-recorded role plays (such as those described in our DVD) that can be analyzed and discussed by accounting tutors; and they then should participate in simulated role plays based on realistic workplace scenarios and receive feedback on their performances. Bringing to life a student's "accounting persona" is an excellent way to see how they approach real-world tasks and deal with them in unprepared, real-time social interactions (i.e. as they would have to do in an actual accounting workplace).

Our study also found strong evidence of the value of stimulated recall in L1. Our preliminary findings, based on an analysis of transcripts supplemented by viewing relevant video clips, were insufficient to truly capture what was happening in the performances of the student accountants. The retrospective interviews provided important triangulation to clarify why students did what they did or said what they said. Yet their commentaries in English tended to be fairly general (e.g. "I'm not good at English") compared to their commentaries in Chinese, which were much more insightful (e.g. "He spoke too quickly for me to understand"; "I wasn't familiar with his accent"). We feel that studies of non-English speaking background students performing in simulated role plays must use a bilingual/bicultural protocol in any later stimulated recall interviews. This will ensure the data is interpreted correctly.

Conclusion

The study reported in this chapter is exploratory. We were interested to see how undergraduate accounting students with a Chinese background performed in simulated accountant–client role plays, and then to compare their performances with professional accountants performing the same role plays with the same client. Our findings have shown a wide gap between these two types of performer. In some cases the gap was due to an insufficient level of general English proficiency to properly perform the role play; in others, the students' familiarity with and effectiveness at applying accounting theory to practice (i.e. academic literacies) was evidently weak; and in others it was more clearly due to them not being aware of appropriate communication skills in an Australian business context. Despite the size of the gap, we feel cautiously optimistic that the differences in levels of performance between professional accountants and student accountants can be bridged by identifying different types of performance and making students aware of their respective appropriateness, and then providing opportunities for students to practice the role of accountant. We believe that only such a "hands-on" approach will help aspiring accountants properly and fully develop the soft skills needed to communicate at an interpersonal level. Such training is at the intersection between university accounting programs and the accounting workplace, and both parties must fully support it. Here we see an important role for applied linguists too, as they are ideally suited to inform this meeting space.

Acknowledgements

We are grateful to Macquarie University for the Provost's Competitive Grant funding that enabled us to undertake this project. We would also like to acknowledge our research colleague, Chris Searchfield, for his contribution to the project.

References

Austin, J. 1962, *How to do things with words*, Oxford: Clarendon Press
Birrell, R. 2006, *The changing face of the accounting profession in Australia*, Melbourne: CPA Australia
Birrell, R. and E. Healy. 2008, "Migrant Accountants—High Numbers, Poor Outcomes", *People and Place* 16(4): 9–22
Birrell, R. and V. Rapson. 2005, *Migration and the accounting profession in Australia.* Report prepared for CPA Australia. Centre for Population and Urban Research, Monash University
Bowles, M. 2010, *The think-aloud controversy*, New York and London: Routledge
Burns, A. and S. Moore. 2007, "Conversation analysis and the accounting classroom: Exploring implications for LSP teaching". In H. Bowles and P.

Seedhouse, eds, *Conversation analysis and language for specific purposes*, Bern, Switzerland: Peter Lang, pp. 183–215

—. 2008a, "Communicating in professional accounting contexts—unexplored territory", *Taxation in Australia* 43(5): 315–17

—. 2008b, "Questioning in simulated accountant-client consultations: Exploring implications for ESP teaching", *English for Specific Purposes* 27: 322–37

Cable, D., M. Dale and R. Day. 2007, "Accounting education: The gap between academic study and professional practice". In N.M. Meyers, B.N. Smith, S.A. Bingham and S.F. Shimeld, eds, *Proceedings of the Second Innovation in Accounting and Corporate Governance Education Conference*, January 31–February 2, Hobart, Tasmania. www.utas.edu.au/business/faculty/conference/documents/Papers/Cable_Dawn_et_al_2007.pdf

Clyne, M. 1994, *Inter-cultural communication at work: Cultural values in discourse*, Cambridge: Cambridge University Press

Devitt, A. 1991, "Intertextuality in tax accounting: Generic, referential, and functional". In Bazerman, C. and J.G. Paradis, eds, *Textual dynamics of the professions: Historical and contemporary studies of writing in professional communities*, Madison, WI: University of Wisconsin Press, pp. 336–57

Forey, G. and D. Nunan. 2002, "The role of language and culture in the workplace. In C. Barron, N. Bruce and D. Nunan", eds, *Knowledge and discourse: Towards an ecology of language*, Harlow: Longman, pp. 204–20

Gass, S. and A. Mackey. 2000, *Stimulated recall methodology in second language research*, New York and London: Routledge

Gray, E. 2010, "Specific oral communication skills desired in new accountancy graduates", *Business Communication Quarterly* 73(1): 40–67

Gray, E. and N. Murray. 2011, "'A distinguishing factor': Oral communication skills in new accountancy graduates", *Accounting Education: An International Journal* 20(3): 275–94

Grice, P. 1975, "Logic and Conversation". In D. Davidson and G. Harman, eds, *The Logic of Grammar*, Encino, CA: Dickenson, pp. 64–75

Hasan, R. 1985, *Linguistics, Language and Verbal Art*, Geelong, Victoria: Deakin University Press

Ho, S. 2006, *Exploring writing strategies employed by accounting finance majors in the university and the workplace*, Unpublished doctoral thesis, Macquarie University, Sydney

Institute of Chartered Accountants. 2007. Candidate enews: http://www.charteredaccountants.com.au/chartered_accountants_program/candidate_enews/articles/A119134999

Jones, A. and S. Sin. 2003, *Generic skills in accounting*, Sydney: Pearson

Jones, K. 1995, *Simulations: A handbook for teachers and trainers*, 3rd ed, London: Kogan Page

Kenny, D. 1998, "Equivalence". In M. Baker, ed, *The Routledge Encyclopaedia of Translation Studies*, London and New York: Routledge, pp. 77–80

Levinson, S. 1983, *Pragmatics*, Cambridge: Cambridge University Press

Moore, S. 2006, "Managing rhetoric in 'smart' journalism: Generic and semantic contours", *TEXT & TALK: An Interdisciplinary Journal of Language, Discourse & Communication Studies* 26: 351–81

Moore, S. and A. Burns. 2008, "NESB accountants and professional communication", *Prospect: An Australian Journal of TESOL* 23(2): 47–59

Moore, S. and H.L. Xu. 2010, *Developing professional communication skills of accounting students self-access DVD*, Sydney: Department of Linguistics, Macquarie University

Murray, N. 2010, "Conceptualising the English language needs of first year university students", *The International Journal of First Year in Higher Education* 1(1): 55–64

Ogilvie, A. 2006, "Conversation comes easy", *Charter* (Sydney: The Institute of Chartered Accountants in Australia): July: 33–35

Rumney, I. 2006, "A matter of linguistics", *Charter* (Sydney: The Institute of Chartered Accountants in Australia): March: 44–45

Sarangi, S. 2007, "Editorial: The anatomy of interpretation: Coming to terms with the analyst's paradox in professional discourse studies", *Text and Talk* 27(5/6): 567–84

Scollon, R. and S. Scollon. 2001, *Intercultural communication: A discourse approach*, Cambridge, U.K.: Blackwell

Searle, J. 1969, *Speech Acts: An essay in the philosophy of language*, Cambridge: Cambridge University Press

Simister, M. 2001, *The new CFO of the future: Finance functions in the twenty first century*, Sydney: The Institute of Chartered Accountants in Australia (ICAA) and KPMG Consulting

Thomas, J. 1983, "Cross-cultural pragmatic failure", *Applied Linguistics* 4(2): 91–112

Walters, K. 2004, "'Soft' skills in demand", *Business Review Weekly*, September, 73: 23–29

Young, L. 1994, *Crosstalk and culture in Sino-American communication*, Cambridge: Cambridge University Press

Appendix—Sample role play

Accountant's role card

You are an accountant working for a small practice dealing with local business people. Among your firm's clients is a bookshop owner/manager who has plans to expand their business. They have arranged an appointment to see you to discuss their plans and to seek your advice.

Some relevant information about their business:

- Located in North Sydney
- Current turnover $250,000 a year
- Manager's salary $80,000 a year
- Profit last financial year approximately $7,000

Client's role card

You own and manage a bookshop in rented premises in North Sydney. The premises next door to your business are currently available for rent, and are owned by the same landlord as your bookshop premises. You are thinking of expanding your business in one of two ways (see below), and need advice from your accountant.

Option 1:   Use all of next door premises as extension of bookshop

Option 2:   Use 50% of next door premises as extension of bookshop, and 50% as bookshop café. [For this option, you would subcontract the café to someone with relevant expertise and experience to run it for an annual fee]

Some figures and estimates for your bookshop business:

	Last financial year	Option 1 estimate	Option 2 estimate
	$	$	$
Bookshop turnover	250,000	400,000	325,000
Café contract fee	-	-	40,000
Book purchases	90,000	140,000	120,000
Premises rent	50,000	100,000	100,000
Manager's salary	80,000	80,000	80,000
Part-time staff	20,000	40,000	25,000
Electricity, water etc	2,000	3,000	3,000
Sundry expenses	1,000	1,000	1,000
Profit/(Loss)	**$7,000**	**$36,000**	**$36,000**

CHAPTER SEVEN

LEARNING SPACES AS MEETING PLACES: ACADEMIC LITERACY IS EVERYONE'S RESPONSIBILITY

ANGELA ARDINGTON

Keywords: approaches to knowledge, flexible learning environments

Abstract

The learning space is a credit-bearing first-year unit of study in engineering at the University of Sydney. The course typically attracts a diverse student cohort, with many students having a first language other than English. The challenges of providing embedded academic literacy support in this course are explored from the perspectives of students and an Academic Language and Learning (ALL) practitioner. Research reported here investigates students' perceptions of their immediate and future communication needs in engineering. Issues examined include conceptions of diversity, cultures, and contexts of learning. Given the predominant curricular focus in engineering on "hard" courses that emphasize computations and technical aptitude rather than communications-based courses that nurture creativity and flexibility in open-ended dialogic learning spaces, how are understandings of academic literacy negotiated and enacted at this disciplinary interface between applied linguistics and engineering? A critical evaluation of existing pedagogies in engineering and academic literacies highlights some tensions, challenges and opportunities. Questionnaires elicited valuable insights for designing future academic literacy programs. A pedagogical shift towards a curriculum that integrates academic literacy centrally in the core curriculum, bringing together collective disciplinary understandings, will more effectively realize the potential of learners and ensure a richer learning experience that will better meet the broader aims of university learning.

Introduction

A specific focus of this chapter is to explore the intersection between the growing research field of Academic Language and Learning (ALL) and other disciplinary approaches to knowledge and enquiry, engineering and architecture, to reveal some of the challenges in scaffolding students' language learning in the provision, design and sustainability of an academic literacy support program embedded in a credit-bearing undergraduate course. The learning space is the core first-year undergraduate unit of study, Professional Engineering, in the Faculty of Engineering, Sydney University. A fundamental question that impacts on the provision of in-discipline literacy support revolves around the place of writing in a practice-based degree such as engineering. Related issues concern the delivery, type, and timing of in-discipline literacy support. Given that language support is typically provided by ALL practitioners, as academic literacy experts, positioned outside the subject discipline (Chanock 2011), this chapter explores the complexities of negotiating this disciplinary interface.

ALL draws on a number of related disciplines: applied linguistics, sociocultural theories of learning, and discourse studies. ALL is a field of enquiry that focuses on the study of academic communication (particularly writing), a core purpose of which is to be an effective communicator. The field recognizes literacies as becoming progressively varied and multilingual (Jones, Turner & Street 1999; Lillis & Scott 2008). Establishing successful integrated language support requires collaboration, cooperation and ongoing commitment; in this case, the nexus between the disciplines of engineering and applied linguistics. ALL practitioners (that is, those responsible for implementing in-discipline academic literacy programs) typically have a formative disciplinary background in linguistics. In revealing some of the complexities of working as an ALL practitioner at the margins of the core university structure (Chanock 2011), a key objective of this chapter is to review the provision of integrated literacy support in *Professional Engineering*, a core first-year unit of study at the University of Sydney, and offer some suggestions. These suggestions will inform and assist in directing future best practice for all those engaged in the student learning experience, to provide more targeted, relevant and equitable support for the increasingly diverse student (and teaching) demographic (Devlin 2011; Kreber 2009).

The diverse learning community

Diversity, which refers to the concept of being different, is not a new phenomenon, but the approach towards it requires reform (Janks 2004; Kostogriz & Godley 2007). Students bring their individual diversity (linguistic, cultural, and religious) and multiple literacies to the learning context (Kimmel & Volet 2012). Key issues addressed here include how we, as agents of educational change and from different disciplinary backgrounds, value and foster these multiple literacies in practice while also meeting the complex professional demands for a global workforce.

More than 150,000 students in Australian universities and high schools grew up in Asia. They could be language teachers, cultural interlocutors and future ambassadors for Australia, but too many pass through our universities as if in a parallel universe. They often return to their home countries without an Australian network of friends and experiences (Low 2012).

Unfortunately, the above criticism rings alarmingly true. All institutions strive to graduate students who are prepared and inspired to contribute to today's multicultural complexity. Few would contest the proposition that the overarching goal of education is to prepare students to embrace differences. But, as yet, we are falling short of this objective. This changing learning space demands that linguistic and sociocultural aspects of diversity are re-examined. Bennett, Volet and Fozdar (2013, p. 2) draw our attention to tertiary contexts, "where English is the language of instruction, monolingual local students rarely mix with students who are not fully proficient in English." Similarly, our shortcomings as educators to exploit the rich potential of the multicultural learning space are highlighted: "Despite the growing linguistic and cultural diversity in tertiary institutions, there is strong evidence of minimal interaction between 'domestic' and 'international' students in classrooms and in wider university contexts" (Cruickshank, Warren & Chen 2012, p. 797).

Recently, the Pro-Vice-Chancellor (Academic Affairs), University of Sydney stated, "our aim is to help students produce not only high quality theses, but for them to be high quality researchers who can be effective thinkers and communicators outside their particular disciplines" (Carroll 2012). While this view acknowledges disciplinary expertise, it emphasizes the importance of global citizenship. The Dean of Engineering at the same University similarly emphasized the importance of the nexus between disciplinary expertise and a broader communicative competence, pointing to key challenges that the profession needs to address: "I see an increased focus of Engineers and IT professionals on the interfaces between people and technology." Indeed, it is timely to focus attention on the "social" side of engineering.

In short, engineering has come to be viewed as diverse as the communities it serves, inextricably linking technical projects with people's needs. The importance of this intersection between education, the technical and the social is succinctly encapsulated in this statement:

"Engineering works. It could work better, however, with improvements in education and an identity in which the social and technical embrace each other with equal prominence" (Trevelyan 2009, p. 1). Researchers have drawn attention to the central place of communication in the daily life of a practicing engineer where some engineers spend up to 60 percent of their time in oral and written communications with a range of participants—contractors, regulators, government agencies and special interest groups (Dym et al. 2005; Trevelyan 2009). Clearly, there is little doubt that many, within and beyond the academy, recognize the need for engineering graduates to demonstrate not only technical competence (a given), but also interpersonal and communication skills that are key employment selection criteria (Dowling, Carew & Hadgraft 2010).[1] Explicit development of students' communicative competence can only be achieved by a review of current engineering curricula and existing pedagogy. Engineers need to be able to not only help solve problems facing communities but also explain them to those communities (King 2008; Sheppard et al. 2009; Trevelyan 2009). The above views locate the university in the wider global community and emphasize the broader aims of university learning, asserting the core values of critical thinking and the communication of ideas beyond the academy in a range of social contexts. Academic literacy therefore, irrespective of discipline, lies at the heart of the successful learning experience. Contemporary higher education is no longer the privilege afforded to an elite; it is a mass education system that invites and attracts a culturally diverse student body. As such, educational institutions have a responsibility to provide their students with a relevant, stimulating and enriching learning experience that will prepare them for success beyond academia.

The following section examines the diversity exhibited in disciplinary approaches to knowledge and enquiry, and its impacts on cultures of learning that govern how knowledge is valued and communicated at institutional, disciplinary, and individual levels.

Cultures of learning

Within an institution, disciplinary epistemologies (theoretical assumptions, methodologies) exert an effect on curricula and pedagogic practices (Becher & Trowler 2001; Lillis & Scott 2008). They represent valued and

---

[1] In 2007, 54.2 percent of Australian graduate recruiters who responded to the graduate Careers Australia survey, ranked "interpersonal and communication skills" as the highest ranked criterion.

powerful ways of engaging with the world that exert an effect on student learning (Jones, Turner & Street 1999; Kreber 2009). According to Becher and Trowler (2001) different "tribes" have different cultures and ways of knowing that generate a respective Community of Practice (CoP).

The concept of the academic "tribe" (Becher & Trowler 2001) requires a sharing of values and acting within specific codes of practice, while CoP emphasizes participation and engagement through learning that can be characterized as a situated learning perspective (Lave & Wenger 1991). This requires more than the simple transfer of knowledge and skills acquired in an academic setting to a professional workplace situation. Learning to communicate in a particular situation, academic or professional, is part of *becoming* a legitimate member of a CoP (Artemeva 2009). It is about *ways of doing, ways of behaving*—making meanings— and writing is a key channel through which meanings are made. A Community of Interest (CoI) is distinct from a CoP as it can be defined by its collective concern with the resolution of a particular problem. Discipline specialists, academic literacy experts, student engineers and potential employers could be considered to be a CoI. A CoP demonstrates group cohesiveness based on homogeneity that is biased towards efficient communication that takes advantage of shared knowledge, established value systems and clear learning trajectories. Patterns of practice are predictable based on shared ideologies. However, a CoP demonstrates limitations due to their "closed" attitude, which effectively suppresses exposure to, and acceptance of, outside ideas. Conversely, a strength of a CoI is its potential for creativity because different perspectives and backgrounds can lead to new insights (Bennis & Biederman 1997). A significant challenge for a CoI is that it may fail to create a shared understanding as it often collaborates only temporarily on a particular project.

The notion of territory indicates tight disciplinary boundaries and still has currency. Yet changes since pose distinct challenges to the notion of discrete disciplinary cultures—challenges that blur boundaries: "Knowledge itself is a social and cultural construct as are the artificial boundaries drawn around packages of knowledge that separate disciplines" (Armstrong 2006, p. 4). The view that discipline boundaries both constrain the sharing of knowledge and exacerbate divisions has led to an emergent focus on the dynamic, uncertain, process-driven quality of learning (Carter 2007). In a marked shift of emphasis from "knowledge" to "knowing," or "becoming," (Carter 2007; Artemeva 2009, p. 166) underscores the inadequacy of acquisition and skill transfer, as not only insufficient, but misleading.

Building on genre-centered approaches of Bazerman (1997) and Miller (1984), genres "are forms of life, ways of being. They are frames for social action. They are environments for learning" (Bazerman 1997, p. 19). They "serve as keys to understanding how to participate in the actions of a community" (Miller 1984, p. 165). They mediate both function—how one acts in a given community—and epistemology—how one comes to understand that community. Genre knowledge is therefore a useful tool for developing a professional identity. The ways that writers present their arguments, control their rhetorical personality, and engage their readers reflect preferred disciplinary practices (Hyland & Tse 2007; Swales 2004). Much of the analysis on disciplinary differences, from the micro level of lexico grammatical features (Hyland 2003; 2008) to the materialized text level (Swales 1990), to the macro level of metagenres (Carter 2007), has identified disciplinary distinctions at the postgraduate level or published academic genres. At the macro level of metagenre, four metagenres or *ways of doing* were identified:[2] "Problem solving" was identified as the dominant metagenre spanning disciplines (Carter 2007), and its potential generalizability can provide a valuable scaffold that is accountable to disciplinary practices, yet transferable across disciplines.

However, learning genres does not occur in a smooth, linear way; it continues through the degree program and into the workplace. First-year undergraduate writers are not yet socialized into the epistemological practices of their disciplines. Existent pedagogies and their impact on interdisciplinary initiatives are discussed in the following section to provide some insights into how we might revise current curricula and interdisciplinary collaborations.

Existent pedagogies

Some of the problems with existent pedagogies concern the constraining nature of packaging knowledge within territorial, rigid discipline boundaries. The silo mentality of "sticky knowledge" (Bartlett & Ghoshal 1998) (that is, residing in one area or silo and not easily moved or manipulated) is a barrier to interdisciplinary initiatives. While the notion of "tribes" (Becher & Trowler 2001) is instructive in focusing attention on the specificities (and so focusing on the differences) of a particular discipline, it tends to foster tunnel vision and hinder interdisciplinary initiatives. By conceiving of boundaries around knowledge as more

---

[2] The four metagenres were problem solving, empirical enquiry, research from sources, and performance.

flexible, opportunities for interdisciplinary collaborations become possibilities. While developing a domain-specific language (syntax, technical lexis) is an important part of demonstrating a disciplinary identity, as educators we should be aware that disciplinary values seem to be expressed as more shared than conflicting. These similarities are reflected in formal requirements or objectives at unit of study, disciplinary and institutional levels; that is, learning outcomes and graduate attributes vary little across faculties. A genuine focus on convergence rather than difference, viewing disciplines as "active ways of knowing" (Carter 2007, p. 387), would optimize these shared values and facilitate negotiated interdisciplinary practice to contribute towards richer learning experiences. These cultures of learning provide the background and contexts of learning for the current research and are examined in the following two sections.

Background to the research

Consider, for example, the combined degree program currently being offered:[3] the Bachelor of Engineering (Civil) and Bachelor of Design in Architecture.[4] This innovative program encourages the combination of developing scientific, analytic, technical, and management skills through the Engineering component with Architectural studies that emphasize the conceptual and aesthetic aspects of the design process. This program shows that disciplinary boundaries are not as fixed as previously supposed. Predominant curricular focus in engineering is on "hard" courses that emphasize computations: solving equations, technical aptitude, product design/structural visualization and modeling processes (Johnston 2006, p. 126). Yet alongside the capacity for technical analysis, core engineering graduate attributes[5] enshrine the broader institutional expectations by emphasizing three non-technical skills: the ability to (1) communicate effectively; (2) function as reflective practitioners on multidisciplinary teams; and (3) participate in the broad education necessary to understand the impact of engineering solutions within a global, economic, and environmental context (Ardington 2011).

A corresponding first-year unit of study, *Architectural Communications*, in the Bachelor of Design in Architecture program in the Faculty of

---

[3] See http://sydney.edu.au/science/fstudent/undergrad/course/bsc-combined.shtml#1
[4] See page 42 of the Engineering Guide at
http://sydney.edu.au/engineering/publications/Engineering-IT-UG-Guide.pdf/
[5] See http://sydney.edu.au/engineering/civil/current/undergraduate/attributes.shtml
Communication

Architecture, Sydney University, "introduces students to fundamental modes of communication used to comprehend, conceive, explore, articulate and document architecture." [6] Curricular emphasis in the Bachelor of Design in Architecture is described as "a creative profession operating at the intersection of art and technology,"[7] is however more likely to value communications-based courses, and so integrate into the degree program "soft" courses that nurture creativity, flexibility and the flow of ideas in open-ended dialogic learning environments. Such environments include studio-based teaching that encourages peer engagement, emphasizes process and self analysis, and forms core learning spaces (Hocking 2010; Reid & Solomonides 2007).

Clearly, genres and approaches to learning (and teaching) differ according to discipline. For example, engineering students will typically write few essays but are likely to be engaged in collaborative, group writing tasks, such as writing technical reports, press releases, and memos. Architectural students will explore domains of sketching, technical drawing, model making, diagramming, photography, and verbal and written communication in the form of the design studio "crit"—a complex, multimodal, (visual-textual-spatial) oral performance genre. While the two disciplines clearly exhibit different curricular focus and assessment activities, in terms of graduate attributes, where values are reflected in contextualized professional practice, [8] they demonstrate remarkable similarities. These interdisciplinary similarities can provide us, as agents of change, with a useful starting point in designing appropriate in-discipline language programs.

Context of learning

The learning context presents a number of challenges. First, many first-year engineering students may be under the common misconception that writing is a relatively minimal component in the degree program. Yet the reality suggests otherwise. Both academics and prospective employers demand highly developed oral and written language skills (Arkoudis, Baik & Richardson 2012). Given that highly developed language competence is a requirement for engineering students, and significant numbers of students do not have English as a first language, the issue of in-discipline language support must be managed. This first-year learning space becomes

---

[6] See http://sydney.edu.au/courses/uos/BDES1012/architectural-communications-1
[7] See http://sydney.edu.au/courses/Bachelor-of-Design-in-Architecture
[8] See http://sydney.edu.au/architecture/about/graduate_attributes.shtml

a meeting place not only of students from a diversity of cultural and linguistic backgrounds. The meeting place is also the site for academics from divergent disciplinary backgrounds and cultures of learning (linguistics and engineering) to negotiate and design relevant language support for this cohort.

A second challenge concerns current perceptions of in-discipline language support underscored by the complexities of working from a marginalized institutional position, often typical, of providers of academic literacy initiatives, located outside the core university structure. Influential studies have demonstrated that perceptions of colleagues can be influenced by disciplinarity and teaching practices (Becher & Trowler 2001; Skillen 2005; Wenger 1998). The status of ALL practitioners is often invisible and low profile within the practices of the institution. As Chanock (2011, p. 50) reports, academic advisors are all too often positioned to "operate at the margins of academic life." The Learning Centre at the University of Sydney [9] is uniquely placed in the structural organization of the institution, lying outside the faculty structure, and this position presents a unique set of challenges and opportunities. On one hand, ALL practitioners are not bound by any one disciplinary epistemology, as their work requires rapid familiarization and immersion in the relevant disciplinary knowledge, values and practices, to build an appropriate language resource. This affords a unique circumstance where potentially strong partnerships can be built within and across disciplines. Conversely, this marginalized institutional position can aggravate underlying tensions between institutional, disciplinary and individual identities and values with regard to the place of literacy support. Language support programs, to an extent, lack the same legitimacy of practice afforded to other disciplines. This can contribute to barriers to consolidating collaborative disciplinary relations and CoP. The following section reports on research that the Learning Centre conducted of a first-year engineering unit of study at the University of Sydney.

---

[9] The major goals of the Learning Centre are to support the enhancement of quality learning and teaching, to support quality research, and to support students from a diversity of social and cultural backgrounds. The main role of the Centre is to help all students develop and enhance their learning and academic literacy (Learning Centre University of Sydney 2011, p. 5).

The research: Professional Engineering ENGG1803

The Learning Centre at the University of Sydney currently provides a 13-hour integrated academic literacy support program: *Professional Engineering, ENGG1803*. This core first-year undergraduate unit of study in Engineering is the result of the Learning Centre being involved with the Faculty of Engineering for more than 10 years.[10] With its emphasis on the social and interpersonal aspects of professional engineering, this learning space is particularly appropriate for the positioning of an embedded academic literacy program. The prescribed Learning Approach as detailed on page 4 of the *ENGG1803 Professional Engineering 1 Unit of Study Manual 2012* states:

> The essence of professional engineering is that you are dealing with people. Different people behave differently in the same, and different situations. The biggest challenge is rarely to work out what to do, but rather to communicate effectively to and motivate a group of people to work out what to do, and how to do it.

Among other non-technical skills, such as being able to function as reflective practitioners on multidisciplinary teams, the ability to communicate effectively, orally and in writing, is a core engineering graduate attribute. The academic literacy program is closely aligned with assessment activities, such as short essays, oral presentations and collaborative report writing. These activities are integrated throughout the semester, using a team teaching approach that involves joint marking of assessments by ALL practitioners and discipline specialists (Ardington, 2011; Arkoudis, Baik & Richardson 2012). Activities and exercises that foreground teamwork mirroring authentic workplace practices are highly relevant. Team teaching brings together the rich expertise of ALL practitioners, and discipline specialists. Doing so optimizes the knowledge base for recipients while simultaneously sharing practices and understandings. This sharing of practice and building disciplinary partnerships can lead to a more sustainable and integrative presence in a degree program.

Theoretical principles that have guided recent Learning Centre intervention in this unit of study draw on a synthesized approach from genre-based pedagogies that foreground situated social practices (Bazerman 1994; Bazerman, Bonini & Figueiredo 2009), *Writing in the Disciplines* (Carter 2007; Hyland 2009) and *Academic Literacies* (Lea &

---

[10] Further details about this partnership are on page 61 of Ardington (2011).

Street 1998; Lillis & Curry 2010), as set out earlier in this chapter in "Cultures of Learning." Improving the current learning space requires that we determine (1) the specific literacy needs of the diverse student cohort; and (2) students' perceptions of their immediate and future communication needs. To address these issues, two research methods were adopted: the MASUS[11] (Measuring the Academic Skills of University Students), and a formal open-ended questionnaire. These two methods are outlined in the following section.

Methods

The MASUS procedure

A total of 157 first-year Engineering students completed the MASUS diagnostic task. On the basis of their MASUS results, 27 students were identified as experiencing literacy related problems and would likely benefit from integrated literacy support. The MASUS is a framework used to inform and structure the staging of the development of students' literacy skills. The MASUS diagnostic is a reliable and established procedure. It is seen as an accurate predictor of students' academic literacy and is used in a variety of disciplines. It is used to assess students writing skills against four criteria: (1) use of source material; (2) structure and development of text; (3) control of academic style; and (4) grammatical correctness. All first-year students enrolled in ENGG1803 must take the assessment in Week 1 of the course.

Early identification of language needs affords the opportunity of reviewing existing curricula and assessment tasks. Early formative feedback proves valuable in ascertaining students' specific language needs to enable timely integration of relevant academic literacy skills into disciplinary content. If the MASUS diagnostic assessment identifies any problem areas, an embedded language support program is implemented from Week 2 of the course. Common problem areas (as reflected in responses to the MASUS diagnostic task[12]) demonstrated that students' close attention to specific detail can cause them to overlook the broader contextual relevance and implications of issues. This means they may

---

[11] The MASUS (Measuring the Academic Skills of University Students) procedure is a diagnostic assessment instrument designed to measure students' academic literacy. It was designed as part of a collaborative process between faculty and Learning Centre staff to identify and develop literacy skills (Bonanno & Jones 2007).

[12] Some examples are on page 65 of Ardington (2011).

focus on the practical rather than the conceptual, and fail to synthesize identified issues into future recommendations. The current engineering curriculum's emphasis on mathematical rather than textual or verbal material tends to reinforce the focus on detail instead of context.

The questionnaire

To determine students' perceptions of their immediate and future communication needs and, more specifically, to probe their understandings of the *place* of academic writing in an engineering degree, a brief questionnaire was distributed to all students enrolled in *Professional Engineering*. The questionnaire comprised six open questions and was designed to: (1) discover students' attitudes, past experience and future expectations, to the *place* of writing in engineering; and (2) refine follow-up language support to better fit the literacy support to the explicit needs of the cohort.

This chapter focuses on only the following two questions about attitudes to writing. Other questions (not included in this chapter) targeted more specific language-related issues that MASUS identified.

1. How important do you think it is for your professional engineering development to write well?

2. What types of writing do you think you are likely to be involved in the future?

Questions focused on students' perception of the position of writing in the engineering degree program and also encouraged students to anticipate future contexts of writing. Importantly, questions also linked to the broader aims of the research—that is reviewing the current narrow curricular focus in engineering, and looking at ways to better negotiate the existing long-established interdisciplinary partnership. Questions also focused on how the tertiary learning experience interconnects with the professional workplace and the wider community. Questions were designed to reflect issues discussed in the literature review and to inform subsequent practice. For example, Question 1 linked developing interpersonal and communication skills in an engineer's academic learning experience with its relevance to wider discourse in the community and professional workplace (Dowling, Carew & Hadgraft 2010). Question 2 refers to genre knowledge and *ways of becoming* (Carter 2007; Swales 1990; 2004) as useful tools for developing a professional identity.

This qualitative data was analyzed by relating responses to genre-based theoretical approaches to language and learning (Bazerman 1994; Kreber

2009; Swales 1990) and interpreted by categorizing responses to Question 1 on a continuum from *very important* to *not important* and for Question 2 by the written genre identified (such as report/article).

Findings

Fifty-five completed questionnaires were returned. Of those completed questionnaires, 48 student responses to Question 1 reported that writing was "very important." One student qualified "very important" by stating that *communication is the most significant part as a good engineer.* Other descriptors included "significant," "critical," and "necessary." Some responses reflected (in an expanded way) on the transformation from intangible to a more tangible form: *because it requires conversion of an idea into a written form,* and, *it allows me to organize my thoughts.* Other responses centered on the issue of relevance: *can see the relevance but still find it difficult.* Yet other responses focused on a more pragmatic aspect of writing: *all projects should be written in detail in order to prevent further dangers with constructions.* Among those 48 responses, the expanded responses showed the students' awareness of links between:

- academic writing and research (reading)
- transformation of ideas into writing
- clear presentation of ideas to a variety of addressees
- writing as an essential communication tool for the sharing of information.

These findings demonstrate that most students in this first-year cohort have a clear appreciation of the centrality and relevance of writing, both in the immediate academic context and in their future professional practice. References to "connections between academic writing and research," "transfer of ideas into coherent text," "clarity," and the centrality of "writing as an essential communication tool" in a range of social contexts, illustrate, even at this early stage in their degree, that students are acutely aware of the demands of their profession and so see the need to cultivate these communicative competences. Of the seven remaining responses, writing was characterized as "not real engineering" and viewed as "peripheral." Other responses referred to "confusion" with respect to expectations and what is valued in writing. Again, these responses are informative to improved program design, as they highlight specific areas of difficulty to target.

Responses to Question 2 reflected an overwhelming reference to the report genre. The "project report, technical report" and "formal academic report" were cited as the most likely writing genres with which they would be engaged. Other genres cited included "project design," "articles," "argumentative essay," "recommendations," and "procedures." These findings demonstrate that most students in this cohort have a clear understanding of the significance of the report genre to their chosen profession. Other responses referred to "official" and "academic," reflecting an awareness of language register.

Responses reflect differing attitudes to academic writing and could be grouped into three categories. Some highlight the standardizing pressures of the academy; others are concerned with issues of relevance; while others point out how certain activities (such as writing drafts, reflective writing, and peer exchange) facilitate how learners construct and shape their responses. The findings are discussed below in terms of specific responses and wider issues for the learning space.

Discussion

Analysis of specific responses

The above responses are insightful for reviewing and evaluating current curricular activities. ENGG1803 now has a reflective component that offers students an opportunity to evaluate their learning experience. Future initiatives could consider using writing drafts in a variety of ways. For example, as graded assignments, they could be used to assess aspects of writing (such as cohesion and argument development). Discussions around co-constructed tasks could result in a more progressive curriculum. Peer exchange seems an obvious resource to use, as it could lead to greater intercultural and interpersonal understandings while simultaneously addressing the argument advanced by Cruickshank, Warren and Chen (2012, p. 797) of failing to exploit the multicultural learning environment.

Effective in-discipline academic language support will use such responses to design and co-construct authentic learning contexts using topical, disciplinary content. Authentic learning spaces could mirror workplace behaviors that encourage sharing information, cultivating understandings, negotiating differences, and integrating relevant experiential knowledge.

Evidence from ongoing programs demonstrates that literacy support is most effective when aligned to assessments embedded in core units of study and relevant to dynamic professional practice (Ardington 2011;

Chanock & Horton 2011; Wingate 2012). Activities based on a genre-based approach (Swales 1990) of language as social action might address (and counter) student claims of writing in engineering being a "peripheral." Group activities would explore a student's knowledge of the variety of common genres that engineers must use daily: notebooks, project documentation, press releases, presentations (to peers and management), conference papers, technical manuals, reports, and proposals. Not all of these genres will be appropriate for a first-year undergraduate cohort. But progressive dialogue between discipline academics and ALL practitioners and a staged development approach for students can help students become familiar with the genres and how to use them. Successful collaborations provide early feedback in a non-threatening context, are responsive to ongoing feedback from students, and adapt current relevant "real world" scenarios as assessment tasks. If we agree that all students can benefit from in-discipline academic language programs, the move for academic literacy from peripheral into core disciplinary curricula is critical.

Wider issues and implications: Synergies not silos

Given that combined degree programs, such as the interdisciplinary program *Bachelor of Engineering (Civil) and Bachelor of Design in Architecture* currently being offered at the University of Sydney, are becoming more commonplace, it would seem opportune to investigate discipline crossing. Instead of focusing attention on distinctions, more progressive approaches to building partnerships across disciplines could usefully investigate how different (though related) disciplinary knowledge, learning spaces and assignment tasks might be fused and used across disciplines. An embedded language program with cross-faculty management could investigate blended genres, and so optimize already discernible links between, for example, the disciplines of architecture and engineering.

Interactions between ALL lecturers and discipline academics could co-construct activities that use and synergize their collaborative expertise. These creative collaborations could result in new curricula developments, such as assessments that encourage self reflexivity, and focus on process/focus on artifact (model/design prototype) or communications-focused tasks (such as group decision making and peer interactions). Exchanging ideas and cultural knowledge could encourage students (and teachers) to explore the multiliteracies in the learning spaces to discover and evaluate different perspectives. Effectively, this would break down "different/outsider" binary notions premised on the "difference is bad" conceptual model. In so doing, learners (and teachers) can benefit from observing, considering, and appropriating learning spaces and assessment practices more traditionally associated with other disciplines. For example, the design studio learning space central to Architecture, with its orientation towards a more flexible, open and dialogic context, could be appropriated as a relevant learning space for a first-year engineering course. The two disciplines have many similarities with regard to learning outcomes, yet how the respective assessment tasks are enacted and managed is quite different.

To improve interdisciplinary communication in the learning space, we must build a culture of mutual respect through the sharing of goals, expertise, and reflective practice. Sharing knowledge, assimilating practices and emphasizing convergent boundaries as meeting places can help to transcend entrenched attitudes. New learning spaces—formal and informal, face-to-face and online environments—incorporate technology and equipment for interactive study, research, and collaboration. Laboratories, teaching spaces and learning hubs all help to generate innovative practice. These learning spaces influence pedagogic change. Openings and dialogues between and across disciplines could provide stimulating discourse that would optimize learning spaces and replace the current arborescent model of learning which uses binary choices. The result would be a more open, non-hierarchical, rhizomatic approach to curriculum design and learning communities—an approach that values the multiplicity of connections (Deleuze & Guattari 1987, p. 21).

Conclusion

Clearly, the meeting place between ALL practitioners, discipline academics and the diverse student cohort presents a challenging and complex web of interconnections. This discussion, using a specific first-year learning space in engineering at the University of Sydney, has revealed some of the tensions and challenges that require ongoing negotiation and commitment to instantiate effective, equitable and sustainable in-discipline academic literacy programs within the core curriculum. Conceptualizing diversity positively is a necessary first step; that is, the divergent composition of learning communities, current student and teacher bodies, the many contexts of learning, and the different domains of knowledge and their intersection. Forging partnerships through close liaison, negotiation, a willingness of faculty and ALL practitioners to engage, and mutual recognition of each other's fields, will enable us to become more informed and better able to manipulate different epistemologies that drive disciplinary rhetorical practices. Valuing the role of language in knowledge creation by expanding the role of language experts in curriculum design demands a commitment to working with attitudinal change. To make learning experiences at university more valuable, we need to develop a coherent vision across disciplines.

The benefits of integrated, in-discipline language programs as constructive initiatives between ALL practitioners and discipline academics are widely reported as effecting change in pedagogic practice (Baik & Greig 2009; Mort & Drury 2012; Skillen et al. 1999; Wingate 2012). While there are glimmers of a pedagogy of hope and openness (Deleuze & Guattari 1987) evidenced in this first-year unit of study at the University of Sydney, in moves towards a more reflexive engineering curriculum (that integrates a broader variety of assignment genres) the shift is incremental, not systemic, and often subject to individual preferences and priorities. Combined degree programs may offer a path towards blended pedagogies. Engaging with academic literacy as a centralized program requires an attitudinal shift. There is much still to achieve, but learning spaces as meeting places afford real possibilities for future collaborations.

References

Ardington, A.M. 2011, "Writing: An essential and powerful communication tool for today's 3 dimensional engineering graduate", EATAW *Journal of Academic Writing* 1: 61–70

Arkoudis, S., C. Baik and S. Richardson. 2012, *English Language Standards in Higher Education*, Camberwell, Victoria: ACER Press

Armstrong, P. 2006, "Location, relocation and dislocation: learning cultures or cultures of learning?" *Conference Proceedings of the 47th Adult Education Research Conference*, May 18–21, University of Minnesota, Minneapolis

Artemeva, N. 2009, "Stories of becoming: A study of novice engineers learning genres of their profession". In C. Bazerman, A. Bonini and D. Figueiredo, *Genre in a changing world: Perspectives on Writing*, Fort Collins, CO: The WAC Clearinghouse and Parlor Press, pp. 158–78

Baik, C. and J. Greig. 2009, "Improving the academic outcomes of undergraduate ESL students: The case for discipline-based academic skills programs", *Higher Education Research and Development* 28(4): 401–16

Bartlett, C.A. and S. Ghoshal. 1998, *Managing Across Borders: The Transnational Solution*, Cambridge, MA: Harvard Business School Press

Bazerman, C. 1997, "The life of genre, the life in the classroom". In W. Bishop and H. Ostrum, eds, *Genre and Writing*, Portsmouth: Boynton/Cook, 19–26

—. 1994, "Systems of genres and the enactment of social intentions". In A. Freedman and P. Medway, eds, *Genre and the New Rhetoric*. London: Routledge, pp. 79-101

Bazerman, C., A. Bonini and D. Figueiredo, eds, 2009, *Genre in a Changing World*, Fort Collins, CO: The WAC Clearinghouse and Parlor Press

Becher, T. and P.R. Trowler. 2001, *Academic tribes and territories: Intellectual enquiry and the culture of disciplines*, Buckingham: Society for Research into Higher Education & Open University Press

Bennis, W. and P.W. Biederman. 1997, *Organizing Genius: The Secrets of Creative Collaboration*, New York: Addison-Wesley

Bennett, R.J., S.E. Volet and F.E. Fozdar. 2013, "'I'd say it's kind of unique in a way': The development of an intercultural student relationship", *Journal of Studies in International Education*.
http://sagepub.comcontent/early/2013/02/05/1028315312474937

Bonanno, H. and J. Jones. 2007, *The MASUS procedure: Measuring the Academic Skills of University Students*, a diagnostic assessment. University of Sydney: Learning Centre Publications

Carroll, M. 2012, "Sydney increases support for PHD students", *Sydney University News*. http://sydney.edu.au/news/84.html?newsstoryid=9413

Carter, M. 2007, "Ways of Knowing, Doing, and Writing in the Disciplines", *College Composition and Communication* 58(3): 385–418

Chanock, K. 2011, "A historical literature review of Australian publications in the field of Academic Language and Learning in the 1980s: Themes, schemes, and schisms: Part One", *Journal of Academic Language and Learning* 5(1): 36–58

Chanock, K. and C. Horton. 2011, "Strange bedfellows: embedding development of skills into discipline curricula", *Tenth AALL Biennial Conference*, November 24–25,University of South Australia, Adelaide

Cruickshank, K., S. Warren and H. Chen. 2012, "Increasing international and domestic student interaction through group work: a case study from the humanities", *Higher Education Research & Development* 31(6): 797–810

Deleuze, G. and F. Guattari. 1987, *A Thousand Plateaus: Capitalism and Schizophrenia*, trans. Brian Massumi. Minneapolis: University of Minnesota Press

Devlin, M. 2011, "Bridging socio-cultural incongruity: conceptualizing the success of students from low socio-economic status backgrounds in Australian higher education", *Studies in Higher Education* 38(6): 939–49.
http://dx.doi.org/10.1080/03075079.2011.613991

Dowling, D., A. Carew and R. Hadgraft. 2010, *Engineering Your Future: An Australasian Guide*, Milton: John Wiley

Dym, C.L., A. Agogino, O. Eris, D. Frey and L. Leifer. 2005, "Engineering design thinking, teaching, and learning", *Journal of Engineering Education* 94(1): 103–20

Hocking, D. 2010, "The discursive construction of creativity as work in a tertiary art and design environment", *Journal of Applied Linguistics and Professional Practice* 7(2): 235–55

Hyland, K. 2009, *Academic discourse*, London: Continuum

—. 2008, "As can be seen: Lexical bundles and disciplinary variation", *English for Specific Purposes* 27(1): 4–21

—. 2003, "Genre-based pedagogies: A social response to process", *Journal of Second Language Writing* 12: 17–29

Hyland, K. and P. Tse. 2007, "Is there an 'Academic Vocabulary'"? *TESOL Quarterly* 41(2): 235–53

Janks, H. 2004, "The access paradox", *English in Australia* 139: 33–42

Johnston, R. 2006, *Professional Engineering 1803*, North Ryde, Sydney: McGraw-Hill

Jones, C., J. Turner and B.V. Street, eds, 1999. *Students Writing in the University: Cultural and epistemological Issues*, Amsterdam: John Benjamins

Kimmel, K. and S.E. Volet. 2012, "University students' perceptions of and attitudes towards culturally diverse group work: Does context matter?" *Journal of Studies in International Education* 16(2): 157–81

King, R. 2008, *Engineers for the future*, Epping, N.S.W.: Australian Council of Engineering Deans. National HE STEM Programme 2010. http://www.hestem.ac.uk/

Kostogriz, A. and A. Godley. 2007, "The construction of academic literacy and difference", *English Teaching: Practice and Critique* 6(2): 1–7. http://education.waikato.ac.nz/research/files/etpc/2007v6n2ed.pdf

Kreber, C. 2009, "Challenges in supporting student learning in the context of diversity, complexity and uncertainty". In C. Kreber, ed, *The University and its Disciplines: Teaching and Learning within and beyond Disciplinary Boundaries*, London: Routledge, pp. 1–18

Lave, J. and E. Wenger. 1991, *Situated Learning: Legitimate Peripheral Participation*, Cambridge: Cambridge University Press

Learning Centre, University of Sydney. 2011, *Annual Report 2011.* sydney.edu.au/stuserv/documents/learning_centre/AnnualReport2011.pdf

Lillis, T. and M.J. Curry. 2010, *Academic Writing in a Global Context: The politics and practices of publishing in English*, London: Routledge

Lillis, T. and M. Scott. 2008, "Defining academic literacies research: Issues of epistemology, ideology and strategy", *Journal of Applied Linguistics* 4: 5–32

Lea, M. and B.V. Street. 1998, "Student writing in Higher education: an academic literacies approach", *Studies in Higher Education* 23(2): 157–72

Low, A. 2012, "Learning more about Asia is smarter than lamenting the language gap", *Sydney Morning Herald*, January 30, 2012. http://www.smh.com.au/federal-politics/political-opinion/learning-more-about-asia-is-smarter-than-lamenting-the-language-gap-20120129-1qnrr.html#ixzz2kIsEGqBE

Miller, C.R. 1984, "Genre as social action", *Quarterly Journal of Speech* 70(2): 151–67

Mort, P. and H. Drury. 2012, "Supporting student academic literacy in the disciplines using genre-based online pedagogy", *Journal of Academic Language and Learning* 6(3): 1–15

Reid, A. and I. Solomonides. 2007, "Design students' experience of engagement and creativity", *Art, Design & Communication in Higher Education* 6(1): 27–39

Sheppard, S.D., K. Macatangay, A. Colby and W. Sullivan. 2009, *Educating Engineers*, Stanford, CA: Jossey Bass Wiley

Skillen, J. 2005, "Teaching academic writing in Australian universities". In L. Ganobscik-Williams, ed, *Academic Writing In Britain: Theories And Practices Of An Emerging Field*, London: Palgrave Macmillan, pp. 37–45

Skillen, J., M. Merten, A. Percy and N. Trivett. 1999, "Integrating the instruction of generic and discipline specific skills into the curriculum: a case study", *Cornerstones: Proceedings of the 1999 HERDSA Conference*

Swales, J. 1990, *Genre Analysis: English in Academic and Research Settings*, Cambridge: Cambridge University Press

—. 2004, *Research Genres*, Cambridge: Cambridge University Press

Trevelyan, J.P. 2009. "Engineering Education Requires a Better Model of Engineering Practice", *Research in Engineering Education Symposium*, July 20–23, 2009; *Engineering Education Requires a Better Model of Engineering Practice*, Research in Engineering Education Symposium: Palm Cove, Queensland

Wenger, E. 1998, *Communities of practice: learning, meaning, and identity*, New York: Cambridge University Press

Wingate, U. 2012, "Using academic literacies and genre-based models for academic writing instruction: A 'literacy' journey", *Journal of English for Academic Purposes* 11: 26–37

CHAPTER EIGHT

THE DEVELOPMENT OF L2 ACADEMIC LITERACY THROUGH ONLINE INTERCULTURAL NETWORKS

HIROYUKI NEMOTO

Keywords: academic literacy, L2 socialization, language management, online intercultural networks

Abstract

Along with the increasing application of multimedia into second language (L2) teaching, e-learning has been reconsidered not only as a tool to help individual language learning but also as a source of providing language learners with authentic sociocultural activities. However, there has been a dearth of research on Computer-Mediated Communication (CMC), which examines the role of online intercultural activities played in L2 literacy development. Based on an email exchange project between learners of English at a Japanese university and learners of Japanese at two Australian universities, this chapter reports on the intersection of applied linguistics with online intercultural networks by illustrating the processes through which Japanese students undertake email interactions with their Australian partners and apply the findings of interactions to their assignment writing in English. From the perspectives of language socialization and the Language Management Theory (LMT) (cf. Duff 2010; Neustupny 1985, 1994, 2004), an in-depth sociocultural and cognitive investigation is made about students' awareness and evaluation of intercultural phenomena, adjustment planning, and implementation of strategies in the processes through which they interact with their Australian partners, formulate and elaborate their questions, interpret their partners' responses, and integrate the elicited information into their own written assignment. The findings suggest that the processes of becoming socialized into L2 academic literacy involve various language management actions triggered by identity transformation, (meta)cognitive development, L1 paraphrasing, inductive reasoning, reader awareness, perception of cross-cultural similarities, and focus-on-form reflection.

Introduction

Along with the increasing application of multimedia into L2 teaching, Computer-Mediated Communication (CMC) has gained higher recognition as a means of incorporating the hybrid modes of academic discourse, including face-to-face and online interactions, into a teaching curriculum. So far, previous research, which dealt with such hybridity, has suggested that CMC highly motivates students to use the target language rather than to simply adhere to L1 and helps them to produce higher-quality discourse while enhancing their equal participation in class activities and collaboration with other students (Cheng 2010; Sullivan & Pratt 1996; Warschauer 1996) In particular, text-based CMC research stresses the advantages of visually displayed written discourse, claiming that such communication reduces peer and time pressure on students and supports both meaning-oriented communication and focus-on-form reflection (Lee 2008).

CMC has also enhanced diaspora and transnational online networks where individuals establish linguistic, social, cultural, political alliances across national borders at the grassroots level (Lam 2008; Miller & Slater 2000). This perspective has led us to reconsider e-learning not only as a means of assisting individual language learning but also as a source of providing language learners with authentic sociocultural activities at the intersections of different cultures. Although several studies in this field examined online language and literacy practices through intercultural CMC (e.g. Lam 2004), an in-depth investigation has not been made about the role of online intercultural activities played in the development of L2 literacy. There has also been a dearth of research that explores the processes in which people deal with different linguistic and social practices and develop L2 literacy in online contexts as well as the mutual sustainment of online and offline interactions (cf. Fayard & DeSanctis 2005; Lam 2008). These shortcomings directed this study to employ a sociocultural approach to applied linguistics in order to analyze students' engagement in sociocultural activities through intercultural CMC.

Focusing on an email exchange project between learners of English at a Japanese university and learners of Japanese at two Australian universities, this study examines the processes through which Japanese students (1) interact by email with their Australian partners, and (2) complete their written assignment in English using the information that they elicited from their partners. The students' management of task-based writing, into which online intercultural interactions are incorporated, is examined from the perspective of socialization into L2 academic literacy (cf. Duff 2010). The Language Management Theory (LMT), which delineates the corrective adjustment processes of language learners' developing interactive competence in intercultural settings (cf. Neustupny 1985, 1994, 2004), is further applied to investigate a student's awareness and evaluation of intercultural phenomena, adjustment planning, and implementation of strategies in the processes in which they interact with their Australian partners, formulate and elaborate their questions, interpret their partners' responses, and integrate the elicited information into their written assignment.

Sociocultural Approaches to Second Language Acquisition

During the last 20 years, a traditional cognition-oriented paradigm in the field of second language acquisition (SLA) has been integrated with sociocultural approaches to language and learning (cf. Zuengler & Miller 2006). Various sociocultural theories have emerged in the area of applied linguistics, including situated learning, legitimate peripheral participation, language socialization, and socio-constructionist genre theory (cf. Duff 1995, 2007; Lantolf 2000; Lave & Wenger 1991; Miller 1984). The theory of situated learning highlights learning through activities in the situations embedded in a certain community (cf. Brown, Collins & Duguid 1989; Lave & Wenger 1991; Wenger 1998). In this theory, to understand what is learned is to see how it is learned within the activity context (Wilson & Myers 2000). Lave and Wenger (1991) elaborated situated learning by proposing a more specific concept, Legitimate Peripheral Participation (LPP). LPP serves as a descriptor of engagement in social practice that entails learning as an integral constituent, stressing the multiple ways that novice members participate in a variety of social situations embedded in a certain community. One significant contribution that LPP has made to applied linguistics is that the site where people struggle to learn the target language is specified as a Community of Practice (CoP). In Lave and Wenger's theory, CoP is regarded as open, conflictual and dynamic rather than autonomous, coherent or static, and the structures of CoP significantly influence social relations of power and legitimacy of learners in the community (Leki 2001; Morita 2004). The emphasis of LPP is therefore placed on the community that learners seek to become members of, learners' social positionings in a community, and the processes of novice members' becoming fuller participants by getting involved with various activities (cf. Belcher 1994).

Another prominent theory that draws on the perspective of learning as situated is language socialization. Although language socialization was first developed in the 1980s as the study of children's social, cultural and first language development through interaction, more attention has recently been paid to L2 learners (cf. Duff & Talmy 2011; Zuengler & Miller 2006). Several researchers define language socialization as the process in which novices engage in language practice and social interactions, and are induced into specific domains of knowledge, beliefs, affect, roles, identities, and social representations (Duff 1995; Schieffelin & Ochs 1986). In this theory, development is construed as culturally situated and mediated and is considered as involving social, cultural, and political meanings as well as propositional or ideational ones (Duff 2010). Therefore, this theory emphasizes language learning through interacting with others who are more proficient in the target language and also with those who explicitly and/or implicitly provide novices with the knowledge of the target language's sociocultural practices and normative ways of using it (cf. Duff, 2007, 2010; Ochs, 1986).

The sociocultural perspectives of applied linguistics have also significantly impacted genre theories and led to the emergence of socio-constructionist genre theory. Freedman and Medway (1994) state that while genres can be characterized by regularities in textual form and substance, current thinking looks at these regularities as surface traces of a different kind of underlying regularity and deems genres as typical ways of engaging rhetorically with recurrent situations. Reinforcing this view, Hyland (2009) has stressed that academic genres are not simply a form of language but forms of social actions, although people focus on the conventional surface features to identify genres. Miller (1984) more concisely explained this theory by claiming that genres are social actions in response to recurring rhetorical situations. Therefore, this theory serves to indicate socially-constructed objects for learners to learn and situated competence for them to develop in relation to the contexts.

These sociocultural perspectives are worthwhile when we consider the role of context played in learning, but we still need to use such perspectives in conjunction with the cognitive aspects of interactions to gain a deeper understanding of "how learners gain control over their own mental activity when they appropriate socioculturally constructed mediational means" (Zuengler & Miller 2006). Therefore, this study also considers LMT, which covers learners' internal representations in the process of undertaking sociocultural activities in contact situations where culturally-different norms tend to conflict with each other (Neustupny 1985, 1994, 2004). Using this theory, Neustupny delineated the corrective adjustment processes of learning, starting from learners' deviations from norms, their awareness and evaluations of these deviations, their adjustment designs, and their implementation of strategies to rectify deviations. Although the traditional model focuses on language management processes triggered by norm deviations, some researchers have more recently indicated that positive intercultural phenomena and positive evaluations may proceed to adjustment planning and the implementation of management strategies (Nekvapil 2011; Nemoto 2004, 2011; Neustupny 2003). The perspective, which integrates the sociocultural into cognitive processes, allows us to see the transformation of learners' metal processes in relation to culturally, socially, and politically shaped communicative contexts.

Conceptual Framework

In Fig. 8-1, as a conceptual model of socialization into L2 academic literacy, this study incorporates sociocultural perspectives into cognitive processes, using the theory of language socialization and LMT. In this study, L2 academic writing tasks and email interactions provide students with recurrent rhetorical situations that students are required to respond to. Student responses to the tasks and student email interactions enable the students to learn academic written genres in L2.

Fig. 8-1: Integration of LMT into L2 Socialization

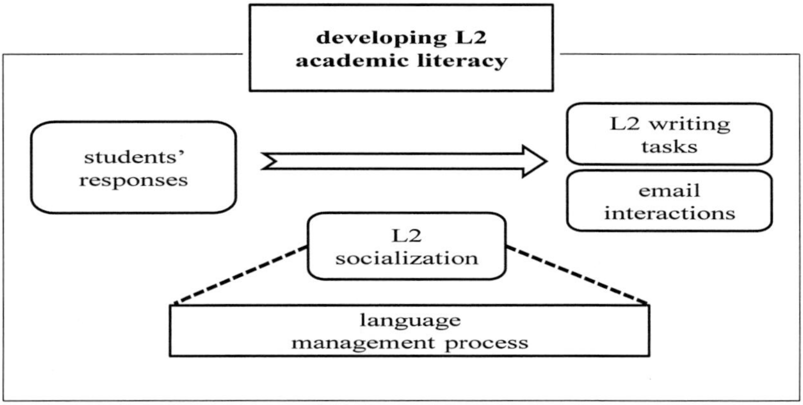

Given that genres are social actions in response to recurrent rhetorical situations (Miller 1984) and that literacy constitutes an integral part of its contexts, something we do, and an activity located in the interactions between people (Hyland 2009, p. 43), the students learn genres and develop L2 academic literacy by engaging in activities. In this study, language socialization represents the actual engagement of students in activities through their interaction with others. However, Duff and Talmy (2011, p. 95) indicate that language socialization represents a broad framework for understanding the development of linguistic, cultural, and communicative competence through interactions with others who are more knowledgeable or proficient. Therefore, considering both sociocultural and cognitive aspects of learning, it is presumed that language socialization will be more effectively employed when it is incorporated into a theory that delineates cognitive processes of L2 learning at the micro level. This study therefore analyzes Japanese students' language socialization into L2 academic literacy in terms of language management.

Language socialization can be considered as involving frequently occurring language management processes in response to various rhetorical situations. Using LMT, the micro-process of students responding to academic writing tasks and online interactions is further illustrated in relation to them encountering cultural contact, noting and evaluating positive and/or negative intercultural phenomena, adjustment planning, and implementing strategies to increase their L2 socialization.

Methodology

Taking into account the limitations of the CoP construct in classroom discourse studies, where some researchers have problematized the tightly circumscribed sense of discourse socialization (Duff 2007, 2010; Haneda 2006; Zuengler & Miller 2006), the email exchange project was implemented on the basis of Zappa-Hollman's (2007) concept of "individual networks of practice." This concept accounts for students' simultaneous engagements with richly distributed human, material and symbolic resources, and relationships with others in their individual networks. The project has been undertaken between a national university in Japan and an Australian university since 2008, with another Australian university joining the project in 2011. The participants from the Japanese university ranged from first-year to third-year students enrolled in English writing classes, while the participants from the two different Australian universities were students enrolled in various levels of Japanese courses. To date, 668 Japanese and 626 Australian students have joined this email exchange project. The project allocated one or two Australian partners to each Japanese student and enabled them to develop online individual networks of practice. The participants were encouraged to use their own target language, but were allowed to change the language code flexibly to interact with each other, except when Japanese students undertook email interviews with their partners in English for their written assignment.

This research focuses on the mid-semester written assignments in the first-year English writing course and the academic writing course, where the Japanese students were required to develop their own arguments and write these down on 2–3 A4 pages. The task procedures involved selecting their own topic in the area of L2 learning or cultural diversity, asking their Australian partners several questions, gaining authentic sociocultural information relevant to the topic, and logically supporting their own arguments using the information that they elicited from their Australian partners. The data collection procedures mostly had two parts: quantitative data collection through a questionnaire survey, and a qualitative case study using diaries and interviews. The questionnaire survey was administered to 305 Japanese students to reveal the whole picture of students' management processes of email interactions and assignment writing. As shown in the Appendix to this chapter, the questionnaire asked seven questions to identify problems that students encountered throughout the project. Students also had to self-evaluate their performances in relation to developing English interactive competence and sociocultural knowledge, eliciting relevant information, interpreting the information, and integrating and organizing text. Although the Appendix presents the English translation of the questionnaire, the original one was written in Japanese to make students more willing to answer the questions and collect precise and specific data.

Based on the Likert scales, the students' responses to closed-ended questions were selected from five options: "very," "somewhat," "undecided," "not really," and "not at all." Each option was scored as one of five grades: *very* = 5, *somewhat* = 4, *undecided* = 3, *not really* =2, and *not at all* =1. Each student's responses were further elaborated upon with open-ended questions that required them to state the specific reason for each answer. These open-format items afforded each participant greater freedom of expression and provided greater richness than fully quantitative data (Dörnyei 2007).

To collect more in-depth qualitative data, a case study of 20 students was conducted using a diary study and follow-up interviews. The diary study, which asked students to keep logs from the day they started the task until the day they completed it, aimed to monitor students' activities and analyze their internal representations of task management. Follow-up interviews were used to supplement the diary study data and elicit detailed accounts of students' engagement in the activities. All interviews for this study were done in Japanese and then the audio-recorded interview data was transcribed. The students' comments shown in this chapter were translated into English, and pseudonyms were used for all Japanese participants and their Australian partners. The data collected from the questionnaire survey, diary study, and interviews was further supplemented by a variety of written documents, including students' brainstorming and outlines of written assignments, draft assignments, returned assignments, and printed copies of email interactions. As a result of reviewing questionnaire findings, transcripts, diary entries, and written documents a number of times, the collected data was inductively analyzed. The salient themes, recurrent patterns, and tentative categories generated by this analysis were tested against the other data until reaching data saturation where "the iterative process of data analysis stops producing new topics, ideas, categories" (Dörnyei 2007, p. 244). Such data triangulation allowed a detailed ethnographic description of each participant and helped this study analyze the micro processes of L2 academic literacy socialization.

Findings and Discussion

Overview of the email exchange project

The macro-level findings as a result of the questionnaire survey, as shown in Table 8-1, suggest the holistic quantitative portrayal of Japanese students' engagement in task-based academic writing through the email exchange project. The quantitative data collected from the first four closed-ended questions reveals high mean scores. This suggests the positive impact of email interactions on L2 learning and assignment writing in L2 (cf. Item 1-4 in Table 8-1). The qualitative data, obtained from students' open-ended answers to Question 1-4, has indicated that such an impact predominantly pertains to their identity transformation and perceptions of (meta)cognitive development in L2. The details of these two factors are discussed in the next section of this chapter.

Table 8-1: The results of the questionnaire survey (n=305)

Item	Mean	SD
1. Enjoyed email exchange project	4.12	.21
2. Improved English skills	4.17	.21
3. Expanded knowledge of other cultures	3.77	.11
4. Positive influence on assignment writing	3.80	.16
5. Difficulties in online interactions	3.79	.21
6. Difficulties in email interviews	3.27	.15
7. Difficulties in integrating partners' information into text	3.00	.09

Very = 5, Somewhat = 4, Undecided = 3, Not really = 2, Not at all = 1

The mean scores of the fifth and sixth questions—3.79 and 3.27—suggest that the online intercultural interactions can be sites of struggle in the processes of L2 literacy socialization by Japanese students (cf. Item 5 and Item 6 in Table 8-1). In particular, the open-ended answers, which students provided to these two questions, enabled this study to find that the Japanese participants faced various problems regarding task management in relation to lack of English vocabulary, translating L1 ideas into English, repeating the same sentence patterns too many times, selecting a topic of the assignment, elaborating ideas based on the selected topic, and formulating questions explicitly enough for partners to provide proper answers. Further, the average score of Question 7 revealed that most of the students did not regard their integration of partners' information into text as either "difficult" or "easy," although the open-ended comments that some students made indicated their struggles to summarize and/or paraphrase their partners' information in their assignment (cf. Item 7 in Table 8-1). Even so, closed-ended and open-ended findings of this question were not fully commensurable with the data from their marked written assignments, which demonstrated their frequent use of illogical text integration. The discrepancy implies that they did not successfully detect their own problems with selecting information suitable for supporting details of their arguments and with evaluating the reliability and validity of information from partners. It also seems that such insufficient awareness of difficulties sometimes caused them to unwittingly compose a descriptive paragraph by copying and pasting their partners' emails excessively. Considering that, as a member of the individual networks of practice, the students tend to experience "inevitable stumblings and violations, which become opportunities for learning rather than cause of dismissal, neglect, or exclusion" (Wenger 1998, p. 101), the processes in which students overcome these difficulties are an inseparable component of their socialization into L2 academic literacy. The processes will be illustrated later in conjunction with the case study data.

Identity transformation and L2 (meta)cognitive development

The case study findings allowed this study to further explore students' identity transformation and L2 (meta)cognitive development, as identified in their open-ended answers to Question 1 to Question 4.

Email exchanges through individual networks of practice enabled the participants to change their perspectives of writing in English and contributed to their identity transformation where "they (re)negotiated a sense of self in relation to the social world and reorganized that relationship in multiple dimensions of their lives" (Norton & McKinney 2011, p. 73). Before participating in the email exchange project, the students construed English writing as a way of decontextualized language learning, including word-for-word translation tasks and short composition exercises. However, through the online interactions with their Australian partners, they gradually regarded English writing as contextualized language use and a tool of interaction in authentic situations. One student commented in the interview:

> Whenever I was required to write English, so far I've only experienced composition exercises, such as translating a couple of Japanese sentences into English, writing several sentences based on an assigned topic. But in email exchanges, I had to communicate with my partner well enough. So, I focused on making myself understood. It was a good practice for me to use English for communicative purposes in casual situations.

The project also offered students multiple identity positions from which they could engage in language practices (Norton 2010). Several students stressed that the authentic online interactive situations allowed them to feel closer to English, and that, towards the end of the semester, they routinely used English in their emails to partners. As the students more clearly noted and evaluated the importance of rapport with their partners through interactions, they changed identities from a learner of English to a non-native but legitimate writer of English.

As Duff (2010) claims, negotiation of power and identity is likely to be inevitably involved in literacy socialization experiences and accounts. Such identity transformation rendered the students more willing to interact with their partners, and mediated both comprehension and construction of the text (Norton 2010). Many students claimed that email interactions were not stressful compared to face-to-face oral communication. Through the project, students who had struggled to orally communicate in English from one identity position were able to frame their relationship with English speakers through online interactions and to claim alternative, more powerful identities from which to interact (Norton & McKinney 2011).

Further, the Japanese students' individual networks of practice through email exchanges provided opportunities to develop cognitive and metacognitive skills in response to authentic interactive situations. The following is a comment from one participant:

> I'm not confident of my English skills and don't like English conversation, but I enjoyed emailing my partner because I have enough time to think about sentence structures, my own opinions, and ideas carefully.

As shown in this comment, the asynchronous nature of email exchanges positively influenced L2 learning on the grounds that it helped students to elaborate on their thoughts and undertake more logical interactions (cf. McLoughlin & Mynard 2009; Yang, Newby & Bill 2005). The asynchronous nature also resulted in students developing self-monitoring skills by looking up English words and expressions in a dictionary more regularly and then paying closer attention to grammatical accuracy and function of a certain word in a sentence. Email interactions further promoted reader awareness in the Japanese students, which contributed to their noting and evaluating writer responsibility. Most participants insisted that they felt the need to accommodate their partners' expectations in their email responses by following linguistic and sociocultural norms and focusing on logical flow and intelligibility. Given that the nature of academic discourse socialization is not only a dynamic, socially situated but also highly intertextual process, it seems that the students' growing awareness of text organization and rhetorical styles through email exchanges enabled them to transfer from informal to formal academic writing in English and facilitated their adjustments to later written tasks (cf. Duff 2010). Indeed, many students stated that their preliminary experiences in writing emails in English made them less anxious about 2-page or 3-page writing tasks.

Reinforcing the intricate relationship between language and a social practice in which experiences are organized and identity negotiated (Norton 2010), the findings in this section indicated that L2 academic literacy is conceptualized as a result of not only gaining linguistic knowledge but of identity transformation, development of cognitive and self-monitoring skills, and reader awareness.

Noting and evaluating norm deviations

The micro-level analysis of L2 socialization from the perspective of LMT helped this study to illustrate that the Japanese students noting and evaluating norm deviations significantly influenced the processes for them overcoming difficulties in online interactions, email interviews and integrating partner information into their written assignment. In particular, when the Japanese participants composed emails, this study found the students' noting and evaluating of norm deviations encouraged them to paraphrase their ideas in L1 before translating them into L2. Such noting and evaluating also played a crucial role in preventing misunderstandings caused by the Japanese students' vague wording in L2 and direct translation from L1 and L2. Hitoshi's drafting process, for instance, revealed that several stages of L1 paraphrasing can occur when students produce L2 expressions. When he composed the sentence shown below, Hitoshi came up with the Japanese word *tokekomu*, which metaphorically represents *fit in with* in Japanese but literally means *melt into* in English.

> If you learn a second language, you can go overseas and *tokekomu* a foreign life. (*melt into*)

After looking up *tokekomu* in a Japanese–English dictionary, Hitoshi noted and negatively evaluated the deviation from appropriate wording in English by finding that *melt into* does not possess the same metaphorical meaning as *tokekomu*. He therefore paraphrased the expression, and used *najimu* (get familiar with) and *nareru* (get used to) for the above sentence. As these verbs were not consistent with what he intended to say in the sentence, Hitoshi decided not to stick to only one verb. Instead he made a longer paraphrase that conveyed more detailed information yet used simple wording. As a result of deliberately imagining specific situations that people living a foreign country might encounter, Hitoshi subsequently came up with two lexical items—*taikennsuru (experience)* and *chishiki wo eru (gain knowledge)*. This led Hitoshi's L1 paraphrasing to produce the following sentence:

> If you learn a second language, you can go overseas, *experience a foreign life, and gain knowledge of the culture.*

Lee (2008) claims that the use of L1 reduces the learners' cognitive burden when they write L2 texts. This study presented further findings about the impact of L1 use on L2 socialization, delineating that L1 paraphrasing before translating ideas into L2 encouraged students to be more aware of contextual meanings and elaborate on their thoughts. Imagining specific situations and considering what occurs in the contexts can lead to L2 literacy development, as this approach allows students to logically reflect on what they intend to state. Given that L1 paraphrasing also prevents students from sticking with abstract concepts in L1 yet enables general-to-specific development of ideas, students can be more sensitive to word choice and produce more appropriate and sophisticated wording in L2.

Furthermore, in this study Japanese students socialized themselves into L2 academic literacy by noting and evaluating deviations from norms of academic writing in English when selecting a topic, interpreting their partner's information, and integrating the information into their own text. Through email interactions with Steve, an Australian male student, who studied Japanese part time at an Australian university, Akiko initially planned to deal with L2 learning strategies for her mid-semester assignment by using her own and her partner's experiences in managing L2 learning. However, after reconfirming the requirements of the assignment, Akiko noted and negatively evaluated potential norm deviation in relation to linking objective ideas with specific examples. Akiko said in the interview:

> I'm afraid that my paragraph is going to be the one that only explains personal information and introduces my partner's details rather than is based on objective ideas.

Therefore, she subsequently sought to specify her ideas by asking her partner several questions and to find a more appropriate and achievable topic for the written assignment. A few days after emailing her questions to Steve, Akiko received comprehensive answers. In particular, one of Steve's emailed answers, shown below, stimulated Akiko's interest:

> Most schools in Australia require compulsory language classes until the early years of high school and then it is up to the individual student as to whether or not they will continue with their language studies. *I have found, personally, that the studying of a second language has actually helped me understand my first language to a greater extent; something which I have found quite interesting.* I enjoy studying Japanese and want to continue to get better at it over time.

Reviewing this section repeatedly, Akiko noted the adequacy of the italicized information for her assignment, but she wondered why Steve gave the answers, commenting, "Because I didn't know why, I didn't think I could use this information in my assignment properly." Based on her deliberate analysis of the noted information, she evaluated the information as too general and insufficient for her to use as a supporting example in her assignment.

To elicit the details of Steve's opinion, Akiko asked further questions that explored the relationship between L2 learning and L1 understanding. She asked:

> Why could you understand your first language to a greater extent thanks to the studying of a second language? And what is something which you have found quite interesting?

Two days later, Steve replied to Akiko, answering her questions.

> By learning a second language it has helped me to understand my first language better. The reason for this is that I have been able to develop a greater understanding of how sentences are constructed in English and why particular grammar is used in certain situations. Instead of just saying things because I know they make sense, I am learning to a greater extent why they make sense also.

In this way, Akiko successfully elicited detailed information about Steve's increasing awareness of L1 sentence construction and grammatical structure by learning Japanese as a second language. This detailed information allowed her to plan topic adjustment for her assignment and to change the topic from "L2 Learning Strategies" to "Advantages of Learning a Second Language." These findings revealed that Akiko's noting and evaluating of potential norm deviations at the stages of topic selection and interpreting her partner's information led her to explore the appropriate topic based on inductive reasoning of the email-interview findings.

Akiko's case has further demonstrated that noting and evaluating appear in the process of socialization into text integration. Although she directly quoted her partner's comment to support one of her main ideas in her written assignment, Akiko noted potential norm deviation in relation to text organization by reviewing the logical flow of this section and discovering that the main idea needed more supporting evidence and that the section seemed unconcluded. She said: "Whenever I email my partner, I check if my text is clear enough. I checked this section in the same way and thought this was a bit unclear." Akiko's comment suggests that her reader awareness, developed through email exchanges, contributed to her applying an analytical lens on her text and enabled such noting and evaluation. After carefully evaluating the significance of the deviation, she supplemented this section with her own interpretations of the main ideas.

The excerpt below is part of Akiko's final draft, and the sentences she added later are in italics.

> Second, it help[s] you to understand your first language better. *When you learn a second language, you will do it in your first language. It deepens your language ability.* For example, my partner, Steve said, "The reason why learning a second language helps me to understand my first language better is that I have been able to develop a greater understanding of how sentences are constructed in English and why particular grammar is used in certain situations." *As he says, it may be a good chance of checking your first language. If you can understand and use your first language correctly, your second language will be also better.*

This section involved some grammatical mistakes and was not perfectly organized in that Akiko used the sentence, which she nearly copied from her Australian partner, as her main idea. It seems that such unsystematic use of outer sources occurred partly due to lower awareness of plagiarism in Japan than Western institutions (cf. Keck 2006). Even so, it is worthwhile noting that Akiko's text-integration approach constituted her adjustment strategy of further consolidating her opinion, and that language management played a significant role in logical text organization and the process of being socialized into L2 academic literacy.

Noting and evaluating positive intercultural phenomena

The Japanese students' socialization into English academic literacy involved language management triggered by not only negative but positive intercultural phenomena that the students encountered through online intercultural interactions. Haruko's case illustrated her strategic elicitation of information relevant to her own topic, "Problems with Learning a Second Language." The following excerpt is part of Haruko's email where she shared her L2 communication problems with her half-Japanese and half-Australian partner, Cathy.

> The problem which I am confronted now is that I can read and write English to some extent but I cannot communicate with people [who] speak English and express what I want to say. Therefore, I think there is a big difference in study skills and communication skills. What do you think?

In the interview, Haruko stated that she wondered if her partner wanted to disclose her struggles to learn Japanese, because she had a Japanese background. Such attention resulted in her introducing her problems first to make her partner more willing to answer her question. Cathy sent a reply the same day she received Haruko's email, and confessed she also found it hard to speak Japanese:

> I'm not good at speaking Japanese, too. Since my childhood, my mum has talked to me in Japanese, but I've always answered in English. So, I don't speak Japanese often even when I'm in Japan. Also, my big sister is a much better speaker of Japanese and she teases me whenever I speak Japanese so I don't want to speak Japanese so much. Also, whenever I listen to Japanese, it takes time to understand it because I have to translate it into English in my brain.

After examining Cathy's answer, Haruko noted the cross-cultural similarity in L2 learning problems, positively evaluated the suitability of her partner's experience as specific supporting information for consolidating one of her arguments, and then planned how to discuss the similarity in her written assignment. The excerpt below shows one of the sections in Haruko's written assignment where she used the above information from her partner (her partner's information is in italics):

> The second main problem is that it is difficult to speak [a] second language actually. I can write or read it to some extent but I can say nothing when I am meeting the foreigner because I do not understand what I may speak so I am quite at a loss. Also, *my partner says that she has [the] ability to speak Japanese but cannot speak actually because she [is] worried [about] the reaction of the surroundings.*

In this section, Haruko's main idea—difficulties in speaking a second language—was consolidated by the first supporting detail where she described her own experience. As the second supporting information, she paraphrased and summarized her partner's comments and integrated the summary into the text. Therefore, Haruko's case delineated that her description and sharing her experiences with her partner led her to identify the similarities in L2 learning, and that identification then facilitated her planning text organization and to develop the text logically.

This study further illustrates the Japanese students' noting and evaluating positive intercultural phenomena, using Kenta's case where his focus-on-form analysis served to enhance his L2 socialization. Kenta approached the topic of cultural diversity and narrowed down the broad topic to cultural differences in using water, because his interest lay in water restrictions in Australia due to his previous experience of a one-week homestay in Australia as a part of school trip. Kenta therefore asked his Australian partner, Tim, some questions about water restrictions and received the following answer:

> Water restrictions are in place by the Water Corporation. We are not allowed to water the garden, which includes hosing or sprinkling until certain periods of time during the day in the season. For example, if we water the garden in winter, then we will be charged a large fine.

Carefully analyzing Tim's reply, Kenta noted the new lexical items in his partner's text and commented as follows:

> I didn't know '*water*' can be a verb and '*fine*' can be a noun, which means the payment for penalty. When I read my partner's email, I recognized a certain word has some different meanings and can be used in different ways.

His noting was followed by positive evaluation of the potential usefulness of the items for both email interactions and his assignment. Then Kenta borrowed these items to ask his partner further questions:

> *Watering your garden* in winter is crime? I feel that it is a crime as you use the word, "*fine*." If so, is it a strict rule?

Kenta stated in his diary entry, "I tried to imitate some expressions to practice and memorize them, and also tried to make my partner want to reply." Such borrowing constituted an adjustment strategy of repeating and actually using the key items to keep the flow going and elicit more details of sociocultural information about water restrictions.

After a while Tim answered Kenta's questions:

> *Watering the garden* isn't a harsh crime, but if you don't *pay your fine* or fee for it, then you will face the court.

Tim's response corroborated not only Kenta's noting and evaluating of the suitability of the expressions for his assignment but also his recognition of the sociocultural differences in water use. Therefore, the findings revealed that content-based and form-focused noting and evaluations occurred at the stage of Kenta interpreting his partner's text. As shown in the excerpt below, these two types of noting and evaluations allowed Kenta to integrate one of the lexical items into his written assignment:

> Third, in Australia, water restrictions make a big influence on people who like gardening. They need to be careful not to *water the garden* excessively. According to my email partner, they are not allowed to water the garden, which includes hosing or sprinkling until certain periods of time during the day in a dry season.

In this section, Kenta intended to emphasize "*water the garden*" as a key word to link his main idea with specific details that included his partner's quotation. The findings indicate that his focus-on-form reflection through online interactions culminated in content-based adjustment planning at the text organization stage, since the reflection led him to organize his text with a greater awareness of the logical development of arguments. The process in which Kenta deliberately analyzed, borrowed and imitated his partner's expressions, therefore, contributed to him socializing himself into L2 academic literacy as well as gaining a deeper understanding of how to use target lexical items in a certain context (cf. Potts 2005).

Conclusion

Integrating the perspective of LMT into Japanese students' socialization into L2 academic literacy, the current study has provided insights into the intersection of sociocultural approaches to SLA with online intercultural networks by illustrating the multimodal, multilingual and situated processes in which Japanese students formulated questions, elicited relevant information from their Australian partners, interpreted their partners' responses, and integrated the partners' information into text. The integrated view also allowed this study to discover that task-based academic writing, including online intercultural interactions, can be a device for enhancing students' goal-driven social actions to learn L2 genres and improve L2 academic literacy, create safe spaces for students to undertake authentic activities, and help students to apply an analytical lens to their own L2 writing. The findings demonstrated that language management actions in the processes of language socialization were enhanced by students' identity transformation, (meta)cognitive development, L1 paraphrasing, inductive reasoning, reader awareness, perception of cross-cultural similarities, and focus-on-form reflection. This study has, furthermore, contributed to expanding LMT by corroborating the positive flow of the language management approach and by suggesting form-focused and content-based noting, evaluations and adjustments.

From a pedagogical perspective, future research must more comprehensively examine how to incorporate online intercultural interactions into L2 literacy teaching as a source of authentic sociocultural activities. Such research would be feasible by focusing not only on CoP but individual networks of practice, and by introducing information-collecting and information-analyzing procedures in assessment tasks. An in-depth investigation of actual discursive practices in this type of task-based learning will contribute to identifying the ways that students adopt heuristic approaches to language socialization and enable schools, universities and instructors to scaffold students' development of L2 academic literacy and their autonomous language management competence.

References

Belcher, D. 1994, "The apprenticeship approach to advanced academic literacy: Graduate students and their mentors", *English for Specific Purposes* 13(1): 23–34

Brown, J.S., A. Collins and P. Duguid. 1989, "Situated cognition and the culture of learning", *Educational Researcher* 18: 32–42

Cheng, R. 2008, "Computer-mediated scaffolding in L2 students' academic literacy development", *CALICO Journal* 28(1): 74–98

Dörnyei, Z. 2007, *Research Methods in Applied Linguistics*, Oxford: Oxford University Press

Duff, P.A. 1995, "An ethnography of communication in immersion classroom in Hungary", *TESOL Quarterly* 29: 505–37

—. 2007, "Problematising academic discourse socialization". In H. Marriott, T. Moore and R. Spence-Brown, eds, *Learning Discourses and the Discourses of Learning*, Melbourne: Monash University ePress, pp. 1.1–1.18

—. 2010, "Language socialization into academic discourse communities", *Annual Review of Applied Linguistics* 30: 169–92

Duff, P.A. and S. Talmy. 2011, "Language socialization approaches to second language acquisition: Social, cultural, and linguistic development in additional languages". In D. Atkinson, ed, *Alternative Approaches to Second Language Acquisition*, London: Routledge, pp. 95–116

Fayard, A. and G. DeSanctis. 2005, "Evolution of an online forum for knowledge management professionals: A language game analysis", *Journal of Computer-Mediated Communication* 10 (4)

Freedman, A. and P. Medway. 1994, *Learning and Teaching Genre*, Portsmouth, N.H.: Boynton/Cook Publishers

Haneda, M. 2006, "Classroom as communities of practice: A reevaluation", *TESOL Quarterly* 40: 807–17

Hyland, K. 2009, *Academic Discourse*, London: Continuum

Keck, C. 2006, "The use of paraphrase in summary writing: A comparison of L1 and L2 writers", *Journal of Second Language Writing* 15: 261–78

Lam, W.S.E. 2004, "Second language socialization in a bilingual chat room: Global and local considerations", *Language Learning and Technology* 8 (3): 44–65

—. 2008, "Language socialization in online communities". In P.A. Duff and N.H. Hornberger, eds, *Encyclopedia of Language and Education, vol. 8. Language Socialization*, Vancouver: Springer, pp. 301–12

Lantolf, J.P. 2000, "Second language learning as a mediated process", *Language Teaching* 33: 79–86

Lave, J. and E. Wenger. 1991, *Situated Learning: Legitimate Peripheral Participation*, Cambridge: Cambridge University Press

Lee, L. 2008, "Focus-on-form through collaborative scaffolding in expert-to-novice online interaction", *Language Learning & Technology* 12(3): 53–72

Leki, I. 2001, "'A Narrow Thinking System': Nonnative-English-Speaking Students in Group Projects Across the Curriculum", *TESOL Quarterly* 35(1): 39–67

McLoughlin, D. and J. Mynard. 2009, "An analysis of higher order thinking in online discussions", *Innovations in Education and Teaching International* 46(2): 147–60

Miller, C.R. 1984, "Genre as social action", *Quarterly Journal of Speech* 70: 151–67

Miller, D. and D. Slater. 2000, *The Internet: An Ethnographic Approach*, Oxford: Berg

Morita, N. 2004, "Negotiating participation and identity in second language academic communities", *TESOL Quarterly* 38(4): 573–603

Nekvapil, J. 2011, "The history and theory of language planning". In E. Hinkel, ed, *Handbook of Research in Second Language Teaching and Learning*, New York, London: Routledge, pp. 871–87

Nemoto, H. 2004, "The cross-cultural academic communication and study management of Japanese exchange students", *Journal of Asian Pacific Communication* 14(1): 113–36

—. 2011, *The Management of Intercultural Academic Interaction: Student Exchanges between Japanese and Australian Universities*, Newcastle: Cambridge Scholars Publishing

Neustupny, J.V. 1985, "Problems in Australian-Japanese contact situations". In J.B. Pride, *Cross-cultural Encounters: Communication and Mis-communication*, Melbourne: River Seine, pp. 44–63

—. 1994, "Problems of English contact discourse and language planning". In T. Kandiah and J. Kwan-Terry, eds, *English and Language Planning: A Southeast Asian Contribution*, Singapore: Times Academic Press, pp. 50–69

—. 2003, "Japanese students in Prague: Problems of communication and interaction", *International Journal of the Sociology of Language* 162: 125–43

—. 2004, "Theory and practice in language management", *Journal of Asian Pacific Communication* 14(1): 3–31

Norton, B. 2010, "Language and identity". In N.H. Hornberger and S.L. McKay, eds, *Sociolinguistics and Language Education*, Bristol: Multilingual Matters, pp. 349–69

Norton, B. and C. McKinney. 2011, "An identity approach to second language acquisition". In D. Atkinson, ed, *Alternative Approaches to Second Language Acquisition*, London: Routledge, pp. 73–94

Ochs, E. 1986, "Introduction". In B. Schieffelin and E. Ochs, eds, *Language Socialization Across Cultures*, Cambridge: Cambridge University Press, pp. 1–13

Potts, D. 2005, "Pedagogy, purpose, and the second language learner in on-line communities", *Canadian Modern Language Review* 62: 137–60

Schieffelin, B. and E. Ochs. 1986, *Language Socialization Across Cultures*, Cambridge: Cambridge University Press

Sullivan, N. and E. Pratt. 1996, "A comparative study of two ESL writing environments: A computer-assisted classroom and a traditional oral classroom", *System* 29: 491–501

Warschauer, M. 1996, "Comparing face-to-face and electronic communication in the second language classroom", *CALICO Journal* 13(2): 7–26

Wenger, E. 1998, *Community of practice: Learning, meaning, and identity*, Cambridge: Cambridge University Press

Wilson, B.G. and K.M. Myers. 2000, "Situated cognition in theoretical and practical context". In D.H. Jonassen and S.M. Land, eds, *Theoretical Foundations of Learning Environments*, Mahwah, N.J.: Lawrence Erlbaum, pp. 57–88

Yang, Y.C., T.J. Newby and R.L. Bill. 2005, "Using socratic questioning to promote critical thinking skills through asynchronous discussion forums in distance learning environments", *American Journal of Distance Education* 19(3): 163–81

Zappa-Hollman, S. 2007, *The academic literacy socialization of Mexican exchange students at a Canadian university*, University of British Columbia, Vancouver

Zuengler, J. and E.R. Miller. 2006, "Cognitive and sociocultural perspectives: Two parallel SLA worlds?" *TESOL Quarterly* 40(1): 35–58

Appendix
Questionnaire Survey of the Email Exchange Project

Q1: How much did you enjoy the email exchange project?
Very   *Somewhat*   *Undecided*   *Not really*   *Not at all*
Please explain the reason why.

Q2: How useful was this project for you to improve your English skills?
Very   *Somewhat*   *Undecided*   *Not really*   *Not at all*
Please explain the reason why.

Q3: How helpful was this project for you to gain a better understanding of Australian and other cultures?
Very   *Somewhat*   *Undecided*   *Not really*   *Not at all*
Please explain the reason why.

Q4: How positively did online writing experiences influence your assignment writing?
Very   *Somewhat*   *Undecided*   *Not really*   *Not at all*
Please explain the reason why.

Q5: How difficult was it for you to interact with your partner(s) through emails?
Very   *Somewhat*   *Undecided*   *Not really*   *Not at all*
Please explain the reason why.

Q6: How difficult was it for you to conduct email interviews to your partner(s)?
Very   *Somewhat*   *Undecided*   *Not really*   *Not at all*
Please explain the reason why.

Q7: How difficult was it for you to use your partner's information in your assignment?
Very   *Somewhat*   *Undecided*   *Not really*   *Not at all*
Please explain the reason why.

CHAPTER NINE

EXPRESSING ONESELF THROUGH DIGITAL STORYTELLING: A STUDENT-CENTERED JAPANESE LANGUAGE LEARNING PROJECT

CAROL HAYES AND YUKI ITANI-ADAMS

Keywords: Japanese language, second language learning, language teaching pedagogy, Digital Storytelling, eLearning

Abstract

Is it possible to include impact within an assessment rubric for intermediate language-learners' oral production? By presenting the results of the Intermediate Japanese Language Digital Storytelling Project conducted at the Australian National University (ANU), this chapter will demonstrate that the answer to this question is yes. This project aimed first to assess the value of using digital stories in Japanese language teaching as an alternative to individual oral presentations or tests, and second to examine methods of encouraging students to become more proactive and to better express their own personal emotions, beliefs, and ideas. Digital stories that combine image, narrative and sound provide a powerful way to develop student communicative skills. These stories mark an intersection between applied linguistics and education, creating a meeting place where pedagogy and practice interact. Digital stories also provide a meeting place where textbook language learning combines with more authentic communication, where teacher-centered and student-centered approaches combine and where the storyteller interacts with their audience. Most of all, digital storytelling addresses student-centered learning expectations in the twenty-first century. It focuses on creative thinking, risk-taking and effective communication, with the added advantage of developing effective technical literacy. It also encourages students to become interactive, collaborative members of their learning community.

Introduction

How do we create a *meeting place* where textbook Japanese language learning combines with a more holistic approach to communication? How do we encourage intermediate learners[1] to look up from the nuts and bolts of the Japanese they are learning, to think about the overall impact or message behind what they are trying to say? How can we encourage students not only to focus on the one-way expression of their own message but also to consider their audience and the social dimensions of language?

Language is so much more than simply stringing words together, for language not only conveys information but also expresses a person's emotions and identity, which is a normal part of human behavior (Maynard 2007, p. 25). Language educators should not forget that language is a *creative* tool, and that we must encourage our students to express their thoughts, emotions and ideas so that their language becomes more meaningful. This is true even at the intermediate level. To achieve this goal, we must push students beyond their comfort zone by helping them develop the skills they need to describe factual experiences and to develop their capacity to communicate the emotions and ideas behind those experiences.

Storytelling provides a creative method of teaching such holistic communication. In today's technical world, this can become even more dynamic through the blended mode of digital storytelling. Digital stories are short 3–4 minute multimedia productions that combine a first-person narrative with image and background music. They are "immersive and participatory" ways of "relating personal, real-life stories—a form of first-person journalism, illustrated by various types of visual material" (Miller 2008, p. xi).

From its inception in 2009, the Australian National University (ANU)'s Intermediate Japanese Digital Storytelling Project (DS Project) was developed to create a space that encourages our students to develop more holistic communicative skills. As the project has progressed, it has become increasingly obvious that student storytellers must focus on the narrative level of their story and consider its *impact* on their audience if they are to effectively *tell* their story and carry their audience with them.

This chapter demonstrates how our DS Project successfully created a space—*a meeting place*—not only between textbook learning and more authentic communication, but also between the student storyteller and the

---

[1] In this context "intermediate" learners refers to tertiary, second-year-level language proficiency. This is equivalent to 220 hours of prior in-class instruction.

viewing audience. We will contextualize our work within the discourse of foreign language teaching and learning, and will demonstrate that the practice of digital storytelling creates an intersection between applied linguistics and education—*a meeting place* where pedagogy and practice connect. We will describe the DS Project in the context of its target intermediate Japanese language course, and discuss how the program has evolved. Drawing on the analysis of several student digital stories, we will then demonstrate why including *impact* in student production is desirable and achievable.

We define the *impact* of a story by the effect it has on its audience. The assessment of impact is something that also concerns teachers of creative writing. For example, Boutler (2004, p. 135) identified the following as criteria relevant to the assessment of impact in that context: "vividness; discernment; control of language; avoidance of cliché; particularized detail; selectivity; originality; economy and coherence of structure; voices that are convincingly and powerfully imitated; persuasiveness; eloquence; writing that is moving; integrity of voice; authenticity; subtle use of language." In the case of our intermediate Japanese language learners, we encourage them to incorporate such elements into their stories: our project has demonstrated that the more they do this; the greater their story's impact. Although we recognize that it is hard to assess impact as it is based on the subjective judgment of the audience/listeners, *real-life* communication requires engagement with more than just words and grammar. So it is vital that we provide students with opportunities to engage with creative communication from the early stages of their language learning.

Digital Storytelling and eLearning

Digital storytelling is increasingly valued as an educational tool to encourage students to participate in "authentic doing," by creating "authentic work that has meaning, virtue, and purpose to a wider audience" (Levin 2012, p. 7). Digital Stories were first developed in the United States in the 1990s, as a means of helping young people to create personal narratives in a contemporary globally accessible mode.

Important websites include British photographer Daniel Meadows (n.d.) with his *Photobus* site, Bernajean Porter (n.d.) with her *DigiTales: The Art of Telling Digital Stories* and Joe Lambert (2006) with *The Center for Digital Storytelling*. Several universities such as the University of Houston (n.d.), the Queensland Institute of Technology (2009) and Georgetown University (n.d.) also make an important contribution to the field with their engaging websites. Their work demonstrates how digital storytelling provides an excellent platform for creative self-expression, for developing digital literacy and for creating a space where educators "can use the emerging technologies to our advantage to foster learning, creativity, and enthusiasm" (Frazel 2010, p. 11). Although there are many published "how-to" guides, with advice on the technical elements and the process of making digital stories (e.g. Frazel 2010; Lambert 2006; Miller 2008), to date little has been published in the area of foreign language teaching. So our research provides an important contribution in this field.

Australian universities are increasingly focused on the role of technology in education and how eLearning can better engage students. Our project explores the possibilities of blending technology with classroom language learning to create a more flexible and inclusive teaching and learning space that allows students with differing learning styles and personalities to participate at their own pace from the comfort of their chosen location.

The pedagogical context of our project

The concept of learner autonomy provides an important framework for our project. First introduced by Holec (1981), this concept is defined as the learner's ability to take charge of their own learning. Barnes (1979) argued that learning involves developing "relationships between what the learner knows already and the new system being presented to him" (p. 82), which can only be done by the learner. Later scholars argue that student autonomy is better achieved if students interact as "members of a learning community" (Little, 2012, pp. 75–76), and stress the importance of the teacher in facilitating this *meeting place* between linguistic skills and the social-interactive-collaborative dimension of language learning.

The promotion of this concept of learner autonomy has also been an important area of ongoing debate within current Japanese language teaching and learning discourse. Ogawa (2007) also stresses the importance of activities that "develop cooperatively from the student's own individual experiences, through proactive and conscious communication" with others (Ogawa 2007, cited in Thomson 2009, p. 23).[2] The fact that we encourage our students to develop their digital stories from their own experiences and to actively consider the impact of their story on their audience reflects this

---

[2] 主観的である個人の経験を、主体的、意識的なコミュニケーション参加によって、協働的に発展させて行く活動 (小川 2007), cited in Thomson 2009, p. 23. Note that all translations from the Japanese in this chapter are our own.

discourse. It draws on the premise that the fundamental goal of language education lies in the self-realization that the learner must "become the protagonist within his or her own story" (Kajita 1998, cited in Thomson 2009, p. 27).[3]

Research into effective output is another important element of our pedagogical framework. Swain argues in her "comprehensible output hypothesis" that it is only through *producing* language (either spoken or written) that language learning can occur (Swain 1993, p. 159). Gathering data from a French-Canadian immersion program, Swain found that despite the students receiving increased *input*, their acquisition of French was less than expected. Swain argued that the each learner's lack of awareness of the importance of structuring their French correctly limited their productive capacity and so their overall acquisition.

In our DS Project, each story provides individual students with a meaningful *output* opportunity, as they are telling a personal story that they have chosen to communicate, rather than more artificial textbook drills and scenario role-plays. This encourages them to develop an understanding of the communicative structures of Japanese and to challenge themselves to use their language to the best of their abilities rather than merely stringing together a series of words or memorized patterns.

Pienemann's research in the area of second language acquisition (SLA) provides another important pedagogical element. He argues that all learners develop incrementally, although at different rates and that they cannot skip any developmental stages, as each stage is a prerequisite for the next (Pienemann 1998, p. 87). Although the university context requires us to group students as Beginners, Intermediate and Advanced, we recognize that each student is at a different stage in their linguistic development. Our project individualizes their learning journey and allows them to work at their current stage. It also allows teachers to provide feedback that targets each student's individual stage of development.

Intermediate Japanese at the Australian National University

At the ANU, introductory and intermediate Japanese language courses are divided into two streams: one focuses on reading and writing, the other focuses on speaking and listening. The target course for the DS Project is

---

[3] 自分が自分自身の主人公でなくては本当に人間であるとはいえない
（梶田 1998), cited in Thomson 2009, p. 27.

JPNS2012 Spoken Japanese 3, which is the Intermediate-level speaking and listening course that a team of four or five teachers teach in the first semester.

Spoken Japanese 3 attracts about 90 students every year and comprises five hours of face-to-face class time each week: one lecture (for all 90 students); two conversational tutorials (15 students in each group); one grammar seminar (30 students in each group) and one multimedia class (15 students in each group). The lecturer works with the textbook to provide an overall introduction to the function(s) and introduces new grammatical points and the socio/cultural background needed in various situations.[4] The two conversational tutorials include some pattern drilling, but mainly focus on encouraging students to speak as much as possible. The grammar seminar uses the workbook that accompanies the main text and provides on-the-spot feedback to student questions. The multimedia class focuses on listening, pronunciation and intonation activities, and uses a variety of supplementary audiovisual materials.

The ANU Intermediate Japanese Digital Storytelling Project

The aim of the DS Project is to encourage students to create a multimedia digital story *from the heart* in their *own* Japanese. The teaching delivery of the project has evolved over the four years, and, by 2012, students had begun to take ownership of the project and reported how much it was helping them to communicate in Japanese:[5]

> *The digital story project was a good way to practice expressing thoughts and emotions in Japanese, and provided an opportunity to focus on intonation and pronunciation without the added stress of public speaking.* (2012)

> *Good way to get creative and work on a topic you are interested it* [sic]. (2012)

---

[4] The course uses the McGraw-Hill textbook *Yookoso! Continuing with Contemporary Japanese* written by Yasu-hiko Tohsaku, and its accompanying *Workbook* (Tohsaku, 2006), as the main texts. These texts are supplemented by other materials, including movie clips and live news broadcasts.

[5] The student comments in this chapter are taken from the anonymous ANU SELT (Student Experience of Learning and Teaching) surveys that the university conducts every year for each course, and an extra DS-focused anonymous online class survey conducted in 2011 and 2012.

In 2012, the DS Project accounted for 25 percent of the overall course assessment for *Spoken Japanese 3*. The remaining assessment was made up of homework (25%). mid-semester online exam (15%), final exam (30%), and participation (5%).

The main learning outcome associated with this assessment task was for students to "develop the ability to express themselves in Japanese by writing and performing creative/imaginative texts." The overall 25 percent assessment of the DS Project was divided into three staged components:

- Digital Storyboard Draft Submission (10%)
- Digital Story Narration Recording (5%)
- Digital Story Final Movie & Revised Storyboard (10%).

This enables teachers to provide targeted feedback, and encourages students to develop their project step by step. Each stage is assessed with a different rubric. The first step of the draft storyboard encourages students to focus on the content and language of their story and assessment is based on linguistic correctness, story structure and content. The second stage focuses on narration delivery, including pronunciation, intonation and verbal expressiveness. The voiceboards and narration activities, presented in Fig. 9-1 and discussed in the next section, prepare the students for the narration assessment.

The final stage lets students focus on the overall composition and audience impact of their completed film. Assessment of the final product emphasizes how students have improved on their earlier draft and successfully drawn their audience into their story. Teachers assess how students have used such aspects as structure, humor, timing, voice, and visuals to create *impact*. While the assessment of such impact is inevitably subjective, we work to quantify our responses in the assessment reports. Our experience has shown that, overall, the individual teachers agree with each other's assessment. The movie night at the end of the semester lets students watch each other's movies, creating a real sense of solidarity and community. Students vote on the most popular, impactful stories. To date, their votes have reflected the teacher's assessment of the interesting and impactful stories.

Fig. 9-1: DS Project Teaching Schedule

Week	DS related course activities and assessment schedule
1	Voiceboard 1
2	Voiceboard 2
3	Narration 1
4	Voiceboard 3 Introduction to Garageband software—how to combine image and sound (multimedia tutorial)
5	Narration 2 • DS Project Introduction (lecture) • Storytelling practice (conversation tutorial) • DS topic brainstorming (multimedia tutorial) • What makes a good DS – structure and content (grammar seminar)
6	Voiceboard 4
7	Midterm Test Voiceboard
	Two week mid-semester break
8	DS small group presentation (multimedia tutorial) Submission of DS Storyboard Draft
9	Narration 3 DS Narration Audio Recording Submission
10	Voiceboard 5
11	DS Final Movie Submission
12	Voiceboard 6
13	DS Movie Night

Student Concerns and Project Evolution

This section discusses a number of issues that the DS Project faced over the four years of the project, and how we resolved them. When we began the project, we focused our attention on the word and sentence level and encouraged students to be more descriptive and therefore to use more adjectival phrases. Teramura (1982, pp. 139–54) argues that Japanese adjectival expression can be divided into two broad categories, referred to as internal and external description. Our analysis of student digital stories, in the first year of the project, showed that students tended to overuse this external type of adjectives ("the shinkansen was *fast*" or "the Golden Pavilion was *beautiful*"), which meant that their stories became simple descriptions of events rather than successfully expressing their emotional engagement with those events (Hayes & Itani 2011, p. 15). Digital stories that focused on sentence level external descriptions tended to become a list of facts and proved less engaging. Some students simply provided a schedule of a trip to Japan full of factual details with little personal engagement. We found ourselves constantly asking students to consider the "why" behind their statements, because as listeners we wanted to know "why" they found a particular experience "interesting" or "beautiful."

We became increasingly aware of the importance of the *impact* of the story and that students needed to consider other devices, such as narration, voice, image and sound, beyond the purely linguistic, to capture their listener's attention (Hayes & Itani-Adams 2014). At first this caused difficulties with some students, who misunderstood our concept of "impact" and felt that they had no interesting story to tell. They worried that only stories that exposed personal details, even intimate secrets, would be judged as having an impact: "*Some people feel comfortable talking about things that are emotional and important but I don't. ... It seemed (to me) like 'books and why I love them' was not going to be a valid topic*" (2011). This was not however the case, as our focus on impact was to encourage the students to think about *how* they told their story, rather than what topic they chose.

In 2012 we introduced several activities to better explain the importance of impact and to provide students with the skills to heighten the impact of their stories. One such activity focused on storytelling skills to help students reflect on what makes an interesting and impactful story and on how their story structure, timing and delivery influenced their audience. Other activities focused on intonation, pronunciation and narration skills, so that students could become more aware of the role and impact of sound and voice on their digital storytelling. The voiceboard activity required students to record a response to an audio question posted by their teacher and to listen to the teacher's recorded feedback. In the short narration activities, students were required to mimic the expressiveness of a pre-recorded narration. These narration activities exposed students to a selection of different speech genres, including colloquial conversations, story narrations, some examples of the onomatopoeic richness of Japanese, interjections and even expletives so as to explore different styles of oral expression. Students were also asked to compare their own recordings with the audio frequency visualizations of their teacher, to become more aware of the pronunciation, intonation and tone of their own audio recordings. This has been positively received in student feedback: *"Using the shadowing technique to improve pronunciation and intonation is effective"* (2012).

As already explained, the DS Project was assessed through three stages. This allowed us to give targeted feedback at each stage: first on the content and language, second on the narration delivery and finally on the overall "impact" of the story. As educators, we need to acknowledge that "second language learning occurs, in part, through the analytic processes that output and feedback can engender" and that "we need to encourage students to be more responsible for their own learning" (Swain 1993, p. 163). To encourage this more active, responsible learning, teachers do not *correct* student errors in the draft storyboard. Instead they highlight problem areas, requiring the students to engage with their mistakes and try to work out what they should say instead. The draft storyboard feedback also allows teachers to comment on the role and effectiveness of image to the overall story. This accords with the approach recommended by Lyster and Ranta (1997, p. 58) who argue that "the feedback-uptake sequence engages students more actively when there is negotiation of form, that is, when the correct form is not provided to the students." Student feedback indicates that some students still found it difficult to take responsibility for their own language learning in this way: *"many mistakes that were highlighted tend to be changed, yet changed incorrectly, without improvement to the overall piece of work"* (2011). Yet most students in 2012 have come to accept this style of content feedback as beneficial for their learning, demonstrating that we are more effectively explaining the goals and steps of the DS Project task:

> *It was good feedback. I admit that I did not understand all of it, but this prompted me to ask the tutors for further explanation, which is better than must getting it [my drafts] back and correcting what was wrong. This helped to improve the quality of my final DS* (2012).

Impact in Student Digital Stories[6]

This section analyzes some specific digital stories to demonstrate how students have tried to express their emotions, beliefs and thoughts and to prove that, even at an intermediate level, students can create impactful

---

[6] Each student has given us permission to reproduce images and text from their digital storytelling productions. Copyright remains with the original copyright holder(s).

dynamic stories. The students have achieved this by employing sophisticated features, not only in the language they use in narration but also in the background sounds and music and in the images they used to create their movies.[7] Some used humor, irony or suspense to draw their audience into their story, while others varied their tone of voice and speech style to create the desired impact. The more impactful digital storytelling managed to draw on a variety of linguistic styles to achieve verbal creativity, such as variation in sentence length or levels of politeness, use of quotations and colloquial exclamations. Many asked their audience some questions, while others created their own metaphors. The non-verbal creativity of some digital stories successfully exploited the potential of the digital movie form such as incorporating *kanji* or *hiragana* into personal photographs or hand-drawn images, using maps, or even using animated features (e.g. morphing personal photos into anime heroes).

Student A and Student B: Humorous beginnings

Student A tells a story of her life in Alice Springs and her subsequent exchange to Japan (Fig. 9-2 to 9-4). Although her DS Project contained many Japanese language errors, on the narrative level she begins strongly. Drawing on stereotypes about Alice Spring (Fig. 9-2)[8] and Australian rural life, she tells her audience humorous falsehoods, such as "in Alice Springs we all live in tin huts and ride kangaroos to school and cook on open fires" (Fig. 9-3), which instantly invites laughter from her listeners. Then telling us that she was "just kidding", in an emphatic joking voice, she successfully uses the rhetorical question "but you all want to come to Alice now don't you?" which draws her listeners into her story (Fig. 9-2 to Fig. 9-4).

Student B also uses humor to tell the story of his early life in a small village in Greece, his subsequent move to Australia and his increasing interest in Japan. He too begins his story in a humorous vein, telling us that life in the small village was all rather uninteresting and that no one talked about anything but goats (Fig. 9-5 and Fig. 9-6). This invites audience laughter and inspires interest in his life story.

---

[7] Some sample stories and information about the DS Project are available on the ANU CAP EngageAsia website at engageasia.anu.edu.au/teach_learn.php

[8] We have included our translation of the student's original Japanese scripts in the main body of the chapter and reproduced them in Japanese in the Appendix to this chapter. All errors or inconsistent expressions made by the students are reproduced as in the original.

Student C: Using Voice

This example demonstrates how the successful use of voice and sound is one of the great strengths of the digital mode of delivery. Student C's story is about his participation in the ANU Inward Bound (IB) 74 km endurance competition (Fig. 9-7). The event takes place over a 24-hour period, which means teams have to navigate in the dark. Early in the run, Student C somehow became separated from his team and lost his way. He cleverly uses short sentences to draw his audience in. Pregnant pauses create an atmosphere of suspense as he tells us about the darkness (Fig. 9-8), the rising mist and distant voices calling out to him (Fig. 9-9).

He effectively uses a softer volume and a ghost-story-like wavering delivery to present these distant voices. His volume then increases as he speaks as the team member who finds him.

Student C also includes an amusing vignette providing tips for male listeners about how hard it is to get a girl (Fig. 9-10). He recommends this sort of endurance event makes a man much more attractive to the opposite sex. He creates a dialogue between himself and an imaginary attractive young woman, and imitates a soft girlish voice to express how worried she is about how he is coping with the race, and then changes his delivery to a very rough masculine voice to tell her that his cuts and bruises are really nothing (Fig. 9-11). Although Student C makes a substantial number of Japanese errors, his overall story has impact due to his success with these devices.

(The students took most of the photographs on the next pages, but web links are included in the chapter's Appendix for Figures 9-2, 9-3, 9-9 and 9-10).

Student D and Student E: Images, scripts, maps, gestures, and poses

Several students managed to sell their message through the use of visuals cues. Student D uses a world map to show the geographic proximity between Japan and her home of Shanghai. She then places hand-drawn figures on the map and used her own hands to emphasize her points as she told us about her favorite hobby Aikido (Fig. 9-12). Her developing relationship with Japan seemed to stall when she came to Australia to university, which she represents with a map of Australia covered in nothing but sheep (Fig. 9-13). Student E tells about her relationship with music. Her opera-singing mother used to tell her that music was her "best" friend. She found this really hard to believe, and she cleverly uses Japanese script to emphasize this point (Fig. 9-14). However, after coming to Australia alone, and rediscovering pleasure in music when she was at her most lonely, she realized that her mother was right. She demonstrates this with an image of her own hands playing the piano (Fig. 9-15).

Student F: Creative metaphors

Student F not only employed all the devices described above, but also created a personal metaphor to express her developing relationship with Japan. Her DS Project, titled "Ten Cups of Green Tea and Me" (Fig. 9-16), tells her evolving relationship with Japan through her developing love of Japanese green tea. She begins her story by telling us her "first cup of green tea," offered to her by her host mother on her first night of a home stay in Japan.

She was not very keen on drinking it as it was bright green, but she managed to hide this response and politely told them it was delicious (Fig. 9-17). This caused great hilarity between her host-parents who then told her that they did not like green tea either, even though they were Japanese (Fig. 9-18). Student F successfully harnessed the multimedia aspect of this task, by animating elements of her drawings to emphasize the points she was making.

As her story unfolds, each cup of tea is used to symbolize the different stages in her life. A mug of green tea sits on her desk as she studies for her final high school exams and it is over a cup of green tea that she first falls in love with her boyfriend. One day she finds herself sitting in her room at university, feeling lonely and missing home. A parcel arrives from her father with a box of green tea bags. Not only does this cheer her up, the *green* of the tea reminds her of her home in Tasmania (Fig. 9-19). She brings her story to an end by telling us that she is now drinking her tenth cup of tea as she creates this digital story (Fig. 9-20).

Conclusion

This chapter began with the question of whether it was possible to include *impact* as a criterion in an assessment rubric for intermediate language-learners of Japanese. By presenting the results of the first four years of our ongoing DS Project, we have demonstrated that the answer to this question is *yes*. There is much ongoing debate about the balance between correctness and communication in language teaching. We recognize that grammatical correctness is important in all language communication. Yet our analysis has found that the overall discourse level of the story, the message and how the message is conveyed are most important in the creation of impactful digital stories. Both teachers and students must learn to recognize the importance of this more holistic view of communication. All too often, in-class time tends to focus on correcting the small linguistic details. Even when in-class activities focus on communication, the scale is rather limited. The DS Project allowed students to focus on the bigger picture and to bring all their *life* knowledge into the space in which they worked in Japanese.

Digital storytelling has the potential to create an effective *meeting place* that brings together a number of features of language teaching and learning, such as language and communication, pedagogy and practice; teacher-centered and student-centered approaches, the interaction between the storyteller and the audience. Most of all, digital storytelling encourages students to become interactive, collaborative members of their learning community. Further, digital storytelling builds a bridge between current and future teaching and learning practice by addressing creative thinking, risk-taking and effective communication. It has the added advantage of developing effective technical literacy, and so reflects one of the key priorities of Australian higher education in the twenty-first century.

Appendix

(the Japanese original for Figures 9-2 to 9-20).

Fig. 9-2
何人かは、アリススプリングスと言うところを知っているかもしれません。
(Image from http://www.flightsaustralia.com.au/images/destinations/Alice_Springs.jpg)

Fig. 9-3
アリススプリングスで砂漠に囲まれているスズの小屋に住んでいます。
そして、カンガルーに乗って学校に行きますよ。
(Image from http://2.bp.blogspot.com/_ewQuGGy0QbI/SwYZ9w9yJLI/AAAAA
AAAAXA/sbGgHlse07E/s320/kanga-school.jpg)

Fig. 9-4
オーブンを使わないのでかわりに外でたき火で料理を作ったりカントリー
音楽を歌ったりします。冗談ですよ！でも、みんないきたくなったでしょ
う。

Fig. 9-5
小さい時に、ギリシャのカストリアという小さい町に生まれ育った。

Fig. 9-6
そこでの生活はあまり面白くなく人々はいつもヤギのことしか話さない。
ヤギを飼うこととか。ヤギのミルクとか、ヤギのチーズとか。

Fig. 9-7
IB2012 と私

Fig. 9-8
キャンベラからひがしかにしかどうか、わかりませんでした。どこに行く
か、わかりませんでした。きたにはしっていることをだけわかりました。

Fig. 9-9
きりにつつまれ、かぜがつよくなりました。わたしのかいちゅうでんとう
がてんめつしはじめて、でんちがしにはじめました。....わたしのなまえが
よばれているのがきこました。
(Image from http://www.bringmebusiness.com.au/reelTime/images/reelTime-dark-
forest.jpg)

Fig. 9-10
どくしんのせいかつはこんなんです。そのしあいはほんとうにむずかしく
しまいましたから、かちにくい。
(Image from http://www.moosehuntinginfo.com/gallery/moose-photo-15.jpg)

Fig. 9-11
あしがいたそうだね。なにをしたの。これ。いたくないよ。

Fig. 9-12
日本と私には縁があります。なぜなら、私の趣味は全部日本に関係が
あるからです。上海の出身なので、日本がとても近いと思います。

Fig. 9-13
私が勉強しているオーストラリア国立大学で合気道クラブもあると分かり
ました。すごく嬉しかったです

Fig. 9-14
いつか、母は　「音楽はじんせいの一番いい友達だ」といいました。
その時には　「音楽.....友達？うそ！」と思いました

Fig. 9-15
ひさばさのピアノえんそうをしました。母におしえてもらった『ジャズ・
チョップスチック』をひいたときには、母と家族がかんじました。母が
「音楽は一番いい友達だ」と言ったこともその時にわかりました。

Fig. 9-16
十杯のお茶と私

Fig. 9-17
にがいと思ったが とてもおいしいと言った。

Fig. 9-18
お母さんとお父さんはわらった。私たちは日本人があまり好きじゃないと
言った。それは一ぱい目のお茶だ。

Fig. 9-19
さびしい時に七はい目のお茶を飲んだ。お茶もタスマニアもみどり色だ。

Fig. 9-20
今、ものがたりを話しながら十はい目のお茶を飲む。うれしい時や
むずかしい時にお茶が私をいつも手伝った。おいしくて熱いお茶が一番
好きだよ！

References

Barnes, D. 1979, *From Communication to Curriculum*, Harmondsworth: Penguin

Boulter, A. 2004, "Assessing the criteria: An argument for creative writing theory", *New Writing: The International Journal for the Practice and Theory for Creative Writing* 1:2, 134–40. http://dx.doi.org/10.1080/14790720408668931

Frazel, M. 2010, *Digital Storytelling Guide for Educators*, Eugene, OR: International Society for Technology in Education

Georgetown University. (n.d.), Digital Storytelling: Multimedia Archive [website] https://pilot.cndls.georgetown.edu/digitalstories//multimedia-distinctive/

Hayes, C. and Y. Itani-Adams. 2011, Gengo gakushū ni okeru 'dijitaru sutōrii teringu' no dōnyū : ōsutoraria kokuritsu daigaku de no kokoromi [「言語学習におけるデジタルストーリーテリング」の導入—オーストラリア国立大学での試み; Introduction of 'Digital Storytelling' into Japanese language learning: Australian National University Trial Project], *2011 Nendo Nihongo Kyōiku Gakkai Kenkyūshūkai: dai nanakai* (2011 年度日本語教育学会研究集会 : 第 7 回; Proceedings from the 7th Research Meeting of The Society for Teaching Japanese as a Foreign Language. Kōnan Daigaku (Kōnan University), September 17. Kobe: Nihongo kyōiku gakkai, pp. 12–15

—. 2014, Inpakuto o nokosu hanashikata no gakushū: Oosutoraria Kokuritsu Daigaku no dejitaru sutōrii teringu purojekuto [「インパクト」を与える話し方の学習：オーストラリア国立大学のデジタル・ストーリー・プロジェクト; Learning to speak with 'impact': The Australian National University's Digital Storytelling Project], *Electronic Journal of Foreign Language Teaching (e-FLT)*, 11:1, 116-135. http://e-flt.nus.edu.sg/v11n12014/hayes.pdf

Holec, H. 1981, *Autonomy and Foreign Language Learning*, Oxford: Pergamon (first published Strasbourg: Council of Europe, 1979)

Lambert, J. 2006, *The Center for Digital Storytelling*: http://www.storycenter.org

—. 2006, *Digital Storytelling: capturing lives, creating community*, 2nd ed, Berkeley, CA: Digital Diner Press

Levin, H. 2012, "Authentic doing: student-produced web-based digital video oral histories". In D. Boyd, S. Cohen, B. Rakerd and D. Rehberger, eds, *Oral history in the digital age*, Institute of Library and Museum Services. http://ohda.matrix.msu.edu/2012/06/authentic-doing/

Little, D. 2012, "Learner Autonomy, the Common European Framework of Reference for Languages, the European Language Portfolio and Language Teaching at University". In P. Alderete-Díez, L.I. McLoughlin, L.N. Dhonnchadha and D.N. Uigín, eds, *Translation, Technology and Autonomy in Language Teaching and Learning*, Oxford: Peter Lang, pp. 73–92

Lyster, R. and L. Ranta. 1997, "Corrective feedback and learner uptake", *Studies in Second Language Acquisition* 19(1): 37–66

Maynard, S.K. 2007, Gengogaku to nihongo kyōikugaku—chi no juyō kara chi no sōzō e [言語学と日本語教育学—知の受容から知の創造へ; Linguistics and Japanese language pedagogy – from passive to creative 'knowledge'], *Nihongo Kyōiku: Journal of Japanese Language Teaching* 132: 27–32

Meadows, D. (n.d.), *Photobus* [website] http://www.photobus.co.uk/?id=1

Miller, C.H. 2008, *Digital storytelling—A creator's guide to interactive entertainment*, Oxford: Elsevier Focal Press

Pienemann, M. 1998, *Language Processing and Second Language Development: Processability Theory*, Amsterdam: John Benjamins

Porter, B. (n.d.), *DigiTales: The Art of Telling Digital Stories* [website]. www.digitales.us

Queensland University of Technology. 2009, *Digital Storytelling* [website]. http://digitalstorytelling.ci.qut.edu.au/

Swain, M. 1993, "The Output Hypothesis: Just Speaking and Writing Aren't Enough", *The Canadian Modern Language Review/La Revue Canadienne des langues vivantes* 50(1): 158–64

Teramura, H. [寺村秀夫] 1982, Nihongo no shintakusu to imi: daiikkan [日本語のシンタクスと意味：第一巻], *Japanese Syntax and Semantics: Vol 1*, Tokyo: Kuroshio Shuppan

Thomson, C.K. [トムソン木下千尋] 2009, *New pedagogies for learner agency: Japanese Language education research and practice in Australia* [学習者主体の日本語教育：オーストラリアの実践研究], Tokyo: Koko Shuppan

Tohsaku, Y-H. 2006, *Yookoso: Continuing with Contemporary Japanese*, 3rd ed, New York: McGraw-Hill

University of Houston. (n.d.), *Educational uses of digital storytelling* [website]. http://digitalstorytelling.coe.uh.edu/index.cfm

CHAPTER TEN

INTEGRATING LITERATURE AND COOPERATIVE LEARNING IN ENGLISH LANGUAGE TEACHING

WAN-LUN LEE

Keywords: literature in ELT, cooperative learning, extensive reading

Abstract

A number of articles and books talk about the benefits or ways of using literature in second or foreign language education, but most of them do not provide empirical evidence to support the claims being made, and few of them target English as a Foreign Language (EFL) students of non-English major. In Taiwan, literary works, often considered too demanding or too impractical, are seldom used in University English courses for these students. This chapter argues that with the help of cooperative learning, literature may enrich these non-English majors' English learning process in a way that "the study of the language alone can not" (Hill 1986, p. 108). The discussion is positioned at the intersection of research into issues surrounding the integration of literature and cooperative pedagogy in English Language Teaching (ELT). A literature-focused, cooperative learning project I designed and used with my Sophomore English courses in a Taiwanese university will serve as an example of such integration, and findings from a mixed methods study conducted to investigate my students' responses to this project will be used as evidence to illustrate in what ways and to what extent the integration has benefited these EFL students of non-English major, especially their English learning processes, experiences, perceptions, motivation and outcomes.

Introduction

Literature was once "relegated to a marginal role" in second and foreign language teaching and learning, but the past few decades have witnessed its return in the language classroom (Paran 2006, p. 1). As Collie and Slater state, literature was once considered ill-suited to language learners and only "reserved for the most advanced level of study" because the "emphasis in modern linguistics on the primacy of the spoken language" made many language teachers "distrust what was seen as essentially a written crystallized form," "far removed from the utterances of daily communication" (1987, p. 2). However, the late 1980s saw a "considerable resurgence of interest in the study of literature in relation to language" (Carter & Long 1987, p. 1). Since then, the resurgence has yielded numerous articles and books advocating potential linguistic, aesthetic, cultural and motivational benefits of using literature with second and foreign language learners, devising various approaches to integrating literature and language, or proposing ways of selecting appropriate literary texts.

Despite such renewed interest in the use of literature in second and foreign language learning contexts, little empirical research exists on this topic. Literary works are still kept out of many language classrooms, especially those in the English as a Second Language (ESL)/English as a Foreign Language (EFL) settings where the purpose for English learning is considered "purely instrumental" (Butler 2006, p. 11). As Paran points out, "most of the writing in this area has been theoretical," and even though more and more interesting practitioner research has been done and documented in recent years, "the number of papers is small," and "the paucity of empirical evidence" cannot fully support the claims that literature "has something unique to contribute to language learning," or contribute to a better understanding of learners' reactions to different types of literary works, approaches, or tasks used in the language classroom (2008, pp. 470–71).

In the field of English Language Teaching (ELT), it is also noteworthy that many teachers still take a suspicious attitude towards integrating language and literature. Some teachers believe that their students need to acquire a more functional kind of English, to achieve such "utilitarian goals" as using the language to communicate with foreigners in business or travel (Fox 1997, p. 30). Other teachers think of literature as "an advanced option" and that their students will find it too difficult to use literature to learn English (Hall 2005, p. 199). Some teachers "see their role as teaching the text" and fear that they do not understand a literary text well enough to teach it or know how to use it well in a language class (Paran 2006, p. 6). Such worries and fears have led to "the conspicuous absence of a place for literature" in most English language classrooms (Belcher & Hirvela 2000, p. 33), where ELT textbooks (most of which rely heavily on information-based, non-literary texts) often are the only tool in the teacher's hands to teach the target language (Tsai 1996).

As an English teacher teaching University English courses for Taiwanese EFL students who do not major in English, I often find similar worries or fears in my colleagues' responses to my idea of using literature with these non-English-major students. Yet my passion for literature and my study of two master degrees—first in English literature (specializing in novels) and then in ELT—has increased my interest and confidence in finding appropriate materials and ways to give literature a useful and significant role to play in my English classes. This enables those of my students not majoring in English, and with little experience or knowledge of literature in English, to enjoy and benefit from the experience.

To avoid any potential misunderstanding, it is worth noting that my intention is never to teach my students how to study literature written in any genre or any form. Instead, I have been more interested in using unsimplified novels intended for native speakers of English as one important component in the university English curriculum to increase the students' exposure to "authentic" and "undistorted" samples of the target language that are often "lost" in texts simplified for their use (Collie & Slater 1987, p. 3, p. 14), and as a valuable resource for stimulating a wide variety of learning activities and tasks that can engage the students "interactively with the text" and with their "fellow students" in English to help them overcome language barriers and promote greater interest, motivation and involvement in the language learning process (Duff & Maley 1990, p. 5).

This chapter explains why I have tried to integrate literature and cooperative learning to achieve my desired goal. The chapter describes how a literature-focused, cooperative learning project has been designed for and used in my *Sophomore English* courses at a Taiwanese University to help those of my students who are not majoring in English. Together the students read *The Lion, the Witch and the Wardrobe* by C. S. Lewis, as a way of learning English. The original text (1998, first published in 1950) is used, for reasons explained later in this chapter. This chapter also presents and discusses the findings of a mixed methods study that used questionnaires, interviews and students' reflective writing to collect and investigate students' responses to the project and their perspectives of the integration of literature and cooperative learning in the university English curriculum. The chapter concludes with comments on the pedagogical potential of such integration and suggestions for further research.

Rationale for Integrating Literature and Cooperative Learning

A careful examination of the discussion in existing publications (such as academic papers and methodology handbooks) about integrating literature and language learning elicits many useful ideas and guidelines about designing language learning activities and tasks based on literary texts, and novels in particular. However, few of them (e.g. Yang 2002) seem to focus on the use of unsimplified English novels in EFL contexts targeted at young adult learners, not to mention undergraduates who are not majoring in English but who are required to take English courses at university. Considering the fact that these non-English majors have no wish to become literature specialists, language-based approaches that aim to use literary texts as a language teaching resource seem to be more suitable for them than literature-based approaches that emphasize the "study" of literary texts. Besides, since these students have no or little experience of tackling any unsimplified work of literature in English on their own, they need support and active help from their teacher and fellow students so that none are "left alone" in the quest for understanding a literary text.

Cooperative learning, which features small group interaction, equal participation, positive interdependence and individual accountability appears to be an ideal approach to the desired goal. Regarded as "a powerful instructional innovation," this approach is much more than just asking students to work together in groups (Jacob 1999, p. 1). Rather, it provides a variety of systematic methods and techniques that can be adapted to instructional uses in "different curriculum areas and classroom settings" to ensure greater success in having students "interdependently linked" to accomplish their shared goals (Gillies 2007, p. 64). In language learning contexts, this approach has been particularly effective in forming a community of students, sometimes with different levels of language proficiency, to "work together on specific tasks or projects" and "benefit from the interactive experience" (Kessler 1992, p. v). If cooperative learning can be implemented as the main organizing scheme for integrating language and literature, various forms of peer cooperation and collaboration, both in and out of class, may contribute to a wealth of active interactions between student and student, student and teacher, and student and text. All such interactions not only help language learners deepen their understanding of a literary work; they also develop their level of English and increase their skills in English.

If integrated carefully in a language class, literature and cooperative pedagogy are very likely to complement each other perfectly. On one hand, all elements of a literary work—theme, plot, character, and setting—give literature the potential to generate "quality" talks characterized by "reflection," "active thinking," and "personal engagement" in cooperative groups; those elements also provide language learners with a rich and meaningful context for peer interaction and cooperation in the process of exchanging alternative perspectives taken on the same literary text (Boyd & Maloof 2000, p. 166). On the other hand, cooperative learning can create a student-centered classroom full of ideas, in which language learners compare and assess diverse opinions and ideas among peers in the group in a "task-oriented way" (Chambers & Gregory 2006, p. 183) and so have better chance to fill in gaps in their understanding of the text and "formulate a sound response" to it (Hall 2005, p. 150). Further, at the intersection of literature and cooperative learning, the attention of non-English-major students can be shifted away from "the minute, intensive attack on a single corner of the text" to "a more extensive concern for gist and overall theme," and so have a less intimidating and more enjoyable experience of learning English through literature (Collie & Slater 1987, p. 14).

A Literature-focused Cooperative Learning Project

To explore the potential benefits of using literature in conjunction with cooperative pedagogy, a literature-focused cooperative learning (LFCL) project was designed for and implemented in my A-level (advanced), B-level (intermediate), and C-level (low-intermediate) *Sophomore English* courses taken by Taiwanese EFL students not majoring in English but in subjects in the fields of medicine, sciences, engineering, management, or social science. All non-English-major students of the Taiwanese university where I conducted this study are required to keep learning and improving their English in the first two years of university by taking *Freshman English* and *Sophomore English* courses suitable for their English language proficiency level. For example, students whose English scores in the nationwide Joint Entrance Examination are above 80 percent among all the examinees can take A-level English courses; those whose scores below 80 percent but above 50 percent take B-level courses; and the rest of the students go to C-level courses.

The literary text I selected to use with the three classes of students is C. S. Lewis's novel *The Lion, the Witch and the Wardrobe* in its original form.

On one hand I let these students read a novel, not only because of my personal interest and knowledge in this literary genre, but also because of two distinct advantages of using novels with language learners. One advantage is that the length of a novel, as Jacobs argues, allows readers to become familiar with the same set of characters, setting and plot, and helps them get accustomed to "a consistent narrative style, vocabulary, and syntax," which makes the progress through the book easier (1994, p. 36). The other advantage is that readers of a novel are often engaged in a procedural and creative process of making interpretations to "grapple with its multiple ambiguities," which makes it more likely for them to develop their "interpretative and sense-making abilities" needed in many real-life situations (Lazar 1993, p. 19).

On the other hand, there are several reasons for my choice of *The Lion, the Witch and the Wardrobe* for the target students, most of whom had no or little experience of reading unsimplified novels in English. First, the book is intended for children or juveniles, so its language is simpler and more straightforward than books written for adults. Also, its length is not too intimidating for my non-English-major students. In addition, the novel is a fable with imaginary and adventurous elements and strong characterization and plot, which can not only pull readers' involvement and imagination from the very first page but also contribute to interesting and thought-provoking discussions. Last but not least, the fact that the book has been adapted into a BBC television series and a good film by Walt Disney is another advantage, because they can be used as visual support to help EFL students with their reading of the novel. They even provide "a good medium" for "extended listening" of the target language (Allan 1985, p. 49).

At the preparatory stage, the students' lack of cooperative learning experience and skills has been taken into consideration in the design of the project whose purpose is to have the students work together, inside or outside the classroom, to complete a variety of cooperative language learning tasks appropriate to each stage of the reading of the novel. In their previous schooling, most of the students had not been taught to work cooperatively with their peers to achieve a common goal. Rather, they were trained to learn within a competitive goal structure where they had to show their individual ability to the teacher. So, although less structured cooperative learning, often referred to as collaborative learning, is considered more appropriate for university students (Bruffee 1995; Panitz 1997), I decided to adopt a more structured cooperative learning approach to help the students get used to this new format of learning and acquire the necessary social skills required to work effectively with others. Further, an orientation session was conducted at the start of the semester to introduce basic cooperative learning skills (e.g. listening actively and disagreeing in an agreeable way) and six discussion roles (discussion director, coordinator and recorder; reporter; summarizer; vocabulary enricher; travel tracer; and cheerleader). A four-skill, cooperative learning-oriented ELT textbook *Super Goal* (2003) was also employed to improve the students' ability to cooperate with others and to use the target language to accomplish all the learning tasks of the project.

Various cooperative learning techniques were used to increase the students' eagerness of participation and involvement in the reading process, and to nurture their language and social skills through different forms of peer cooperation. The techniques included three-step interviews, think-pair-share, roundtables, jigsaws, student teams-achievement divisions, cooperative integrated reading and composition, group investigation, and group discussion. All were incorporated in the cooperative learning activities centered on the novel.

One example was a post-reading activity using the jigsaw technique to help students go beyond the basic comprehension of the novel as an example. A long article with critical comments on different aspects of the novel was divided into six sections for this activity and assigned to each of the six members in each group. Those getting the same section to read had to gather together as an expert group to read and discuss the content of the section before returning to their home groups to share what they had learned from the discussion on that part of the text with the others. This jigsaw reading activity requires a great deal of active listening and speaking as students read and discuss the content of the assigned material. It also enhances positive interdependence and individual accountability, because each student has to teach and be taught by the other group members to do well on a reading comprehension quiz used to see how well each student has understood the main points of the whole article.

Particularly noteworthy is that each of my three *Sophomore English* classes met only once a week for 100 minutes. This meant that the literature-focused, cooperative learning activities of this project were presented as take-home worksheets and in-class tasks to give my students more chance to work on the novel cooperatively in and out of class. For convenience, I divided the novel into five sections, each consisting of three or four chapters. The students were allowed two weeks to finish their home reading of each section, accompanied by a supportive bi-weekly worksheet devised around that part of the novel. Each group of six students had to meet regularly out of class to discuss the novel and complete the worksheet. If it was not easy for them to meet face to face after class, the students were encouraged to communicate with each other electronically using online discussion tools (e.g. MSN and Skype). These tools, as noted by Chambers and Gregory, not only break the limitations of time and space to make it more convenient for them to "discuss the issues, organize themselves, distribute tasks, negotiate the outcomes and, together, structure and present the final piece of work;" they also yield "an accurate record" of what was said and by whom to help the teacher "assess individual contributions" (2006, p. 188). By completing their home reading and worksheets before class, the students were ready for the in-class cooperative learning activities. Then, while as busily engaged in various forms of peer cooperation and interaction in the cooperative group, they used the language and thought of the literary text to develop their knowledge of the target language, improve their understanding of the content, and practice the four skills of the target language.

Researching into Students' Responses to the LFCL Project

As a teacher–researcher conducting this practitioner research in my own university English classes, I have adopted a mixed methods approach that aims to avoid "biases inherent in any single method" (Creswell 2003, p. 15) and to use words to "add meaning to numbers" and use numbers to "add precision to words" (Dörnyei 2007, p. 45). It was hoped that qualitative and quantitative data collected from different research instruments would help me explore my students' responses to the integration of literature and cooperative learning in an English language class and to investigate the following research questions more thoroughly:

1. From non-English major EFL students' perspectives, to what extent and in what ways do those students benefit from the integration of literature and cooperative learning?

2. From non-English major EFL students' perspectives, what are the effects of and their responses to this LFCL experience, and what are the factors perceived to influence these?

Quantitative and qualitative data were collected sometimes concurrently, but mainly sequentially during the whole semester. The order followed was quantitative and qualitative (pre-course questionnaire), qualitative (semi-structured focus group interviews and students' reflective writing), and finally quantitative and qualitative (post-course questionnaire). The following sections illustrate respectively the data collection instruments employed in this study and the way each type of data is analyzed and integrated with the findings from the other data sources.

Questionnaires

At the start and the end of the semester, 146 students in my three *Sophomore English* classes (65 in A-level, 29 in B-level, and 52 in C-level class) were asked to complete two questionnaires anonymously. The pre-course questionnaire was used to collect background information about the students' experiences with and attitude toward literature and cooperative learning. That questionnaire was made up of 25 Likert-scale statements (e.g. "I enjoyed reading the assigned English graded readers" and "Learning alone is better than learning together") for the respondents to rank for agreement on a scale of 1 to 4. The post-course questionnaire was designed to get the students' responses to the different elements of this LFCL project, including the novel, cooperative learning tasks and activities, and their learning experience. That questionnaire was made up of 55 polarized, yes/no questions (e.g. "Have you read through the whole novel?" and "Did cooperative learning make it easier to learn English through the novel?"). Each question contained "a single idea that is not subject to debate" to make the results of the yes-no rating more reliable (Dörnyei 2003, p. 42). In addition, at the last part of both questionnaires the students were encouraged to write down any suggestions or comments they wished to make.

Focus Group Interviews

Eighteen semi-structured focus group interviews were conducted at different times. Each interview targeted one of the three classes and one of the six CL discussion roles (e.g. students of the A-level class playing the role of discussion director were interviewed together). The length of each interview was one to two hours, depending on the number of interviewees, which varied with class size. Though some students did not show up for various reasons, 52 of 65 students in the A-level class, 24 of 29 in the B-level class, and 40 of 52 in the C-level class participated in the focus group interviews. I chose to interview one student from each group in a semi-structured way to reduce the "inequitable role relationship of interviewer-interviewee" to some extent (Hall 2005, p. 219), collect data "through group interaction on a topic determined by the researcher" (Morgan 1996, p. 130), impose a certain amount of "direction and structure" to move the discussion along for "greater coverage of topics" of interest in the time available (Stewart et al. 2007, p. 91), and to yield richer information than unstructured or structured interviews (Dowsett 1986). Further, having students playing the same discussion role interviewed together allowed them to share their "work experience" with each other. This not only contributed to cooperative learning among cross-group interviewees, I also found it easier to detect and deal with the problems existing in individual groups.

Reflective Writing

To get rich and valuable text-based information for "in-depth qualitative understanding" of their responses to the project (Hall 2005, p. 230), I also collected the reflective writing from 146 students, including their weekly feedback on the cooperative learning activities done in and out of class and their end-of-semester essays where they wrote about their reflections on this learning experience. Using this data collection instrument had two advantages. One advantage was that different pieces of reflective writing had their own stories to tell, so they would throw up new issues or provide written complements to the spoken data from the focus group interviews. The other advantage was that students were able to express themselves more freely, without the pressure from face-to-face interaction with the teacher or the other students in the interviews. It is also worth pointing out here that I also kept a record of my own reflections on the practice and effects of the project so that I could make timely changes to my pedagogical design and implementation and generate ideas of the guided questions for the interviews and the post-course questionnaire items.

Data Analysis and Integration

All the qualitative and quantitative data collected from different research instruments were first analyzed respectively. The questionnaire quantitative data was processed and turned into bar charts using *Microsoft Excel* to make the descriptive statistical analysis easier and make comparisons of the results of the questionnaires administered in my three classes before and after the implementation of the project. The qualitative data, from the respondents' written comments to both questionnaires, was reduced to a handful of categories or key points, to allow for comparisons with results or findings from other data sources. The interview qualitative data was transcribed, condensed, and analyzed for themes or categories with the help of "electronic scissors"—NVivo. The qualitative data from students' reflective writing was first read carefully to look for themes or patterns repeatedly revealed in them. Once an initial list of potential codes was built up, NVivo was used to identify and categorize chunks of text exemplifying the codes.

The integration of the findings from various data sources started during analysis. On one hand, similar themes or categories related to the research questions, such as language outcomes, were applied to the coding process of the qualitative data collected from the questionnaire comments, interviews and reflective writing. On the other hand, since this study needs qualitative depth to answer the research questions, greater priority was given to the qualitative data, and quantitative results were "included with qualitative data in thematic or pattern analysis" to "assist in the interpretation of qualitative findings" (Creswell 2008, p. 235).

Research Discussions and Findings

The purpose of this practitioner research is to evaluate the effects of integrating literature and cooperative learning in the university English curriculum from my students' perspectives. So the discussion of the major research findings drawn from different data types and sources will focus on the students' perceptions of the benefits and the problems of such integration.

First, the qualitative and quantitative data shows evidence that the majority of the students considered the cooperative way of learning English through literature beneficial in the following five ways.

1. Improving reading comprehension and critical thinking skills

Of the 116 interviewees, 49 interviewees mentioned that learning English through the novel in such a cooperative way had let them get answers to their reading comprehension questions related to the novel, exchange ideas and opinions with each other, learn new or fresh ideas from the others, study the story from different angles, or pay attention to things previously unnoticed. This outcome improved their understanding and interpretation of the literary text and improved their critical thinking skills. The post-course questionnaire data show that about 85 percent of respondents greatly enjoyed their group discussion time. Further, many students commented in their reflective essays about how much they enjoyed exchanging ideas with group mates, getting new or interesting thoughts from the others, or looking at things from various perspectives. They also commented how doing these group activities had helped them develop their own critical responses to the content of the novel. This is in line with my reflections on my classroom observations, and with what Jacobs, McCafferty and DaSilva Iddings claim when talking about the advantages of cooperative learning: "The purpose of cooperative learning is not to get everyone to think alike, but to get everyone to think and to share and to develop their own thinking through engagement with others" (2006, p. 16).

2. Strengthening confidence and motivation to learn English through literature

The results of the pre-course questionnaire show that the students' lack of experience in tackling any unsimplified literary text in English had made many of them, especially students in C-level courses, worry about the linguistic problems presented in the novel reading task. Yet, during interviews some students told me that this uncertainty of their own English ability had made them welcome the idea of learning together in small groups. In other words, adding the cooperative learning component to the reading task had given these students stronger confidence and motivation to deal with the potential linguistic difficulties even before they started to read the novel. In interviews and students' reflective writing, it was not uncommon to hear or read similar comments such as "I could never finish reading the novel without working with my group members" and "I am really grateful for all the help from my group."

Even so, the students' fondness for the novel increased their personal involvement with the story and their motivation to continue to read it to find out what happens next regardless of its linguistic difficulties. There were 31 positive comments about the novel in the interview data, and 28 positive comments about the novel in the students' reflective writing. The quantitative data from the post-course questionnaire survey also support these findings from these qualitative instruments, as they show that the majority of the respondents enjoyed reading the novel and learning English from it. Further, both qualitative and quantitative data of this study reveal that for those with no interest in the novel or who lost interest in it at some point, the cooperative learning activities, group discussions, and peer support or pressure motivated them to go on the reading journey. This implies that with the help of cooperative learning, even those students who do not like the literary work still feel like keeping up with the reading schedule to get involved in the process of peer cooperation.

Particularly noteworthy is that if these findings are examined under the theory of *intrinsic* versus *extrinsic* motivation, it is clear that more students were intrinsically rather than extrinsically motivated to read the novel.

First, their love for the story and curiosity about what happens next gave them intrinsic motivation to read the novel for pleasure and satisfaction. Second, working cooperatively on the novel and the learning activities related to it allowed them to "take learning initiatives and more control of their learning process" and developed in them a greater "sense of peer-group solidarity" and "shared responsibility," all of which contributed to "the appropriate psychological conditions for intrinsic motivation" (Ushioda 1996, p. 46).

3. Fostering the development of learner autonomy

As Dörnyei expounds, cooperative groups are "by definition autonomous," for they have to "work a lot without the immediate supervision of the teacher" (2001, p. 101). The interview data shows that many students made great efforts to play their discussion roles well by taking the initiative in improving their English language skills, searching for useful resources, and asking the other interviewees playing the same role for advice. In addition, many students felt that they had learned how to act independently of the teacher and become more capable of managing their own learning in the process of reading the novel and working with other students on the learning activities related to the novel. These findings are in line with the post-course questionnaire survey in which about 88 percent of the respondents agreed that they had learned to take more responsibilities for their own learning, and 75 percent agreed that this learning experience had made them become more active English learners.

4. Developing English language ability and social competence

I did not use a pre-test or post-test to measure the effect of the project on improving the students' English ability, but evidence from different data sources showed that most students believed their English had improved due to this learning experience. In interview, eight interviewees mentioned that they had learned and used "real" English from the novel to improve their own writing; thirteen interviewees commented that intergroup interactions had helped them become more capable of thinking in English or speaking English in front of other people; and three interviewees believed the novel reading had improved their reading skills, enlarged their vocabulary, and increased their reading speed. In their reflective essays, a number of students attributed the improvement of their English reading ability, their habit of reading in English, and the increase in the amount of their English vocabulary to their reading of the novel. Some students also wrote how their speaking ability improved in the process of discussing the novel or doing the activities in English. Further, in the post-course questionnaire survey, about 75 percent of the respondents agreed that their English had improved, and that they had learned many new words from the novel. In addition, about 90 percent of them considered it a good way to learn English through the unsimplified novel, and 80 percent agreed that they would continue to improve their English by reading other unsimplified novels in the future.

In addition to language learning gains, both qualitative and quantitative data also reveal the impact of this cooperative learning experience on the students' mastery and use of social skills. During interviews, the students often took the initiative in talking about the factors that they thought had influenced their intergroup cooperation. In reflective essays, many students wrote about the social outcomes they had benefited from this learning experience, such as having more courage to express their opinions in front of people, knowing how to cooperate with others, how to communicate with others, how to express their opinions, and how to negotiate with people having different opinions. Other social outcomes included how to recognize the importance of being responsible for one's share of work, how to listen to others, and how to respect divergent views. According to the post-course questionnaire data, 77 percent of the respondents practiced their interactive skills in group discussions, 80 percent of respondents agreed that their negotiating and interaction skills had improved, and 86 percent noted that this cooperative learning experience had taught them how to work better in a group.

5. Increasing interest in English language learning

In the students' reflective writing, the most frequently-used adjectives are "good" (59 times) and "interesting" (50 times). During interviews, the interviewees often mentioned how much this LFCL project had changed their attitude toward learning English. Most of the students had no or little experience of tackling unsimplified English novels and had not even heard of cooperative learning before the project started. Even so, they made many positive comments on this cooperative way of learning English through the novel in the interview and reflective writing data. The post-course questionnaire data also indicates that 65 percent of the respondents agreed that the use of the novel and the cooperative learning activities had added a lot of fun and pleasure to the English learning process, and 70 percent of students felt that this cooperative learning experience had greatly increased their interest in learning the target language. All this feedback is in line with my own reflections on the classroom atmosphere, where words like "fun" and "excitement" were often used to describe what was going on in class and in the small groups.

Factors Perceived to Influence the LFCL Experience

The findings of the present study also show that the effects of and the students' responses to the LFCL project were greatly influenced by time-related, material-related and group-related factors as well as their personal preferred learning style.

1. Time-related factors

Most of the students responded positively to learning English through the novel, but one student in the B-level course and several students in the C-level course complained about how they have found it time-consuming and difficult to keep up with the reading schedule for the novel. For students with poorer English language proficiency, the time factor inevitably influenced their attitude toward the reading task. In addition, the time factor also affected some students' attitude toward cooperative learning. Thirty-six students complained in their reflective essays that they spent "too much time" out of class for this project, and that sometimes it could be extremely difficult for the whole group to meet outside the classroom, whether online or face to face. These qualitative findings explain why the majority of respondents to the post-course questionnaire survey preferred to do cooperative learning activities in class.

2. Material-related factors

Although the majority of my students liked the novel I had chosen for them, inevitably the novel appealed more to some students than to others. Six students made it clear in their reflective essays that they had no interest in fantasy, so they did not really enjoy reading the Narnia story. By contrast, the interview data and the feedback on individual activities show that not all the students had the same preferences. This meant some students might find an activity fun or easy, while others might find an activity boring or hard. For example, some students preferred to do activities that required them to take a closer look at the text, while others favored activities that allowed them to use their imagination and creativity. Both qualitative and quantitative date provide evidence that these material-related factors would affect the students' feedback to the LFCL project to some extent. The more they liked the book or the activities, the more positive responses they gave about them.

3. Group-related factors

The qualitative data showed several group-related negative comments. Some interviewees complained that they had to play more than one discussion role or were given more work to do if anyone in the group was absent; some wished that others in their group had been more responsible for their share of work. It is not surprising that those students who did not think that others in their group had contributed enough to the group work tended to consider cooperative learning a disappointing rather than beneficial way of learning. These students needed to do a lot of extra work to make the group function properly.

4. Personal preferred learning style

Although a lot of evidence showed that most of the students took a very positive attitude toward cooperative learning, unfortunately this learning format did not appeal to all students. Some 23 percent of respondents to the post-course questionnaire survey did not think this learning experience made them like learning together more than learning alone. There is no doubt that their preferred learning style would affect their motivation to cooperate with others as well as their feedback to this project. What is worse, their negative attitude toward cooperative learning sometimes damaged the cooperative work in their groups and even their group mates' responses to this format of learning.

Conclusion

The importance (or innovation) of the current study lies in its attempt to fill in research and pedagogical gaps at the intersection of literature and cooperative learning in the field of ELT. Paran argues that much of the discussion on literature in language education is "not in English," so research is "urgently needed" on what approach English teachers are taking to using literature in the language classroom, how their students are reacting to it, and what they feel to be the advantage (2006, pp. 9–10). The limitations of this study, such as the small number of participants with similar sociocultural and linguistic backgrounds, the short-term intervention period (18 weeks), and my role as the teacher of the target students may reduce the possibility to yield richer and more meaningful or valid results.

Even so, the study carries useful and significant implications for integrating literature and cooperative learning in EFL contexts. For example, the findings provide an assurance that, with the help of cooperative learning, English teachers need not worry so much about choosing the wrong literary text. The students who do not really like the text can still be highly motivated to go on the reading journey as they share and discuss what they read with others and work together on the cooperative learning activities centering on the novel. In addition, it is advised to engage in diverse activities so as to vary the cooperative learning process and satisfy different students' needs and interests. Last but not least, teachers who want to use a similar LFCL project with non-English major students have to give careful consideration to the total amount of time and work required to finish the reading and the cooperative work because these students may not wish to invest a great deal of time and energy in English learning tasks.

Future research may compare the effects of using a simplified novel and an unsimplified novel with non-English majors, or study the outcomes of integrating literature and cooperative learning in ELT in primary and secondary school settings. Further, in the current, small-scale, semester-long study, the participants all attended one university in Taiwan, taking my 18-week long *Sophomore English* course. So, it is also suggested that future research be extended on a larger scale to compare how non-English majors in different learning, linguistic or culture contexts may respond to the integration of literature and cooperative learning differently. Or the LFCL project could be used with the same group of language learners for a longer period of time to trace its long-term effects on their English learning interest, motivation and performance.

My students' positive responses to the LFCL project have encouraged me to share this cooperative way of using literature in ELT with teachers who are also interested in using literature with their students but still wondering how to do it effectively. As Showalter points out, "the best way to learn how to teach is to try to show someone else how to do it" (2003, p. viii). It is hoped that a complete picture of the literature-focused, cooperative learning approach has been drawn clearly enough to lay the "foundations" and offer "support, validation, and a sense of renewal" for those who are ready to unleash the potential of literature and cooperative learning in their language classrooms (DaSilva Iddings 2006, p. 180).

References

Allan, M. 1985, *Teaching English with Video*, Harlow: Longman

Belcher, D. and A. Hirvela. 2000, "Literature and L2 composition: Revisiting the debate", *Journal of Second Language Writing* 9(1): 21–39

Boyd, M. and V.M. Maloof. 2000, "How teachers can build on student-proposed intertextual links to facilitate student talk in the ESL classroom". In J.K. Hall and L.S. Verplaetse, eds, *Second and Foreign Languages Learning through Classroom Interaction*, Mahwah, N.J.: Erlbaum, pp. 163–82

Bruffee, K.A. 1995, "Sharing our toys: cooperative learning versus collaborative learning", *Change* January/February: 12–18

Butler, I. 2006, "A brighter future? Integrating language and literature for first-year university students". In A. Paran, ed, *Literature in Language Teaching and Learning*, Alexandria: TESOL, Inc., pp. 11–25

Carter, R. and M.N. Long. 1987, *The Web of Words: Exploring Literature through Language*, Cambridge: Cambridge University Press

Chambers E. and M. Gregory. 2006, *Teaching & Learning English Literature*, London: Sage

Collie, J. and S. Slater. 1987, *Literature in the Language Classroom*, Cambridge: Cambridge University Press

Creswell, J.W. 2003, *Research Design: Qualitative, Quantitative, and Mixed Methods Approaches*, 2nd ed. Thousand Oaks, CA: Sage

—. 2008, *The Mixed Methods Reader*, Los Angeles: Sage

DaSilva Iddings, A.C. 2006. "Conclusion". In S.G. McCafferty, G.M. Jacobs and A.C. DaSilva Iddings, eds, *Cooperative Learning and Second Language Teaching*, Cambridge: Cambridge University Press, pp. 177–80

Dörnyei, Z. 2001, *Motivational Strategies in the Language Classroom*, Cambridge: Cambridge University Press

—. 2003, *Questionnaires in Second Language Research: Construction, administration and processing*, London: Lawrence Erlbaum Associates

—. 2007, *Research Methods in Applied Linguistics*, Oxford: Oxford University Press

Dowsett, G. 1986, "Interaction in the semi-structured interview". In M. Emery, ed, *Qualitative Research*, Canberra: Australian Association of Adult Education, pp. 50–56

Duff, A. and A. Maley. 1990, *Literature*, Oxford: Oxford University Press

Fox, T.R. 1997, "Refuting the skeptics: the argument for literature in the language Classroom", *Hwa Kang Journal of English Language & Literature* 3: 29–37

Gillies, R.M. 2007, "Structuring co-operative learning experiences in primary school". In R.M. Gillies and A.F. Ashman, eds, *Co-operative Learning: The social and intellectual outcomes of learning in groups*, London and New York: RoutledgeFalmer, pp. 36–53

Hall, G. 2005, *Literature in Language Education*, New York: Palgrave Macmillan

Hill, J. 1986, *Teaching Literature in the Language Classroom*, London: Macmillan

Jacob, E. 1999, *Cooperative Learning in Context: An Educational Innovation in Everyday Classrooms*, New York: State University of New York Press

Jacobs, G.M., S.G. McCafferty and A.C. DaSilva Iddings. 2006, "Roots of cooperative learning in general education". In S.G. McCafferty, G.M. Jacobs and A.C. DaSilva Iddings, eds, *Cooperative Learning and Second Language Teaching*, Cambridge: Cambridge University Press, pp. 9–17

Jacobs, R.A. 1994, "A Place for Literature in the Language Classroom?" *Guidelines* 16(2): 29–37

Kessler, C. ed. 1992, *Cooperative Language Learning*, Englewood Cliffs, N.J.: Prentice Hall Regents

Lazar, G. 1993, *Literature and Language Teaching*, Cambridge: Cambridge University Press

Lewis, C.S. 1998, *The Lion, the Witch and the Wardrobe*, London: HarperCollins

Morgan, D.L. 1996, "Focus Groups", *Annual Review of Sociology* 22: 129–52

Panitz, T. 1997, "Collaborative versus cooperative learning: comparing the two definitions helps understand the nature of interactive learning", *Cooperative Learning and College Teaching* 8(2): 5–7

Paran, A. 2006, "The Stories of Literature and Language Teaching". In A. Paran, ed, *Literature in Language Teaching and Learning*, Alexandria: TESOL, Inc., pp. 1–10

—. 2008, "Literature in foreign language learning and teaching", *Language Teaching* 41(4): 465–96

Santos, M.D. 2003, *Super Goal Student Book 6*, New York: McGraw-Hill Education

Showalter, E. 2003, *Teaching Literature*, Oxford: Blackwell Publishing

Stewart, D.W., P.N. Shamdasani and D.W. Rook. 2007, *Focus Groups: Theory and Practice*, 2nd ed, Thousand Oaks, CA: Sage

Tsai, Y.H. 1996, "Classification of Textbooks for Freshman English Classes in Taiwan: Contents and Language", *Hwa Kang Journal of Foreign Languages & Literature* 3: 151–79

Ushioda, E. 1996, *Learner Autonomy 5: the Role of Motivation*, Dublin: Authentik

Yang, A. 2002, "Science fiction in the EFL class", *Language, Culture and Curriculum* 5(1): 50–60

Chapter Eleven

The Importance of Writing in Mathematics: Quantitative Analysis of U.S. English Learners' Academic Language Proficiency and Mathematics Achievement

Rosalie Grant, Rita MacDonald, Aek Phakiti and H. Gary Cook

Keywords: academic language, ACCESS, English learners, mathematics

Abstract

It is often said that mathematics has its own language. The challenge to English language learners of mathematics' multisemiotic nature, with symbols, equations, and graphs, has been clearly described by Schleppegrell (2007). But what about the language itself? Can knowledge about the language of mathematics assist U.S. educators facing persistent achievement gaps between English Learners (ELs) and proficient English speakers (Goldenberg & Coleman 2010)? How can our understanding of academic language contribute to this effort?

Structural equation modeling (SEM), a quantitative methodology examining relationships and underlying structures among measures, was applied to measures of academic language and mathematics. The analysis revealed clear relationships between writing skill and mathematics achievement. The strength of the observed relationships calls for the development of an approach supporting the integration of writing and mathematics instruction.

This chapter discusses this intersection of applied linguistics and mathematics education in relation to a growing need for cross-disciplinary collaboration. Combining new resources (CCSSO 2012b & 2012c) with strategies derived from Systemic Functional Linguistics (SFL) (Halliday 1994; Schleppegrell 2004), we outline meaning-centered writing activities that can easily be integrated into mathematics lessons to provide students with essential practice in the careful, precise writing needed to effectively articulate complex mathematical thinking.

Introduction

Educators in the United States face the combined challenges of a persistent achievement gap between fluent English speakers (FES) and English learners (ELs), rapidly increasing growth of the EL subgroup in K-12 classrooms, and training that has not prepared teachers to integrate second language instruction into content disciplines and mainstream classrooms. Added to this is a national initiative focused on developing advanced literacy skills across all disciplines for all students, including ELs.

Given these challenges, it is important to identify which aspects of academic language contribute most significantly to academic achievement. This research examines that question through structural equation modeling (SEM), a quantitative methodology that examines relationships and underlying structures among measures, applied to measures of academic language and mathematics. The analysis revealed skill in writing to be foundational to mathematics achievement.

The strength of the observed relationships calls for the development of an approach that supports the integration of writing and mathematics instruction. This chapter calls for collaboration among language specialists and mathematics educators to develop mathematics-focused writing strategies, and offers examples of such strategies that can easily be embedded into mathematics lessons.

Challenges to academic performance among English learners

This chapter discusses a research foundation for, and suggested implementation of, strategies to improve English learners (ELs)' mathematics achievement in U.S. classrooms—a context in which educators face a set of challenges for which they are ill-prepared. The number of ELs in K-12 classrooms is growing at a rate far surpassing that of the FES population, with more than 20 percent of school-age children having a native language other than English (Planty et al. 2009). More than 10 percent of the total K-12 population have limited English language proficiency (ELP) and consistently rank lower than FES peers in academic performance (Goldenberg 2008). Related research consistently emphasizes the importance of specialized content instruction and systematic academic language development (August & Shanahan 2006; Goldenberg 2008;

Goldenberg & Coleman 2010), yet most teachers have had little training in teaching ELs (National Staff Development Council 2009). Further complicating this context is that, in many states, educators who support ELs are scattered thinly across many school districts: 75.3 percent of districts assessing EL students in a 27 state EL assessment consortium in 2011–12 enrolled fewer than 100 ELs (WIDA 2012, p. 13). In these low-incidence areas of the country, school budgets often do not support the hiring of sufficient English language development (ELD) specialists to adequately address the needs of this group. As a result, many ELs in these low incidence districts are placed immediately into general education, or "mainstream," classrooms, with little or no ELD specialist support available to them or to their teachers as they face the dual challenge of learning new content and learning it in a new language.

Call for increased academic literacy

Added to these difficulties for teachers is an increasing national awareness of the need for advanced literacy development for all students, FES and ELs. The *Common Core State Standards for English Language Arts, Literacy, and Literacy in History/Social Studies, Science, and Technical Studies* (CCSS) (National Governors Association for Best Practices and Council of Chief State School Officers 2010a) and the *Common Core State Standards for Mathematics* (CCSSM) (National Governors Association for Best Practices and Council of Chief State School Officers, 2010b) adopted in the United States by 45 states, the District of Columbia, and four territories, emphasize literacy training that goes beyond that of the English language arts (ELA) classroom to include reading and writing across all subjects—again calling for pedagogical content knowledge regarding writing, with which few teachers outside early elementary or ELA classrooms have been equipped.

The relationship between ELP and academic achievement

As educators revise curricula and instruction to meet these newly articulated expectations, it is critical to attend to the needs of ELs. Given the realities of the lack of teacher training in ELD and the scarcity of ELD specialist resources in many districts, it is important to equip mathematics, science, and social studies teachers with tightly focused strategies for the development of ELs' discipline-specific language proficiency. Toward that end, SEM analyses recently completed at the WIDA Consortium can assist in identifying high-leverage strategies by examining the relationships between ELP and academic achievement. This chapter reports the examination of the relationship of the elements of ELP to achievement in mathematics, discusses the importance of integrating writing into mathematics curricula, and offers brief, mathematics-focused writing strategies that can easily and quickly be incorporated into mathematics lessons. An overview of relevant research follows.

Research on ELs' writing proficiency and mathematics achievement

Academic ELP refers to the ability to successfully use language for communication and learning in the classroom and school environment (Anstrom et al. 2010). This is essential for ELs' academic success in the classroom and on standardized, high-stakes tests administered in schools (Francis et al. 2006; Snow & Kim 2007).

Although research examining the contribution of academic ELP to ELs' mathematics performance has found that students with limited ELP performed significantly less well than FES (e.g. Abedi & Lord 2001; Francis & Rivera 2007), few studies to date have investigated the predictive validity of English language tests for ELs' subsequent mathematics success. Butler and Castellon-Wellington (2000/2005) examined Grades 3 and 11 ELs' ELP and mathematics achievement as assessed by standardized tests. The English-only group outperformed ELs on language and content assessments, suggesting that ELP could account for one quarter of ELs' academic performance on another content measure. Kim and Herman (2008), through hierarchical linear modeling, found strongly positive associations between ELP and content-area achievement (including mathematics) across three states. On the Assessing Comprehension and Communication in English State-to-State for English Language Learners assessment (ACCESS for ELLs®; hereafter ACCESS), Cook, Hicks, Lee and Freshwater (2009) found strong positive relationships between ACCESS ELP scores and scores on mathematics content assessments for ELs in Grades 3-5. Another study by Parker et al. (2009) shows that ACCESS reading and writing scores are significant predictors of reading, writing, and mathematics scores on large-scale content assessments for Grades 5 and 8 ELs. The current study investigates more closely the differential contributions of the language domains (i.e. speaking, listening, reading and writing) to achievement on state mathematics tests.

Analytical method for the study

SEM was selected as an appropriate methodology with which to investigate the relationship between academic language and mathematics achievement. The goal was not to establish causality, but to increase understanding of a complex set of relationships between ELs' ELP and mathematical achievement across different contexts. The study deals with multivariate, complex issues, and the data used were non-experimental. As Kaplan (2009) notes, SEM enables assessment of complex patterns of relationships between underlying constructs (latent variables or factors). A myriad of variables and constructs influence the development of ELP and academic achievement. The interaction among these language proficiency and mathematics variables and constructs is the subject of this study. Advantages of SEM over other possible techniques, such as multiple regression, include constructs being inferred from several observed variables and free of random error, and investigating variables simultaneously rather than sequentially (Alavifar et al. 2012). Both direct and indirect relationships between constructs can be identified and analyzed using SEM. The conventional approach to SEM uses hypothetico-deductive reasoning in which theories are confirmed or refuted by testing observable predictions under experimental conditions. Spanos (1995) argues that, with respect to econometrics, the use of the hypothetico-deductive approach to modeling is not well suited to non-experimental data because experimental design reasoning is applied to purely observational, not experimental, data.

Alternative approaches to conventional hypothetico-deductive modeling in the social sciences include those proposed by Kaplan (2009) and Haig (2009). For Haig, the hypothetico-deductive approach values logic and evaluates theories according to their predictive success. His approach to modeling not only emphasizes logic, but also values the explanatory power and worth of the model. Bearing in mind the varying views of the appropriateness of the conventional hypothetico-deductive approach to SEM with non-experimental data, the authors adopted an analytical approach, which was consistent with approaches proposed by Kaplan and Haig.

Setting, participants, and data

Setting and participants

The research question was investigated using data from 30,776 ELs in two grade-level clusters (Grades 3–5 and 6–8) in one U.S. state. The state had over 300 school districts and between 46,000 and 47,000 ELs in Grades K–12. These data were sufficient to form eight cohorts of students in various situations. The native language of most students was Spanish; the second most common native language was Hmong. Males made up a slight majority of the student population in each grade-level cluster.

English language proficiency assessment (ACCESS)

ACCESS is a large-scale assessment of academic ELP. Tests are administered in the second half of each school year, with test items based on *WIDA's English Language Proficiency Standards* (Gottlieb et al. 2007). WIDA's standards describe the expectations that educators have of ELs in five different grade-level clusters (K, 1-2, 3-5, 6-8, and 9-12); in five content areas: social and instructional language, language arts, mathematics, science, and social studies; and in four language domains: listening, speaking, reading, and writing.

Different test formats are used to assess academic ELP. Speaking tests are locally scored by trained raters within schools using an adaptive assessment methodology (where students start sections at appropriate levels and stop when they reach their "ceilings"). Listening and reading tests are multiple-choice, group administered, and machine scored. Trained raters score the writing assessment. The arrangement of the 20 ACCESS measures of the five ELP standards used for analyses across the four language domains is shown in Table 11-1. The array of 20 measures shown in Table 11-1 comes from teacher reports provided with assessment results. For more detail on these measures, see WIDA (2014). Note that listening and reading measures are combined for each standard, reflecting receptive language skills. Measures of three aspects of writing are provided: language complexity, language control, and vocabulary usage. These measures are combined for language arts and social studies. Speaking measures for the languages of mathematics and science, and of language arts and social studies, are also combined. To accommodate the wide range of ELP levels, ACCESS tests are divided into three distinct tiers: A, B, and C. Tier A forms are administered to the lowest ELP levels,

Tier B to intermediate levels, and Tier C to the highest levels. Students are placed in the tiers that best match their ELP levels.

Table 11-1: ACCESS variables: English language proficiency standards across language domains

English Language Proficiency Standards					
Language domain elements	Mathematics	Science	Language/ Arts	Social studies	Social and Instructional
Listening/ reading	X	X	X	X	X
Writing					
Linguistic complexity	X	X		A	X
Language control	X	X		A	X
Vocabulary usage	X	X		A	X
Speaking		A		A	X

Note: Linguistic complexity is the amount and quality of writing in a given situation. Language control is the comprehensibility of the communication level based on the amount and types of errors. Vocabulary usage is the specificity of words or phrases for a given context (Gottlieb et al. 2007). A is a measure that is an aggregate of two ELP standards.

Test validity can be understood in terms of arguments related to evidence and use (Bachman & Palmer 2010; Kane 2006), with validity understood as a measure of the extent to which decisions based on test results are supported by evidence and theory. For ACCESS, the main inferences made are whether an EL has sufficient academic ELP to participate in a mainstream classroom without English language support and whether a child has made meaningful progress in developing ELP. Test developers for ACCESS provide several pieces of evidence to support that use. For example, Kenyon (2006) details how test developers grounded the items in the *WIDA English Language Proficiency Standards* (Gottlieb et al. 2007). Items produced for the test are rigorously reviewed to ensure that the content and language are appropriate for particular student groups (see MacGregor et al. 2009 for a description of these reviews).

State Mathematics Assessment

The state mathematics test consisted of multiple-choice, short answer and/or constructed response test items. Depending on grade level, between 14 percent and 20 percent of the score points came from short answer and/or constructed response items. Measures of six mathematics content strands were available (e.g. mathematical processes, numbers and operations, statistics and probability, and algebraic relationships).

The state education department establishes the reliability and validity of the mathematics test through a structured process of expert review, field testing, and analyses. Acceptable reliability indices are established using Cronbach's α statistic or the associated estimated Item Response Theory (IRT)-based reliability index. Several procedures provide evidence of content validity. All items are calibrated using IRT and these items are used to scale the items and students onto a common framework.

Assessment data

Data were available for eight models established from eight cohorts with matched ACCESS and state mathematics assessment (see Table 11-2). The study analyzed data comprised of two grade-level clusters, two tiers, across two consecutive school years. Complete datasets were established by matching the ELP scores from the year-end administration in one school year with the standardized scores of the same students in the following year-onset administration of the state mathematics tests. Each cohort was judged homogenous and representative of the relevant population. The numbers in each cohort are shown in Table 11-2.

Table 11-2: Number of students in each cohort

Grade-level Clusters	School year 1		School year 2	
	Tier B	Tier C	Tier B	Tier C
3–5	3,590	3,701	3,801	4,038
6–8	3,942	4,319	2,623	4,762

Although all students in the population took the mandatory tests, ACCESS and mathematics, some data were missing from the datasets provided. Whether particular data points were missing randomly, in part, completely, or related to observed variables or latent constructs, or any combination of these possibilities, could not be identified. SEM assumes that the units of analysis are complete (Kaplan 2009, p. 92). To deal with missing data, the authors considered whether they had sufficient information from which to impute the missing data by means and regression imputation as discussed by Muthén and Muthén (2010). However, given that it could not be determined whether any particular data point was missing due to randomness or some other reason, there was insufficient information with which to justify imputation decisions for the 20 ELP measures, 6 mathematics measures, and 3 variables identifying the 8 cohorts. Further influencing the authors' decision was the study's purpose as theory forming, aimed at providing insights into the relationships between ELP and mathematics achievement for ELs from varied situations. Consequently, it was deemed prudent to establish complete datasets relying only on the information provided, subject to adequate cell sizes. Population proportions captured in each dataset are shown in Table 11-3.

Table 11-3: Percentages of eligible students within each cohort

Grade-level Clusters	School year 1		School year 2	
	Tier B	Tier C	Tier B	Tier C
3–5	59.1	74.6	63.3	74.5
6–8	89.8	97.0	89.7	97.7

Overview of the SEM process

A 3-step modeling process (Hatcher 2007) established models for each cohort. Data were analyzed with the software programs SAS 9.3 and Mplus 6.12. To identify the nature and number of underlying constructs in the data, exploratory factor analyses (EFAs) were first undertaken with each cohort. In the second step, confirmatory factor analyses (CFAs) were performed to reveal relationships between these constructs. For the final step, structural models were created to identify the pattern by which particular constructs relate to, or predict, or are associated with, other constructs, and to identify the relative strengths of those predictive relationships. Models show how the constructs work in concert with each other. It is important to remember that, in this study, the models do not lead to longitudinal analyses. They do not show the development of constructs over time, but rather the constructs operative at the time when these students were tested. So, in this study, SEM was used to identify the constructs students needed to bring to bear to succeed in the testing situation, and which constructs were more salient than others as related to mathematics achievement. Decisions to modify and accept a model as final were guided by whether it was meaningful conceptually, not just statistically. As a rule, more parsimonious structures were preferred and judged as being credible by linguists and mathematics educators.

Results

Constructs from Exploratory and Confirmatory Factor Analyses

The EFA results for all of the eight cohorts indicated that the academic ELP and mathematics achievement variables could be grouped into seven meaningful constructs. The language proficiency constructs were based primarily on the language domains rather than the specific academic languages of the content areas, although the constructs for writing did separate out by content areas. These constructs included all the mathematics variables and 19 of the 20 ACCESS measures of ELP. (One ACCESS measure, reading/listening in social and instructional language, was omitted due to small construct loadings.) Ideally, measures for reading and listening would have been analyzed separately, but, as shown in Table 11-1, individual measures were not available.

Given the theories underpinning the development of ACCESS measures, particularly those related to the interdependence of language domains (Boals et al. 2009), the authors expected EFA and CFA models to include all four language domains. While it was anticipated that proficiency in mathematics and science academic languages would have some common characteristics and be included in the models, the CFAs indicated that the final models were likely to include proficiency in other academic language areas as well, including social and instructional language. Although the magnitudes of the relationships differed for each cohort, the same ACCESS and mathematics measures were revealed in all models. Having found preliminary evidence to address the research question ("Are some elements of ELP more closely related to mathematics achievement than others?"), the analyses proceeded to investigate the directions and magnitudes of the structural relationships among the constructs.

Final SEM models for eight cohorts

All SEM models retained the same language proficiency and mathematical achievement measures and constructs found in the CFA models, and all had acceptable fit statistics and were meaningful conceptually. More parsimonious models were preferred. While the magnitudes of the standardized path coefficients between individual constructs and fit statistics varied across the models, a consistent pattern in the structural arrangement of the constructs emerged across cohorts.

Fig. 11-1: Structural model, Grade-level Cluster 3-5, Tier B, School Year 1 (N= 3,590)

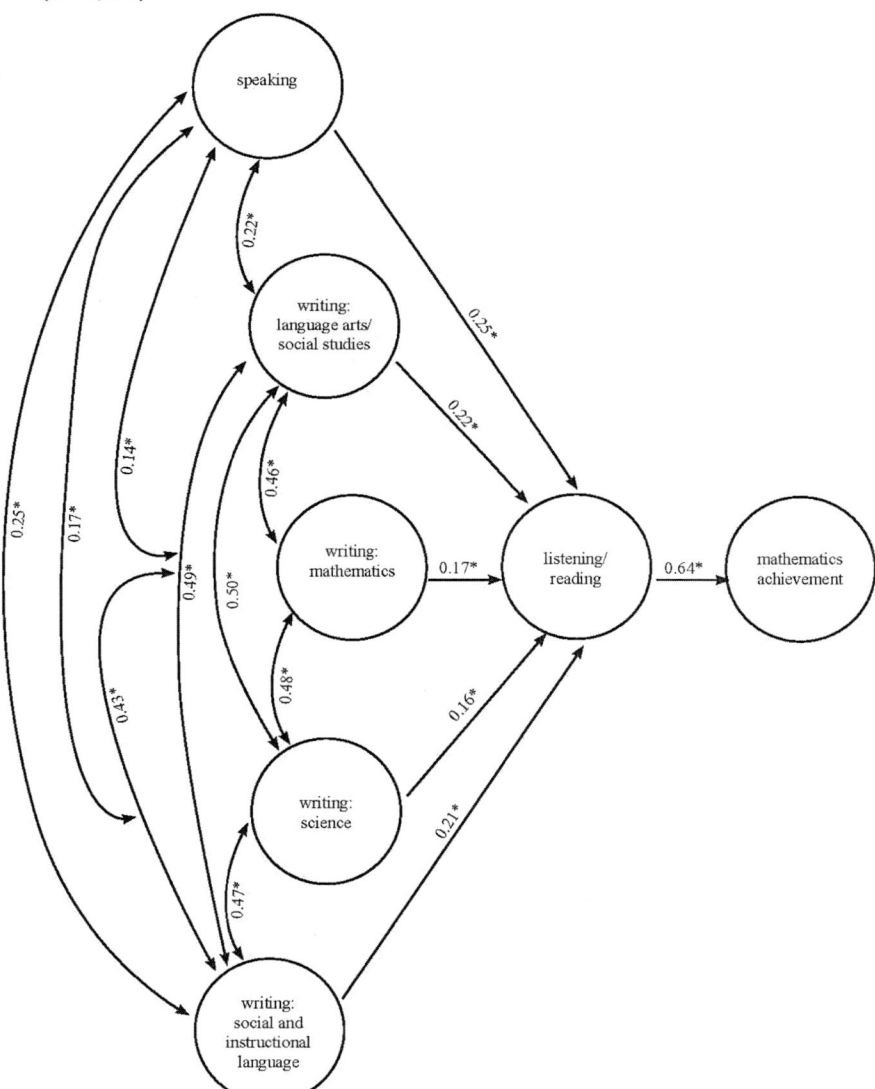

Note: (1) * = p<0.05; (2) Goodness of fit indices with MLR estimator: Chi-square test of model fit = 538.4, d.f. = 259; RMSEA = 0.017 with 90% CI = 0.015 to 0.019; CFI = 0.992; TLI = 0.991; and SRMR = 0.019.

Fig. 11-1 is an example of the magnitudes and directions of the relationships among the constructs for one cohort, Grade-level Cluster 3–5, Tier B, and School Year 1.

The authors found that writing skills in all of the academic languages of the five content areas, together with speaking skills, directly influenced reading/listening, which directly influenced mathematics achievement. Although there was some variability in the strength of the relationships in different models, the directions of those relationships were the same in six of the eight models and the overall pattern of relationships was consistent across the models. The outliers were models for cohorts in Grade-level Cluster 3–5, Tier C, and School Years 1 and 2. In each of those models, the path between writing in mathematics and reading/listening was not statistically significant. Further modeling for these two cohorts revealed two writing constructs (language arts/social studies, and social and instructional language) that directly influenced the other two writing constructs (mathematics and science). These two constructs in turn directly influenced reading/listening. Even so, models for all eight cohorts explained between 27 percent and 50 percent of the mathematics performance variances. Given the many variables purported to influence ELs' mathematics achievement, and that 80 percent to 86 percent of the score points were allocated to multiple-choice items, these percentages were considered high.

Measuring impact on mathematics achievement

This general pattern across the models can be viewed through the lens of productive and receptive language skills. Interestingly, the productive language skills (writing and speaking) directly influence the receptive language skills (reading and listening). The models suggest that proficiency in the written aspects of academic languages and in speaking underpins proficiency in the receptive language domains and subsequently influences mathematics performance.

The importance of writing skills in mathematics achievement can be seen by comparing the indirect effects of different constructs on mathematics achievement. The indirect effects, shown in Table 11-4, indicate that speaking does not seem to have salient discipline-specific characteristics. Similar relationships were found in the other models, except for Grades 3–5, Tier C, and Year 1 in which the effects of the combined writing skills and speaking on mathematics were the same. The form of the test could have influenced the result for this particular model. The overall results could be explained in part by ACCESS writing items being more finely differentiated, and the assessment of writing being more reliable than for speaking. However, although both speaking and writing constructs incorporated the same academic languages—mathematics, science, language arts, social studies, and social and instructional languages—the analysis identified four distinct writing constructs, not just one construct as for speaking.

Table 11-4: Indirect effects of productive language constructs on mathematics achievement, Grade-level Cluster 3–5, Tier B, School Year 1

Construct	Indirect effects
Individual constructs	
speaking	0.16
writing: language arts/social studies	0.14
writing: social and instructional language	0.13
writing: mathematics	0.11
writing: science	0.10
All writing constructs	0.48
Ratio (all writing/speaking)	3.00

Enhancing the explanatory power

Given the unexpected nature of these relationships, particularly writing's strong influence on mathematics achievement, the authors were interested in enhancing the explanatory power of the models. One strategy is to investigate whether there is evidence for a more generalized construct in the models—a higher-order construct, in SEM terminology. Higher-order constructs represent a higher level of abstraction than do constructs identified from examining observed responses from students to test items, the observed variables. Evidence of higher-order constructs is not obtained directly from observed variables, but indirectly through the variables of lower-order constructs. As noted earlier, the concept of academic English language involves a set of complex linguistic, cognitive, and sociocultural relationships.

Fig. 11-2: Structural model for Grade-level Cluster 3—5, Tier B, School Year (N=3,590)

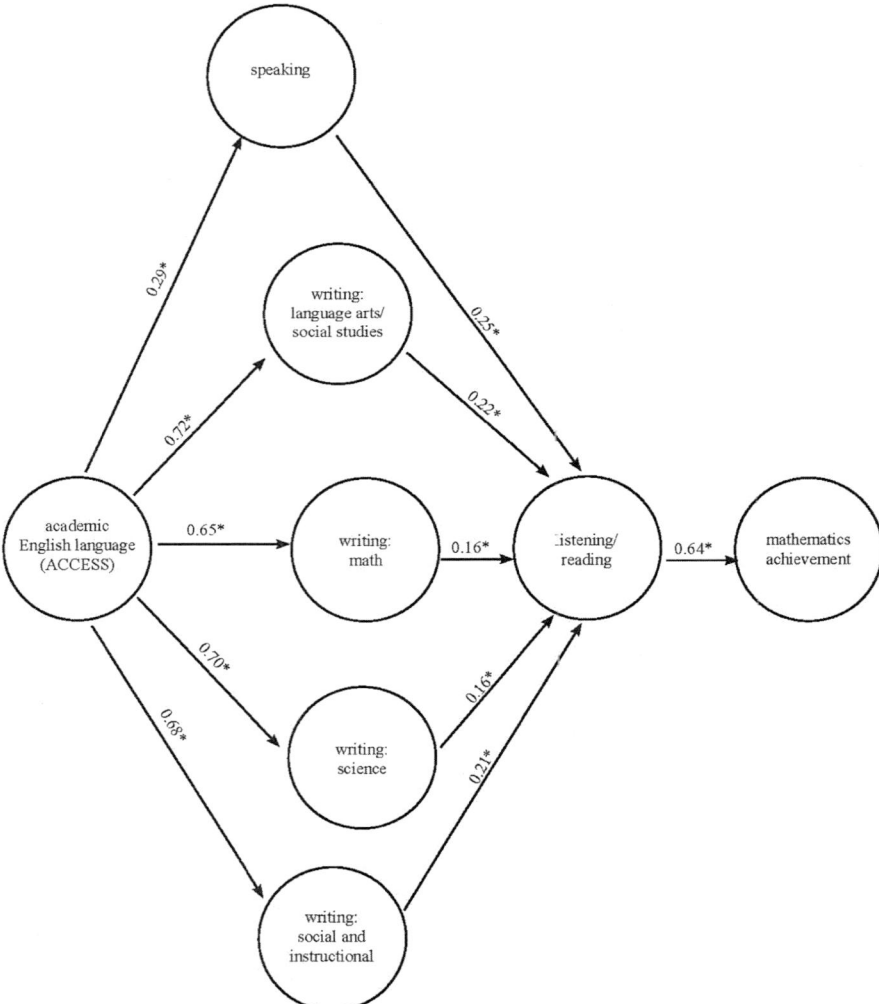

Note: (1) *=p<0.05; (2) Goodness of fit indices with MLR estimator: Chi-square test of model fit = 560.1, d.f. = 264; RMSEA = 0.018 with 90% CI = 0.016 to 0.020; CFI = 0.992; TLI = 0.991; and SRMR = 0.020

Fig. 11-3: Schematic representation of SEM relationships

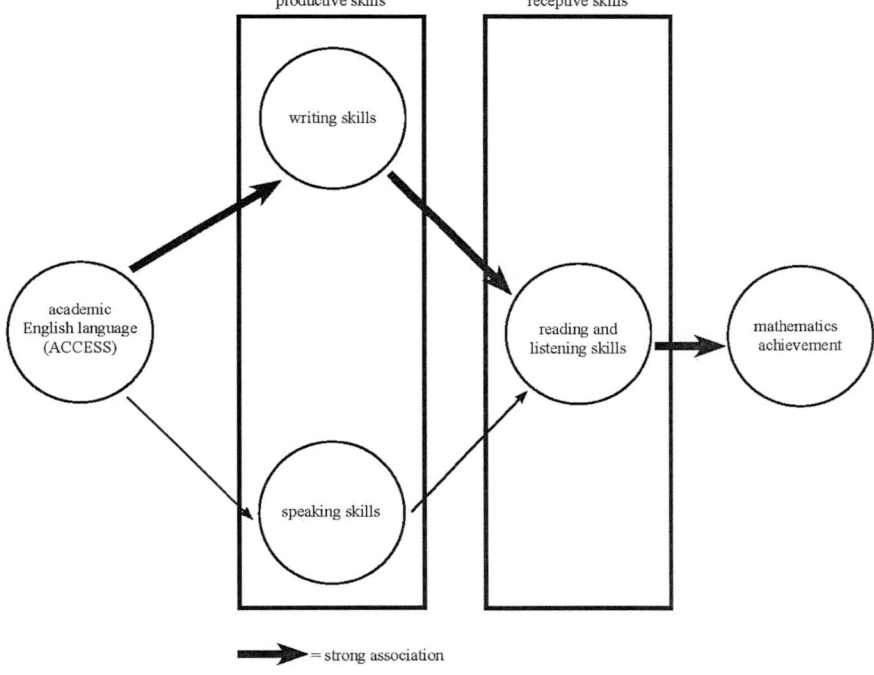

Despite this complexity, if ACCESS is intended to measure academic ELP, then analyses should reveal at least indicative evidence of a higher-order construct. The authors postulated that evidence of a higher-order construct would be linked directly to all or some language proficiency constructs and not directly to mathematics achievement.

Analyses revealed evidence of a higher-order construct the authors have named *Academic English Language as measured by ACCESS* (Academic English Language (ACCESS)). This construct directly influences the productive skills of speaking and writing and indirectly contributes to the receptive skills of reading/listening and, ultimately, to mathematics achievement, as shown in Fig. 11-2 for the cohort, Grade-level Cluster 3–5, Tier B and School Year 1. Fig. 11-2 shows a schematic representation of those same SEM relationships. When considering the degree to which certain constructs influence mathematics achievement, the higher-order construct has an important role. Evidence of the relative strength of its influence on productive language skills is obtained by considering the magnitudes of its association to each of the productive language skills constructs. Across all models, the average effect of the higher-order construct on each writing construct ranges from 2.4 to 2.9 times larger than its effect on speaking. Similar results were found through analyses of a second state's data.

Discussion

These results highlight the directly predictive role of receptive skills in ELs' mathematics achievement, and the foundational role of writing to receptive skills. Across eight settings (two school years, each with two grade-level clusters representing six grades, and two language proficiency levels), SEM revealed a strong association between ELP and mathematics achievement, with writing as fundamental to that relationship. While receptive skills are correctly thought to be closely associated with mathematics achievement and have significant instructional time devoted to them, including attention to vocabulary and word problems, our findings, consistent with other research (Butler & Castellon-Wellington 2000/2005; Huang & Nomandia 2007; Johanning 2000; Kim & Herman 2008) suggest that there may be much to gain by helping students produce mathematics language, in speech and in writing.

The authors found that the higher-order construct called Academic English Language (ACCESS) directly influenced the written and spoken aspects of ELs' academic ELP and, ultimately, mathematics achievement. The authors postulate that the higher-order construct may capture aspects of academic ELP as proposed by the Boals et al.'s (2009) theoretical model of academic language. Yet general characteristics, such as strategic competence and other cognitive or meta-cognitive strategies, which underpin performance on mathematics tests more broadly, may also be involved. Further, characteristics of test formats on ACCESS and state mathematics tests may feature in this underlying construct. The attributes of writing assessed by the state mathematics tests would be consistent with, but not necessarily duplicate, those represented in ACCESS-written ELP assessments. Given that state mathematics tests are designed, for example, to assess students' ability to connect and integrate mathematical processes with conceptual knowledge, mathematics rubrics for constructed response items could be expected to stress the importance of students demonstrating their understanding and communicating their ideas and conclusions effectively. While these attributes are also part of assessing written ELP,

ACCESS rubrics measure other attributes such as language control and linguistic complexity (Gottlieb et al. 2007).

Although SEM allows for a better understanding of the relationship between academic ELP and academic content achievement, it is not the only window into ELs' cognition. While the models linked different aspects of academic ELP to mathematics achievement, care should be taken not to generalize the models to other populations or curriculum areas. The results were based on data from one content area, mathematics, and the assumption was that the relationships were manifested in the same way across the grades within a grade-level cluster and for ELs with different characteristics, such as linguistic background. Particular limitations to note include (1) the time difference between assessing students' academic ELP and mathematics assessments; (2) any imprecision due to the aggregation of some ACCESS measures; and (3) the different methods used to assess speaking and non-speaking academic ELP tasks. Even so, it is critical to understand that all constructs in these statistical models are important and influence mathematics achievement. It would be incorrect to presume that focusing only on the writing of mathematics would be needed to improve ELs' mathematics achievement. Academic ELP constructs work in concert and influence one another.

Further research, using item-level analyses of the ELP and the mathematics assessment, would provide more specific information about the relationship of writing to mathematics achievement. Even so, the consistency of the present findings and the high percentage of variance in mathematics achievement predicted by the observed relationships make clear that simply having a detailed knowledge of mathematical concepts is insufficient for ELs' achievement in mathematics. To demonstrate their knowledge, students must know how to write. As state mathematics tests change to address the CCSS-related expectation that students demonstrate competence in explaining their reasoning, justifying conclusions, and specifying relevant conditions and constraints, the need for students to do so in writing will certainly increase. The results of these SEM analyses make clear the importance of providing explicit instruction in writing across the content areas.

Implications

This focus on writing would represent a change for mathematics teachers. While writing as an instructional strategy has not been completely absent in mathematics or other classrooms, the prevalence of writing in U.S. classrooms has been very low, consisting primarily of sentence completion and list-making, with some instances of multi-paragraph writing found mainly in English language arts and focused on personal narratives (Graham & Perin 2007). Recent promotion of mathematics-related discourse in K-12 classrooms remains focused on oral discourse (Celedón-Pattichis & Ramirez 2012; Herbel-Eisenmann & Cirillo 2009), with little attention to writing. Given the realities of the lack of teacher training in ELD and the scarcity of ELD specialist resources in many low-incidence districts, this call to integrate writing to support EL's mathematics achievement would require that mathematics teachers draw on resources not readily available. Faced with the need to close the FES-EL achievement gap in mathematics, we must consider whether limiting instruction to the customary focus on vocabulary and on reading and listening may be limiting ELs' mathematics achievement. Given writing's strong foundational role, the integration of writing into mathematics instruction may provide ELs critical opportunities.

Given many teachers' lack of pedagogical content knowledge related to writing for ELs, mathematics teachers will need help. Classroom-based research on the integration of academic writing into science classrooms (MacDonald et al. 2012) emphasizes that writing instruction must not be positioned as an optional "add-on," but as a method by which students learn content. It is important, therefore, that writing strategies for the mathematics classroom be deeply contextualized, tied tightly to mathematical understanding and practice, and easily embedded into mathematics lessons. The remainder of this chapter offers examples of strategies that integrate mathematical writing in a deeply contextualized, content-focused manner.

Writing strategies for mathematics

Key characteristics of mathematical language are its density and its precision (Fang & Schleppegrell 2008). Central to the new CCSSM are eight Standards for Mathematical Practice (SMPs) (National Governors Association for Best Practices and Council of Chief State School Officers, 2010b, pp. 6–8), all of which engage students in complex thinking and complex language, and all of which could be supported by regular attention to writing. We will focus our suggested writing activities on Standard 6: *Attend to precision*. Similar strategies can be devised to support other SMPs.

The linguistic construction of precise description is important in a variety of mathematical situations: understanding definitions, identifying specific entities, and describing the situation under which certain assumptions apply or do not apply. Consider these examples of precise mathematical language:

A tessellation is *a set of plane figures in a pattern covering the plane completely, with no gaps or overlaps.*
Calculate *the length of the longer of the two parallel lines intersecting the hypotenuse of the right triangle in the drawing above.*

Notice the italicized long noun phrases in the sentences above. Constructing precise meaning through long noun phrases is common in mathematics and science (Fang & Schleppegrell 2008; Fang, Lamme & Pringle 2010) and is extremely challenging for many students, especially ELs.

Writing activities can provide students with helpful practice of long noun phrases. Teachers can help students to develop precise, one-sentence descriptions of relevant features of a diagram, as shown in Fig. 11-4.

Fig. 11-4: A writing activity focused on precision in naming entities

Choose one of the bold lines in this drawing, and write a sentence telling someone to draw a circle around it.

Tell him or her, in one sentence, <u>exactly</u> which line you mean.

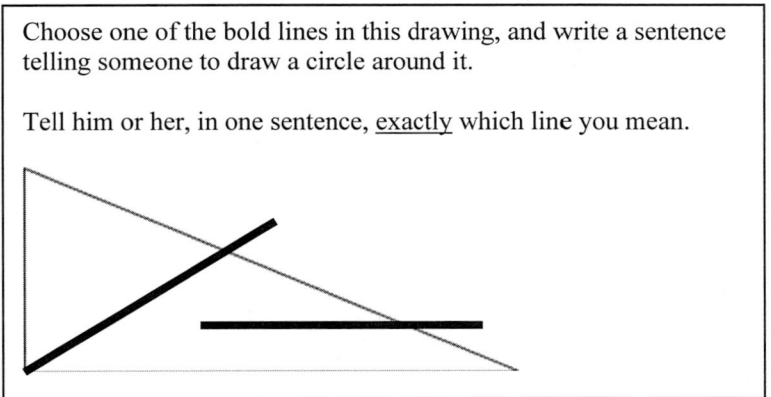

The writing activity provides practice in precisely naming mathematical entities, focuses on the mathematical concepts and the vocabulary and, through the stipulation to write only one sentence, on the construction of long noun phrases.

Similar writing activities can assist students to develop precision in naming circumstances and constraints—a skill critical to argumentation in mathematics. Students can be assigned to write one sentence naming the precise circumstances under which a four-sided figure is a square, and a companion sentence naming the circumstances under which it is not a square. The stipulation that the meaning be compacted into one written sentence provides essential practice with the long noun phrases so common to mathematics.

An additional writing activity, focused on teaching long noun phrases, involves engaging small groups of students in breaking a sentence with a long noun phrase into as many smaller sentences as possible and then reconstructing it. For example, the concise definition of a tessellation shown above might be deconstructed as:

> *A tessellation is a kind of pattern. Imagine a flat square. We call that a plane in mathematics class. The square is all filled up with this one kind of pattern, over and over. There aren't any holes left anywhere, and nothing overlaps.*

Groups compare their unique sets of sentences to make sure all essential elements defining tessellations are included. Following this, they recombine their own or another group's sentences by writing one long, "reconstituted" sentence similar in pattern to—but different from—the original. As students write to transform short, simple sentences back into more concise, densely packed "mathematics language," they will be practicing and learning from one another patterns that construct the long noun phrases common to the academic language of mathematics. Repeated practice transitioning between conversational and technical language has been described as central to learning the meaning-making patterns of mathematics (Lemke 2003).

During all of these writing activities, students are examining and practicing language while also gaining a deep understanding of mathematical concepts. These focused writing activities can be easily embedded into mathematics lessons, and provide the mathematics teacher simple means by which to incorporate into the curriculum the writing shown by the research described in this chapter to be a strong contributor to mathematics achievement.

Conclusion

This chapter has reported the use of SEM to identify the relative contributions of particular aspects of academic language to mathematics achievement for ELs. The analysis revealed skill in writing to be foundational to mathematics achievement. Additional research is needed to develop, implement, and assess the effects of writing strategies such as those suggested in this chapter. However, given the strength of these findings, it is clear that continued collaboration among applied linguists and mathematics instructors can prove helpful. Given the rigorous new standards adopted by many U.S. states, mathematics teachers need effective strategies to increase ELs' proficiency in language and in mathematics. Continued collaboration between mathematics educators and applied linguists can offer effective means by which to address the challenges that mathematics teachers, and the ELs they teach, face.

References

Abedi, J. and C. Lord. 2001, "The Language Factor in Mathematics Tests", *Applied Measurement in Education* 14(3): 219–34

Alavifar, A., M. Karimimalayer and M.K. Anuar. 2012, "The first and second generation of multivariate techniques", *Engineering Science and Technology: An International Journal* 2, 2: 326–29

Anstrom, K., P. DiCerbo, F. Butler, A. Katz, J. Millet and C. Rivera. 2010, *A Review of the Literature on Academic English: Implications for K-12 English Language Learners*, Arlington, VA: The George Washington University Center for Equity and Excellence in Education

August, D. and T. Shanahan, eds, 2006, *Developing Literacy in Second-Language Learners: Report of the National Literacy Panel on Language-Minority Children and Youth*, Mahwah, N.J.: Lawrence Erlbaum

Bachman, L. and A. Palmer. 2010, *Language Assessment in Practice*, Oxford: Oxford University Press

Boals, T., M. Gottlieb and A. Spalter. 2009, *The WIDA Consortium's conceptualization of academic language proficiency: A model rooted in language education theory and research*, Unpublished manuscript, University of Wisconsin-Madison

Butler, F., and M. Castellon-Wellington. 2000/2005, *Students' Concurrent Performance on Tests of English Language Proficiency and Academic Achievement* (Final Deliverable to OERI, Contract No. R30B60002). (In CSE Tech. Rep. No. 663), Los Angeles: University of California, National Center for Research on Evaluation, Standards, and Student Testing

Celedón-Pattichis, S. and N. Ramirez. 2012, *Beyond Good Teaching: Advancing Mathematics Education for ELLs*, Reston, VA: National Council of Teachers of Mathematics

Cook, H. Gary, E. Hicks, S. Lee and R. Freshwater. 2009, *Methods for Establishing English Language Proficiency using State Content Language Proficiency Assessments*, Unpublished manuscript: University of Wisconsin–Madison

Fang, Z., L. Lamme and R. Pringle. 2010, *Language and Literacy in Inquiry-based Science*, Thousand Oaks, CA: Corwin

Fang, Z. and M. Schleppegrell. 2008, *Reading in Secondary Content Areas: A Language-Based Pedagogy*, Ann Arbor, MI: University of Michigan Press

Francis, D. and M. Rivera. 2007, "Principles Underlying English Language Proficiency Tests and Academic Accountability for ELLs". In J. Abedi, ed,

English Language Proficiency Assessment in the Nation: Current Status and Future Practice, University of California, Davis: School of Education, pp. 13–29

Francis, D., M. Rivera, N. Lesaux, M. Kieffer and H. Rivera. 2006, *Practical Guidelines for the Education of English Language Learners: Research-based Recommendations for Instruction and Academic Interventions*. Portsmouth, N.H.: RMC Research Corporation, Center on Instruction

Goldenberg, C. 2008, "Teaching English Language Learners: What the Research Does—and Does Not—Say", *American Educator* 32(2): 8–23, 42–44

Goldenberg, C. and R. Coleman. 2010, *Promoting Academic Achievement among English Learners: A Guide to the Research*, Thousand Oaks, CA: Corwin

Gottlieb, M., M.E. Cranley and A. Oliver. 2007, *English Language Proficiency Standards and Resource Guide, PreKindergarten through Grade 12*, Madison, WI: Board of Regents of the University of Wisconsin System on behalf of the WIDA Consortium

Graham, S. and D. Perin. 2007, *Writing Next: Effective Strategies to Improve Writing of Adolescents in Middle and High Schools*, A report to the Carnegie Corporation, Alliance for Excellent Education. http://www.all4ed.org/files/WritingNext.pdf

Haig, B. 2009, "Inference to the best explanation: A neglected approach to theory appraisal in psychology", *American Journal of Psychology* 122(2): 219–34

Hatcher, L. 2007, *A step-by-step approach to using SAS® for factor analysis and structural equation modeling*, Cary, NC: SAS® Institute

Herbel-Eisenmann, B. and M. Cirillo. 2009, *Promoting Purposeful Discourse: Teacher Research in Classroom Mathematics*, Reston, VA: National Council of Teachers of Mathematics

Huang, J. and B. Normandia. 2007, "Learning the Language of Mathematics: A Study in Student Writing", *International Journal of Applied Linguistics* 17: 294–318

Johanning, D.L. 2000, "An Analysis of Writing and Postwriting Group Collaboration in Middle School Pre-algebra", *School Science and Mathematics Journal* 100: 151–60

Kane, M. 2006, "Validation", *Educational Measurement*, 4th ed, (R. Brennan ed), Westport, CT: Greenwood Publishing, pp.17–64

Kaplan, D. 2009, *Structural Equation Modeling: Foundations and Extensions*, 2nd ed, Los Angeles, CA: Sage

Kenyon, D. 2006, *Development and field test of ACCESS for ELLs®* (WIDA Consortium Technical Report No. 1)

Kim, J. and J. Herman. 2008, "Investigating ELL assessment and accommodation practices using state data", *Providing Validity Evidence to Improve the Assessment of English Language Learners*. (CRESST Report 736), Wolf, et al. eds. Washington, D.C: U.S. Department of Education, Institute of Education Sciences, National Center for Education, Evaluation and Regional Assistance, Regional Educational Laboratory Northeast and Islands, pp. 81–104

Lemke, J. 2003, "Mathematics in the Middle: Measure, Picture, Gesture, Sign, and Word". In M. Anderson, A. Saaenz-Ludlow, S. Zellweger, and V.V. Cifarelli, eds, *Educational Perspectives on Mathematics as Semiosis: From Thinking to Interpreting to Knowing*, Brooklyn, N.Y., and Ottawa, Ontario: Legas, pp. 215–23

MacDonald, R., J. Nagle, T. Akerley and H. Western. 2012, "Double-teaming: Teaching Academic Language in High School Biology". In A. Honigsfeld and M. Dove, eds, *Coteaching and Other Collaborative Practices in the EFL/ESL Classroom: Rationale, Research, Reflections, and Recommendations*, Charlotte, N.C.: Information Age Publishing, pp. 91–100

MacGregor, D., M. Louguit, X. Huang and D. Kenyon. 2009, *Annual Technical Report for ACCESS for ELLs® English Language Proficiency Test, Series 103, 2007-2008 Administration* (WIDA Consortium Annual Technical Report No. 4)

Moschkovich, J. 1999, "Supporting the Participation of English Language Learners in Mathematical Discussions", *For the Learning of Mathematics* 19(1): 11–19

Muthén, L. and B. Muthén. 2010, *Mplus Short Courses, Topic 4, Growth Modeling with Latent Variables Using Mplus: Advanced Growth Models, Survival Analysis and Missing Data*. Slide 168.
http://www.statmodel.com/download/Topic4-v.pdf

National Governors Association for Best Practices and Council of Chief State School Officers. (2010a), *Common core state standards for English language arts and literacy in history/social studies, science, and technical subjects*, Washington, D.C.: Author.

National Governors Association for Best Practices and Council of Chief State School Officers. (2010b), *Common core state standards for mathematics*, Washington, D.C.: Author.

National Staff Development Council. 2009, *Professional Learning in the Learning Profession: A Status Report on Teacher Development in the United States and Abroad*, Darling-Hammond, L., R.C. Wei, A. Andree, N. Richardson and S. Orphanos. learningforward.org/docs/pdf/nsdcstudy2009.pdf

Parker, C., J. Louie and L. O'Dwyer. 2009, *New Measures of English Language Proficiency and their Relationship to Performance on Large-scale Assessments.* (Issues & Answers Report, REL. 2009-No. 066). Washington, D.C: U.S. Department of Education, Institute of Education Sciences, National Center for Education, Evaluation and Regional Assistance, Regional Educational Laboratory Northeast and Islands.
http://ies.ed.gov/ncee/edlabs/projects/project.asp?projectID=172&productID=125

Planty, M., W. Hussar, T. Snyder, G. Kena, A. Kewal Ramani and J. Kemp. 2009, *The Condition of Education 2009.* (NCES 2009-081). Washington, D.C.: U.S. Department of Education National Center for Education Statistics, Institute of Education Sciences

Snow, C. E. and Y. Kim. 2007, "Large Problem Spaces: The Challenges of Vocabulary for English Language Learners". In A.M.R. Wagner and K.K. Tannenbaum, eds, *Vocabulary Acquisition: Implications for Reading Comprehension*, New York: Guilford Press, pp. 123–39

Spanos, A. 1995, "On Theory Testing in Econometrics Modeling with
  Nonexperimental Data", *Journal of Econometrics* 67: 189–226

WIDA 2012 Annual Report. 2012, WIDA Consortium at Wisconsin Center for
  Education Research, University of Wisconsin-Madison

WIDA, 2014. *ACCESS for ELLS® Interpretive Guide for Score Reports, Spring
  2014.* http://www.wida.us/get.aspx?id=25

CHAPTER TWELVE

ABORIGINAL ENGLISH AND BI-DIALECTAL IDENTITY IN EARLY CHILDHOOD EDUCATION

ELIZABETH M. ELLIS

Keywords: Aboriginal English, bidialectal identity, early childhood, preschool

Abstract

Aboriginal English is a powerful marker of identity for many Aboriginal people, but in schools it is still often seen as "poor English." This chapter reports a study of the impact of Aboriginal English on learning outcomes for Indigenous children in preschools in the Australian Capital Territory (ACT). Data from one family's home interactions and from Koori and mainstream preschool interactions are presented. Little evidence was found of grammatical and lexical features of Aboriginal English, but prosodic features of interactional style are suggested to form an integral part of Aboriginal identity. The findings suggested that there may be dissonance between Indigenous children's home and preschool language experiences that includes, but exceeds, the linguistic features of Aboriginal English. We suggest that, particularly in contexts where a "light" form of Aboriginal English is used, identity is indexed by features of prosody and interactional style that are characteristic of Aboriginal ways of being, doing and knowing. Combining our understanding of Aboriginal ways of talking and of effective preschool pedagogies forges links between Applied Linguistics and Early Childhood Education that can contribute to improving outcomes for young Indigenous learners.

Background and rationale for the study

This chapter reports selected findings of a study conducted for the Australian Capital Territory Department of Education and Training (ACT DET) into the impact of Aboriginal English (AE) on the learning outcomes for Indigenous children in preschools (Ellis, Edwards & Brooks 2010). Although Indigenous children in the ACT have the best outcomes of all States and Territories for attendance and academic achievement, overall they still lag behind their non-Indigenous peers (ACT DET 2009a). Comparisons generated from both Performance Indicators in Primary Schools (PIPS) and National Assessment Program Literacy and Numeracy (NAPLAN) testing reveal that Indigenous children achieve outcomes comparable to those of non-Indigenous students in Year 3, but after Year 3 their achievement drops. It is increasingly accepted that Early Childhood Education (ECE) is foundational to the building of learning skills that enable children to engage successfully with the school system. So ACT DET was keen to find out whether language issues in preschools were helping or hindering Indigenous students' access to such engagement. The project aimed to find out whether and how AE featured in ACT preschools and whether and how Aboriginal children were helped to become bidialectal in AE and Standard Australian English (SAE).

Early discussions with senior educators revealed their concerns that preschool staff could be doing more to prepare children for the SAE of the primary classroom, as the following quote shows:

> ... the main thing that concerned us [was that] there wasn't any talk—kids were playing, or eating, but when a kid had a car, well no one was saying to the kid 'oh that's a lovely blue car you've got there, or 'which colour are you going to choose next?' or... you know, the kid's in the sand—you know, 'you can make a bridge over this....' (ACT DET key informant).

This quote gives a clear example of the kind of social language extension that leads to learning (Painter 1999). Play is central to early childhood learning, but children's solitary or group play activities need to be scaffolded by adult carers and teachers. By engaging with children in play, commenting on materials and actions, asking questions and posing problems to be solved, adults can help children to extend what they know and learn to articulate their activities and experiences, first orally and later through images and text, in developing early literacy practices.

Another key informant asked "how relevant is Aboriginal English and what might we be doing about it?" (ACT DET informant). Language and dialect issues in the preschool are closely interwoven with pedagogical practices and the home practices which children bring, and so the direction of the project was established as being "[to] map the linguistic landscape of preschool and [map] the linguistic landscape of the home ... and look at what that might mean. The maps might be different" (ACT DET informant).

Aboriginal English in ACT preschools

At the time of the study the Indigenous population of the ACT, according to the 2006 Census, was 4,282 (ABS 2008) and includes Indigenous peoples from other States and Territories as well as the local Ngunnawal people, with a mobility rate of 14%–18%. The ACT Indigenous population has a higher rate of participating in secondary and tertiary education than the Australia-wide Indigenous average (FaHCSIA[1] 2009).

In 2009 the ACT had 79 mainstream preschools and five Koori (Aboriginal) preschools in which Indigenous Home School Liaison Officers (IHSLOs) team-teach with non-Indigenous teachers. Four-year-old Indigenous children can attend mainstream preschool 12 hours each week and an extra 9 hours in Koori preschool. Younger children can attend Koori preschool if a parent or carer goes with them and their presence contributes to the distinctive family-friendly atmosphere of Koori preschool. Koori preschool is seen as an adjunct to mainstream preschool; it does not replace it. So Koori children either attend both, or mainstream only. In 2009 the ACT had 112 Indigenous students enrolled in preschool, and about 65 students enrolled in the 5 Koori preschools (ACT DET 2009b).

AE is a non-standard variety of English that is the "first language or home language of many Aboriginal children in New South Wales and throughout the whole of Australia" (Eades 1995, p. 3). Most Aboriginal Australians speak AE and it is the second or third language for those Aboriginal people who still speak a traditional Aboriginal language as their first language. It functions as a *lingua franca* between all Aboriginal people living in Australia today and is a powerful marker of Aboriginal identity (Priman 2002). AE is not a single language; it has many varieties that "differ in systematic ways from Standard Australian English at all levels of linguistic structure and which are used for distinctive speech acts, speech events and genres" (Malcolm et al 1999, p. 22). SAE is "the dialect of English which is spoken by the more powerful, dominant groups in society and which therefore has become the language of education, the media, government and law" (Eades 1993, p. 2). Speakers of Aboriginal English are frequently judged negatively by SAE speakers; McRae (1994, p. 8) quoted teachers saying, for example: "the [Aboriginal] kids here all

---

[1] On September 18, 2013, the Australian Government established the Department of Social Services. That Department took over most of the responsibilities of the Department of Families, Housing, Community Services and Indigenous Affairs (FaHCSIA). The Department of the Prime Minister and Cabinet took over FaHCSIA's indigenous affairs functions.

speak English. Bad English, of course, lazy English, but English," and concluded: "it is obvious that Aboriginal English is still a misunderstood and stigmatised language, best left outside the school fence" (1994, p. 6).

The literature has noted several regional varieties of AE, ranging from "light" varieties spoken in southern Queensland and New South Wales, described by Eades (1988), to "heavy" Central Australian AE, described by Harkins (1994) and Koch (2000). "Light" and "heavy" here refer to mutual intelligibility with other dialects of English. Since we found no studies on AE done in the ACT, we focused as far as possible on research done in contexts with at least some parallels—urban or small-town populations where Indigenous languages were hardly spoken—before looking at studies from remote Australia where AE occurs alongside Indigenous languages and creoles. We found little on AE among preschoolers and so focused on studies with primary school children such as Malin (1990). A recent focus in educational linguistics has been on how AE encodes an Aboriginal worldview, and embodies different "cultural schemas" (Sharifian 2001, 2005). Schemas have been described as

> … the building blocks of our knowledge. These are derived from our various experiences and guide us in our interpretations and communication. For example, people may have a schema for 'restaurant' in their mind, which is based on their various experiences of going to different restaurants (Western Australia DET 2007, p. 11).

Malcolm (2000, p. 58) notes that the cultural schemas of children living in Western Australia who speak AE include; *image schemas, event schemas,* and *story schemas*. He claims (p. 61) that "classroom communication is often characterized by exchanges in which the teacher calls for responses to an elicitation which is no longer explicit in the discourse." These responses often cause problems for bidialectal learners. For example, a teacher might say in a sing-song tone: "I'm waiting!" Students who have grown up with a schema of instructional relationships that expect children to be quiet and listen to adults, will interpret this utterance as meaning "you know my expectations are that you will sit down and be quiet before I begin to talk. You are not fulfilling those expectations, and I am getting cross." A child who has grown up with a schema common in some Aboriginal societies, where children are not expected always to listen to and obey directives from adults (Harrison 2008), may not be able to interpret the meaning behind this utterance. So some authors are calling for a bidialectal approach to engaging Aboriginal students in school learning: one that goes beyond looking at differences in phonological and grammatical forms, to considering "worlds of linguistic and cultural imagery which have a long history of opposition to one another" (Malcolm & Koscielecki 1997, p. 85).

Young Aboriginal speakers of AE "encounter in the English of White people an alien way of thinking and their communication and learning is correspondingly inhibited" (Malcolm 1994, cited in Wilson 1996, p. 4). Yet it is generally accepted that in urban Aboriginal contexts, where light forms of AE are spoken, it is not lexico-grammatical features but communication strategies, pragmatics and prosodic aspects that distinguish Aboriginal interactional style. Walsh (1997) has found significant differences between how Indigenous people at Wadeye interact with each other and how non-Indigenous Australians interact with each other. Even so, we cannot extrapolate directly from such research to the ACT where few Indigenous people have fluency in a traditional language. Yet Walsh points out that Eades (1981) found distinctive interactional style among South East Queensland Aboriginal people who spoke English as their first language, as did Wilson (1996) and Hitchen (1992). Walsh suggests that "[a] distinctive interactional style may well be the last thing to survive from Aboriginal language after nearly all the vocabulary and the details of the grammar are lost" (Walsh, 1997, p. 17). This is likely in the ACT, where many Aboriginal people have largely lost the language(s) spoken by their forebears. This distinctive interactional style provides a powerful basis for the expression of Aboriginal identity, solidarity and survival.

Key features of Early Childhood Education

Early childhood, defined as the period from birth to 8 years of age, lays the foundation for learning; so ECE is more than just preparing the child for formal schooling (UNESCO 2012). A MCEETYA[2] report stated that early childhood is

> … a period of critical physical, emotional, intellectual and social growth … high quality early education programs have a profound effect on children's development, influencing their ability to learn, their acquisition of pre-literacy and numeracy skills and their capacity to regulate emotions… (MCEETYA 2006, p. 18).

---

[2] In January 2012, the Council of Australian Governments (COAG) announced the launch of the Standing Council on School Education and Early Childhood (SCSEEC). SCSEEC replaced the Ministerial Council for Education, Early Childhood Development and Youth Affairs (MCEECDYA).

We know that Aboriginal children arrive at school as "fluent and competent communicators (Eades 1993, p. 5), with well-developed visual skills (Christie 1984, p. 213; Kearins 1986), that their motor-coordination is honed in informal real-life contexts (Harris 1980), that they are encouraged from infancy to function as autonomous beings, that they value their independence, and that they form strong peer bonds (Hamilton 1981; Malin et al 1996). Their upbringing means that they enter the school system with a great many practical skills (Malin 1990).

Quality ECE emerges from close relationships between home and school (Hill & Nichols 2009). It follows that the skills and knowledge that Indigenous children bring to preschool must be recognized, valued and built upon. Martin (2008) presents a compelling framework for valuing Aboriginal children's multiliteracies and talks of "Aboriginal ways of knowing, ways of being and ways of doing," claiming that

> the essence of Aboriginal worldviews is *relatedness*, defined as sets of conditions, processes and practices that occur among and between elements of a particular place, and across contexts that are physical, social, political and intellectual (Martin 2008, p. 61).

Martin (2008, p. 70) argues that Aboriginal students must not be silenced by a curriculum using only SAE that reflects Western culture, and that "translating" Aboriginal literacies into an SAE form diminishes their meanings. This notion chimes with the work of Sharifian (2001, 2008), Malcolm (2000) and others noted above on the topic of "cultural schemas." Despite knowing it is important that teachers recognize the literacies that children bring from home and value the language of the lifeworlds of those children, we know that Indigenous children are largely not succeeding. Malin's study of children in a transition/Year 1 class (1990) shows how dissonance between Aboriginal home practices and school expectations led to those children quickly becoming alienated from schooling. Another study supports this idea that failure begins very early:

Teacher:	Some had given up, totally. Kindergarten—given up … some kids even at a very early age, who come to school, and they're gone,
Interviewer:	*For all intents and purposes educationally they're gone?*
Teacher:	Ah yeah, they're gone

(Munns & McFadden 2000, p. 67)

We conclude that there must be a serious mismatch between what young Indigenous children experience at home and what they experience in ECE for them to "switch off" to education. Something goes wrong; and it goes wrong very early.

Method

The ideal approach for a study of this kind would be ethnographic and longitudinal, but time, distance and budget constraints did not permit this. The next best option was to gather as much rich data as possible over four field trips—two of two days and two of one week. After an initial "scoping visit," the research team spent a total of 29 person-days observing, filming and interviewing in four Koori preschools and four mainstream preschools; conducted two focus groups with IHSLOs and with preschool teachers; and attended one workshop and conducted another. Twenty-five interviews were held with key informants, teachers and IHSLOs. Key informants included staff of ACT DET, elders of the Ngunnawal people and school principals. A key plank of the research method was to recruit four Aboriginal families to use a digital video-camera to record "home literacy activities" with their preschool child. This powerful research method has the potential to give researchers access to natural interaction in the home without their imposing on the private sphere (Fleer 2004). "We view our participant [families] as co-researchers and put the visual tools [of cameras] in their hands to enhance our understanding of their everyday …. practices" (Kendrick & McKay 2009, p. 56). Footage was obtained from only one family, but this was extensive and extremely valuable.

Detailed field notes were kept of all preschool visits and observations. All interviews were audio-recorded and many of the preschool observation hours were video-recorded. Interviews were transcribed and analyzed for key themes and insights about the use of AE and SAE. Video footage was viewed several times and key incidents were extracted and transcribed. The home video footage was viewed and discussed with the Indigenous mother who recorded it, and the discussion was itself recorded, transcribed and analyzed. The multidimensional data was then read iteratively using an interpretive and qualitative approach to extract salient and recurrent themes.

Findings and Discussion

Three aspects of the findings are reported here:

- the attitudes and reported practices of using AE and SAE in preschool and in families, gathered from interviews
- language data from one family
- samples of interaction from Koori and mainstream preschools.

Attitudes to Aboriginal English

We found a variety of attitudes towards AE among those interviewed, ranging from an in-depth understanding of how important it is to support AE and build bridges to SAE, to a reluctance to acknowledge that AE exists. Understandably, from their own experience the IHSLOs were the most informed about Aboriginal ways of speaking, yet their views varied considerably. One person preferred to think of Aboriginal ways of speaking as "just the way we talk," and this is indeed a useful rubric.[3] This range of views echoes those found by Hitchen (1992) in the town of Moree in northern New South Wales.

Many skilled bilinguals or bidialectals find it hard to talk about their languages and dialects which are so much a part of their identity. Non-standard dialects are even harder to talk about, because they are less widely recognized, and history has viewed them as a deficient version of the standard (Holmes 2008). Discussion of the language that AE and SAE speakers use is fraught with historical and cultural background that renders the topic uncomfortable or even dangerous. The fact that the relationship between AE and SAE does not form part of normal professional discussion in the preschool system, we suggest, reflects an Australia-wide lack of understanding of how languages and dialects function *and* the turbulent historical relationship between Indigenous and non-Indigenous Australians.

Some informants who speak AE in their private lives found it hard to consider it as a legitimate dialect due to their own bad experiences in the past, such as being told at school that speaking AE was a "lazy" or "bad" way to speak. One IHSLO reported a mother telling her that her daughter "speaks broken English at home." For others, AE is a private aspect of identity and no business of non-Indigenous people. For this reason, some families do not want preschool staff to "correct" children's AE. Others

---

[3] In educational terms, "rubric" means a standard of performance for a defined population.

only want staff to teach the children SAE so that they can get ahead in the system. Most families in the study thought that teachers should model SAE and validate AE, and that it is important not to "correct" particular words from an Aboriginal language. One IHSLO did not accept the label "Aboriginal English," but was happy to talk about "Aboriginal ways of talk" as being equally valid.

A strong theme was the importance of preschool and school reflecting the experiences of Aboriginal children and families, in ways of talking but also in representations in books, toys and artefacts, as shown in the following excerpt. A parent explained how her child had started kindergarten with great excitement but gradually became withdrawn and depressed, until an incident that helped him to see himself reflected in the materials:

> .... part of it was racism on the second day and straight away school wasn't the safe place—that he thought it was going to be—but the other part was that his world wasn't being reflected, so part of it is the language that we use at home wasn't reflected—and even meanings—different meanings of words and things like that and so I had a yarn with his teacher [who supplied some Indigenous readers] .... the last sentence in the book was 'my mum is Koori' and when he read that he said 'that's us Mum!' so you know, totally engaged!!

Language in the home

Family 1 returned valuable footage of home interaction between parents and children (mother, father, son aged 9, preschool son aged 4, and baby). There were 39 minutes of footage, in 19 clips of one to four minutes each. The clips showed a range of family activities taking place in the lounge and dining room, including card games; Garth[4] (the preschool child) dancing to a music video and interacting with older brother Jack and Dad; the family commenting on a kids' TV program; Garth drawing freehand pictures in a sketchbook on the floor, encouraged and helped by Mum and Dad; and Garth tracing numbers, writing his name and coloring in animals while Jack does homework. Those utterances judged to be examples of light AE are indicated in bold, while those judged to be examples of heavier AE are in bold italics.

---

[4] All names are pseudonyms.

Clip 006	*Garth is dancing to TV music video clips. Jack is holding the camera and Dad is on the couch.*
Dad:	you don't want this song? **whaddaya gonna dance ter?**
Jack: (Garth blocks the camera with a book)	**no dancin' no lookin'—dance!**
Dad:	show us what you got now—**full dance floor**—that was a good one—up now—**show'm show me**
Jack:	go Garth!!
Jack:	***goo(d) c(g)amera dis!***
	eh, wan' me t' turn t'off?
Garth:	*that* song!
Jack: (to camera)	**'e keeps on wan'in' ter change sooongs** (humorous chiding of Garth)
Clip 0012	Garth is sitting on the floor with pencil and a drawing book. The pencil has a decorative fluffy end, and a light, which is supposed to come on when pressure is put on it. The baby is bouncing in her bouncinette in frame, a kids' learning program is on TV.
Mum:	What else can you draw? ... How abo...ut ... a circle?
Garth:	a circle
Mum:	**whad else?**
Garth:	triangle!
Mum:	triangle, OK ... very good ... **whad else?** what about the star? Can you draw the star?
	the light on Garth's pen appears to give out
Garth:	**wha's wha's the light doin'?**
Mum: (reassuring tone)	**iss wo..rkin'**
Garth:	watch...
Mum:	ah, must be flat, the batteries must be flat—never mind
Garth:	**maybe dey is**
Mum:	**yea...h ..but finish drawin' the king**

Clip 0014	Garth is drawing in his book again on the floor: Mum is filming, the baby is on her back on the floor partly in frame, the TV is on. Dad helps Garth draw trucks and cars, questioning, commenting and joking. The atmosphere is cheerful, warm and highly interactive, featuring mock scolding, laughing and physical closeness.
Mum:	**what are yer drawin'?**
Garth:	**t' uck .... see, dat and de wheels**
Dad:	do the truck ah
Garth:	**aaaaand da doors ... da's da doors—see?**
	...
Mum:	do the truck
Dad:	do the truck
	(Garth sneezes)
Dad:	do the truck, *(sneeze)* **don't do da sneeze, do da truck!**

The suggestions of AE here occur in the following aspects of pronunciation:

- substituting the final /n/ for /ŋ/ in "drawing," "doing," "working," "dancing," and "looking"
- eliding the "t" in "wan(t)in(g)" and in "what"
- eliding the "r" sound in "truck"
- eliding the "d" sound in "good"
- substituting voiced form "g" for unvoiced form "c" in "camera": "good camera" becoming "goo' gamra"
- substituting the "d" sound for the "th" sound in "the," "they," "this," and "that"
- elongating some vowels—"soooooongs"
- shortening of some long vowels—"floor"
- putting less aspiration on the stops "p," "b," "t," "d," "k," and "g"
- assimilating sounds in connected phrases: "whaddaya gunna" (what are you going to...).

The video showed only one example of a grammatical characteristic of AE: the subject-fronting of "good camera this" from Jack.

Neither the above aspects of pronunciation nor the single grammatical example are exclusive to AE: all are also found in Broad Australian English, and in other dialects of English. It is not only the sounds but the prosodic aspects—tempo, loudness, pitch, stress and intonation—of some of the speech transcribed here that is distinctively Aboriginal. "It ain't what you say, it's the way that you say it" claim Burridge and Mulder (1998, p. 65). It can be argued that particular combinations of tempo, loudness, pitch, stress and intonation combine to form distinctive AE rhythms. These rhythms are evident in the utterances marked AE in the above data. These characteristic rhythms are also evident to other speakers of the same dialect; so Aboriginal people can recognize another Aboriginal person from "their way of talking" regardless of appearance (Eades 1995, p. 17). A respondent in Hitchen's study of AE in Moree explained how, on meeting strangers at sports events or conferences, "we wait till they speak—ah yes, they Aboriginal" (Hitchen 1992, p. 75). The characteristic rhythms of AE combine with Aboriginal interactional style to establish an Aboriginal identity, which is performed and reproduced within the family and among friends (Eades 1995; Hitchen 1992). Interactional style includes "the use of humour, the way that adults talk to kids, or don't talk to kids, the things that people tease about, what requests or demands are seen as reasonable…" (Eades, personal communication, October 2009).

The parents and two older children in this family are able to switch easily from SAE to a light form of AE. The mother, later reviewing the recording with us, spoke entirely in SAE. The limited evidence here does not allow us to draw definitive conclusions, but the switches seem to happen at the most intimate family moments. Examples of this are first when Mum reassures Garth that the light on his pen is working and second when Dad teases Garth about his sneezing: ("don't do the sneeze, do the truck!"). An example of how a sudden switch into AE can function as a bonding device came in one of the key informant interviews, which was otherwise conducted entirely in SAE. The three researchers and two Indigenous informants (A and B) were present, and the following private exchange took place between the two informants, referring to A's intention to continue working at the university until her niece finishes her studies there:

A:	*(addressing B)*	I only promised to stay [at this university] until X [my niece] finishes
B:		**she ever gunna finish?**
A & B:	*joint laughter*	

B's response came hot on A's utterance and was spoken rapidly, with the lack of aspiration characteristic of much AE speech. It was clear that X's prolonged studies had been discussed before, and constituted the basis for the teasing displayed here. The use of AE (elision of auxiliary "be"; contraction of "going to" but, more importantly, the tempo and lack of aspiration) establishes that it is a friendly joke. Had B said 'Is she ever going to finish?' in SAE, the question might have been construed as a criticism. The use of AE also serves to exclude the three researchers, making it clear that this is a private joke about someone known to A and B. This form of speech accommodation called *divergence* is used to exclude someone or to emphasize different allegiances (Holmes 2008, pp. 230–32). So AE, like any dialect, can be used to emphasize shared understanding or to emphasize difference: to include or to exclude. The people interacting do not think about the prosodic elements and interactional style of their discourse. The data samples of naturally occurring Aboriginal family talk that we were able to collect for this study are insufficient for an analysis of interactional style. Yet the effect of subtle prosodic and interactional features is powerful: even if most people cannot describe *how* someone speaks, they know the effect of their speech. It may be to make us feel that the speaker is above or below us on the social scale, is being overly familiar or overly distant, is arrogant, is withholding information, or is being deliberately obtuse. This is because speech communities use prosody and an interactional style to convey meaning. So they may fail to understand each other if they use different interactional styles. This often happens between speakers of different dialects. So when an Aboriginal child is socialized in "one way of talking" at home and then encounters "another way of talking" at preschool, even though most of the words and the grammar are the same, we suspect the child can read the difference, but has no way of responding to it, other than to withdraw, become silent and not participate.

Preschool observation data

From our observations of the four Koori and four mainstream preschool programs, we found the mainstream preschools to be much more structured in their approach than the Koori ones. Indoor activities were largely teacher-fronted and teacher-controlled, and teacher–student interaction was mostly of the IRF format (initiation—response—feedback) characteristic of much mainstream classroom discourse. An example follows of Indigenous and non-Indigenous children, in a mainstream preschool class, attempting to deal with an unfamiliar interaction style and an underlying cultural schema. The following excerpt is not given to criticize the teacher, but to show that the interactional style and cultural schema they used, as a way to be friendly, were very different from what Indigenous children might find at home.

Mainstream preschool teacher and non-Indigenous teacher aide are conducting a group session that includes several Koori children. The children are sitting in a circle on the floor, all wearing name tags, since it is early in the preschool year, and the children have each said their names, as have the visiting researchers.

Teacher:	*(looking intently around the group)*	Now, are you going to be clever enough to remember all those names?
Children:	*(sit in silence, with uncomfortable and uncertain glances at others)*	
Teacher:	*(long pause and meaningful looks around the group)*	... because I'm not!
	(laughs)	It's hard to remember people's names—that's why we give you labels.

This episode relies on an adult humorous discourse that is typical of an Anglo-Australian interactional style, and a cultural schema that says we are all bad at remembering people's names, and that we jokingly chide ourselves for it. The teacher places the children in an awkward situation by asking if they can remember all the names. It is a rhetorical question that leaves the children confused and unsure what to say. The teacher resolves the confusion by revealing that the children are not expected to remember every name—it's a hard thing to do. According to Martin (2008), naming people and their interrelationships is important in Indigenous society. This interchange may be highly perplexing to an Indigenous child who has not grown up with this Anglo-Australian discourse. The question seems to set *all* children up for the wrong answer—it's a trick question, impossible to answer (Yes—means I am saying I'm clever (that is, bragging). No—means I'm not clever and also maybe I'm not doing what the teacher appears to want—remembering all the names). The teacher's answer reveals the joke, leaving the children off the hook but possibly confused and wondering what the question really meant.

We noted several instances where children's responses or initiatives were ignored or deflected, when they could have provided fertile material for developing language and concepts.

In the following example from Koori preschool, the teacher is a non-indigenous teacher.

T:	*The children sat in a circle on the floor and sang the "Five little ducks" song, using fingers for numbers. After that the teacher showed a picture of ducks.*	
Child 1:	(unprompted)	ducks in water!
T:	(ignores child 1 comment)	what kind of animal is it?
Child 1:	(repeats)	ducks in water!
T:		yes, they live in water, but what kind of animal are they?
Child 2:		Birds
T:		yes, they're birds, aren't they? So 'Jane' was right when she said "flap flap"—birds fly.
	A few minutes later…	
Child 3:	(pointing out the window)	There's a birdy!
T:	shhhhhhhhhh…	

This excerpt demonstrates lost opportunities for learning, and talk that is counter-productive to the learning of Child 1 and Child 3. Child 1's spontaneous contribution was clearly relevant and informative and could have led to a discussion about how ducks are adapted to water, and what other birds/animals live in/on water. Instead, Child 1's utterance was first ignored, then on repetition, briefly acknowledged but deflected as not being "on the agenda." The child does not know the teacher's agenda and may well conclude that the teacher hasn't rejected their comment but them as a person. The teacher also praises "Jane" for an earlier comment ("flap flap") because this tied in with the teacher's agenda of classifying ducks as birds, even though none of the children knew this was her intention at the time the child spoke. Then Child 3 sees a real bird through the window and excitedly shares this information, only to be shushed. So Child 1 and Child 3 may be left wondering what it was about their attempts to contribute that were so wrong. It seems like a guessing game where the rules are unknown. After all, "Jane" was right on the mark with something she said five minutes ago—why was the teacher so pleased with that? She accepts answers from some children and not others. All young children are equipped to learn through the "here and now" and one of the functions of preschool and school is to gradually equip them to move towards more abstract thought. There is some suggestion that the familiar experiences of Aboriginal children make them more likely to talk about the "here and now," and to relate learning to the real world: animals, plants and landscapes around us and how all are connected (the concept of "relatedness" in Martin 2008, p. 61). So the rejection of the contributions of Child 1 and Child 3, which were based on observation and real world knowledge, may also constitute a rejection of the kind of learning they brought from home and be a further disincentive to participate in future. As with the "names" episode (above), children may conclude that teachers are unpredictable and it is best to keep quiet. This data does not feature AE as such, even though these children may well use AE at home: rather it suggests a possible mismatch between an Indigenous interactional style and that of the mainstream (non-Indigenous) teachers, even when, as in the second example, the interaction happens within a Koori preschool context.

Conclusion

Although the study found very little AE spoken in either Koori or mainstream preschool, it was clear that "Aboriginal ways of knowing, being and doing" were more in evidence in the Koori preschools than in the mainstream preschools. IHSLOs used AE in songs and reading stories to the children, but otherwise it featured hardly at all, at least in the researchers' hearing, over many days. Yet "Aboriginal ways of talk" were recognized by all stakeholders, suggesting that there are distinctive Aboriginal patterns of communication that may be characterized more by prosodic features and interactional style than by particular grammar or lexis. If, as our family data suggests, code-switching is frequent in the home but is absent in the preschool, this may contribute to the "dissonance" we referred to in the introduction. The report made seven recommendations about language and pedagogy in ACT preschools, of which two are relevant to this chapter.

One recommendation was for staff to undertake action research to reach an understanding within the ACT preschool system, of *how to talk about* AE and SAE in an educational context. There is a need to develop a meta-language that Indigenous and non-Indigenous families and staff feel comfortable using. Without this shared meta-language, it is hard to develop and implement a coherent policy for including AE and for helping children to expand their verbal repertoire to include AE and SAE. Non-Indigenous teachers stated they were keen to develop inclusive practices, and talked comfortably about including different cultural perspectives with children from immigrant backgrounds, but were clearly unsure how or whether to include aspects of Indigenous communication and cultures. This, as noted above, comes from the unspoken historical tensions between Indigenous and non-Indigenous Australia: to the Anglo-Australian teacher, Aboriginal culture is "other" but not "foreign," and cannot be treated in the same way as that of Indonesia or Japan. Whatever terms are chosen to use, they must be chosen after discussions with teachers and families in the area, and then adopted system-wide through professional development activities.

A further recommendation was that the ACT gives priority to the training and support of fully-qualified Indigenous preschool teachers. This proposal is often made in reports on Indigenous education, but it is critical for two key reasons. First, the only Indigenous staff that children see are the IHSLOs, who sometimes lead activities in the Koori preschools, but who in other contexts are (by their own reports) sometimes under-used, sometimes marginalized and always under the control of the qualified (non-Indigenous) teacher. So children see the representative of their language and culture acting as "handmaiden." Second, IHSLOs' level of cultural and language knowledge is what all teachers ideally should possess. It is much more effective to train biculturals as teachers than to teach monolinguals to teach biculturally. It is only by children seeing *fully-qualified* Indigenous preschool teachers comfortably switching from AE to SAE and back again that they will learn that both dialects are valid and have their specific uses. This strategy is much more likely to bring the results intended than the strategy of training non-Indigenous teachers to overtly flag the differences between the dialects.

Acknowledgements

The author thanks the preschool teachers, IHSLOs and parents who took part in the study, her co-researchers Dr. Helen Edwards and Dr. Margaret Brooks and Mr Ron Reavell, CARSS research manager.

References

Australian Bureau of Statistics 2008, 2006 Census data.
www.abs.gov.au/ausstats/abs@.nsf/Latestproducts/3238.0.55.001Main%20Fea
tures1Jun%202006?opendocument&tabname=Summary&prodno=3238.0.55.0
01&issue=Jun%202006&num=&view=.j

Australian Capital Territory Department of Education and Training. 2009a. *Performance in Indigenous Education Report to the Legislative Assembly of the Australian Capital Territory Annual Report 2008*, Canberra: ACT DET

Australian Capital Territory Government. 2009b, *Performance in Indigenous Education. Interim Report to the Legislative Assembly of the Australian Capital Territory, January–June 2009*, Canberra: ACT DET

Burridge, K. and J. Mulder. 1998, *English in Australia and New Zealand: An introduction to its history, structure and use*, Oxford: OUP

Christie, M.J. 1984, *The Classroom World of the Aboriginal Child*. Ph.D thesis, University of Queensland

Eades, D. 2009, Personal communication with author (October)

Eades, D. 1981, "'That's our way of talking': Aborigines in South East Queensland", *Social Alternatives* 2(2): 11–14

Eades, D. 1988, "They don't speak an Aboriginal language, or do they?" In I. Keen, ed, *Being black: Aboriginal "cultures" in settled Australia*, Canberra: Aboriginal Studies Press, pp. 97–15

—. 1993, "Aboriginal English", *PEN* 93: 1–6

—. 1995, *Aboriginal English*, Sydney: N.S.W. Board of Studies

Ellis, E.M., H. Edwards and M. Brooks. 2010, *The impact of Aboriginal English (or Torres Strait Creole) on learning outcomes for Indigenous children in ACT preschools and preschool programs*. Report prepared for the ACT DET. CARSS, University of New England: Armidale

FaHCSIA: Department of Families, Housing, Community Services and Indigenous Affairs. 2009, *Finding our feet: first findings from Footprints in Time—a longitudinal study of indigenous children*. www.fahcsia.gov.au/about-fahcsia/publications-articles/research-publications/longitudinal-data-initiatives/footprints-in-time-the-longitudinal-study-of-indigenous-children-lsic

Fleer, M. 2004, "The cultural construction of family involvement in early childhood education: some indigenous perspectives", *The Australian Educational Researcher* 31(3): 51–68

Hamilton, A. 1981, *Nature and nurture: Aboriginal child-rearing in north-central Arnhem Land*, Canberra: Australian Institute of Aboriginal Studies

Harkins, J. 1994, *Bridging two worlds: Aboriginal English and cross-cultural understanding*, St Lucia: University of Queensland Press

Harris, P. 1980, *Measurement in tribal Aboriginal communities*, Darwin: Department of Education

Harrison, N. 2008, *Teaching and learning in Indigenous education*, Melbourne: Oxford University Press

Hill, S. and S. Nichols. 2009, "Multiple pathways between home and school literacies". In A. Anning, J. Cullen and M. Fleer, eds, *Early Childhood Education Society and Culture*, 2nd ed, Los Angeles: Sage, pp. 169–84

Hitchen, M. 1992, *Talkin' Up: Aboriginal English in Moree*. M.Litt. thesis. Armidale: University of New England

Holmes, J. 2008, *An introduction to sociolinguistics*, 3rd ed. Harlow, Essex: Longman

Kearins, J. 1986, "Visual spatial memory in Aboriginal and white children", *Australian Journal of Psychology* 38 (3): 203–14

Kendrik, M.E. and R.A. McKay. 2009, "Researching literacy in young children's drawing". In M. Narey, ed, *Making Meaning Constructing Multimodal Perspectives of Language, Literacy, and Learning Through Arts-based Early Childhood Education*, Pittsburgh: Springer, pp. 53–70

Koch, H. 2000, "Central Australian Aboriginal English; In comparison with the morphosyntactical categories of Kaytetye", *Asian Englishes* 3(2): 32–58

Malcolm, I. 1994, "Issues in the maintenance of Aboriginal languages and Aboriginal English". Paper presented to the 10th National Languages Conference of the Australian Federation of Modern Language Teachers' Associations, Perth

Malcolm, I.G. 2000, "English and Inclusivity in Education for Indigenous Students", *Australian Review of Applied Linguistics* 22(2): 51–66

Malcolm, I., Y. Haig, P. Konigsberg, J. Rochecouste, G. Collard, A. Hill and R. Cahill. 1999, *Two-way English: towards more user-friendly education for speakers of Aboriginal English*, Perth: Western Australia Department of Education

Malcolm, I.G. and M.M. Koscielecki. 1997, *Aboriginality and English: Report to the Australian Research Council November 1997*, Mt Lawley: Centre for Applied Language Research, Edith Cowan University

Malin, M. 1990, "The visibility and invisibility of the Aboriginal child in an urban classroom", *Australian Journal of Education*, 34(3): 312–29

Malin, M., K. Campbell and L. Agius. 1996, "Raising children in the Nunga Aboriginal way", *Family Matters* 43 (Autumn): 43–47. www.aifs.org.au/institute/pubs/fm/fm43mm.pdf

Martin, K. 2008, "The intersection of Aboriginal knowledges, Aboriginal literacies, and new learning pedagogy for Aboriginal students". In A. Healy, ed, *Multiliteracies and Diversity in Education: New pedagogies for Expanding Landscapes*, South Melbourne: Oxford University Press, pp. 58–81

MCEETYA 2006, *Australian Directions in Indigenous Education 2005-2008*, Carlton South: Ministerial Council on Education, Employment and Youth Affairs

McRae, D. 1994, *Langwij comes to school: promoting literacy among speakers of Aboriginal English and Australian Creoles*, Canberra: DEET

Munns, G. and M. McFadden. 2000, "First chance, second chance or last chance? Resistance and response to education", *British Journal of Sociology of Education* 21(1): 59–75

Painter, C. 1999, *Learning through language in early childhood*, London: Continuum

Priman, B. 2002, "Aboriginal English: an Aboriginal perspective", *Ngoonjook*, 28(1): 19–24

Sharifian, F. 2001, "Schema-based processing in Australian Speakers of Aboriginal English", *Language and Intercultural Communication* 1(2): 120–33

—. 2005, Cultural conceptualization in English words: A study of Aboriginal children in Perth. *Language and Education* 19(1): 74–88.

—. 2008, Aboriginal English in the classroom: An asset or a liability? *Language Awareness* 17(2): 131–38

UNESCO. 2012, Statement on Early Childhood Education.
    www.unesco.org/new/en/education/themes/strengthening-education-
    systems/early-childhood/mission

Walsh, M. 1997, *Cross Cultural Communication Problems in Aboriginal Australia*. Discussion paper 07/1997. Canberra: ANU Research Unit

Western Australian Department of Education. 2007, *Ways of being, ways of talk*, East Perth: W.A. DET

Wilson, G. 1996, *Only Nungas talk Nunga English*, M.Litt. Armidale: University of New England

CHAPTER THIRTEEN

MEETING PLACE OF CULTURES: ABORIGINAL STUDENTS AND STANDARD AUSTRALIAN ENGLISH LEARNING

IAN G. MALCOLM

Keywords: Aboriginal English, cultural schema theory, idea unit analysis, bidialectal education, aural comprehension

Abstract

Schooling in Australia necessarily involves the use of Standard Australian English (SAE) for the expression and accessing of meanings. This is not problematic for most Australians, who are familiar, at least, with Standard Australian Colloquial English. In Aboriginal communities, however, the primary in-group means of communication is Aboriginal English and the use of SAE may carry negative associations.

The intersection of applied linguistics with cultural linguistics in two recent research projects has yielded an investigative technique to enable the examination of the ways in which (a) Aboriginal and non-Aboriginal educators interpret the oral expression of Aboriginal students; and (b) Aboriginal and non-Aboriginal students interpret SAE texts. An analysis of the idea units retained in recalls in both cases suggests the pervasive influence of cultural schemas in cross-dialectal interpretation.

This chapter draws together information on these research projects, which have already been separately reported, but showing how their findings complement one another. The chapter suggests how the application of cultural schema theory may lead to procedures that will make the educational setting for Aboriginal students more culturally inclusive.

Introduction

The classroom is a meeting place of cultures. Put this way, this would seem to be a positive and affirming statement. However, there are implications. What are the respective roles of the meeting cultures in the classroom? What culture brings its own language into the classroom? What culture owns the linguistic medium in which knowledge is conveyed and accessed? What culture defines the speech acts within which learning takes place? What culture controls the medium in which what is learned is expressed and evaluated?

It is easy in Australia to say the language and culture of the classroom are Australian. There is an Australian Language and Literacy Policy carrying the name *Australia's Language* (Dawkins 1991). But what *is* Australia's language? Even if we agree that it is English, there are three main contenders:

- Standard Australian English (SAE), which is always what is assumed in the policy documents, and which, in its sub-variety, Standard Australian Colloquial English, is, according to Pawley (2008, p. 365), "strongly linked to middle class upbringings, occupations and aspirations"
- Australian Vernacular English, the basilectal form which, according to Pawley (2008, p. 362), characterizes informal speech, especially among "working class and country men"
- Aboriginal English, which is the carrier, for most Aboriginal students, of Aboriginal culture.

My focus here is upon Aboriginal English, in relation to SAE, but there is room for similar research to be carried out in relation to speakers of Australian Vernacular English. The questions that arise include: What are the implications of the way in which language and culture (albeit, English-speaking and Australian) interact in the classroom? What does it mean for the Aboriginal English speaker if learning can only be accessed, and learning outcomes only validated, in SAE? And what does it mean for the teacher who does not know Aboriginal English if learners are using Aboriginal English when interacting and expressing their learning?

Questions such as these are typically not addressed because of the pervasive assumption that to know English, for an Australian, is to know SAE. The question of how much is lost in translation when Aboriginal English speakers are present in classrooms where SAE is spoken had, until recently, not been directly addressed.

Research on cross-dialectal understanding

Research done in Western Australia over some decades has inevitably led in the direction of posing this question. Progressively, the English discourse of Aboriginal speakers, especially those in schools, has been analyzed at the linguistic level (Kaldor & Malcolm 1979), at the level of speech use, discourse and genres (Malcolm 1994; 2001; Rochecouste & Malcolm 2003), at the level of the history of its development within Aboriginal speech communities (Malcolm & Koscielecki 1997; Malcolm 2000) and at the level of its underlying conceptualizations (Malcolm & Sharifian 2002). There have been studies of the ways in which it finds expression in youth culture (Malcolm et al. 2002) and of the way in which it is, or is not, represented in school literacy materials (Malcolm et al. 2003). So the question naturally arose: if Aboriginal English is not represented—at least officially—in school, and yet is ever-present in the lives of Aboriginal participants in learning situations, what are the consequences of this for learning? As communication passes between Aboriginal English speaking students and SAE-speaking teachers, how much might be lost, and what might be the consequences of this?

Methodology of the first study (Sharifian et al. 2004) into text comprehension

The author first advocated applying cognitive and cultural linguistic concepts in research into the use of Aboriginal English in the late 1990s (Malcolm 1998; Malcolm et al. 1999). The author has continued to be involved, with Farzad Sharifian and colleagues, in the ongoing implementation of such research. This chapter reports on some of the more recent developments. In 2002 Sharifian devised a system of exploring the potential loss in cross-dialectal communication by employing the concept of idea units, which had been developed by Kroll (1977) and used by Johns and Mayes (1990) and others in analyzing the writing of university students. Idea units are units of discourse in which a single complete element of thought is expressed. Johns and Mayes classify idea units into eight types on the basis of their linguistic form. For example, main clauses, relative and adverbial clauses, phrases set off from the sentence by commas, gerundives and infinitival constructive are examples of separate idea units. The idea of Sharifian and his team was to take eight existing Aboriginal English oral narrative texts from the database at the Centre for Applied Language and Literacy Research at Edith Cowan University in Perth, Western Australia, and, with due regard to the way the dialect works, analyze them into their idea units. We then invited teachers of Aboriginal students, and Aboriginal and Islander Education Officers (AIEOs), separately, to listen to the oral narratives and provide oral recalls of them, which were recorded. This means that the idea units in the original versions could be compared with those in the recalled versions, and the recalls of the non-Aboriginal teachers and the AIEOs could be compared. The Western Australian Department of Education and Training funded the research, which was published in the report *Improving Understanding of Aboriginal Literacy: Factors in Text Comprehension* (Sharifian et al. 2004).

Analysis of the recalls revealed five ways of dealing with the idea units (Sharifian et al. 2004, p. 13):

1. correct recall, where the essential idea from the narrative is reproduced

2. partial recall, where the idea is recalled with something missing (e.g. "The uncle was chasing something" for "My uncle was chasing a kangaroo")

3. distortion or re-interpretation, where another idea is substituted for the original

4. addition, where the original idea is extended

5. omission, where the original idea is not recalled.

After having been given two attempts to listen to and recall the narratives, participants were given a transcript of the narrative to read. Then they were invited to comment on how they had gone about attempting to recall what they had originally listened to.

Findings of the first study

It was apparent that the non-Aboriginal teachers did not, on the whole, interpret the Aboriginal English narratives with confidence. Many partially recalled idea units, with expressions like "somebody," "something," "something about," and "something like" being used to give vague expression to the idea. In such cases, the teachers seemed to be dependent on bottom-up processing, where they were taking a recalled word but not knowing how it fitted into the whole. On other occasions the teachers attempted to interpret what they had heard, but interpreted it in a distorted or re-interpreted form.

Below is the transcript, in idea units, of Text 1, in which a 13-year-old Aboriginal boy is telling his Aboriginal Education Specialist Teacher what went wrong when, at a school event, the teacher cooked a kangaroo.

1	...Did you um try the kangaroo tails last year?
2	Yeah.
3	Mr March cooked 'em.
4	They were half raw...
5	They weren't nice at all...
6	Only part was cooked would be the onion.
7	I was sitting there trying to eat it too.
8	It's sand too much sand.
9	Needed to cook longer.
10	One little piece was [cooked].
11	E should of done it in the morning early.
12	But e done it about ten or something.
13	It's too late.
14	E should of dug the hole day before,
15	cook the wood,
16	'cause the wood took a long time.
17	Leave the ashes there,
18	thas what e shoulda done,
19	Thas what my Dad said.
20	He didn't have time.
21	E shoulda asked for help.
22	Me and Lawrie woulda 'elp im.
23	We had lots of helpers.
24	They weren't very good at digging pits.
25	It took a lot longer [digging].
26	Maybe next year you can help.

A teacher's attempted recall reduced idea unit 6 to "something about the onion," and so exhibited the use of bottom-up processing on a minor detail. This led to the teacher missing the main point about the rawness of the meat. The same respondent also changed idea unit 14 to "The pit wasn't dug deep enough," showing unawareness of the fact that the roasting of the kangaroo requires a shallow hole and the covering of the carcass with ashes. It is time, rather than the depth of the hole that is the essential element in the cooking.

There were many examples of such misconstrued meanings of texts which relied on schemas well-known to Aboriginal speakers. Text 5, which is a tale about a 14-year-old girl's family's encounter with a molesting spirit, included the idea unit "One of my nannas could feel these little fingers an' that choking 'er." This was recalled by the teacher as "It was the smoke choking her." In addition, there were some completely new ideas introduced in the teacher recalls and many of the original idea units not recalled. Text 2, which related to travel alongside a "water pond" looking for a kangaroo was recontextualized as "They were in a cave."

The teacher recalls also demonstrated a tendency to re-order the content of the narratives to bring the material into a more chronological sequence. In other words, the expression of the Aboriginal speakers was guided not only by content schemas but by formal schemas that determined the ordering of the material presented, and teachers in their recalls were guided by different formal schemas which presuppose linear chronological ordering. Typically, Aboriginal speakers will not provide information in advance of when it is relevant to the narrative, when they will introduce it with a retrospective clause beginning with "cause." So Text 4 concludes with the clause, referring to a dog: "cause it was tied up but it got undone," which explained how the dog had broken loose and got in the way of shooting the kangaroo. The non-Aboriginal recalls placed this information earlier in the account.

By contrast with the non-Aboriginal teachers, AIEOs tended to approach the narratives from a "holistic" perspective, recognizing more quickly the overall intent of the narrative rather than trying to make sense of it by picking up details. Sometimes the AIEOs verbalized the strategies they were using, explaining to the researcher how the event being described takes place. For example, in accounting for the spirit visitation underlying Text 5, an Aboriginal listener explained:

> Yeah this one is a bit hard. Um like she said they- she was stayin at her uncle's an 'e woke up one night and something was cooking obviously but it wasn't anyone, it was a spirit, yeah, musta been someone that lived there before and ah well back in the old days they say travelling spirit travelling

through the house. 'Cos it comes through like stop and then move on a couple of days later or something. Yeah are but yeah it's hard one as they sayin leavin the window open, s- so the spirit just cos he tryin to go-hopefully he's just pass through and to the next resting spot wherever it's gonna go before it gets to its destination. By the cooking smelling that's just a, it wasn't cooking it's just a scent you that sorta pick up for travelling spirits, you know feeling, yeah.

In accounting for the occurrence described in Text 2 where, in the course of the hunt, the car went too close to the fence, the Aboriginal listener relates the event to his own schema as he says: "in the car chasing down the fence line, *like most of us do*, most of the kangaroos head toward the fence line anyways to jump it and to get away yeah."

Interpretation of the first study

To account for what was revealed in this study, it is necessary to go beyond the linguistic elements in the narratives. This was particularly apparent from the way in which the AIEOs approached the interpretive task. They sought clues from the text that would signal a familiar scenario in which to locate the action. In other words, the Aboriginal English narratives derived from schemas, familiar to Aboriginal people, in which experience is organized. Schemas can be seen as "*cognitive* structures that can be determined by *cultural* experiences and are reflected in *linguistic* expression" (Sharifian 2001, p. 125; Sharifian et al. 2012). In analyzing oral narratives from the Yamatji people in Western Australia, Malcolm and Rochecouste (2000) suggested that they were very often organized according to four prototypic schemas, identified as travel, hunting, observing, and encountering the unknown (this latter title being subsequently changed, at the suggestion of Aboriginal research assistants, to "scary things"). These schemas, and others like them, are, as it were, scripts (Schank & Abelson 1977, p. 41) which help in the organization of perceptions and the interpretation of discourse. Access to the relevant schemas seemed to be what differentiated the non-Aboriginal teachers from the AIEOs in interpreting the Aboriginal English oral narratives.

Sometimes, knowing that a schema is shared, a narrator will leave details out as redundant, or perhaps allude to them with a phrase like "and that." In Text 5, for example, in which the narrator assumes the "scary things" schema, they use the expression "an' that" three times in a single sentence: "She feel this choking and when she like finished an' that she 'ad to finish the praying an' that 'cause it's choking 'er an' that an' they noticed it 'cause it in 'er voice an' they had kept on praying an' got over it an' the spirit's not there anymore." This is what Sharifian (2001) has called schema-based referencing. Sometimes a single word or phrase, like *Wudachi* or "there's a bush" may summon up a schema which, to the Aboriginal listener doesn't need to be elaborated, resulting in what Sharifian (2001) termed "minimal verbal processing," which, of course makes the interpretive task harder for the non-Aboriginal listener.

The question arises, of course, as to whether or not the non-Aboriginal teachers were using schemas derived from their cultural background in interpreting, or re-interpreting what they were listening to. The nature of the additions, omissions and re-interpretations in the recalls certainly led in this direction, though we have not undertaken any investigation of non-Aboriginal schemas.

The second study (Sharifian et al. 2012)

An Australian Research Council (ARC) Discovery Grant to Sharifian and the present author made it possible for the team, which had looked at how teachers interpret Aboriginal English narratives, to look in the other direction and investigate how students in schools interpret the standard English literacy materials with which they are confronted. This project involved 44 Aboriginal and 20 non-Aboriginal students and their teachers, from five Perth metropolitan and two rural primary schools. The team examined literacy materials that those surveyed used widely. From these materials, the team selected five written narratives of varying genres:

- fairytale: *Puss in Boots* (Deverell 2002, adapted from Frances Sargent Osgood, 1842)
- Aboriginal folklore: The *Magic Colours* (Cecilia Egan & Elizabeth Alger, 2006)
- non-Aboriginal fable: *The Story about Ping* (Marjorie Flack & Kurt Wiese, 1981)
- non-Aboriginal fiction: *John Brown, Rose and the Midnight Cat* (Jenny Wagner, 1980)
- realistic fiction: *Bushfire* (Marguerite Hann Syme, 2000).

The Aboriginal and non-Aboriginal students individually listened to their teacher reading each story, in separate sessions. The students were not allowed to see what book the teacher was reading. The student would leave and, after a break, return to the teacher and, in a recorded session, provide their oral recall of what had been read to them. Then the teacher would probe with further questions. As in the previous project, the original texts and the recalls were analyzed into idea units. Then the idea units in the recall protocols and the original texts were compared.

Findings of the second study

The Institute for Professional Learning of the Education Department of Western Australia published the second report as *"Understanding stories my way": Aboriginal-English Speaking Students' (Mis)understanding of School Literacy Materials in Australian English* (Sharifian et al. 2012).

As in the earlier project, it was evident that those surveyed recalled few of the idea units from the original texts. It was also apparent that the Aboriginal and non-Aboriginal students had quite different additions and patterns of recall of idea units.

To illustrate, one story, *John Brown, Rose and the Midnight Cat* by Wagner is shown below. In summary, the story is as follows:

> Rose, a widow, and her dog, John Brown, happily live together. They rely on each other for company, but when a cat appears in the garden, John Brown refuses to acknowledge it. Rose, however, is quite taken by the cat. Eventually Rose falls ill, and this distresses John Brown. He reluctantly chooses to welcome the cat into the home to help Rose get better (Sharifian et al. 2012, p. 32).

In seeking to understand the Aboriginal responses to the text, the team depended heavily on input from its Aboriginal member who, like the AIEOs in the first study, was sensitive to the overarching schemas which were informing the students' interpretations. Two types of schema were involved: a schema that provides the orientation to the situation to be anticipated; and schemas that entail propositions about elements in the story. For example, in *John Brown, Rose and the Midnight Cat* the title already alerts the Aboriginal listener to the fact that midnight and a cat are involved, and these are triggers to what Aboriginal consultants have suggested we call the "scary things" schema. The overall schema is "scary things," and the fact that Rose's husband has died and that Rose falls ill compounds this impression. However, there are also propositions entailed in some of the elements in the story. A proposition associated with a dog, for instance, is that a dog can be a protector, especially where spirits are involved. A cat, on the other hand, whose eyes shine in the night, may be a messenger of the spirit world, perhaps warning of something bad to come, while fire may protect against pursuing spirits.

Table 13-1 attempts to show the levels of association involved in the story for Aboriginal listeners. The story is summarized due to space constraints.

Table 13-1: Level of association for Aboriginal listeners

Story	Trigger	Schema (orientation)	Association/ Proposition Schema
Rose, a widow, and her dog, John Brown, happily live together sitting by the fire, but when a cat appears in the garden one night, John Brown refuses to acknowledge it. Rose, however, is quite taken by the cat. Eventually Rose falls ill, and this distresses John Brown. He reluctantly chooses to welcome the cat into the home to help Rose get better.	widow	sickness, death, scary things	Tormenting spirits cause illness
	dog		Dog may be spiritual care-giver
	fire		Fire protects you from tormenting spirits
	cat		Cat: spirit connection (eyes). Warning?
	night		Spirits are active at night
	falls ill		May have been foreseen by cat

Now, presumably, none of these associations was intended by the authors of the story, or might be foreseen by the teachers who select it as a literacy resource. It is an endearing story of a dog which has to give up its aversion for cats to keep the woman who feeds it happy. However, when Aboriginal students attempted to recall the story, the omissions, additions and revisions were non-random.

The main point of conflict in the original story—the opposition between Rose and John Brown about admitting the cat—was often not mentioned. Most Aboriginal students recalled the death of Rose's husband and Rose falling ill. Sitting by the fire was, for some Aboriginal students, a significant point of resolution. One even implied that Rose got better by sitting by the fire. One Aboriginal student included in his recall that a ghost had tipped over the cat's milk. Another Aboriginal student said that the cat came to them as a warning that they might get shot or arrested. When the teacher attempted to probe for more from this student he was silent, in that he was frightened to talk more about it.

When the idea units recalled by the Aboriginal students were compared with those recalled by the non-Aboriginal students, the salience of the idea units to the two groups differed by a minimum of 15 percent. Key idea units recalled by the Aboriginal students but not the non-Aboriginal students were: Rose's husband died, there was something out in the bushes, and they ended up sitting by the fire. Key idea units recalled by the non-Aboriginal but not the Aboriginal students were: Rose lived with a dog, Rose and the dog argued over giving milk to the cat, the dog missed out on his breakfast, and the dog eventually let the cat in.

To understand the respective ways that the two groups of listeners understood the text, it is necessary to recognize that one effect of depending on a schema for the interpretation of material encountered is that some elements in the text will be foregrounded and some elements backgrounded (Sharifian et al. 2012, p. 37). Elements in the story of *John Brown, Rose and the Midnight Cat* foregrounded by Aboriginal listeners included the death of Rose's husband, the association of the cat with midnight, and the reassuring presence of the fire. In contrast, the antipathy of the dog towards the cat, and the relationship between Rose and the dog—key elements to non-Aboriginal listeners—tended to be backgrounded by Aboriginal listeners.

Interpretation of the second study

In interpreting the findings on this project, the key concept that emerges is what the researchers have called *reschematization*. This is the re-interpretation of a text by applying to it different interpretive schemas from those that first informed it. While limitations of space mean only a small portion of the data from this study is shown, the findings on this story are consistent with those on the five others included in the investigation, as shown in detail in Sharifian et al. (2012).

It seems likely, on the basis of this study, that Aboriginal English speaking students may rely heavily on reschematization to understand the texts with which they are confronted. In the light of the earlier study, we can recognize that teachers are doing the same thing when they attempt to understand Aboriginal English narratives. If this is, as is reasonable to assume, a regular feature of communication in classrooms where Aboriginal students and non-Aboriginal teachers are communicating, it could have a significant effect on the learning that is taking place.

Implications of this research

While cultural schema theory has been applied across a range of disciplines for more than half a century (Sharifian et al. 2012, p. 10), only now has it been brought to bear on the interface between Aboriginal and non-Aboriginal cultures in classrooms. The work reported on in this chapter is preliminary and limited by it taking place in a limited number of locations, with a relatively small number of participants. It is not, then, possible to make confident, wide-ranging recommendations from the research. However, it should alert us to a number of factors that could better inform our understanding of the Aboriginal classroom as a meeting place of cultures.

This research helps to show that education is necessarily a cross-cultural process, and that in cross-dialectal communication the possibilities for misunderstanding lie not only at the linguistic level but at the conceptual level. Ideally, Aboriginal learners should have the opportunity to respond to texts in their own dialect and in SAE. But, even where all texts are in SAE, it cannot be assumed that Aboriginal and non-Aboriginal students will give those texts the same "reading" , since it is by way of cultural schemas that all students will arrive at their understanding.

It is apparent that, in cross-dialectal situations, Aboriginal English-speaking students are actively involved in seeking to make meanings from what is presented to them in SAE, although the meanings they arrive at may easily lead to the wrong inference that those students are not attentive or lack ability. Rather than not attending, they may have been attending to cues that escaped the teacher's attention. At the early stages of this research, the term "distortion" was used to refer to changed versions of texts in teacher recalls. The term is no longer seen as appropriate. Rather, it is recognized that reschematization occurs whenever a text from one culture is interpreted on the basis of a schematic framework acquired in another culture.

The research shows that, where the communication between teacher and student seems to break down, the reluctance of Aboriginal students to respond to the teacher's questions may well relate to the student getting implications from the communication that the teacher fails to recognize. This, for example, was the case with *John Brown, Rose and the Midnight Cat*, where students who were wary of the role of tormenting spirits in this story resisted the teacher's questioning about how they had come at the interpretation of the story they had given.

In addition, the projects discussed here highlight the reciprocal nature of reschematization. Teachers cannot assume that the conceptual implications of texts they use in the classroom (including texts claiming to have indigenous subject matter) are unproblematic. Teachers need to develop ways of questioning texts with students in a way that lets cross-cultural interpretations emerge and become recognized. At the same time, teachers need to recognize the need to make explicit the SAE schemas which are assumed by the texts they use. What is needed is a cross-cultural critical literacy.

The Department of Education and the Department of Training and Workforce Development in Western Australia has recognized the relevance of this research to the professional development of teachers, trainers and AIEOs working with Aboriginal students. Those departments have published *Tracks to Two-Way Learning* (Königsberg, Collard & McHugh 2012), a training resource that Aboriginal and non-Aboriginal teaching teams can use, in which 2 of the 12 focus areas are "How we represent our world" and "How we shape experience."

Materials such as these can lead to a greater recognition of the need for culturally-inclusive approaches to education and for increasingly open approaches to the interpretation of texts that will give room for the emergence of cross-cultural interpretations and the negotiation of meanings on a basis of equal respect.

The place of Applied Linguistics in enabling a meeting place of cultures

The education of minorities has long been bedevilled by what Wolfram (2001, p. 345) has called a "language subordination ideology." From the 1960s, as sociolinguistic research had extended knowledge of non-standard dialects in the United States, applied linguists such as Shuy, Wolfram and Riley (1968) and Baratz (1969) sought to embed the dialects of the learners in the education process which privileged only the culture of SAE speakers. Yet when attempts are made to institutionalize true recognition of non-standard varieties in education, they encounter entrenched resistance as detailed in Adger, Christian and Taylor (1999) and May (2012). Instead of being meeting places of cultures, schools are pressured to be strongholds of the prevailing culture. On the basis of the research outlined in this chapter, applied linguists can counter this pressure in a number of ways.

First, applied linguists need to reconceptualize the "gap" that must be bridged so that Aboriginal students can be successful in the education system. Dixon has observed (2013, p. 302) that "the *Closing the Gap* initiative (Commonwealth of Australia 2009) explicitly defines the "gap" as between non-Indigenous and Indigenous students—rather than in terms of what Indigenous students' own goals are for *their* futures..." The idea that Aboriginal students need to catch up to non-Aboriginal students fails to recognize that there is, as the two research projects discussed here show, a gap to be bridged on *both* sides: Aboriginal students do not fully understand the material in SAE they are exposed to, and non-Aboriginal teachers do not fully understand what their Aboriginal students are communicating to them. Educational systems need to recognize a responsibility to enhance the skills of teachers of Aboriginal students in understanding the dialect these students use.

Second, we now know, through the application of cognitive and cultural linguistic research to Aboriginal educational settings, that Aboriginal English and SAE differ not only linguistically but in terms of mental imagery. Students are being disadvantaged because insufficient account is being taken of the schemas that lie behind the way in which they construe experience, in terms both of their production and reception of language. Teachers need training in how to bring to a level of explicitness the schemas both they and their Aboriginal students depend on when they use English.

Third, we need to get rid of the idea that subordinating one culture to another is acceptable. Education, for Aboriginal students, must be a meeting place of cultures. This implies that such education should give Aboriginal students the opportunity to express themselves and use existing cultural knowledge on the way towards acquiring new cultural knowledge. In the course of such learning, when assessment does takes place, it will be consistent with the bicultural nature of the learning process, instead of treating Aboriginal students as de facto native speakers of SAE.

Acknowledgements

The research reported in this chapter is the product of the joint efforts of Farzad Sharifian, Patricia Königsberg, Judith Rochecouste, Adriano Truscott, Glenys Collard and the author. I wish to express my indebtedness to all these colleagues, and also to the teachers, AIEOs and students from 11 schools who made the research possible.

References

Adger, C.T., D. Christian and O. Taylor, eds, 1999, *Making the Connection: Language and academic achievement among African American students*, McHenry, IL: Center for Applied Linguistics and Delta Systems Co., Inc.

Baratz, J.C. 1969, "Teaching reading in an urban Negro school system". In J.C. Baratz and R.W. Shuy, eds, *Teaching Black Children to Read*, Washington, D.C.: Center for Applied Linguistics, pp. 92–116

Dawkins, J. 1991, *Australia's Language: The Australian Language and Literacy Policy*, Canberra: Australian Government Publishing Service

Deverell, C. 2002, "Puss in Boots". In *Classic Fairy Tales for Bedtime Reading*, Linden, N.J.: Grand Dreams (adapted from F.S. Osgood, *Puss in Boots*, 1842)

Dixon, S. 2013, "Educational failure or success: Aboriginal students' non-standard English utterances", *Australian Review of Applied Linguistics* 36(3): 302–15

Egan, C. and E. Alger. 2006, *The Magic Colours*, Marleston, South Australia: Gecko Books

Flack, M. and K. Wiese. 1981, *The Story About Ping*, London: William Clowes Ltd

Johns, A.M. and P. Mayes. 1990, "An analysis of summary protocols of university ESL students", *Applied Linguistics* 11(3): 253–71

Kaldor, S. and I.G. Malcolm. 1979, "The language of the school and the language of the Western Australian Aboriginal schoolchild: Implications for education". In R.M. and C.H. Berndt, eds, *Aborigines of the West: Their past and their present*, Perth: University of Western Australia Press, pp. 406–37

Königsberg, P., G. Collard and M. McHugh. 2012, *Tracks to Two-Way Learning*. Perth, W.A.: Department of Education and Department of Training and Workplace Development

Kroll, B. 1977, "Combining ideas in written and spoken English: A look at subordination and coordination". In E.O. Keenan and T.L Bennett, eds, *Discourse across Time and Space*. Number 5 in Southern California Occasional Papers in Linguistics. Department of Linguistics, University of Southern California, Los Angeles, pp. 68–108

Malcolm, I.G. 1994, "Aboriginal English inside and outside the classroom", *Australian Review of Applied Linguistics* 17(2): 147–80

—. 1998, "Aboriginal English: Some perspectives from cognitive linguistics". Paper presented to the Annual Conference of the Australian Linguistic Society, Griffith University, Brisbane, 3–5 July

—. 2000, "Aboriginal English: From contact variety to social dialect". In J. Siegel, ed, *Processes of Language Contact: Case Studies from Australia and the South Pacific*. Montreal: Fides, pp. 123–44

—. 2001, *Aboriginal English Genres in Perth*. Mount Lawley, W.A.: Centre for Applied Language and Literacy Research, Edith Cowan University

Malcolm, I.G., E. Grote, L. Eggington and F. Sharifian. 2003, *The Representation of Aboriginal English in School Literacy Materials*, Mount Lawley, W.A.: Centre for Applied Language and Literacy Research, Edith Cowan University

Malcolm, I., Y. Haig, P. Königsberg, J. Rochecouste, G. Collard, A. Hill and R. Cahill. 1999, *Towards More User-Friendly Education for Speakers of Aboriginal English*, Mount Lawley: Centre for Applied Language and Literacy Research, Edith Cowan University and Education Department of Western Australia

Malcolm, I.G., P. Königsberg, G. Collard, A. Hill, E. Grote, F. Sharifian, A. Kickett and E. Sahanna. 2002, *Umob Deadly: Recognized and Unrecognized Literacy Skills of Aboriginal Youth*, Mount Lawley, W.A.: Centre for Applied Language and Literacy Research and Institute for the Service Professions, Edith Cowan University

Malcolm, I.G. and M.M. Koscielecki. 1997, *Aboriginality and English*. Report to the Australian Research Council. Perth, W.A.: Centre for Applied Language Research, Edith Cowan University

Malcolm, I.G. and J. Rochecouste. 2000, "Event and story schemas in Australian Aboriginal English discourse", *English World-Wide* 21(2): 261–89

Malcolm, I.G. and F. Sharifian. 2002, "Aspects of Aboriginal English oral discourse: an application of cultural schema theory", *Discourse Studies* 4(2): 169–81

May, S. 2012, "Educational approaches to minorities: context, contest and opportunities". In A. Yiakoumetti, ed, *Harnessing Linguistic Variation to Improve Education*, Oxford, U.K.: Peter Lang, pp. 11–43

Pawley, A. 2008, "Australian vernacular English: some grammatical characteristics". In K. Burridge and B. Kortmann, eds, *Varieties of English: The Pacific and Australasia*, Berlin: Mouton de Gruyter, pp. 362–97

Rochecouste, J. and I.G. Malcolm. 2003, 2nd ed, *Aboriginal English Genres in the Yamatji Lands of Western Australia*, Mount Lawley, W.A.: Centre for Applied Language and Literacy Research, Edith Cowan University

Schank, R.C. and R.P. Abelson. 1977, *Scripts, Plans, Goals and Understanding: an Inquiry into Human Knowledge Structures*, Hillsdale, N.J.: Lawrence Erlbaum Associates

Sharifian, F. 2001, "Schema-based processing in Australian speakers of Aboriginal English", *Language and Intercultural Communication* 1(2): 120–34

Sharifian, F., J. Rochecouste, I.G. Malcolm, P. Königsberg and G. Collard. 2004, *Improving Understanding of Aboriginal Literacy: Factors in Text Comprehension*, East Perth: Department of Education and Training

Sharifian, F., A. Truscott, P. Königsberg, I.G. Malcolm and G. Collard. 2012, *"Understanding stories my way": Aboriginal-English Speaking Students' (Mis)understanding of School Literacy Materials in Australian English*, Leederville, W.A.: Institute for Professional learning, Department of Education

Shuy, R.W., W.A. Wolfram and W.K Riley. 1968, *Field Techniques in an Urban Language Study*, Washington, D.C.: Center for Applied Linguistics

Syme, M.H. 2000, *Bushfire*, Richmond: Scholastic Australia

Wagner, J. 1980, *John Brown, Rose and the Midnight Cat*, Camberwell, Vic: Penguin Australia

Wolfram, W. 2001, "Reconsidering the sociolinguistic addenda for African American English: The next generation of research and application". In S.L. Lanehart, ed, *Sociocultural and Historical Contexts of African American English*, Amsterdam: John Benjamins, pp. 331–62

PART III

Chapter Fourteen

Anomalous Data about Aboriginal and Torres Strait Islander Language Ecologies

Denise Angelo and Sophie McIntosh

Keywords: contact language demographics, language data collection, census language data, Aboriginal and Torres Strait Islander languages, Australian contact languages, contact language ecologies

Abstract

This chapter presents in-depth case studies that reveal the skewed nature of Census data collected or reported about the vernaculars of many Aboriginal and Torres Strait Islander people in remote Queensland communities. It is argued that issues relating to inconsistent and inaccurate data have arisen largely due to complexities surrounding widespread language shift towards contact languages. In such contexts, collected language data can be misunderstood and miscoded, because naming and classifying a "language spoken at home" is predicated on (pre-existing) language awareness and recognition, as well as standardized—or at least well-recognized—nomenclature. The chapter also shows that Census categories for contact languages—and the compilations drawing on them—require considered attention to ensure greater validity. This is particularly pertinent at the present time, as data-driven government reforms for improving Indigenous outcomes require data of the highest quality to be effective.

Introduction

This chapter demonstrates that languages spoken by Aboriginal and Torres Strait Islander people in Queensland are not always recorded accurately in collected and disseminated language data, such as for the Australian Census. While Indigenous languages perhaps lack visibility in the Australian public domain in general, the "contact languages" used by many Indigenous Australians appear to have even less acknowledgement and status (Berry & Hudson 1997). This is despite these *newer* languages having much larger numbers of speakers than any traditional Indigenous language in Queensland (HoR 1992). The lack of recognition and awareness about these contact languages seems to allow anomalous language data into the public domain.

Reliable and valid data about Aboriginal and Torres Strait Islander people's language use is important. Information about the languages spoken by Indigenous families may be necessary for ascertaining community needs, delivering targeted services, and analyzing outcomes, especially with data-driven Government systems. The current National Indigenous Reform Agreement—otherwise known as Closing the Gap (COAG 2008)—for example, represents an intervention process aiming to reduce disparities between Indigenous and non-Indigenous Australians, and data collection and analysis play a central role (p. A-33). Clearly, accurate data—and informed interpretations—are pivotal to the success of evidence-based models of reform. In light of this, it is especially concerning that language data may not reflect actual language use in some Indigenous communities.

Clarifying information about contact languages with students, communities, and institutions is a mediated process, influenced greatly by overlays of mutual understandings, attitudes and beliefs, and shared language(s) and terminology (Sellwood & Angelo 2013). (Potentially) misleading language data in the public domain has not assisted. Rather than being futilely critical, however, the intentions of this chapter are to compare and contrast available information to show how anomalous data about contact language situations can be revealed, and to make constructive observations and practical suggestions about issues encountered. To this end, the chapter first briefly describes the contemporary Indigenous language situation in Queensland. Case studies illustrating inaccuracies and/or inconsistencies in language data that are publicly available then follow. After summarising apparent recurring issues, the chapter finally puts forward suggestions to improve the collection and representation of language data.

Several conventions adopted throughout this chapter require explanation here. First, the term "Indigenous" is used with the intention of respectfully including Aboriginal *and* Torres Strait Islander peoples. Second, double quote marks are used to indicate that language names or data categories are exactly as they appear within source language data, as in "Torres Strait Creole." In addition, the compilations of Census data called "Time Series Profile" provide a useful starting point for each place-based case study because they provide material across three Censuses (2001, 2006 and

2011), not because their language data displays contain *more* anomalies than other compilations. Finally, it is important to note the following differing uses of the term "other," as employed on the Australian Bureau of Statistics (ABS) website:

- the expression "Other Languages" denotes a diverse range of languages classified under 9000 codes, which include "African Languages" and "Oceanic Pidgins and Creoles" (see ABS 2011b, pp. 111–12)
- the phrase "speaks other language" is generally used on the ABS website to indicate a "language spoken at home" other than "English only" (e.g. ABS 2012a)
- however, in some data tables, the term "other" includes "languages not identified individually," "inadequately described" and "non-verbal so described" (e.g. ABS 2012a, T10, footnote d).

Overview of Indigenous languages in Queensland relevant to the Case Studies

Traditional languages connected to specific lands and islands were once spoken by Indigenous peoples across the Australian continent, but the punitive, assimilatory and marginalizing practices imposed since British invasion and settlement have resulted in these languages suffering a marked loss of speakers (HoR 2012; McConvell & Thieberger 2001; Schmidt 1990). However, new languages have also emerged and developed as a result of this forced language contact. Communication niches created in post-contact multilingual speech communities (Munro 2005; Shnukal 1988) were filled by language contact varieties, some of which expanded into creoles—languages in their own right.

In Queensland there are three broad chains of creoles, although research is still required into the exact nature of the relationships between these:

- *Yumplatok* (or Torres Strait Creole) is a creole spoken throughout the Torres Strait, parts of northern Cape York and in towns with significant Torres Strait Islander populations (Crowley & Rigsby 1979; Ober 1999; Shnukal 1991)
- *Kriol* is a creole predominately linked to the spread of the cattle industry, and unnamed varieties associated with it are spoken in parts of western Cape York, of the Gulf and of far western Queensland

(Graber 1987; Munro 2000, 2005; Sandefur 1990; Sandefur et al. 1982; Schultze-Berndt et al. 2013)

- *Yarrie Lingo* is the name attributed to a creole spoken at Yarrabah (Sellwood & Angelo 2013; Yeatman et al. 2009), with related forms spoken at Palm Island, Woorabinda and Cherbourg.

Queensland has witnessed such immense language shift towards these (and other) contact languages that traditional languages are now only commonly spoken in a few remote areas (HoR 2012, p. 38). Creoles differ markedly and systematically from English across their syntactic, morphological, semantic, pragmatic and phonological systems, rendering them mutually incomprehensible with this language (Sandefur 1984; Shnukal 2002). Despite this, they can go unrecognized in language data collected for purposes such as the Census, because they can be erroneously perceived as (often substandard) versions of the mainstream language of power, Standard Australian English (SAE), due to being English-lexified (McIntosh et. al. 2012, p. 451). Dialects of English resulting from language contact have also been documented in Queensland—Aboriginal English (Eades 1983) and Torres Strait English (Shnukal 2001)—but these are not a focus for the Census as they are not "a language other than English," unlike creoles.

The significant changes in language use across Indigenous speech communities in Queensland have actually created *more* complexity in regards to the accuracy of language-related data collection and analysis, adding to issues already identified with collecting data about traditional languages (McConvell & Thieberger 2001, pp. 40–41; Morphy 2002, pp. 45–46). Indeed, the compilations of data analyzed in this chapter show difficulties encountered by many Indigenous individuals in Queensland in answering the Census question: "Does the person speak a language other than English at home?" (ABS 2011a) and/or in having their responses accurately rendered.

Data

The following case studies examine language data relevant to specific locations and/or specific languages. The methodology employed combines discussion of selected language data issues alongside explanations of local language ecologies.

Case Study One: A gentle glide?

At Yarrabah, an Aboriginal community in far north Queensland, data available on the ABS website as a *Time Series Profile* (ABS 2012a, shown in Fig. 14-1) shows a decline in the number of people reporting that they speak "English only" between the 2006 and 2011 Censuses and a corresponding increase in those indicating that they speak "Australian Indigenous Languages." These changes mirror each other (shifting 14 percent respectively), which seems to suggest that there has been a gentle glide towards a situation where more residents apparently speak "Australian Indigenous Languages."

Fig. 14-1: Responses categorized as "Australian Indigenous Languages" and "English only" to "language spoken at home" at Yarrabah, as a percentage of total residents

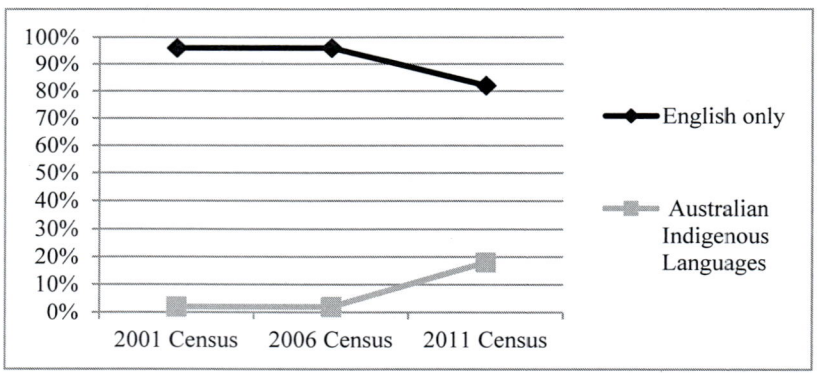

Data source: ABS, 2012a, "T01 Selected person characteristics", "T10 Language spoken at home (a) by sex".

The number of children born to residents of Yarrabah between 2006 and 2011 make up 13 percent of the total 2011 population, very close to this percentage of shifted language use. Yet additional language data, displayed by age in the same *Time Series Profile* (ABS 2012a, T11), shows that children born between these Censuses are not the sole source of the apparent shift in language. Fig. 14-2 depicts (only) people reporting proficient use of "other language" to show how numbers increased markedly across all age groups between these Censuses.

Fig. 14-2: Responses to "Speaks other language" at Yarrabah, as numbers of residents, by age (in 2006 and 2011)

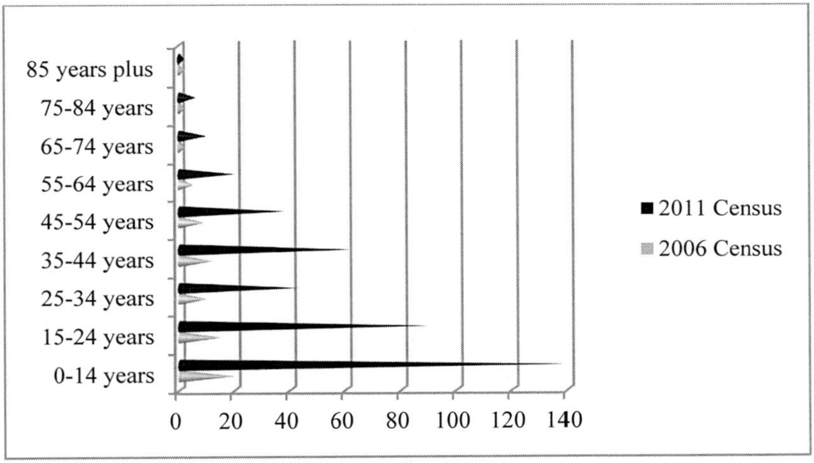

Data source: ABS, 2012a, "T11. Proficiency in spoken English/language by age".

The 2011 Census *QuickStats* for Yarrabah (ABS 2012b) provides a further public source of information about residents' language use. This includes a table titled "Language, top responses (other than English)," which are listed as: "Kriol," 15.4%; "Other Australian Indigenous languages, nec" (i.e. not elsewhere classified), 0.7%; "Yumplatok (Torres Strait Creole)," 0.2%; and "Guugu Yimidhirr," 0.1%. All of these languages would be termed "Australian Indigenous languages" according to the ABS. And all the named languages except "Guugu Yimidhirr" (a traditional language) could be described as contact languages by linguists. Small variations due to different data compilations are a likely reason that the total percentage of collective Indigenous language responses is 16% here as opposed to 14% above. (This *QuickStats* display is compiled from Census data included by "place of usual residence," not "place of enumeration" as for the *Time Series Profile* cited above.)

Problems

These publicly available datasets would lead most viewers to assume— erroneously—that a small but significant proportion of the Yarrabah community changed from speaking "English only" to speaking "Australian

Indigenous Languages" (predominantly "Kriol"), between 2006 and 2011. In actual fact, language usage in Yarrabah was shifting from traditional languages to a contact language a century ago. The resulting local creole, increasingly called "Yarrie Lingo," is, however, not Kriol (see Sellwood & Angelo 2013; Yeatman et al. 2009).

Case Study Two: A rapid cross over?

At Kubin, on Moa Island in the western Torres Strait, selected Census data available in a *Time Series Profile* (ABS 2012d) appears to show a steep rise in residents declaring that they speak "Australian Indigenous Languages" as their "language spoken at home." This seems to correspond closely to a dramatic fall in the responses compiled under "Other" languages (see Fig. 14-3), in contrast to the decreasing "English only" responses at Yarrabah. (In fact, the percentage of total residents at Kubin who declared they spoke "English only" was just 8% in both 2001 and 2006, and 5% in 2011.)

Fig. 14-3: Responses categorized as "Australian Indigenous Languages" and "Other" languages to "language spoken at home" at Kubin Village, as a percentage of the total number of residents

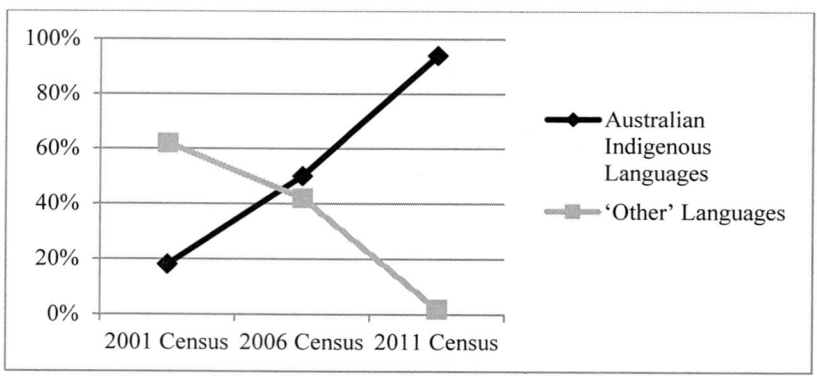

Data source: ABS, 2012d, "T01 Selected person characteristics" and "T10 Language spoken at home (a) by sex".

Considering that responses categorized as "Other" languages are displayed separately to "Australian Indigenous Languages," the data displayed in Fig.14-3 raises questions about the possible identity of the formerly widely-claimed "Other" language(s). Indeed, despite the fact that Kubin residents are primarily Indigenous (comprising 86%, 94%, 99% of Kubin's total population in 2001, 2006, 2011 respectively), data from this *Time Series Profile* suggests that many Kubin residents were, until recently, declaring they spoke a language (at least one) which was categorized as neither an "Australian Indigenous Language" nor "English only."

In the 2011 Census *QuickStats* for the statistical local area of Kubin (ABS 2012e), a table displaying "Language, top responses (other than English)" shows that the local traditional language—"Kalaw Kawaw Ya/Kala Lagaw Ya"—and the contact languages—"Yumplatok (Torres Strait Creole)" and "Kriol"—were the only responses for "language spoken at home" (see the right column in Table 14-1). This data represents a language ecology consistent with this part of the western Torres Strait (Shnukal 1989).

Moving to the 2006 Census *QuickStats* for Kubin (Indigenous Community) (ABS 2007a), there is a significant gap in language data. Other than "English only" (8.4%), just "Kalaw Kawaw Ya/Kala Lagaw Ya" (31.7%) and "Torres Strait Creole" (16.8%) are displayed (see the center column in Table 14-1). The blurb beneath this data also declares they are "the only two languages other than English spoken at home." Taken together, the responses total only 56.9 percent of residents, so it is clear that just under half the population of Kubin is not even visible in this source of "language spoken at home" data. The "missing" proportion is very similar to that categorized as speaking "Other" languages (again not including "Australian Indigenous Languages") in 2006, as reproduced in Fig. 14-3.

An alternate public source of 2006 Census data for the Local Government Area of Kubin is in *The People of Queensland* (Dept. I & C 2008, p. 304), which seems to have compiled more extensive information on "languages other than English spoken at home" and presents more (labeled) categories than the portrayals of 2006 Census data on the ABS website. In addition to the traditional language "Kalaw Kawaw Ya/Kala Lagaw Ya" and the contact language "Torres Strait Creole," it reports responses of Kubin residents categorized under "Creole, nfd" (i.e. not further defined) (see the left column in Table 14-1).

Table 14-1: Responses to "language spoken at home" (other than "English only") at Kubin Village, as a percentage of the total number of residents, in 2006 and 2011, languages identified

Language designation	2006 Census *People of Queensland* (Dept. I & C, 2008)	2006 Census *QuickStats* (ABS, 2007a)	2011 Census *QuickStats* (ABS, 2012e)
Traditional language			
'Kalaw Kawaw Ya/Kalaw Lagaw Ya'	34.5	31.7	34.6
Contact languages			
'Yumplatok (Torres Strait Creole)'	17.8	16.8	56.2
'Creole, nfd'	42.5	-	-
'Kriol'	-	-	1.9
Total	**94.8%**	**48.5%**	**92.7%**

Data sources: Dept. I & C (2008, p. 303) Table 2.75.5 "Languages Other than English Spoken at Home by Gender"; ABS (2007a) "Language spoken at home"; ABS (2012e) "Language, top responses (other than English)".

Overall, it is evident that a very similar percentage of Kubin residents are classified as speaking "Creole, nfd" in one public source of 2006 Census language data (Dept. I & C 2008), as are missing from language data reported in another (ABS 2007a), and as are categorized as speaking "Other" languages in another (ABS 2012d) (in Fig. 14-3). So it seems highly probable that the treatment of the responses classified as "Creole, nfd" (in 2006) has caused these glitches. To date, other publicly available compilations of 2001 Census data about "language spoken at home" at Kubin have not been located and, without the ability to cross-reference, it can only be surmised that a problematic handling of "Creole, nfd" pertained to an even greater extent at that time (see Fig. 14-3).

Problems

Despite an appearance of people in Kubin shifting away from speaking what are classed as "Other" languages (Fig. 14-3), no such languages have been in widespread use. The language shift underway is actually *between* different "Australian Indigenous Languages." Areas of the western region of the Torres Strait, such as Kubin, have seen a shift away from exclusively using Kalaw Lagaw Ya (KLY), the local traditional language, towards Yumplatok, the lingua franca of the Torres Strait. Indeed, this creole has been reported in the language repertoires of students from the western Torres Strait islands since the 1980s, along with KLY and English (Shnukal 1989, p. 43). As in Yarrabah, then, the language shift at Kubin did not begin this decade, nor has it accelerated as rapidly as might be interpreted from Fig. 14-3.

As nomenclature for Yumplatok is not standardized, expressions denoting it vary, including "Broken," "Pizin," "Ailan Tok," and "Creole" (e.g. Shnukal 1988, p. 3). It is quite possible, then, that the source of these anomalies is a misinterpretation of the labels that Kubin residents were using to report their use of Yumplatok. In other words, the alternate names were likely not understood and/or not classified under "Australian Indigenous Languages" in these ABS website compilations of 2001 and 2006 Census data. Further, while "Australian Indigenous Languages" are coded in the 8000s and "Other Languages" are coded in the 9000s, "Creole, nfd" appears as 0005 under the "Supplementary codes" (ABS 2006a, pp. 100–106). This coding probably renders it less likely to be included in data compilations drawing on "Australian Indigenous Languages."

Although the data in Table 14-1 above could be interpreted as depicting a stable proportion of KLY speakers at Kubin, this assumption too could be flawed. The Census question about speaking "a language other than English at home" allows only a single response, so, where KLY, Yumplatok and English are all spoken—for example—it is unknown how residents select which language to declare.

Case Study Three: A flip?

On Poruma Island, in the central Torres Strait, Census data displayed in the *Time Series Profile* (ABS 2012f) about residents' declared "language spoken at home" appears to indicate a complete community-wide flip between 2001 and 2006. Excluding responses of "English only," "not stated" and "overseas visitor," 100 percent of responses in 2001 were classed as "Other" languages, while, in 2006 and 2011, 100 percent were classed as "Australian Indigenous Languages" (see Fig. 14-4). On first impressions, this suggests that the language used by an entire speech community shifted within the space of 5 years—a shift even more dramatic than that depicted for Kubin.

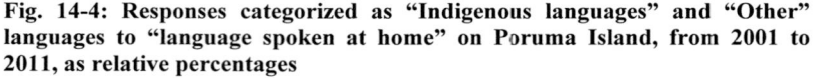

Fig. 14-4: Responses categorized as "Indigenous languages" and "Other" languages to "language spoken at home" on Poruma Island, from 2001 to 2011, as relative percentages

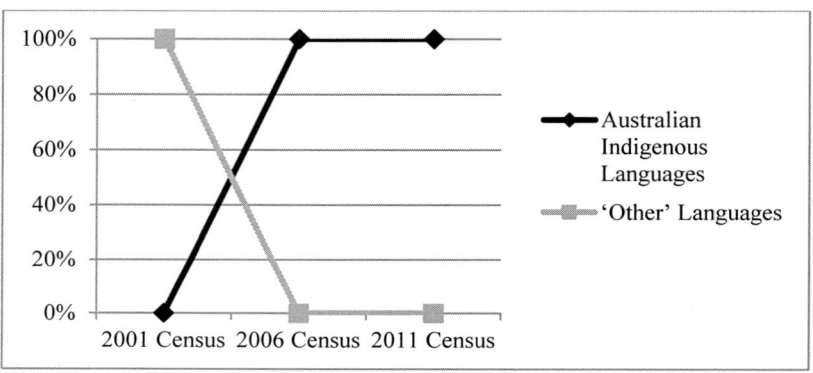

Data source: ABS (2012f) "T10 Language spoken at home (a) by sex".

It is striking that no Poruma residents' responses were classified as "Other" languages in Censuses after 2001. An *Indigenous Profile* (ABS 2007c) for Poruma, one of the many compilations of 2006 Census data, classifies all responses to "language spoken at home" as "Torres Strait Island Languages." In contrast, many responses contained in Kubin's *Indigenous Profile* (ABS 2007d) show up as "Speaks 'other' language" (as per the final definition of "other" listed in this chapter's Introduction) and not as "Australian Indigenous Languages," nor as any of its subcategories, such as "Australian Indigenous Languages, nfd," "Torres Strait Island Languages," or even "Other Australian Indigenous Languages."

QuickStats displays of Census data available for Poruma (ABS 2007b, 2012g) also contrast with Kubin's Census data. Poruma residents' language responses align with population figures (i.e. language responses are not missing as in Table 14-1), and they consistently indicate the regional creole—"Torres Strait Creole" (in 2006) or "Yumplatok (Torres Strait Creole)" (in 2011)—as the only "language[s] spoken at home" apart from English. At the level of publicly available information, it might not be possible to clarify why Poruma's data provides such a contrast to Kubin's data. Were Poruma residents' responses in 2006 and 2011 somehow clearer (perhaps using recognizable nomenclature), or were their responses classified more appropriately? Either way, the more cuts, displays and compilations of the 2006 Census data that are examined for

Kubin and for Poruma, the more it becomes clear that the nature of residents' responses and/or their interpretation led to different classifications of the same linguistic entity.

Problems

The language data about Poruma available in the public domain (in Fig. 14-4) could lead viewers to assume that, after 2001, a dramatic change in language use occurred, involving almost the entire population on the island. The only record of widespread language shift actually recorded on Poruma, however, was when children were noted to be speaking "Broken"—nowadays also known as Yumplatok or Torres Strait Creole—in the 1930s (Shnukal 1988).

Classification of responses indicating "Torres Strait Creole" appears to have been absolute in 2006 in the case of Poruma, but not of Kubin. Perhaps the greater time depth of the language shift away from traditional language(s) and over to Yumplatok (over 80 years on Poruma) generated different levels of awareness and acceptance of this contact language at a community level. Conceivably, as a result, Poruma residents might have labeled Yumplatok more consistently or recognizably in their Census responses.

Case Study Four: A back flip?

In the far northwest of the Torres Strait, on Saibai, the proportion of the 2006 Census responses for "language spoken at home" that are categorized under "Other" languages appears to shrink considerably compared to 2001, but bounces back again in 2011 (ABS 2012h, *Time Series Profile*). Concurrently, the number of speakers of "Australian Indigenous languages" appears to increase significantly in 2006, but actually recedes in 2011 to a level similar to the 2001 Census (see Fig. 14-5), which runs counter to the trend in cases previously outlined (see Figs. 14-1, 14-3 and 14-4).

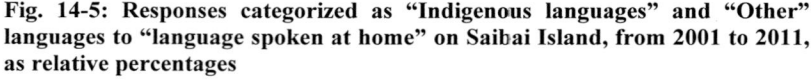

Fig. 14-5: Responses categorized as "Indigenous languages" and "Other" languages to "language spoken at home" on Saibai Island, from 2001 to 2011, as relative percentages

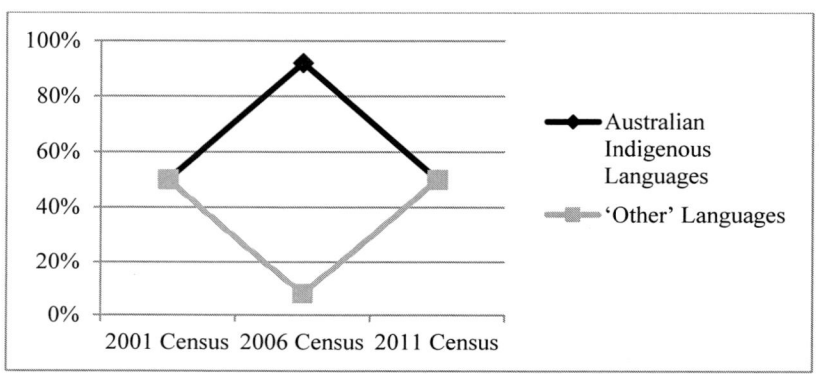

Data source: ABS (2012h) "T10 Language spoken at home (a) by sex".

The 2006 *QuickStats* data (see left-hand column in Table 14-2) shows a similar proportion of people declaring to speak "Australian Indigenous languages" as in the 2006 *Time Series Profile* data (Fig. 14-5), with *Kiwai*—a Papuan language—presumably the source of "Other" language speakers. The data from this year is relatively reflective of the expected language ecology for this part of the Torres Strait, where Yumplatok is reportedly gaining speakers (Ober 2008). However, the 2011 *QuickStats* "language spoken at home" data (see the right column in Table 14-2) does not align with 2011 Census data from the *Time Series Profile*. The 2011 Census data shows a considerable proportion of "Other" languages responses. As with Kubin's *QuickStats*, languages categorized as "Other" appear to have gone missing from Saibai's 2011 display (the responses show only 38.5 percent), although the accompanying explanatory note gives no indication of this:

> 3.8% of people only spoke English at home. The only other responses for language spoken at home were Kalaw Kawaw Ya/Kalaw Lagaw Ya 28.3%, Kriol 3.1%, Yumplatok (Torres Strait Creole) 2.7% and Kiwai 0.6%.

Further, the 2011 *QuickStats* data for Saibai appears illogical considering almost 90 percent of households are said to be multilingual.

An examination of Table 14-2 also indicates a decrease in reported speakers of Contact language(s) generally, and Yumplatok specifically, in

2011. Such figures are unlikely, given that Ober (2008) describes how Saibai Island, over the past four decades, has developed into a multilingual speech community inclusive of Yumplatok (to such an extent that action is required to maintain the local traditional language, Kalaw Kawaw Ya (KKY)). This means that, if anything, *more* Yumplatok speakers would be expected in 2011—certainly more than Kriol speakers. It can only be hypothesized that, as with Yarrabah, responses classified under "Kriol" might instead indicate an alternate designation for the regional creole on Saibai, Yumplatok. Other non-standard, unrecognized responses might have been categorized as "Other" languages and, on account of this, not displayed in the 2011 *QuickStats* data at all.

Table 14-2: Responses to "language spoken at home" on Saibai Island, as percentages of the total number of residents, in 2006 and 2011, languages identified

Language designation	2006 Census *QuickStats* (ABS, 2007e)	2011 Census *QuickStats* (ABS, 2012i)
Traditional language		
'Kalaw Kawaw Ya/Kalaw Lagaw Ya'	58.5	28.3
Contact language		
'Kriol'		3.1
'Yumplatok (Torres Strait Creole)'	12.8	2.7
Papuan language		
'Kiwai'	4.5	0.6
'English only spoken at home'	9.5	3.8
Total	**85.9%**	**38.5%**
Households where two or more languages are spoken	no indication	89.2%

Data sources: ABS (2007e) "Language spoken at home"; ABS (2012i) "Language, top responses (other than English)".

Problems

Publicly available language data about Saibai Island might incline viewers to believe—incorrectly—that a shift to Yumplatok is *not* occurring, despite its increasing use on the island over the past four decades (Ober 2008). Viewers might well note that the greatest number of responses is consistently assigned to KKY, while contact languages seem to represent only a relatively small proportion of residents' responses. Depending on the data display, viewers might even assume "Kriol" (the creole spoken from western Queensland through to the Kimberley region) has more speakers on Saibai than "Yumplatok," the lingua franca of the Torres Strait.

In contrast, other publicly available language data, the *Time Series Profile* (ABS 2012h), could be interpreted as showing *two* dramatic shifts in language use within the past decade on Saibai Island: the use of "Australian Indigenous Languages" apparently almost doubling from 2001–2006, then almost halving from 2006–2011. Ironically, 2006 Census language data for Saibai (see Fig. 14-5 and Table 14-2) more closely approximates the expected language ecology for this part of the Torres Strait, yet viewers might—erroneously—assume this year's data is anomalous in comparison with 2001 and 2011.

Case Study Five: A mistaken identity?

Across Australia in 2001, 199 people recorded their "Main language spoken at home" as Mauritian Creole (ABS 2006b), a French-lexified contact language from the island of Mauritius in the Indian Ocean. The 2001 Census figures reveal 65 putative speakers of Mauritian Creole in Queensland, on the Torres Strait islands of Badu (48), Iama (5) and Mer (3), and at Bamaga on northern Cape York (9) (ABS 2006b, c, d, e). Such figures appear to indicate more than one-third of all people speaking Mauritian Creole lived in remote parts of Queensland. As with Yarrabah, Kubin and Saibai, it is proposed that responses of "Creole," attempts at indicating the local contact language, have been miscoded, this time to a specific overseas creole.

As speakers of Mauritian Creole would have represented 7 percent of the Badu population in 2001 (if accurate), some indication from other reported personal characteristics would be expected to confirm their backgrounds, such as "Countries of birth." But this is not the case. Through just such a process of cross-referencing, the ABS diagnosed and reported on a reverse situation in the 2006 Census, with 1,755 people who were born overseas coded to "Australian Indigenous Languages." Of those codes confirmed as errors, "199 persons who reported that they spoke 'Creol' or 'Kriol' at home were miscoded to Aboriginal Creol which is included in the language group Kriol (8924)" (ABS 2006f). It is noteworthy that nomenclature of creoles caused the topmost miscoding error in this document. Indeed, it is openly acknowledged that a variation of the term "creole" could be used to designate a number of different *overseas* creoles (ABS 2006f).

Problems

Some language data in the public domain might cause viewers to believe that a particular overseas language, Mauritian Creole, is spoken in several Indigenous communities when, in fact, it is not. Viewers who are not informed about local language contact ecologies and creoles may not be able to critically interpret Census data, nor the sometimes anomalous results of non-standardized nomenclature interacting with data collection processes.

Case Study Six: A flutter?

At Kowanyama, on the lower western coast of Cape York, the *Time Series Profile* (ABS 2012j) indicates that most of the community report speaking "English only." There is also a discernible "flutter" of between 9 percent and 18 percent of other responses, the composition of which varies at each Census (see Fig. 14-6): Responses categorized as "not stated" are highest in 2001, while those recorded as "Australian Indigenous Languages" are most noticeable in 2006, but reduced in 2011.

QuickStats displays of these Censuses for Kowanyama (ABS 2006g, 2007f, 2012k) reveal that "Australian Indigenous Languages" responses consist either of a small percentage of speakers (≤5%) of individual traditional languages from the region, or of languages that have been classed as "Cape York Peninsula Aboriginal, nec" (i.e. not elsewhere classified) (see Table 14-3). No mention is made of any contact language.

Fig. 14-6: All responses to "language spoken at home" at Kowanyama, excluding overseas languages (apart from English), shown as relative percentages, from 2001 to 2011

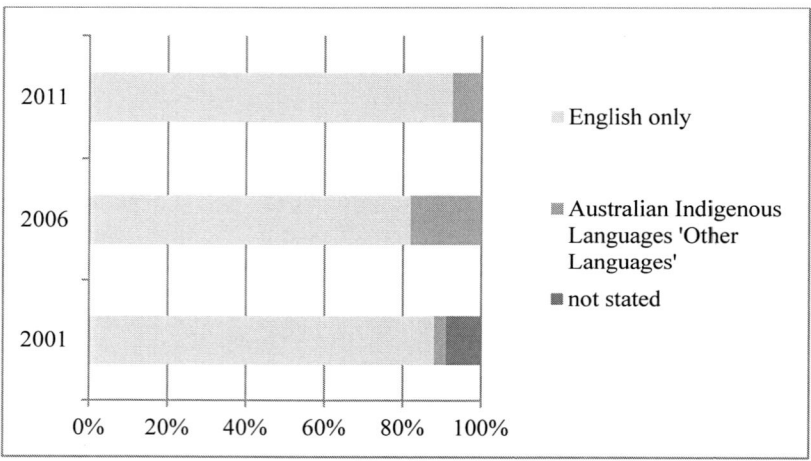

Data source: ABS (2012j) "T10 Language spoken at home (a) by sex".

Table 14-3: Responses to "language spoken at home" at Kowanyama categorized as "Australian Indigenous Languages," as a percentage of total number of residents, from 2001 to 2011

Language designation	2001 Census *QuickStats* (ABS, 2006g)	2006 Census *QuickStats* (ABS, 2007f)	2011 Census *QuickStats* (ABS, 2012k)
Traditional language			
'Cape York Peninsula Aboriginal, nec'	0.9	4.8	2.9
'Kok(o)-Bera'	-	5.7	2.7
'Guugu Yimidhirr'	-	5.2	0.3
'Kuk Thayorre'	-	0.6	-
Total	**0.9**	**16.3**	**5.9**

Data sources: ABS (2006g) "Main language spoken at home"; ABS (2007f) "Language spoken at home"; ABS (2012k) "Language, top responses (other than English)".

To date, no Census data reflects Kowanyama's actual contact language ecology (see Mühlhäusler 1996; Sandefur et al. 1982). However, there is an alternative (though general) public source of language data which draws on a different dataset than the ABS Census: the *MySchool* website. School principals are responsible for ensuring this student information is accurate (ACARA 2012, p. 49). On the *MySchool* website for 2011, Kowanyama State School (the only school in the community) reports that 98 percent of the students sitting the National Assessment Program Literacy and Numeracy (NAPLAN) had a "Language Background Other Than English" (LBOTE) (ACARA 2011). This category is not the exact equivalent of an individual claiming a "language spoken at home," because a student can be identified as having a LBOTE "if either the student, or the student's parents or carers, speaks a language other than English at home" (ACARA 2011, Glossary). So, assuming that up to 98 percent of Kowanyama students and/or their parents/carers have a "language spoken at home" other than English (extrapolating that the 2011 NAPLAN cohort's language backgrounds would not differ substantially to other students), this is a language situation certainly not reflected in the ABS data.

Problems

Viewers of the Census data presented in this case study would assume—incorrectly—that most of Kowanyama's residents speak "English only." They might also infer a shift away from traditional languages. However, they will not be alerted to the contact language ecology here, where a local creolized variety has been reported for decades. Moreover, this creole is mutually comprehensible with Kriol (Mühlhäusler 1996; Sandefur et al. 1982). *MySchool* LBOTE data for Kowanyama indicates that a language other than English is spoken by at least one person in almost all students' homes, but contains no more details. So while a comparison of ABS data with ACARA data for Kowanyama shows a huge discrepancy, neither captures the language contact ecology nor the actual contact varieties that residents speak.

Summary of issues

In the above case studies, naming and classifying contact languages appears to have been highly and consistently problematic. This is hardly surprising considering that new languages generated by language contact do not come with standardized names (Simpson & Wigglesworth 2008). Sometimes, terms such as "pidgin" or "creole" are used to refer to a particular contact language. However, other descriptive ways of referring to contact languages are also common, such as their speakers (e.g. Murri, meaning 'Queensland Aboriginal'), their location (e.g. Yarrie Lingo, meaning 'the local Yarrabah way of talking') or their non-standard nature (e.g. Broken, Slang, Creole) (DET 2011). Apparently, such responses can be construed and coded in numerous ways.

Of course, any response to a "language spoken at home" requires that a language first be recognized, acknowledged and claimed. Due to the existence of some apparently shared linguistic material, creoles are liable to be considered "poor" versions of their lexifier, thereby generating responses of "English only."

Responses to Census language questions denoting contact languages have apparently been categorized differently at different times and in different locations, leading to the many inconsistencies illustrated in the case studies. Inconsistencies occur at very broad category levels, such as whether a response belongs to "Australian Indigenous Languages" (8000s), "Other Languages" (9000s) or "Supplementary codes" (0000s), down to specific language codings "Kriol," "Yumplatok (Torres Strait Creole)," "Mauritian Creole," "Creole, nfd," and so on (ABS 2012c, 2006a).

In the Queensland context, a tension possibly exists about perceived purposes for enumerating traditional languages versus (mostly contact language) vernaculars: language maintenance and revival on one hand; communication needs and service delivery on the other. In any case, some selection process is involved where a single language response is required from a speaker with complex multilingual resources. Recommendations addressing both issues appear in McConvell and Thieberger (2001, p. 7). Although focusing on data collection for traditional languages, these particular points pertain to contact languages too.

Classification of language responses can impact greatly on any subsequent use of data. Whether contact languages are included—or omitted—in totals of "Australian Indigenous Languages" has *serious* ramifications on the validity of correlations and claims that can be made with these data. By way of illustration, the ABS (2011c) media release titled *Speaking an Indigenous language linked to youth wellbeing* addresses a serious issue, and the quality of its Indigenous language data will affect the reliability of its findings.

Unrecognized and/or misclassified languages in data in the public domain have real-world implications for language planning for Indigenous communities. Decision-making related to the provision of interpreting and translating, the need for English as an Additional Language/Dialect curriculum and pedagogy in schools, and targeted employment of local, like-language speaking community workers depends on the clear and consistent visibility of languages other than English.

Ways forward

As the data inaccuracy can partly be attributed to the public invisibility of rich and complex contemporary Indigenous language ecologies, including contact languages, the way forward clearly requires carefully targeted public education. This would aim to change social attitudes towards embracing contact languages as acceptable, useful and, appropriately, even a prestigious expression of identity.

The collectors and analysts of language information also need an awareness of the language contact contexts being described. If no standardized name exists for a contact language, then its existence should be described to an audience able to understand and interpret the context. The ABS is already supporting people with local expertise and relationships in the role of Census collectors (HoR 2012, p. 41), so relevant (site-specific) training would optimize language data.

In addition, the contact language categories require considered and specialist attention. At the very least, a generic creole code such as "Creole, nfd" is required within the category of "Australian Indigenous Languages," but consideration should also be given to the relative merits of generic codes at regional levels. Methodology for effectively capturing non-standard language designations must be trialled and developed, at both the point of collection and during analysis and quality control procedures. Further, the various compilations and displays of language data should undergo cross-comparisons to assist consistency. External points of reference, such as linguistic research or other data sources, would also provide useful cross-checking mechanisms.

Finally, the speech community, with its on-the-ground experiences and specialist insider knowledge, is integral to any process aiming to obtain quality responses to "language spoken at home." The field of applied linguistics can help by providing the conceptual underpinnings to foster language awareness, critically interpret language data, undertake community-based or academic research and communicate linguistic findings. The authors of this chapter have tried to meet these professional responsibilities in ways that will hopefully help to ensure the visibility of contact languages and the increased validity of the language data that is drawn upon in evidence-based service provision.

Acknowledgements

The authors acknowledge Dr. Cath Hudson who, many years ago, encouraged the first draft of the paper on which this chapter is based.

References

References from the Australian Bureau of Statistics: website: www.abs.gov.au

2012a, "Yarrabah (S) (350107600)", *2011 Census of Population and housing Time Series Profile*, cat.no. 2003.0

2012b, "Yarrabah (S) 350107600 (SLA)", *2011 Census QuickStats All people - usual residents*

2012c, "Language spoken at home (LANP)" *2011 Census classifications*

2012d, "Torres Strait Island (R)—Kubin (350106978)" *Census of Population and housing Time Series Profile*, cat.no. 2003.0

2012e, "Torres Strait Island (R)—Kubin (Moa Island) Code 350106978 (SLA)", *2011 Census QuickStats All people—usual residents*

2012f, "Torres Strait Island (R)—Poruma (350106986)", *Census of Population and housing Time Series Profile*, cat.no. 2003.0

2012g, "Torres Strait Island (R)—Poruma Code 350106986", *2011 Census QuickStats All people - usual residents*

2012h, "Torres Strait Island (R)—Saibai (350106992)", *Census of Population and housing Time Series Profile*, cat.no. 2003.0

2012i, "Torres Strait Island (R)—Saibai Code 350106992", *2011 Census QuickStats All people - usual residents*

2012j, "Kowanyama (S) (350104420)", *Census of Population and housing Time Series Profile*, cat.no. 2003.0

2012k, "Kowanyama Code UCL 315051", *2011 Census QuickStats All people - usual residents*

2011a, *Household form 2011Census*

2011b, *Census Dictionary. Australia 2011.* cat. no. 2901.0 Canberra: Commonwealth of Australia

2011c, "Speaking an Indigenous language linked to youth wellbeing", *Media release*, 29 April 2011

2007a, "Kubin (IC) (SLA) Loc. Code 350104430", *2006 Census QuickStats*

2007b, "Poruma (IC) (LGA) Loc. Code LGA 36100", *2006 Census QuickStats*

2007c, "Poruma (IC) (LGA 36100)", *Indigenous Profile, 2006 Census Community Profile Series*, cat. no. 2002.0

2007d, "Kubin (IC) (LGA 34430)", *Indigenous Profile, 2006 Census Community Profile Series*, cat. no. 2002.0

2007e, "Saibai (IC) (SLA) Loc. Code LGA 350106470", *2006 Census QuickStats*

2007f, "Kowanyama (UCL) Loc. Code UCL 333200", *2006 Census QuickStats*

2006a, *Census Dictionary-Australia* cat. no. 2901.0, 2006 (Reissue), Canberra: Commonwealth of Australia

2006b, "Badu Island (L) (UCL) Loc. Code UCL 302700", *2001 Census QuickStats*

2006c, "Yam Island (L) (UCL) Loc. Code UCL 362150", *2001 Census QuickStats*
2006d, "Murray Island (L) (UCL) Loc. Code UCL 343100", *2001 Census QuickStats*
2006e, "Bamaga (L) (UCL) Loc. Code UCL 303000", *2001 Census QuickStats*
2006f, "Language spoken at home—Characteristics' *Census Dictionary*, Short Definitions and classifications—2006, cat. no. 2901.0, 2006 (Reissue)"
2006g, "Kowanyama (L) (UCL) Loc. Code UCL 333200", *2001 Census QuickStats*

Other references:
Australian Curriculum Assessment and Reporting Authority (ACARA). 2012, *National Assessment Program Literacy and Numeracy Handbook for Principals*.
www.qsa.qld.edu.au/downloads/early_middle/naplan12_hbook_principals.pdf
Australian Curriculum Assessment and Reporting Authority (ACARA). 2011, "Kowanyama State School, Kowanyama, Qld", *MySchool*.
www.myschool.edu.au/MainPages/SchoolProfileRep.aspx?SDRSchoolId=467 16&DEEWRId=0&CalendarYear=2011&RefId=DHoffHqFBpF%2btKlDyDl6 qg%3d%3d20Features12001?OpenDocument
Berry, R. and J. Hudson. 1997, *Making the Jump*, Broome, W.A.: Catholic Education Office
Council of Australian Governments (COAG). 2008, *National Indigenous Reform Agreement*, updated September 2012.
www.federalfinancialrelations.gov.au/content/npa/health_indigenous/indigeno us-reform/national-agreement_sept_12.docx
Crowley, T. and B. Rigsby. 1979, "Cape York Creole". In T. Shopen, ed, *Languages and their status*, Philadelphia: University of Pennsylvania Press, pp. 153–207
Department of Education and Training (DET). 2011, "Aboriginal and Torres Strait Islander languages statement". deta.qld.gov.au/indigenous/pdfs/abtsi-language-statement.pdf
Department of Immigration and Citizenship (Dept. I&C). 2008, *The People of Queensland, vol. 2. Statistics from the 2006 Census*, Canberra: Commonwealth of Australia
Eades, D. 1983, "English as an Aboriginal Language in Southeast Queensland", Ph.D thesis, Brisbane: University of Queensland
Graber, P. 1987, "Kriol in the Barkly Tableland", *Australian Aboriginal Studies* 2: 14–19
House of Representatives Standing Committee on Aboriginal and Torres Strait Islander Affairs (HoR). 2012, *Our land, our languages. Language learning in Indigenous communities*, Canberra: Parliament of the Commonwealth of Australia
House of Representatives Standing Committee on Aboriginal and Torres Strait Islander Affairs (HoR). 1992, *Language and culture— a matter of survival. Report of the inquiry into Aboriginal and Torres Strait Islander language maintenance*, Canberra: Australian Government Publishing Service

McConvell, P. and N. Thieberger. 2001, *State of indigenous languages in Australia. Australia State of the Environment Second Technical Paper Series (Natural and Cultural Heritage)*, Canberra: Department of the Environment and Heritage.
www.environment.gov.au/system/files/pages/30bedb2e-29d7-4733-b45d-835b1bf2bef3/files/indigenous-languages.pdf

McIntosh, S., R. O'Hanlon and D. Angelo. 2012. "The (In)visibility of 'language' within Australian educational documentation: Differentiating language from literacy and exploring particular ramifications for a group of 'hidden' ESL/D learners". In R. Baldauf, ed, *Future directions in applied linguistics: Local and global perspectives—35th Applied Linguistics Association Australia Congress*, Brisbane: University of Queensland Press, pp. 447–68

Morphy, F. 2002, "When systems collide: the 2001 Census at a Northern Territory outstation". In D. Martin, et al., eds, *Making Sense of the Census. Observation of the 2001 enumeration in remote Aboriginal Australia*, Research monograph no. 22, Canberra: Centre for Aboriginal Economic Policy Research, Australian National University, pp. 29–75. http://epress.anu.edu.au?p=32061

Mühlhäusler, P. 1996, "Pidgins and creoles in Queensland". In S. Wurm, et al., eds, *Atlas of languages of intercultural communication in the Pacific, Asia and the Americas, Trends in Linguistics, vol. II*. Berlin: De Gruyter Mouton, pp. 67–82

Munro, J. 2005, "Substrate language influence in Kriol: The application of transfer constraints to language contact in northern Australia", unpublished Ph.D thesis, Armidale: University of New England

—. 2000, "Kriol on the move: A case of language spread and shift in northern Australia". In J. Siegel, ed, *Processes of language contact: Studies from Australia and the South Pacific*, Montreal: Fides, pp. 245–70

Ober, D. 2008, "Younger generations losing fluency in Kawaw Kalaw Ya", Indigenous Language Institute 2008 Keynote Speakers.
www.lingfest.arts.usyd.edu.au/ILIPlenaries.pdf

—. 1999, "Yumplatok". In T. Balzer, et al., eds, *Pidgin: The languages of Oceania*, Melbourne: Lonely Planet, pp. 141–47

Sandefur, J. 1990, "Kriol and Torres Strait Creole: Where do they meet?", *The Occasional Bulletin* 4: 1–13

—. 1984, "A language coming of age: Kriol of North Australia", unpublished M.A. thesis, Perth: University of Western Australia

Sandefur, J., M. Gumbuli, D. Daniels and M. Wurramara. 1982, "Looking for Kriol in Queensland", *AIAS Newsletter* 17: 35–40

Schmidt, A. 1990, *The loss of Australia's Aboriginal heritage*, Canberra: Aboriginal Studies Press

Schultze-Berndt, E., F. Meakins and D. Angelo. 2013, "Kriol". In S. Michaelis et al., eds, *Atlas of Pidgin and Creole Language Structures, vol 2: The language surveys*, Oxford: Oxford University Press

Sellwood, J. and D. Angelo. 2013, "Everywhere and nowhere. Invisibility of Aboriginal and Torres Strait Islander contact languages in education and Indigenous language contexts", *Australian Review of Applied Linguistics* 36(3): 250–66

Shnukal, A. 2002, "Some language-related observations for teachers in Torres Strait and Cape York Peninsula schools", *The Australian Journal of Indigenous Education* 30(1): 8–24

—. 2001, "Torres Strait English", In D. Blair and P. Collins, eds, *English in Australia*, Amsterdam: John Benjamins, pp. 181–200

—. 1991, "Torres Strait Creole". In S. Romaine, ed, *Language in Australia*, Cambridge: Cambridge University Press, pp. 180–94

—. 1989, *Language shift and maintenance in Torres Strait. Vol 3*, pp. 41–47

—. 1988, *Broken: An introduction to the creole language of the Torres Strait.* Pacific Linguistics Series C, Number 107. Canberra: Australian National University

Simpson, J. and G. Wigglesworth. 2008, *Children's language and multilingualism: Indigenous language use at home and school*, London: Continuum

Yeatman, B., et al. 2009, "At da Crick", poster, Cairns: Far North Queensland Indigenous Schooling Support Unit

CHAPTER FIFTEEN

MAKING AN EXAMPLE OF ARIZONA: ANALYZING A CASE OF RESTRICTIVE LANGUAGE POLICY FOR LANGUAGE MINORITY RIGHTS

KAREN E. LILLIE

Keywords: language minority, language policy, education, law, language rights, Arizona

Abstract

For the past 20 years, Arizona has been a state to watch in regard to how they create, change, and implement language policies for language minority (LM) students, policies which do not reflect the best practices for teaching English language learners (ELs). The question of whether or not ELs are receiving an equal education still remains (Rios-Aguilar & Gándara, 2012a; Gándara & Orfield 2012b; Lillie et al. 2012). This chapter first presents a backdrop of language education in the United States, including an overview of Arizona's model, and discusses legal decisions which have been made regarding language rights. It then details the major events that have led to the language policy of Arizona that is in place today largely because of one court case: *Flores v. Arizona*. There follows a synthesis of research over the past five years since Arizona's model was implemented. Finally, the chapter examines the most recent events of and decision in *Flores*. The outcome of the case may not only have long-lasting effects on ELs in Arizona, but also on the educational rights of ELs throughout the United States. These events may also serve as a cautionary reminder to scholars in related fields.

Introduction

Arizona has a language policy in place unlike any other in the United States. The policy enacted in Arizona, known there as *structured English immersion* or the "SEI model," is an example of what can happen after prior legislation regarding language education, and decades of court decisions and ensuing appeals. One of these has recently been decided: *Flores v. Arizona*. Once a bilingual state in terms of educational policy, for the past five years Arizona classrooms have been almost exclusively English-only because of propositions and legal mandates resulting in decisions being made by those who are not experts in the field of language education (Faltis & Arias 2012; Gándara & Orfield 2012b). Scholars have lamented the decisions made by Arizona, largely because the policies in place do not reflect what research has shown is best practice for English language learners (ELs) (see e.g. Arias & Faltis 2012; Moore 2014; Rios-Aguilar & Gándara 2012a, 2012b[1]). However, the state has the right to make these decisions because while courts have given opinions on language rights, they often defer to states in deciding which type of educational language program is best. This can be problematic when those deciding are not "experts" or claim to use theories that are "sound," even though research in the field suggests otherwise (Faltis & Arias 2012; Krashen et al. 2012). This chapter, therefore, looks at a trajectory of prior court decisions on language education in the United States, the ever-changing language policies in Arizona due to some of these decisions, and the resulting schooling practices in place for ELs in the state of Arizona. It also discusses the idea of "experts" and "expertise" when determining language programs and what happened in Arizona during *Flores* regarding use of expert knowledge as a cautionary tale to academics worldwide. The decisions made about policy and therefore the manner in which those decisions have been implemented in Arizona schools could have far-reaching implications for not just the educational experiences of ELs in the United States, but also serve as an example for the field of applied linguistics.

Language minority education in the United States

Although some countries may have national or central language policy in place, as well as languages that have official status, the United States has neither a federal language policy nor an official language policy (Gándara & Orfield 2012b). The United States has never been monolingual and English is not the official language, contrary to popular belief (Crawford

---

[1] Rios-Aguilar and Gándara (2012a, 2012b) are the introduction articles to two special issues dealing with Arizona policy. The 2012a reference is for the *Teachers College Record* special issue (vol. 114, issue 9), and 2012b refers to the thematic issue of *Language Policy* (vol. 11, issue 1).

2004; Wiley 2013; Wiley & Wright 2004). While English is the *de facto* language of the country, it is not *de jure*.[2] The creators of the Constitution did not mandate English as the language of the land (Baker 2011). America is multilingual, yet educational systems have not always reflected this. Despite its linguistic diversity, throughout American history political and educational stakeholders have been predominantly focused on promoting the acquisition of only English, particularly on those for whom English is not the first language (Baker 2011; Wiley 2013). "English-only" ideologies in society have been widespread throughout America's history (Crawford 2004; Wiley 2004) and language policies have vacillated from those of *promotion-oriented* to *repression-oriented* (Wiley 2013; also Kloss 1977/1998). The ideologies within society and politics therefore are played out in the educational system and, as such, there has always been a variety of educational programs for language minority (LM) students.

Educational programs for LM students in the United States

Schools across the United States have a variety of language programs in place, ranging from bilingual education (e.g. transitional, two-way immersion) to those focused on acquiring only English (e.g. immersion, or English as a second language, known as ESL). Bilingual education and instruction using the native language has been present in schooling of American children for centuries (Wiley 2013), but it has not always been supported or consistent. As Wright (2011) notes, "there has been neither total centralization nor full devolution to states in bilingual education" (p. 184). While the Bilingual Education Act in 1968 showed that the federal government acknowledged this form of instruction as an option for ELs, it was not a mandate.[3]

On the other side of the language program spectrum is what is known as immersion. One form of this is "sheltered English immersion" or SEI.[4] Research on SEI as an educational model has been contested and very few have shown SEI to be beneficial or effective for ELs (Combs 2012; Combs et al. 2005; Mahoney et al. 2004; Martinez-Wenzl et al. 2012). SEI originated from *structured immersion*, which was posited as being more

---

[2] Some states currently have English-only policies, but not necessarily regarding schooling (Crawford 2004).

[3] Wright (2011) gives a concise history of bilingual education in the United States.

[4] Arizona calls their program the "SEI model", but their depiction of SEI is different from what the term SEI intended originally, as will be evidenced shortly.

successful than bilingual education based on a report by Baker and de Kanter in 1981. One major concern over this report stems from the fact that the case studies on which the researchers based their recommendation for SEI over transitional bilingual programs were French Canadian immersion models, which are very different from the SEI programs in the United States (Baker 2011). Some key differences include the length of time devoted to the program, the use of native languages during instruction, and having bilingual teachers. In short, SEI promotes monolingualism in English, while Canadian immersion program goals are bilingualism and biliteracy (Faltis & Arias 2012[5]). Arizona's "SEI" as a term is inconsistent with Baker's and de Kanter's definition of SEI; Arizona's policy is conceptually different and is more restrictive. Their report defined SEI as learning language and content simultaneously, which is not done in Arizona (Crawford 2004).

Arizona's "SEI" stands for *Structured English Immersion*. Contrary to claims by Arizona's Department of Education (ADE) that this is sound in theory, again, research on best practice for ELs does not include this type of instruction or model (Krashen et al. 2012). Arizona's version of SEI requires that all LM students not proficient in English must be segregated into proficiency-based groups (away from native-speaking peers), and enrolled in English classes for four hours a day, every day. These classes are to be conducted only in English, with the instructional focus on English language skills at the detriment of learning content (Lillie et al. 2010, 2012). The question is how this model came to be and what events led to the implementation of such an arguably destructive model. A convergence of laws, court mandates, and "expert" decisions have led us to where education in Arizona is today.

Choosing a Language Program: Setting precedence?

Courts are traditionally against choosing or naming any type of language program as being the best for students. Instead, individual states have the power to determine which language(s) may be used in the schools and the federal government often defers to states in educational matters (Gándara & Orfield 2012b; Wiley 2013). As Wiley (2013) notes, "recent court decisions are allowing states broader authority in determining policy and practice for the education of [LM] children" (p. 77). When looking at Supreme Court cases throughout U.S. history, few have attempted to

---

[5] A descriptive table is included in the chapter by Faltis and Arias (2012) comparing the two programs.

tackle language rights for LM students. The cases in this chapter have not set precedence for the type of schooling that must be enforced for ELs, but they have ensured that LM rights are upheld and that all children are receiving an equal education, regardless of their native tongue (Del Valle 2003).

Earlier cases on language

Meyer v. Nebraska (1923) and *Farrington v. Tokushige* (1927) were two cases that dealt with language. In *Meyer*, a teacher was fined and fired for teaching in a foreign language, which was against Nebraska law at the time. The Supreme Court decided in favor of Meyer. The opinion stated that the 14th Amendment upheld Meyer's right to teach in a foreign language (in this case, German), and that parents were allowed to make the decision as to whether their children could learn languages other than English (Del Valle 2003; Wiley 2013). As Del Valle (2003) notes,

> in a single simple phrase, the Supreme Court undermined the perception of language as tied to loyalty, citizenship and rights...[they] saw the language-restrictive legislation for what it was—free-floating fear converted into xenophobic legislation. (p. 38)

The precedence here for LM rights, however, was weak. Also, this case was heard during peace time (after the First World War) and scholars have noted that had this been heard earlier, they may not have ruled in favor of Meyer (Del Valle 2003; Wiley 2013). The opinion acknowledged that while schools had the right to determine certain regulations "including a requirement that they shall give instructions in English" (*Meyer v. Nebraska*, 1923), they were not to deny rights to LMs that were afforded to others.

Farrington (1927) was similar in that the case was about whether or not heritage language schools were allowed to provide additional instruction to compensate for the English-only education students received at school in Hawai'i. Farrington was the Governor of Hawai'i and was attempting to restrict these private schools from operating without a permit and demanded a fee for every student who attended. Justice McReynolds stated in the opinion that

> enforcement of the Act probably would destroy most, if not all, of them; and, certainly, it would deprive parents of fair opportunity to procure for their children instruction which they think important and we cannot say is harmful. (273 U.S. 284)

The Supreme Court used the *Meyer* decision as support and ruled that parents were allowed to decide what type of instruction they felt was best for their children, and that to dismantle foreign language schools would be damaging (Del Valle 2003).

Later Cases on Language Rights in Public Schools: *Lau*, the EEOA, and *Castañeda*

One of the most important and significant cases about LM education occurred in the 1970s: *Lau v. Nichols* (1974). Parents of Chinese-descent LM students initiated a class action suit against the district, claiming that the ELs were not being provided an equal education, thus violating the 14th Amendment and §601 of the Civil Rights Act of 1964 (414 U.S. 563). Lower courts had consistently sided with the school districts and took a very deficit perspective to ELs. In one such statement, the excuse for discrimination towards the Chinese students was not a fault of California law but of the "deficiencies created by the [students] themselves in failing to [learn] the English language" (Del Valle 2003, p. 238). The Supreme Court found otherwise, stating that providing a curriculum to the LM students via the same resources, materials, and teachers does not mean students are receiving an equal education, especially if they cannot understand the instruction being provided to them because of their non-proficiency in English. In short, same does not mean equal.

This case did not decide that bilingual education was what schools had to offer, but it did require that some sort of acceptable language program be used in schools so that students would have a chance of receiving an equal education (Gándara et al. 2010; Wiley 2013). A troubling remark from Justice Blackmun was made when he stated "this is a very substantial group that is being deprived of any meaningful schooling" and noted that if the number of students affected had been smaller, the decision might have been different (Del Valle 2003, p. 240). The implication is that for a case to be considered detrimental, large numbers of children must be affected. This is precisely what is occurring in Arizona today.

The Equal Education Opportunities Act (EEOA) also passed in 1974. Within the EEOA, §1703(f) requires that schools take "appropriate action to overcome language barriers that impede equal participation by its students in its instructional programs" (20 USC §1703). This stipulation is useful, but the question then is what is considered to be "appropriate action" when deciding on language programs. In 1981, a case known as *Castañeda v. Pickard* established a three-prong test for helping to determine whether or not there is compliance with the EEOA under

§1703(f). These three prongs are that the language program (1) must be based on a sound, research-based methodology of second language acquisition (SLA); (2) must be properly funded so as to implement the program successfully; and (3) shows evidence that ELs are learning English and mastering subject matter. This third prong has yet to be tested in a court of law. These three prongs, however, have been asserted (by the plaintiffs) as not being met throughout the case that was ongoing during the design and implementation of Arizona's restrictive language policy and the SEI model: *Flores*.

Flores v. Arizona

Flores v. Arizona[6] started in 1992 and the March 2013 decision may have severe effects on the educational rights of LM students. This case was initially a trial over equitable funding but evolved into a case examining the quality and equity of the education ELs are receiving. In 1992, parents of Miriam Flores filed a class action lawsuit claiming that Arizona had violated the EEOA. Ultimately, *Flores* did show that EL programs were not being provided with enough funding and therefore Arizona was not meeting the requirement under the EEOA (*Flores v. Arizona*, 2000; see also Combs 2012; Hogan 2008). The cost analysis of how much the state was paying for each EL against how much they should be paying for each student showed a significant difference of a few hundred dollars (Hogan 2008; Wightman 2010). Judge Marquez ruled that the funding for the language program was "arbitrary and capricious" (*Flores v. Arizona*, 2000).

In 2000, the Flores Consent Order was enacted. This mandated that the language program be defined so that it could be funded appropriately. Unfortunately, like many court decisions before it, the type of program was not determined (Lillie et al. 2012). The state was left to decide if the program should be bilingual, a form of ESL, or immersion. The Consent Order, however, did stipulate five key points: (1) that the Superintendent must choose a proficiency assessment to be used; (2) that LM students who exit the program are monitored for two years; (3) that if students do not meet a satisfactory level of academic achievement after exiting the program, they are provided with compensatory instruction (e.g. after-school tutoring); (4) that ELs must receive daily instruction that is at their

---

[6] *Flores v. Arizona* in later years subsequently evolved into *Horne v. Arizona*, but, for the purposes of clarity, in this chapter *Flores* captures the entire two decades of litigation.

appropriate level of achievement and language proficiency; and (5) that the program itself is comparable in amount, scope and quality to that of native English-speaking peers (*Flores v. Arizona*, Consent Order). This Order was mandated only four months prior to a law that would dictate the type of program to be implemented: Proposition 203.

Proposition 203

Compounding the issue of educating LM students, Proposition 203[7] was passed with 63 percent of the vote in November of 2000, and it effectively dismantled bilingual education in Arizona. This proposition is what required the use of a poorly-defined and contentious model called Sheltered (eventually Structured) English Immersion (aka, SEI) (see also, Wright 2005).

Arizona's Proposition 203 followed the assumptions held in California's Proposition 227[8] that to help make children "productive members of society," children should be immersed in English as the medium of education. The proposition upheld the mistaken belief that "young immigrant children can easily acquire full fluency in a new language, such as English, if they are heavily exposed to that language in the classroom at an early age" (http://www.azed.gov/wp-content/uploads/PDF/PROPOSITION203.pdf, see Section 1) and the statutes dictated that this learning period should not "normally...exceed one year" (A.R.S. §15-752). This is problematic for the two major assumptions inherent in the statute about language learning and ELs: (1) that all ELs are immigrants and (2) that the English language can be learned in a one-year timeframe. The latter is especially counter to what research says about SLA (Krashen et al. 2012; Long & Adamson 2012).

Proposition 203 did not stipulate what this SEI model should include, other than to mandate English-only instruction. Following the passage of 203, the state struggled to develop a clear model to be used in classrooms with ELs, thereby ensuring wide variation in implementation and practice (Davenport 2008, 2011). The decision for a specific model came six years later with House Bill 2064 (H.B. 2064), which was part of the ongoing *Flores* case.

---

[7] Proposition 203 ultimately became Arizona Revised Statutes (A.R.S.) §15-751 through §15-757.
[8] Proposition 227 passed in 1998 with 61 percent of the vote, and much has been written on the topic (Gándara & Hopkins 2010).

H.B. 2064

In 2006, H.B. 2064 was passed in an effort to address the mandates stemming from the Consent Order and the confusion over the language program required since Proposition 203 was enacted. H.B. 2064 decreed that the state must develop a *statewide*, cost-effective model in which all ELs would be enrolled that was to be comparable in amount, scope and quality to that of their non-EL peers. H.B. 2064 still did not describe what the instruction for ELs would look like. An English Language Learner Task Force was established and charged with this undertaking (A.R.S. §15-756.01). The passage of this bill in conjunction with Proposition 203 created a "one-size fits all" (Wright & Choi 2006) prescriptive SEI model, and that is how it came to be that ELs were required to have English instruction for four hours *every day*.

Implementation of Arizona's "SEI"

The SEI model was fully implemented in 2008. Again, the model consists of prescribed English language development (ELD) classes, which are broken into four separate hours of instruction including reading, writing, grammar, and academic vocabulary and conversational English. All teachers are required to get SEI training where they are informed of the ways to teach English language skills as the primary focus (Murri et al. 2012). The ADE describes the ELD classes as being those where content is not to be the focus because the stress should be on the English language skills that students need to acquire.

To get into this 4-hour block, students are questioned on the Home Language Survey (HLS). Initially three questions, the ADE briefly reduced it to one, only to return to the original three questions after the Office of Civil Rights stepped in and found it to be in violation of Title VI of the Civil Rights Act (Goldenberg & Rutherford-Quach 2012; Rios-Aguilar & Gándara 2012a). If an answer of anything other than in "English" is provided to any of the three questions, students are required to take the Arizona English Language Learner Assessment (AZELLA). This test is grouped into grade bands (i.e. K, 1-3, 4-5, 6-8, 9-12th, respectively). Should a child not pass as English proficient on the test, they are labeled as one of four designations: Pre-Emergent, Emergent, Basic, and Intermediate. The SEI model calls for all students to be grouped preferably by grade-level and proficiency-designation or, if there are not enough numbers to make up one class, cross-grade level bands with similar proficiency levels or, finally, across both grade and proficiency levels. This means that a child can be a 12th grade Intermediate EL and if there are not enough students of the same designation to make up one classroom, the student could be grouped with 9th grade Basic ELs. To exit the program, students must pass the AZELLA. Should they pass as proficient, they are then labeled as reclassified fluent English proficient (RFEP) and are tested on the AZELLA again for another two years. This fulfills the 2-year monitoring mandate stipulated in the Consent Order.

Synthesis of research on Arizona's SEI model since 2008

For the past five years, scholars have investigated the implementation of SEI from various perspectives now that the implications of the restrictive language policy are beginning to be evidenced and to be measurable. Mahoney et al. (2010b) did a comprehensive study on the effectiveness of the SEI model as tested against *Castañeda*'s third prong and found that the state is not meeting the standard set forth in *Castañeda*. García et al. (2012) looked at the achievement gap between ELs and non-ELs post-SEI implementation and also found no substantial progress in reducing this gap. Rios-Aguilar et al. (2012) similarly found dismal results when looking at the academic achievement of ELs under the SEI model.

Arias (2012), Murri et al. (2012), and Wright and Sung (2012) look at the impacts Proposition 203 and the SEI training requirement have had on teacher preparation. Some studies have questioned the validity of using one test to determine ELs' proficiency in English (Florez 2012; Mahoney et al. 2010a). Rios-Aguilar et al. (2012a) report on the ensuing effects on teacher practice post-implementation of the SEI model. Grijalva (2009) examined principals' understanding of and considerations around the implementation of the SEI model. She found that principals felt that (a) it violates segregation laws, (b) there is a lack of funding, and (c) there was fear over the potential ramifications for not implementing the mandate. Leckie et al. (2012) analyzed the discourse around the reclassification process for ELs, noting that Arizona's attempt to meet the "one year" exit goal is paramount compared to whether or not ELs are ready to be reclassified. Others have examined the detrimental effects the policy has had on segregation of students (Gándara & Orfield 2012a). One study looked systematically at the policy as put into practice within the ELD classrooms (Lillie et al. 2010, 2012), while another surveyed the students who were and had been experiencing the SEI model (Lillie 2011).

All of the studies that have examined the model in the years after its initial implementation have reported negative effects of the policy as practiced. Four key themes emerge from the research:

- SEI, as defined by Arizona, is not superior to or beneficial for language acquisition, nor are students exiting the program in one year as stipulated by law (Gándara & Orfield 2012a; Krashen et al. 2012; Martinez-Wenzl et al. 2012)
- ELs are not receiving an equal education to that of their mainstream peers, largely due to the limited exposure to content and age-grade appropriate curricula and reduced resources[9] (Iddings et al. 2012; Lillie et al. 2010; Rios-Aguilar et al. 2012b; Rios-Aguilar et al. 2012)
- ELs are segregated from their non-EL peers, which further helps to stigmatize these students and is noticed by both the children and the adults who work with them (Gándara & Orfield 2012a; Rios-Aguilar et al. 2012a, 2012b)
- a typical four-year timeframe for graduation of secondary-level ELs may be hindered (Lillie et al. 2010, 2012; Rios-Aguilar et al. 2012a, 2012b).

Ultimately, studies are showing that ELs in Arizona are precluded from full access to their school community, both socially and academically, and are barred access to an equal education.

Flores today

In 2009, the Supreme Court[10] overturned earlier decisions on *Flores* and remanded the case back to the District Court level. The majority opinion remarked that because of the many changes since the beginning of *Flores*, particularly implementation of the new SEI model and more federal funding to schools, there were enough changes made since the earlier decisions which potentially impact the instruction of ELs. Now, at District Court level, the focus shifted to whether or not the instruction of ELs was meeting the *Castañeda* test and therefore satisfying the EEOA (Wightman 2010).

Meeting the three-prong test is complex. For one, *Flores* was initially tried arguing that Arizona was not meeting the second prong: proper funding. In the remand, the focus was now on the first and third prong. The task, then, falls on the plaintiffs to prove that, contrary to ADE's

---

[9] Typical school days are 6–7 hours; with 4 of those hours devoted to the ELD classes, ELs are not getting much time for anything else during the day.

[10] The case before the Supreme Court was known as *Horne v. Flores*.

claims that the SEI model is "research based" and sound in theory,[11] research does not support this model and that, in practice, it is not meeting the needs of ELs.

In the Autumn of 2009/Spring of 2010, UCLA's Civil Rights Project/Proyecto Derechos Civiles put together a team of expert scholars who were charged with researching the effects and implementation of the SEI model in practice. Nine peer-reviewed research studies resulted from this collaboration and none found evidence in support of SEI. Hogan, the plaintiff's lawyer for *Flores*, read these studies. He asked some authors to be expert witnesses and testify to their study's findings. The defendants (the ADE) issued subpoenas to some of the authors at Arizona State University and the University of Arizona, specifically over three of the studies. This act alone called into question the idea of "expertise" and threatened confidentiality of the research participants.

Expertise and confidentiality

I was one of the authors whose work was subpoenaed. The subpoena asked for everything that we had, including:

> all documents... reflecting the name, school, district and grade of each teacher...recordings...of any and all interviews, observations of any school professionals...all drafts of the report and the final report... emails...reflecting communications between any...authors of the report and Tim Hogan...emails...to and from any employees of any and all school districts and schools...[and] the entire file of the authors... containing all data, records, emails, recordings...[and] other material used in preparing the report. (see http://www.edweek.org/media/ ps_motion.pdf, Exhibit A)

While subpoenas are standard practice in litigation for the legal profession, this was astounding for us as academics and we met with our university lawyers. Hogan immediately issued a motion for a protective order on August 2, 2010, in an attempt to protect the confidentiality of the participants. While I cannot speak as to what transpired at the University of Arizona, I can attest to the support we received.[12] My colleagues and I

---

[11] The SEI model was initially developed by Kevin Clark, who is not a language education expert (Gándara & Orfield 2012b).

[12] We were largely supported because of one line in our consent forms: "No identifiable information will be released to anyone other than the researchers involved in the study. All observations and any responses to informative questions asked by the researcher will remain confidential."

began the arduous task of redacting any potentially identifiable information from every single piece of data that we had, regardless of the form (e.g. electronic, paper), to maintain confidentiality. We were under a tight deadline, knowing there was a risk of being held in contempt of court if the documents were not delivered on time. Ultimately, Hogan made the decision to forgo using any of the studies in the hearings, for it could not be guaranteed that we would be able to protect our participants' anonymity. This unfortunately meant that the data from our study which was arguably damaging to the defendant's case would not be heard and documented in court. The hearing ended on January 11, 2011 and a decision was announced on March 29, 2013. The court decided in favor of the defendants and an appeal has been filed.

Concluding remarks

It is true that this happened in Arizona and that therefore much of what is reported here is specific to the Arizona sociocultural and sociopolitical climate. The lessons to be learned from Arizona, however, are great and should encourage scholars to engage in a public debate about matters related to LM students and language rights. The passage of an English-only, voter-initiated proposition occurred quickly and has changed the course of education in Arizona. If other states, and therefore the voters, are not careful and attentive, similar laws could take effect or be placed on the ballots for consideration. The ensuing confusion over a top-down policy and the years it took to implement the SEI model also signal disconnect between law and policymakers and the education field. Even the Task Force only had two educational experts on the team (Faltis & Arias 2012). The effect of the policy being created without joint effort from all parties involved is becoming more obvious with the dismal reports from the field.

The *Flores* case lasted for over 20 years, and the implications from this recent decision could impact schooling for ELs across the United States by setting precedence for what type of instruction meets the three-prong test of *Castañeda* and therefore the EEOA. While the outcome may only affect the schooling of ELs in Arizona, it is not a Supreme Court decision (e.g. Gándara & Orfield 2012b). This means that the themes which led to Arizona's policy could be replicated anywhere LM students or LM rights are repressed.

It is important that lawyers and other legal personnel continuously look at research being done in the areas from which their trials and cases stem. The issue then becomes, of course, how to get publications readily accessible (in cost and language) for all those who might be interested in reading them. It is equally important to be sure that scholars are reading work outside of one's specialty, to increase the likelihood that research is shared across disciplines. Unfortunately, while Hogan did read peer-reviewed publications during *Flores,* the subpoenas ultimately blocked him from using the studies.

The subpoena and revoking of witnesses for the evidentiary hearings between September 2010 and January 2011 are significant to the wider field of applied linguistics in another way too, as it calls into question the idea of what research counts when courts are determining what might be best for the education of ELs, and, in a larger sense, who is an "expert" in matters related to those called in for judicial proceedings. Further, when scholars create confidentiality agreements with participants it is expected that this will remain secure. To have that expectation questioned creates a tenuous environment for all scholars in conducting research, particularly that which might be politically or legally sensitive. It means we may need to think more deeply about the type of language to include in the consent forms, not to mention the idea of possibly needing to consistently maintain anonymity throughout the data collection process. It also reinforces the importance of making research accessible and readable for the wider public (who may end up on juries or, at the very least, as voters), particularly if that research is barred from being presented in a case and/or that case continues on through appeals.

The themes emerging not just in U.S. legal history but in the events of Arizona should cause all disciplines to stop and reflect about LM rights, LM schooling, and how to prevent restrictive policies from being designed in the first place. When research shows that the type of restrictive policy in place is detrimental to ELs, it is important to remember that the argument has never been whether or not students need to know English. Rather the argument is that the manner in which some schools may be teaching English is wrong and so institutional and policy reform must occur. In the 20 years since *Flores* began, an entire generation of students has been impacted. All we can do now is wait to see the effect the recent decision and upcoming appeal will have on the generations of LM students to come.

Acknowledgements

While the work presented here is entirely my own, I would like to respectfully acknowledge Professor Terrence G. Wiley, President of the Center for Applied Linguistics, Washington, D.C., and Professor Emeritus, Arizona State University, for the initial contribution to this chapter's theme and content.

References

Arias, M.B. 2012, "Language policy and teacher preparation: The implications of a restrictive language policy on teacher preparation". In M.B. Arias and C. Faltis, eds, *Implementing educational language policy in Arizona: Legal, historical, and current practices in SEI*, Buffalo, N.Y.: Multilingual Matters, pp. 3–20

Arias, M.B. and C. Faltis, eds, 2012, *Implementing educational language policy in Arizona: Legal, historical, and current practices in SEI*, Buffalo, N.Y.: Multilingual Matters

Arizona Revised Statutes. 2000, Article 3.1 §15-751 to 15-757: English Language Education for the Children in Public Schools.
http://www.azleg.state.az.us/ArizonaRevisedStatutes.asp?Title=15.

Baker, C. 2011, *Foundations of bilingual education and bilingualism*, 5th ed, Bristol: Multilingual Matters

Castañeda v. Pickard, No. 79-2253, 989, United States Court of Appeals, Fifth Circuit. Unit A, 648F.2d 989; 1981 U.S. App. LEXIS 12063

Combs, M.C. 2012, "Everything on its head: How Arizona's structured English immersion policy re-invents theory and practice". In M.B. Arias and C. Faltis, eds, *Implementing educational language policy in Arizona: Legal, historical, and current practices in SEI*, Buffalo, N.Y.: Multilingual Matters, pp. 59–85

Combs, M.C., C. Evans, T. Fletcher, E. Parra and A. Jiménez. 2005, "Bilingualism for the children: Implementing a dual-language program in an English-only state", *Educational Policy* 19(5): 701–28

Crawford, J.W. 2004, *Educating English learners: Language diversity in the classroom*, 5th ed, Los Angeles: Bilingual Education Services, Inc.

Davenport, D.K. 2008, *Baseline study of Arizona's English language learner programs and data, fiscal year 2007*, State of Arizona Office of the Auditor General.
http://www.auditorgen.state.az.us/Reports/School_Districts/Statewide/2008_April/ELL_Baseline_Report.pdf

—. 2011, *Arizona English language leaner program, fiscal year 2010* (Report No. 11-06). State of Arizona Office of the Auditor General.
http://www.azauditor.gov/Reports/School_Districts/Statewide/2011/ELL_Report.pdf

Del Valle, S. 2003, *Language rights and the law in the United States: Finding our voices*, Clevedon: Multilingual Matters

Faltis, C. and M.B. Arias. 2012, "Research-based reform in Arizona: Whose evidence counts for applying the Castaneda test to structured English immersion models?" In M.B. Arias and C. Faltis, eds, *Implementing educational language policy in Arizona: An examination of legal, historical and current practices in SEI*, Buffalo, N.Y.: Multilingual Matters, pp. 21–38

Farrington v. Tokusighe, 273 US 284. (1927)

Flores v. Arizona, 172 F.Sup.2d 1225, 1238-39 (D. Ariz. 2000)

Flores v. Arizona, Consent Order. U.S. District Court of Arizona, CIV 92-596 TUC ACM (2000)

Florez, I.R. 2012, "Examining the validity of the Arizona English language learners assessment cut scores", *Language Policy* 11(1): 33–45. doi: 10.1007/s10993-011-9225-4

Gándara, P. and M. Hopkins, eds, 2010, *Forbidden languages: English learners and restrictive language policies*, New York: Teachers College Press

Gándara, P. and G. Orfield. 2012a, "Segregating Arizona's English learners: A return to the 'Mexican room'", *Teachers College Record* 114(9): 1–27

—. 2012b, "Why Arizona matters: The historical, legal, and political contexts of Arizona's instructional policies and U.S. linguistic hegemony", *Language Policy* 11(1): 7–19. doi: 10.1007/s10993-11-9227-2

Gándara, P., D. Losen, D. August, M. Uriarte, M.C. Gómez and M. Hopkins. 2010, "Forbidden language: A brief history of U.S. language policy". In P. Gándara and M. Hopkins, eds, *Forbidden language: English learners and restrictive language policies*, New York: Teachers College Press, pp. 20–33

García, E.E., K. Lawton and E.H. Diniz de Figueiredo. 2012, "The education of English language learners in Arizona: A history of underachievement", *Teachers College Record* 114(9): 1–18

Goldenberg, C. and S. Rutherford-Quach. 2012, "The Arizona home language survey: The under-identification of students for English language services", *Language Policy* 11(1): 21–31. doi: 10.1007/s10993-011-9224-5

Grijalva, G.G. 2009, *Implementing language policy: Exploring concerns of school principals* (Doctoral dissertation), ProQuest Dissertations and Theses

Hogan, T. 2008, "*Flores v. State of Arizona*". In J.M. González, ed, *Encyclopedia of bilingual education*, Thousand Oaks, CA: Sage Publications, pp. 307–12

Horne v. Flores. No. 08-28, No. 08-294, Supreme Court of the United States, 557 U.S. 433; 129 S. Ct. 2579; 174 L. Ed. 2d 406; 2009 U.S. LEXIS 4733; 77 U.S.L.W. 4611; 21 Fla. L. Weekly Fed. S 1020

Iddings, A.C.D., M.C. Combs and L. Moll. 2012, "In the arid zone: Drying out educational resources for English language learners through policy and practice", *Urban Education* 47(2): 495–514. doi: 10.1177/0042085911430713

Kloss, H. 1977/1998, *The American bilingual tradition*, Center for Applied Linguistics and Delta Systems: Washington, D. C. and McHenry, IL. Original work published in 1977, Rowley, MA: Newbury House Publishers

Krashen, S., J. MacSwan and K. Rolstad. 2012, "Review of 'research summary and bibliography for structured English immersion programs' of the Arizona English language learners task force", In M.B. Arias and C. Faltis, eds, *Implementing educational policy in Arizona: Legal, historical and current practices in SEI*, Bristol: Multilingual Matters, pp. 107–18

Lau v. Nichols. No. 72-6520, U.S. Supreme Court, 414 U.S. 563; 94 S. Ct. 786; 39 L. Ed. 2d 1; 1974 U.S. LEXIS 151

Leckie, A.G., S.E. Kaplan and E. Rubinstein-Ávila. 2012, "The need for speed: A critical discourse analysis of the reclassification of English language learners in Arizona", *Language Policy* 12(2): 159–76. doi: 10.1007/s10993-012-9242y

Lillie, K.E. 2011, *Giving the students a voice: Surveying students about Arizona's structured English immersion restrictive language policy* (Doctoral dissertation). Retrieved from ASU Electronic Dissertations and Theses

Lillie, K.E., A. Markos, M.B. Arias and T.G. Wiley. 2012, "Separate and not equal: The implementation of structured English immersion in Arizona's classrooms", *Teachers College Record* 114(9): 1–33

Lillie, K.E., A. Markos, A. Estrella, T. Nguyen, K. Peer, K. Perez, A. Trifiro, M.B. Arias, and T.G. Wiley. 2010, *Policy in practice: The implementation of structured English immersion in Arizona*, Los Angeles, CA: Civil Rights Project: University of California, Los Angeles

Long, M.H. and H.D. Adamson. 2012, "SLA research and Arizona's structured English immersion policies". In M.B. Arias and C. Faltis, eds, *Implementing educational language policy in Arizona: Legal, historical, and current practices in SEI*, Buffalo, NY: Multilingual Matters, pp. 39–55

Mahoney, K., T. Haladyna and J. MacSwan. 2010a, "The need for multiple measures in reclassification decisions: A validity study of the Stanford English language proficiency test". In T.G. Wiley, J. Sook Lee and R.W. Rumberger, eds, *The education of language minority immigrants in the United States*, Tonawanda, NY: Multilingual Matters, pp. 240–62

Mahoney, K., J. MacSwan, T. Haladyna and D. García. 2010b, "Castañeda's third prong: Evaluating the achievement of Arizona's English learners under restrictive language policy". In P. Gándara and M. Hopkins, eds, *Forbidden languages: English learners and restrictive language policies*, New York: Teachers College Press, pp. 50–64

Mahoney, K., M. Thompson and J. MacSwan. 2004, *The condition of English language learners in Arizona: 2004*, Tempe: Education Policy Studies Laboratory, Arizona State University. http://epsl.asu.edu/aepi/EPSL-0405-106-AEPI.pdf

Martinez-Wenzl, M., K.C. Pérez and P. Gándara. 2012, "Is Arizona's approach to educating its ELs superior to other forms of instruction?" *Teachers College Record* 114(9): 1–32

Meyer v. Nebraska, 262 U.S. 390; 43 S. Ct. 625; 67 L. Ed. 1042; 1923 U.S. LEXIS 2655; 29 A.L.R. 1446

Moore, S.C.K., ed, 2014, *Language policy implementation as process and consequence: Arizona case studies*, Bristol: Multilingual Matters

Murri, N., A. Markos and A. Estrella. 2012, "Implementing structured English immersion in teacher preparation in Arizona". In M.B. Arias and C. Faltis, eds, *Implementing educational language policy in Arizona: An examination of legal, historical and current practices in SEI*, Buffalo, N.Y.: Multilingual Matters, pp. 142–63

Rios-Aguilar, C. and P. Gándara. 2012a, "*Horne v. Flores* and the future of language policy", *Teachers College Record* 114(9): 1–13

—. 2012b, "(Re)conceptualizing and (re)evaluating language policies for English learners: The case of Arizona", *Language Policy* 11(1): 1–5. doi:10.1007/s10993-011-9228-1

Rios-Aguilar, C., M.S. González-Canche and L.C. Moll. 2012a, "A study of Arizona's teachers of English language learners", *Teachers College Record* 114(9): 1–33

—. 2012b, "Implementing structured English immersion in Arizona: Benefits, challenges, and opportunities", *Teachers College Record* 114(9): 1–18

Rios-Aguilar, C., M.S. González-Canche and S. Sabetghadam. 2012, "Evaluating the impact of restrictive language policies: The Arizona 4-hour English language development block", *Language Policy* 11(1): 47–80. doi: 10.1007/s10993-011-9226-3

Wightman, J. 2010, "ELL education in Arizona: Unconstitutional segregation nor just inappropriate?" *Texas Hispanic Journal of Law and Policy* 16(121): 123–51

Wiley, T.G. 2004, "Language policy and English-only". In E. Finegan and J.R. Rickford, eds, *Language in the USA: Perspectives for the twenty-first century*, Cambridge: Cambridge University Press, pp. 319–38

—. 2013, "A brief history and assessment of language rights in the United States". In J.W. Tollefson, ed, *Language policies in education: Critical issues*, 2nd ed, New York: Routledge, pp. 61–90

Wiley, T.G. and W.E. Wright. 2004, "Against the undertow: Language-minority education policy and politics in the 'age of accountability'", *Educational Policy* 18(1): 142–68. doi:10.1177/0895904803260030.

Wright, W.E. 2005, "The political spectacle of Arizona's proposition 203", *Educational Policy* 19: 662–700

—. 2011, "Historical introduction to bilingual education: The United States". In C. Baker, ed, *Foundations of bilingual education and bilingualism*, 5th ed, Bristol: Multilingual Matters, pp. 182–205

Wright, W.E. and D. Choi. 2006, "The impact of language and high-stakes testing policies on elementary school English language learners in Arizona", *Education Policy Analysis Archives* 14(13): 1–75 http://epaa.asu.edu/ojs/article/viewFile/84/210

Wright, W.E. and K. Sung. 2012, "Teachers' sheltered English immersion views and practices". In M.B. Arias and C. Faltis, eds, *Implementing educational language policy in Arizona: Legal, historical, and current practices in SEI*, Buffalo, N.Y.: Multilingual Matters, pp. 86–106

Chapter Sixteen

Mother Tongue Education as a Legal Right for Indigenous Children

Molly Townes O'Brien and Peter Bailey

Keywords: mother tongue instruction as a human right, legal right to mother tongue instruction, bilingual education, international law and language of instruction, indigenous languages, non-English speaking education

Abstract

Education is a fundamental right, but not always an unqualified good. For indigenous peoples around the world, education has historically failed to deliver fully on its promise of economic and social advancement. Instead, it has often worked to deprive indigenous children of their sense of cultural identity and value. In some cases, education has been an instrument of cultural destruction and has operated to endanger traditional languages (Rubio-Marín 2003, pp. 70–73). This chapter sketches the history and reasons for the denial of mother tongue education and discusses how assimilationist education derives from a mono-cultural outlook. It then examines the right to bilingual education in international law, arguing that the voice of a pluralist international community is clear: Mother tongue education is the child's right. Language preservation is the minority community's right. The chapter then examines Australia's domestic approach to legal rights and argues that some statutory protection of the right to bilingual education will be required to secure an appropriate education for indigenous-language-speaking children. Taking account of the legal rights of indigenous children in Australia, the work of applied linguists is relevant to shaping educational policy and curriculum.

Why teach traditional languages?

Indigenous Australian children who arrive in primary school speaking a language other than Standard Australian English (SAE) are in a precarious educational situation. If they cannot understand their teachers, they cannot access the curriculum. They are likely to fall behind in literacy and numeracy, and will simultaneously lose self-confidence and a positive sense of their cultural identity (Kymlicka & Patten 2003, p. 146). Currently, indigenous peoples rank significantly behind non-indigenous Australians in educational achievement, in employment, in life expectancy, and in other measures of wellbeing. [1] If provided with an English immersion program (Lucas & Katz 1994, p. 537), they may be successful in gaining literacy and numeracy skills in English. But their overall achievement is likely to be lower than their English-speaking counterparts, who, while struggling to learn new concepts, do not have to struggle simultaneously to understand the language of instruction. Moreover, their new language skills are often associated with loss of their ability to speak their mother tongue. Loss of their language undermines indigenous communities and depletes cultural diversity.

Teaching endangered indigenous languages in schools is an important step toward preserving endangered cultural heritage. It not only nurtures linguistic heritage, but also sustains indigenous knowledge and identity.

> Language is at the core of cultural identity. It links people to their land, protects history through story and song, and the key to kinship systems and to the intricacies of tribal law including spirituality, secret/sacred objects and rites. Language is a major factor in people retaining their cultural identity and many say "if the Language is strong, then Culture is strong" (ATSIC 2000, p. 161).

The link between language and identity can hardly be overstated. One Native American woman, commenting on the importance of maintaining her indigenous language, said:

> If we're able to keep our language going, we'll be able to pass on knowledge, from generation to generation. Without it, we're going to lose so much. We're going to be just like everybody else. We can tell them…this is how it was…. We used to dance, but we don't know our songs. We used to have these traditional activities, but we can't do them no more, because we can't talk. We would lose so much without our language (Rock, as quoted in Dussias 2008, p. 5).

Programs that maintain, preserve or revitalize indigenous languages are also "widely accepted as a means of assisting in the general well-being of the indigenous population" (Purdie, et al. 2008, p. 12). Indigenous language programs promote a sense of fairness and equality, relieve some of the sense of oppression experienced by indigenous people, and act to

---

[1]Australian Bureau of Statistics:
www.abs.gov.au/websitedbs/D3310114.nsf/home/Home?opendocument

soothe the degree of alienation experienced (Kibbee 2008, p. 92). For school-age children, language maintenance programs may also contribute positively to "[c]ultural literacy in English, cognitive development, self-concept, verbal intelligence, mental creativity, adaptability, self-confidence" (Nicholls 1994, p. 14).

In other words, for indigenous children whose mother tongue is a traditional Australian language or a creole, a curriculum presented only in English denies them equal access to the fundamental right to education afforded all other children. The standard curriculum must be adapted to meet the needs of non-English speaking indigenous children. Evidence from around the world is that the most effective way to attain literacy is to introduce reading and writing in the mother tongue of the student. If literate in their mother tongue, the student learns English literacy skills more readily and is more likely to reach desired educational outcomes (Magga, et al. 2005, p. 4). It has also been established that bilingualism has additional cognitive benefits, including mental flexibility, greater intelligence and, in old age, protection from dementia (Bialystok 2011). Yet, despite overwhelming evidence that bilingual education is effective for indigenous children, it can be a political football.

Perhaps because language plays a central role in perpetuating minority culture and identity, it is subject to political pressures in many countries. The associated policy conflicts are frequently emotional and highly pitched, reflecting the identity politics of the majority (Skutnabb-Kangas 2008, pp. 117–19). Disputes about the use of Corsican in France, Basque in Spain, Spanish in the United States, the Uyghur language in China, and Kurdish in Turkey, for example, have been at the center of recent political controversy and even civil unrest. Bilingual education policies in Australia are similarly subject to pressures from ill-informed or politically motivated actors. Bilingual education programs have suffered from inadequate resourcing, inconsistent support and threats of abolition (Nicholls 2005, p. 162).

Australian states have a greater responsibility to guarantee the linguistic rights of indigenous peoples than those of immigrant minorities, who can usually rely on contacts in their country of origin for support in maintaining their language. Foreign languages (such as French, German, and Spanish) are taught more pervasively in Australian schools than indigenous languages (Purdie, et al. 2008, pp. 50–90), while indigenous language programs have been fading or phased out. Since 1978, for example, the Northern Territory government has reduced funds for indigenous language programs, the number of specialist staff and the number of bilingual schools (Devlin 2011a, p. 261). Further, the main goals for indigenous bilingual programs have changed to focus on English literacy (McKay 1996, pp. 113–14). Withering financial and policy support eventually led to an end to bilingual education in 1998 (Devlin 2009). After a short-lived reinstatement of bilingual education in 2005, the Northern Territory government replaced it with a "four-hours-of-English" policy based on what Devlin has labelled "dishonest manipulation of data" to show falsely the inferior literacy results of bilingual compared with monolingual programs (Devlin 2011b, p. 65). Australian education policy has failed to deliver a cognitively and culturally grounded education for indigenous students.

Being taught in the mother tongue is a duty— not a charitable gift

In spite of Australia's failure to reliably deliver mother tongue education to indigenous children, the argument for a special duty in relation to indigenous languages is strong, supported by earlier successful programs and by the decades of discriminatory laws implementing assimilation through, among other things, language suppression. Further, Australia has acknowledged the importance of education and of mother tongue education by endorsing many international legal conventions that describe those rights. So Australia has recognized the fundamental rights of indigenous children to education on equal terms and to maintain their heritage and culture. Table 16-1 contains a list of relevant international instruments endorsed by Australia with references to the paragraphs that relate to educational rights.

Table 16-1: International Covenants and Declarations relevant to the Right to Education

Acronym or initialism	Convention, Declaration or Covenant	Operative
CCITPIC	Convention concerning Indigenous and Tribal Peoples in Independent Countries (ILO No. 169), 72 ILO Official Bull. 59, Article 28	5 September 1991
CRC	Convention on the Rights of the Child, 1577 UNTS 3, Articles 3; 12; 27; 28(b),(c); 29(c),(d); Article 30 (has a complaints committee) Opened for signature 20 November 1989	2 September 1990

Acronym or initialism	Convention, Declaration or Covenant	Operative
DRC	Declaration of the Rights of the Child, GA Res 1386 (XIV)	20 November 1959
DRPBNERLM	*Declaration on the Rights of Persons Belonging to National or Ethnic, Religious and Linguistic Minorities*, UN Doc A/Res/47/135, Article 4(3)	18 December 1992
ICCPR	*International Covenant on Civil and Political Rights*, 999 UNTS 171, Articles 24, 25, 27 (has a complaints committee) Opened for signature 16 December 1966	23 March 1976
ICERD	*International Convention on the Elimination of all forms of Racial Discrimination*, 660 UNTS 195, Article 5 (has a complaints committee) Opened for signature 7 March 1966	4 January 1969
ICESCR	*International Covenant on Economic, Social and Cultural Rights*, 993 UNTS 3. Articles 2, 5, 13, 14, 15, 27 (has a complaints committee) Opened for signature 16 December 1966	3 January 1976
UDHR	*Universal Declaration of Human Rights*, GA Res 217 (III), UN GAOR, 3rd Sess, Supp No. 13, UN Doc A/810, Articles 2; 26; 27	10 December 1948
UNDRIP	*United Nations Declaration on the Rights of Indigenous People*, GA Res 61/295, UN GAOR, 61st Sess, 107th plenary meeting, Supp No 49, UN Doc A/Res/61/295, Articles 1-3; 8.1; especially 13; 14; 17.2; 23	13 September 2007
UNESCO	United Nations Educational, Scientific and Cultural Organization, *Convention Against Discrimination in Education*, 14 December 1960	22 May 1962

For example, primary and secondary education is internationally declared a fundamental right in the 1959 Declaration of the Rights of the Child (DRC), which Australia supported. It is part of the Australian Human

Rights Commission (AHRC)'s Charter, and provides that "the child is entitled to receive education, which shall be free and compulsory, at least in the elementary stages." The right to education is also recognized in Article 13 of the International Covenant on Economic, Social and Cultural Rights (ICESCR), to which Australia is a party:

> The States Parties to the present Covenant recognize the right of everyone to education. They agree that education shall be directed to the full development of the human personality and the sense of its dignity, and shall strengthen the respect for human rights and fundamental freedoms. They further agree that education shall enable all persons to participate effectively in a free society, promote understanding, tolerance and friendship among all nations and all racial, ethnic or religious groups, and further the activities of the United Nations for the maintenance of peace (ICESCR, Article 13).

Education is a fundamental right and can "unlock other rights" (Tomasevski 2001, p. 12), such as access to the labor market, and the ability to assert human rights. "Its denial can lead to compounded denials of other human rights and the perpetuation of poverty" (Tomasevski 2005, p. 74). Education is intended to be a right of empowerment that will "enable all persons to participate effectively in a free society" (UDHR, preamble).

Education can also be a powerful engine for socioeconomic development, achieving responsible citizenship, and developing national identity and patriotism. School policymakers often view the forging of a national identity as a central function of state-provided education (Kaestle 1983, pp. 4–7). Education has also been called "the most widespread form of institutionalized socialization of children" (Tomasevski 2005, p. 74). The DRC states it will enable the child "to develop physically, mentally, morally, spiritually and socially in a healthy and normal manner in conditions of freedom and dignity" (DRC, Principle 2).

The socialization and identity-formation aspects of schooling are not "add-on" or optional. Even when the educational approach is deliberately bicultural or multicultural, children cannot be given knowledge without values. No knowledge is value-free. What counts as knowledge is itself a distillation of the values of a particular culture. Although education is necessarily assimilationist to some extent, it does at least pass on to children the culture, values and skills of the adult teachers.

Historical experience in Australia and other countries

Perhaps the most extreme examples of forced assimilation of indigenous minorities through education are found in the boarding school programs of Canada, the United States and Australia. In Canada, for example, Native American children were subject to a decades-long federal government policy that removed them from their families and forced them to live in residential schools (Miller 1996). In a 2008 apology for the policy, Prime Minister Stephen Harper admitted that the residential school education had been designed to effect cultural annihilation:

> Two primary objectives of the residential schools system were to remove and isolate children from the influence of their homes, families, traditions and cultures, and to assimilate them into the dominant culture. These objectives were based on the assumption that aboriginal cultures and spiritual beliefs were inferior and unequal. (Harper 2008)

Similarly, Native American children in the United States were taken from their families and taught in "Indian schools" between 1885 and the mid-twentieth century in an effort to "dissolve Native Americans into the great American melting pot" (Dussias 2008, p. 12). Between 1910 and 1974, the Australian Government also employed education to eliminate ethnic difference, taking thousands of Aboriginal and Torres Strait Islander children from their families to be educated at boarding schools.[2] In Australia and North America indigenous children were forcibly taken from their families to residential schools where they were inculcated with the dominant white culture. They were required to adopt a new language, a new religion, a new mode of dress and hair style. They were given unfamiliar beds and foods and required to leave behind their customs and traditions and spend their days in unfamiliar spaces doing unfamiliar tasks.

When viewed from a comfortable historical distance, it is easy to understand how this educational policy inflicted harm. By depriving the children of their family, culture, and a large part of their identity, assimilationist education not only created a rift in indigenous communities, but also imposed life-long emotional and social burdens on thousands of indigenous children (HREOC 1997). Seen through the eyes of its proponents at the time, however, residential education was a charity, a good work, a gift, that offered the benefits of civilization, advancement and opportunity. The education offered by the boarding schools placed no

---

[2] Prime Minister Kevin Rudd formally apologized in 2008 for the policy (Rudd 2008).

value on indigenous knowledge, language, experience, values, families or community ties. Instead, attributes of indigenous culture were seen as a problem to be eliminated through education. It was thought that once provided with the rudimentary elements of white culture, these children might climb the rungs of the white social ladder and become participants in the dominant culture. The children and their descendants would no longer be members of an outcast and inferior class. According to Cecil Cook, the Northern Territory Protector of Natives between 1927 and 1937:

> Generally by the fifth and invariably by the sixth generation, all native characteristics of the Australian Aborigine are eradicated. The problem of our half-castes will quickly be eliminated by the complete disappearance of the black race, and the swift submergence of their progeny in the white. (Rudd 2008)

Few in the indigenous language policy discussion argue against teaching English to indigenous language-speaking children. Around the globe, however, indigenous children are less likely to be enrolled in school and have higher drop out and illiteracy rates than non-indigenous children (Committee on the Rights of the Child, General Comment No. 11 (2009), para 59). Conversely, they are disproportionately to be imprisoned (Tonry 1997, p. 19). All have been shown to have negative educational and social outcomes in dominant language educational systems (Bewicke 2009, p. 135; Skutnabb-Kangas & Dunbar 2010, pp. 44–56).

As noted earlier, while there may be multiple causes for minority children to lag behind majority children in educational and socioeconomic outcomes (such as lack of high-quality educational programs, low expectations, poor attendance, family poverty, distance from school, and lack of a place and time to study), a growing body of research indicates that instruction in the child's mother tongue is an essential ingredient of an appropriate education:

> There is overwhelming technical evidence that the most efficacious approach to attaining literacy—a fundamental goal of mass education—is to introduce reading and writing in the mother tongue of the student, followed, if desirable, by a transition to literacy in a national language (Sutton 2005, p. 104).

While it is not possible for education to avoid all assimilation, it is possible to assimilate the child to a bicultural or pluralist culture. Mother tongue instruction requires a shift in one's educational mindset from a mono-cultural orientation to a pluralist one. The shift toward a pluralist concept of citizenship and culture is a shift that national policy initiatives have already recognized in a number of ways, including through a national apology. The benefits of diversity and a pluralist culture for a contemporary democracy are well known. Unfortunately, however, the impulse to blame the minority culture for social problems and to expect minorities to assimilate into the mainstream mono-culture remains strong.

International Mother tongue instruction obligations

International law and declarations (see Table 16-1) do not sit on the fence in the debate over mother tongue instruction. The international community is pluralist—ready to acknowledge and support the value of a variety of cultures. International provisions recognize that education can alienate a child from their family and culture and are worded to guard against that possibility. CRC expresses the right to education in terms that prioritize the child's family cultural heritage and promote multicultural affinity. Article 29 requires that education must (among other things) be directed to:

> (para (b)) The development of respect for the child's parents, his or her own cultural identity, language and values, for the national values of the country in which the child is living, the country from which he or she may originate, and for civilizations different from his or her own;
> (para (c)) The preparation of the child for responsible life in a free society
> …

Article 29(c) also emphasizes how important it is that free societies respect national values. The Article indicates that internationally agreed human rights values should be embodied in the content of education in each country. Whatever curricula choices are arrived at by local school authorities, those values must be involved in guiding the curriculum, and be communicated to the child. Article 30 further requires that an indigenous child not be "denied [the right to] use his or her own language…" Low-quality instruction or instruction that does not prepare the child to participate in the political and cultural life of their country (which necessarily includes literacy and proficiency in the language of the dominant culture) would also fall short of fulfilling the requirement in Article 29(d) of "preparation of the child for responsible life in a free society."

Article 29 does not specifically address mother tongue instruction but, taken with recent comments by the Committee on the Rights of the Child, it could be argued that instruction in the mother tongue is the child's right. The right of equal opportunity in education is further supported in international law by Article 5(e)(v) of the ICERD. That Article imposes a duty on state parties "to guarantee the right of everyone, without distinction as to race, colour, or national or ethnic origin, to equality before the law … in the enjoyment of the right to education and training."

When a child who does not speak English begins school in Australia, equality of opportunity cannot be achieved in an "English only" instruction regime. In *Lau v. Nichols*, 414 U.S. 563, 565 (1974)—a landmark US case in 1974—the U.S. Supreme Court considered the educational rights of non-English speaking children of Chinese ancestry who were in school in California, where the school's teachers spoke only English. The Court pointed out:

> [T]here is no equality of treatment by providing students with the same facilities, textbooks, teachers, and curriculum; for students who do not understand English are effectively foreclosed from any meaningful education.

Similarly, the High Court in Australia has long acknowledged that the achievement of equality may require more than formal equality: special measures may be required "to achieve effective and genuine equality." (For example, see *Gerhardy v. Brown* (1985) 159 CLR 70, 129, Brennan, J.) Further, it can be persuasively argued that an English-only curriculum is not "accessible" to a non-English speaking child, in violation of Article 5 of the Convention Against Discrimination in Education, which recognizes in Article 51 "the right of members of national minorities" to use or teach "their own language." In 2009 the CRC Committee explained:

> Article 30 of the Convention establishes the right of the indigenous child to use his or her own language. *In order to implement this right, education in the child's own language is essential* (CRC Committee, General Comment No. 11, para 62 (italics supplied)).

Other UN declarations and international conventions affirm the language rights of indigenous children. Article 27 of the ICCPR ensures the rights of linguistic and cultural minorities "to enjoy their own culture, to profess and practise their own religion, or to use their own language." Article 4(3) of the *Declaration on the Rights of Persons Belonging to National or Ethnic, Religious and Linguistic Minorities* provides that

> States should take appropriate measures so that, wherever possible, persons belonging to minorities may have adequate opportunities to learn their mother tongue or to have instruction in their mother tongue (47/135.DRPBNERLM).

Article 14(3) of the UNDRIP similarly requires that

> States shall, in conjunction with indigenous peoples, take effective measures, in order for indigenous individuals, particularly children, including those living outside their communities, to have access, when possible, to an education in their own culture and provided in their own language.

The voice of the international community is neither unclear nor ambiguous. And it has been directed critically and explicitly at Australia. For example, in 2010 the ICERD Committee explicitly expressed concern over the apparent elimination of bilingual education programs in the Northern Territory and urged the government to conduct a national inquiry into the issue of bilingual education. It recommended that the state "adopt all necessary measures to preserve native languages and develop and carry out programmes to revitalize indigenous languages and bilingual and intercultural education for indigenous peoples" and "consider providing national minorities with adequate opportunities for the use and teaching of their own language."[3]

In sum, the views of the international community are explicitly behind mother tongue education for indigenous children. For example, Article 14(3) of the UNDRIP provides that indigenous children have a right to access, when possible, "to an education in their own culture and provided in their own language."

No right without a remedy—the lack of effective and enforceable domestic legislation

In spite of vigorous endorsement of the educational and linguistic rights of indigenous children, the Commonwealth has not guaranteed reliable protection through any specific domestic legislation or policy. Although the Commonwealth has promoted various indigenous language policies and indigenous language support initiatives and a National Indigenous Language Policy (http://arts.gov.au/indigenous/languages), none provides an enforceable right to mother tongue instruction.

There is a timeless legal adage, *ubi jus ibi remedium,* which translates as "There is no right without a remedy." Said another way, this means that without an effective remedy for the violation of a right, the existence of

---

[3] ICERD/C/AUS/CO 15-17 (2010)—Consideration of reports submitted... (Australia) paragraph 21.

the right itself is questionable.[4] There are no modes of enforcement for international law provisions, even those written in strong, mandatory language. International conventions are not domestically enforceable without implementing domestic legislation.

At present, Australia does not have domestic legislation implementing the right of non-English speaking children to education in their mother tongue, and a recently developed curriculum for teaching indigenous languages does not guarantee mother tongue instruction. Although some aspects of the CRC Committee comments have been incorporated into domestic law (Ruddle & Nicholes 2004), the provisions for mother tongue instruction of CRC Articles 28 and 29 have not been included. While CRC had been annexed to the charter of HREOC,[5] that does not confer legal power to implement it. All it can do is submit a report to the Minister, and publish it.

Of the international treaties mentioned above, only the ICERD has been implemented through domestic legislation in the Racial Discrimination Act 1975 (Cth).[6] A complaint alleging discrimination based on race could be made to the AHRC, if on the basis of "race, colour, descent or national or ethnic origin," a person engaged in an activity within an area protected by the Act did something that had the "purpose or effect of nullifying or impairing the recognition, enjoyment or exercise" of a human right "on an equal footing" (Racial Discrimination Act 1975, section 9(1)).

Only two complaints relating to an Aboriginal school program have been brought under the Racial Discrimination Act 1975 (Cth), and neither specifically raised the mother tongue issue. The first complaint, heard by HREOC in 1992,[7] concerned the Traeger Park Primary School in the Northern Territory. But even in the sensitive and lengthy reasons for decisions handed down by the HREOC Inquiry, the Inquiry Commissioner

---

[4] See *Nulyarimma v. Thompson* [1999] FCA 1192; *Chow Hung Ching v. The King*, (1948) 77 CLR 449, 478; and *Bradley v. Commonwealth*, (1973) 128 CLR 557, 582.

[5] Australian Human Rights and Equal Opportunity Commission Act 1986, section 47 (since 2007 the Australian Human Rights Commission).

[6] Anti-discrimination provisions of the ICCPR and ICESCR are domestically implemented in part through the Racial Discrimination Act 1975 and various state and territory discrimination laws, but not directly in relation to mother tongue languages. ICESCR, ICCPR and CRC have not been enacted into domestic law, although certain aspects of the rights recognized in the ICCPR (in addition to non-discrimination provisions) can be found in common law decisions and various statutory provisions. See *Minogue v. Williams* [2000] FCA 125 [23]-[25].

[7] Heard by Commissioner W. Carter QC, 1992 EOC 92-415.

held that there had been no racial discrimination in closing the Aboriginal school. Although he would have preferred to find discrimination, the Commissioner found there had been none, because of the absence of certain requirements of the Racial Discrimination Act (RDA 1975).

In the second case, *Sinnapan and Others v. State of Victoria*[8] the issue involved the closing of a government school that included a significant group of local "Aboriginal" children. A "whole-of-school" approach had provided special services for the indigenous group, with much of the emphasis on preserving their "culture and traditions." The Supreme Court held that education was a "service" for racial discrimination purposes and found that neither it nor the Board could determine the policy aspects. There had been no unlawful discrimination. In sum, the prospects of protecting bilingual education by way of either Commonwealth or a State or Territory racial discrimination legislation are unlikely to produce results supportive of mother tongue initiatives.

Issues of cost, culture and a high burden of proof (de Plevitz 2003) make litigation an unwelcoming pathway for seeking redress. Further, even when the school authorities have been shown to act in violation of the law, some courts have been reluctant to decide on educational issues. For example, in a case seeking sign language instruction for a deaf child, the court found a violation of the Anti-Discrimination Act 1991 (QLD), but questioned the appropriateness of litigation:

> In my opinion, it is a misconception to think that legal proceedings of this kind are the appropriate vehicle to introduce changes into the education system (Dickson 2005, quoting the judge in the case).

Similarly, resort to international education rights may be unavailing. Following a 1998 announcement by the Northern Territory Government that it was phasing out bilingual education programs in Aboriginal communities, HREOC reviewed international law and commentary on the issue of bilingual education and concluded:

> For many Indigenous people, the decision of the Northern Territory government to phase out bilingual education programs in government schools in Aboriginal communities amounted to a denial of their right to

---

[8] *Sinnapan and Others v. State of Victoria*, EOC 92-499 Aboriginal Students Support Committee Complaint Traeger Park Primary School (1993—original stay in SC); 567 (1993—main initial hearing by EOB Vic); 568 (1994) initial hearing by SC Vic; 663 (1995—final hearing by SC Vic); 699 (1995—final consent orders by EOB).

choose the mode of education for their children and threatens the viability of remaining languages (Australian Human Rights Commission 2000).[9]

As a result of the report and public pressure, bilingual education was given a temporary reprieve. Even so, bilingual education programs were continuously scaled back throughout the subsequent decade and funding for English as a Second Language programs decreased (Simpson, et al. 2011).

How can Australia move forward?

If neither international pressure nor domestic legislation nor litigation offer viable remedies for the denial of linguistic rights, how can they be secured? Given the current lack of any comprehensive regime for enforcement of rights, legislation is the most viable option. The linguistic rights of indigenous peoples of Australia need the protection of a specific, national statutory scheme. Also needed are the committed efforts of applied linguistics professionals, who could train bilingual teachers and design various mother tongue curricula.

Statutory protection of mother tongues could provide not only important support and opportunities for protection for individual students, but also a strong incentive for States to develop appropriate language instructional programs in bilingual education and mother tongue instruction. Around the world, it is becoming clear that the linguistic and educational rights of indigenous children cannot reliably be left for implementation by unassisted local groups or governments. A number of nations have recently enacted statutes to protect indigenous children's right to be educated in their mother tongue. An international best practice model is the legal architecture for the protection of Sami languages in Norway. Sami are the indigenous people of territory situated across the State borders of Norway, Sweden, Finland and Russia. The Sami Language Act of 1990 officially classifies six municipalities as bilingual, and so requiring all municipal offices to offer their services (including schooling) in both Norwegian and Sami.

The Commonwealth has sufficient legislative power to give effect to its international obligations. [10] National legislation would have the

---

[9] It should be noted that the judge's ruling was overturned on appeal and deaf children in Queensland have been provided with Auslan interpretive services. See "Delivering quality educational outcomes for deaf and hearing impaired students: the transition to Auslan" at
http://education.qld.gov.au/studentservices/staff/workshops/auslan.html
[10] See *Koowarta v. Bjelke-Petersen* (1982) 152 CLR 168.

advantage of providing a single and compelling approach to language
rights issues and would place those rights out of reach of the vagaries of
identity politics at the local level. Various measures to protect indigenous
languages and to develop viable language programs (such as measures
relating to teacher training, for local consultation, for the development of
culturally appropriate materials) can and should be tackled by applied
linguists and addressed at the state and territory level. [11] But the
foundational right to indigenous mother tongue education should be
recognized in a national statute that provides a clear and meaningful
statement of the right and how it must be implemented.

Conclusion

Australia's national policy on education has, "in principle", supported
indigenous language instruction for many years. Even so, progress in
providing appropriate language instruction to the children who most
desperately need it has been slow and sometimes subject to substantial
backsliding. Failure to provide appropriate language instruction to the
small minority of indigenous children for whom English is a second
language is discriminatory and fails to live up to Australia's declared
ideals. Statutory protection would go a long way toward putting
indigenous-language-speaking children on an equal footing as they enter
school and toward closing the achievement gap. Statutory protection
would also ensure that educational rights are nationally recognized and
achieved reliably, equally and predictably. Perhaps most importantly, such
legislation, if broadly intentioned and creating obligations, would also help
to preserve endangered indigenous languages and help to protect
Australia's diverse cultural heritage. We need a regime of rights that
includes a statute that specifically protects and provides a remedy for the
denial of a child's right to education in their mother tongue.

---

[11] These include the Education Act 1990 (N.S.W.); Education and Training Reform
Act 2006 (Vic); Education (General Provisions) Act 2006 (Qld); School Education
Act 1999 (WA); Education Act 1972 (SA); Education Act 1994 (Tas) Education
Act 2004 (ACT); and Education Act (NT).

References

Aboriginal Students Support and Parents Awareness Committee Traeger Park Primary School v. Minister for Education. 1992, Northern Territory of Australia, HREOCA 4

Aboriginal and Torres Strait Islander Commission (ATSIC). 2000, *Submission to the House of Representatives Standing Committee into the Needs of Urban Dwelling Aboriginal and Torres Strait Islander Peoples*, Canberra: Commonwealth of Australia

Australian Bureau of Statistics. 2006, 4221.0—Schools, Australia. http://www.abs.gov.au/AUSSTATS/abs@.nsf/Previousproducts/4221.0Main%20Features22006?opendocument&tabname=Summary&prodno=4221.0&issue=2006&num=&view

Australian Human Rights Commission Act. 1986, Section 47, Section 11 (k) and (m)

—. 2000, *International Review of Indigenous issues in 2000: Australia.* http://www.humanrights.gov.au/social_justice/native_title/nt_issues/index.html

Bailey, P. 2009, *The Human Rights Enterprise in Australia and Internationally*, Chatswood, N.S.W.: LexisNexis

Bewicke, E. 2009, "Silencing the Silk Road: China's Language Policy in the Xinjiang Uyghur Autonomous Region", *San Diego International Law Journal* 11: 135–69

Bialystok, E. 2011, "Reshaping the mind: The benefits of bilingualism", *Canadian Journal of Experimental Psychology/Revue Canadienne de Psychologie Expérimentale* 65(4): 229–35

Bradley v. The Commonwealth (1973) 128 CLR 557

Chow Hung Ching v. The King (1948) 77 CLR 449

Committee on the Rights of the Child (CRC), General Comment No. 11. 2009, paragraph 59

Devlin, B. 2009, "Bilingual education in the Northern Territory and the continuing debate about its effectiveness and value". http://www.abc.net.au/4corners/special_eds/20090914/language/docs/Devlin_paper.pdf

—. 2011a, "The Status and Future of Bilingual Education", *Australian Review of Applied Linguistics* 34: 260–79

—. 2011b, "A Bilingual Education Policy Issue: Biliteracy versus English only Literacy". In N. Purdie, G. Milgate and H.R. Bell, eds, *Two Way Teaching and Learning: Toward Culturally Reflective and Relevant Education*, Camberwell: ACER Press, pp. 49–70

de Plevitz, L. 2003, "The Briginshaw 'standard of proof' in Anti-Discrimination Law: Pointing with a wavering Finger", *Melbourne University Law Review* 27(2): 308–33

Dickson, E. 2005, "Case Note: The Instruction of Students with Hearing Impairments in Auslan: *Hurst and Devlin v. Education Queensland*", *Australia and New Zealand Journal of Law and Education* 10(1): 4

Dussias, A.M. 2008, "Indigenous Languages under Siege: The Native American Experience", *Intercultural Human Rights Law Review* 3: 5–78

Gerhardy v. Brown (1985) 159 CLR 70, 129 Brennan, J.

Harper, S. (Prime Minister of Canada), June 11, 2008. http://www.pm.gc.ca/eng/news/2008/06/11/prime-minister-harper-offers-full-apology-behalf-canadians-indian-residential

Human Rights and Equal Opportunity Commission (HREOC). 1997, *Bringing them Home: Report of the National Inquiry into the Separation of Aboriginal and Torres Strait Islander Children from their Families* (1997). http://www.humanrights.gov.au/social_justice/bth_report/index.html

International Convention on the Elimination of all Forms of Racial Discrimination (ICERD), 4 January 1969. http://www.unhchr.ch/tbs/doc.nsf/898586b1dc7b4043c1256a450044f331/150a5789fc5e8499c1256fc5003dc6c2/$FILE/G0540634.pdf

Kaestle, C. 1983, *Pillars of the Republic: Common Schools and American Society 1780-1860*, Madeira Park, B.C.: Douglas & McIntyre

Kibbee, D.A. 2008, "Minority Language Rights: Historical and Comparative Perspectives", *Intercultural Human Rights Law Review* 3: 79–136

Koowarta v. Bjelke-Petersen (1982) 153 CLR 168

Kymlicka, W. and A. Patten, eds, 2003, *Language Rights and Political Theory*, Oxford: Oxford University Press

Lau v. Nichols (1973) 414 U.S. 563

Lucas, T. and A. Katz. 1994, "Reframing the Debate: The Roles of Native Languages in English-Only Programs for Language Minority Students", *TESOL Quarterly* 28: 537–61

Magga, O.H., I. Nicolaisen, M. Trask, T. Skutnabb-Kangas and R. Dunbar. 2005, *Indigenous Children's Education and Indigenous Languages* (Report Commissioned for the United Nations Permanent Forum on Indigenous Issues [UNPFII]). http://www.tove-skutnabb-kangas.org/pdf/PFII_Expert_paper_1_Education_final.pdf

McKay, G. 1996, *The Land Still Speaks*, Commissioned Report No 44, National Board of Employment, Education and Training, Canberra: Australian Government Publishing Service

Miller, J.R. 1996, *Shingwauk's Vision: A History of Native American Residential Schools*, Toronto: University of Toronto Press

Minogue v. Williams (2000) FCA 125

Nicholls, C. 1994, "Vernacular language programmes and bilingual education programmes in Aboriginal Australia: issues and ideologies". In D. Hartman and J.K. Henderson, eds, *Aboriginal languages in education*, Alice Springs, N.T.: IAD Press, pp. 3–58

—. 2005, "Death by a Thousand Cuts: Indigenous Language Bilingual Education Programmes in the Northern Territory of Australia, 1972–1998", *International Journal of Bilingual Education and Bilingualism* 8(2–3): 160–77

Nulyarimma v. Thompson (1999) FCA 1192

Purdie, N., T. Frigo, C. Ozolins, G. Noblett, N. Thieberger and J. Sharp, J. 2008, *Indigenous Language Programmes in Australian Schools: A Way Forward*,

Australian Council for Educational Research (ACER), Commonwealth of Australia. http://research.acer.edu.au/indigenous_education/18/

Rubio-Marín, R. 2003, "Language Rights: Exploring the Competing Rationales. In W. Kymlicka and A. Patten", eds, *Language Rights and Political Theory*, Oxford: Oxford University Press, pp. 25–75

Rudd, K. "Apology to Australia's Indigenous Peoples, House of Representatives", February 13, 2008, Parliament House, Canberra. http://www.aph.gov.au/house/Rudd_Speech.pdf

Sydney Morning Herald, "Kevin Rudd's Sorry Speech", February 13, 2008. http://www.smh.com.au/articles/2008/02/13/1202760379056.html

Ruddle, L. and S. Nicholes. 2004, "B & B and Minister for Immigration and Multicultural and Indigenous Affairs: Can International Treaties Release Children from Immigration Detention Centres?", *Melbourne Journal of International Law* 5(1): 256–79

Simpson, J., J. Caffery and P. McConvell. 2011, "Gaps in Australia's Indigenous Language Policy: Dismantling bilingual education in the Northern Territory", AIATSIS Discussion Paper Number 24. http://www.aiatsis.gov.au/research/docs/dp/DP24.pdf

Skutnabb-Kangas, T. and R. Dunbar. 2010, "Indigenous Children's Education as Linguistic Genocide and a Crime Against Humanity? A Global View", *Journal of Indigenous Peoples Rights* 1: 1–122. http://www.e-pages.dk/grusweb/55/

Skutnabb-Kangas, T. 2008, "Language Rights and Bilingual Education. In J. Cummins and N. Hornberger", eds, *Encyclopedia of Language and Education, vol. 5. Bilingual Education*, 2nd ed, New York: Springer, pp. 117–31

Sutton, M. 2005, "The Globalization of Multicultural Education", *Indiana Journal of Global Legal Studies* 12: 97–108

Tomasevski, K. 2001, "Human rights obligations: making education available, accessible, acceptable and adaptable", *Right to Education Primers No. 3*, Buenos Aires: Latin American Council of Social Sciences

—. 2005. "Globalizing What: Education as a Human Right or as a Traded Service?", *Indiana Journal of Global Legal Studies* 1–79

Tonry, M. 1997, "Ethnicity, Crime and Immigration", *Crime and Justice* 21: 1–29

UN Educational, Scientific and Cultural Organization (UNESCO). 1960. Convention Against Discrimination in Education. http://www.unhcr.org/refworld/docid/3ae6b3880.html

LIST OF ABBREVIATIONS

ABS	Australian Bureau of Statistics
ACER	Australian Council for Educational Research
ACT	Australian Capital Territory
ACT DET	Australian Capital Territory Department of Education and Training
ADE	Arizona Department of Education
AHRC	Australian Human Rights Commission
AIEO	Aboriginal and Islander Education Officer
ALL	Academic Language and Learning
ANU	Australian National University
ARC	Australian Research Council
ATSIC	Aboriginal and Torres Strait Islander Commission
AZELLA	Arizona English Language Learner Assessment
C1	first culture
C2	second culture
CCSM	Common Core State Standards for Mathematics
CCSS	Common Core State Standards
CFAs	confirmatory factor analyses
CMC	Computer-Mediated Communication
COAG	Council of Australian Governments
CoI	Community of Interest
CoP	Community of Practice
CRC	Convention on the Rights of the Child
Dept. I & C	Department of Immigration and Citizenship

DET	Department of Education and Training
DRC	Declaration of the Rights of the Child
DS Project	Digital Storytelling Project
ECCHo	Effective Clinical Communication in Handover
ECE	Early Childhood Education
ED	emergency department
EEOA	Equal Education Opportunities Act 1974
EFAs	exploratory factor analyses
EFL	English as a Foreign Language
EL	English learner (also called English language learner)
ELA	English language arts
ELD	English language development
ELP	English language proficiency
ELT	English Language Teaching
ESL	English as a Second Language
ESP	English for Specific Purpose
FaHCSIA	Families, Housing, Community Services and Indigenous Affairs
FES	Fluent English Speakers
HLS	Home Language Survey
HREOC	Human Rights and Equal Opportunity Commission
IB	Inward Bound (ANU)
ICAA	Institute of Chartered Accountants in Australia
ICCPR	International Covenant on Civil and Political Rights
ICERD	International Convention on the Elimination of all forms of Racial Discrimination
ICESCR	International Covenant on Economic, Social and Cultural Rights

IELTS	International English Language Testing System
IHSLO	Indigenous Home School Liaison Officer
ILO	International Labour Organisation
IRT	Item Response Theory
KLY	Kalaw Lagaw Ya
L1	first language
L2	second language
LBOTE	Language Background Other Than English
LFCL	literature-focused cooperative learning
LM	language minority
LMT	Language Management Theory
LPP	Legitimate Peripheral Participation
LWP	Language in the Workplace Project
MASUS	Measuring the Academic Skills of University Students
MCEECDYA	Ministerial Council for Education, Early Childhood Development and Youth Affairs
MYOB	Mind Your Own Business
NAATI	National Accreditation Authority for Translators and Interpreters
NAPLAN	National Assessment Program Literacy and Numeracy
PIPS	Performance Indicators in Primary Schools
RDA	Racial Discrimination Act 1975
RFEP	reclassified fluent English proficient
SAE	Standard Australian English
SCSEEC	Standing Council on School Education and Early Childhood
SEI	Structured English Immersion
SEM	Structural equation modeling

SFL	Systemic Functional Linguistics
SLA	second language acquisition
SMPs	Standards for Mathematical Practice
UDHR	Universal Declaration of Human Rights
UNDRIP	United Nations Declaration on the Rights of Indigenous People
UNESCO	United Nations Educational, Scientific and Cultural Organization

CONTRIBUTORS

Denise Angelo is a visiting fellow at the Australian National University. She is an educator, language teacher, ESL specialist and linguist who has worked in primary, secondary and tertiary settings. She has worked with teams teaching traditional Aboriginal languages across northern Australia; training Aboriginal interpreters and translators; researching contact language varieties; building educator capacity; and developing resources to support classroom learning for Indigenous students with complex "contact language" backgrounds. Contact language varieties—their historical and present day development, their role for communities, families and individuals, the recognition and attitudes assigned to them, and their impact in education—are a major research interest. Recent publications include "Sad stories. A preliminary study of NAPLAN practice texts analysing students' second language linguistic resources and the effects of these on their written narratives" in M. Ponsonnet, L. Dao and M. Bowler, eds, *Proceedings of the 42nd Australian Linguistic Society Conference—2011* (2012), and papers in *Papers in Language Testing and Assessment* and the *Australian Review of Applied Linguistics*.

Angela Ardington is a senior lecturer in the Learning Centre at the University of Sydney. Her linguistic research interests cover Writing Across the Disciplines, with an emphasis on Visual Arts, Architecture and Engineering students' approaches and attitudes to academic writing as effective communication. Other areas of research interest include politeness phenomena in conflict negotiation, especially in the public domain. She is the author of "Alliance building and identity work in early adolescent girls' talk; Conversational accomplishments of playful duelling" in A. Duszak and U. Okulska, eds, *Language, Culture and the Dynamics of Age* (2011); and "Tourist advertising of Australia: impolite or situation-appropriate? Or a uniquely Aussie Invite Lost in Translation" in B.L. Davies, A.J. Merrison, M. Haugh, eds, *Situated Politeness* (2011). She has also written for the *Journal of Language Aggression and Conflict*.

Peter Bailey is an adjunct professor at the College of Law, Australian National University. He received his LL.M from the University of Melbourne and his M.A. from Oxford University. He was awarded an OBE in 1972 and an AM in 1999. He was CEO of the Human Rights

Commission (Commonwealth) from 1981 to 1985 (the predecessor of the Human Rights and Equal Opportunity Commission and the AHRC). He joined the ANU as a visiting fellow in 1987. Since then he has taught human rights and discrimination law and public law in undergraduate and graduate courses. His main recent books are *The Human Rights Enterprise in Australia and Internationally* (2009) and *Human Rights Law* (2012). He has also published numerous articles and was editor of and contributor to "Human Rights", vol. 21 in (1995–99) *The Laws of Australia.*

Julie Bradshaw is an adjunct senior research fellow in linguistics at Monash University. She received her D. Phil. from the University of York. She is interested in the linguistic consequences of migration and language contact, multilingualism, language maintenance and loss, and language and identity. Her publications include papers in the *International Journal of the Sociology of Language*, the *International Journal of Bilingualism and Bilingual Education*, and the *International Journal of Multilingualism*. She is joint editor of *The Palgrave Companion to English Language and Linguistics.*

H. Gary Cook is director of research for the WIDA Consortium, Wisconsin Center for Education Research, University of Wisconsin-Madison. His recent research interests focus on alignment of standards and assessments, and national policy and evaluation issues associated with Title III, the U.S. Government's program, "Language Instruction for Limited English Proficiency and Immigrant Students in the Elementary and Secondary Education Act". He has written widely, including *National Evaluation of Title III Implementation Supplemental Report: Exploring approaches to setting English language proficiency and performance criteria and monitoring English learner progress,* published by the U.S. Department of Education.

Marisa Cordella is an associate professor in Spanish linguistics at the University of Queensland. She received her Ph.D in linguistics from Monash University. She has conducted research, published extensively and supervised postgraduate students in the areas of medical communication, intercultural communication, interactional sociolinguistics, critical discourse analysis, pragmatics, teaching methodologies and translation studies. Her latest publication (with A. Poiani) is *Behavioral Oncology: Psychological, communicative and social dimensions* (2014).

Suzanne Eggins taught and researched in professional writing, linguistics and children's literature at the University of New South Wales for 15 years. She has since worked in editing and publishing and as a health communication Research Fellow with the University of Technology Sydney. She received her B.A. (Hons) and Ph.D in Linguistics from the University of Sydney and has postgraduate degrees in journalism, professional communication and applied linguistics. She is the author of *An Introduction to Systemic Functional Linguistics* (2nd ed., 2004) and co-author (with D. Slade) of *Analysing Casual Conversation* (1997).

Elizabeth Ellis is a senior lecturer in linguistics at the University of New England. She holds a Ph.D and has written widely, including in *TESOL Quarterly*, *Voces Hispanas*, *Language Awareness iFirst*, *University of Sydney Papers in TESOL*, *Current Issues in Language Planning* and *Sociolinguistic Studies*.

Farzana Gounder is a postdoctoral fellow at the University of Waikato, Hamilton. She received her Ph.D from Massey University. Her research focuses on the intersection of linguistics, media, and transnationalism. Her publications include *Indentured identities: Resistance and accommodation in plantation-era Fiji* (2011). She is currently editing a book titled *Narrative and identity constructions in the Pacific Islands*, and a special edition of the New Zealand Linguistic Society's official journal, *Te Reo*, on narrative definitions in Aotearoa.

Rosalie Grant is a quantitative researcher for the WIDA Consortium, Wisconsin Center for Education Research, University of Wisconsin-Madison. She has broad experience in educational measurement, research, evaluation and accountability at the state and federal government levels. Her current research includes advancing academic English language development and academic achievement for English learners, including Native American students.

Kirsten Hanna is a senior lecturer in the School of Social Sciences and Public Policy at AUT University, Auckland. She received her Ph.D in Linguistics from the University of Auckland. Her research currently focuses on child witnesses who testify in the criminal courts and, in particular, the language used in the examination and cross-examination of children. She now teaches within the Criminology programme at AUT.

Carol Hayes is a senior lecturer in Japanese language and literature in the College of Asia and the Pacific at the Australian National University. She holds a Ph.D in Japanese Literature from the University of Sydney. She teaches both Japanese language and courses about Japan in English ranging from literature to culture and film. Her research focuses on modern and contemporary Japanese cultural studies, literature and film. She was awarded an OLT National Teaching Excellence Award in 2013 and the ANU Vice Chancellor's Teaching Excellence Award also in 2013. She also has a strong research interest in eLearning and Japanese language teaching pedagogy, focusing on the relationship between flexible, online learning to student motivation and second language acquisition. She has written widely, including in the *Electronic Journal of Foreign Language Teaching* (e-FLT).

Janet Holmes is emeritus professor of linguistics at Victoria University of Wellington where she directs the Language in the Workplace Project: see www.victoria.ac.nz/lwp. She is a fellow of the Royal Society of New Zealand. She has published on a wide range of topics, including New Zealand English, language and gender, sexist language, pragmatic particles, compliments and apologies, and most recently on aspects of workplace discourse. Her most recent books are *Gendered Talk at Work* (2006), *Leadership, Discourse, and Ethnicity* (2011), and the 4th edition of *Introduction to Sociolinguistics*. Her research team is currently investigating the discourse of skilled migrants as they enter New Zealand workplaces and analyzing the language used on construction sites and in elder care facilities to help refugees who seek to work in these areas.

Yuki Itani-Adams is a lecturer in Japanese language and a digital learning developer in the College of Asia and the Pacific at the Australian National University. She received her Ph.D in Applied Linguistics from the University of Western Sydney. She has taught a variety of subjects in the fields of languages and applied linguistics at a number of Australian universities. Her research interests cover such areas as bilingual and second language acquisition with particular reference to Japanese and English, and second language teaching pedagogy. She was awarded the ANU Vice Chancellor's Award for Teaching Excellence in 2012, and an OLT National Citation for Outstanding Contribution to Student Learning in 2013. She has written widely, including a recent article in the *Electronic Journal of Foreign Language Teaching* (e-FLT) and her book *One Child and Two Languages: Acquisition of Japanese and English as bilingual first languages* (2013).

Wan-lun Lee is an assistant professor in the English Department at Fu Jen Catholic University, Taiwan. She holds two M.A. degrees—one in English Literature and the other in English Language Teaching—and a Ph.D in Applied Linguistics and ELT. Her research interests include using literature in ELT, computer-assistant language learning, and cross-cultural communication. She has published articles in journals such as *Languages and International Studies* and conference papers such as "Using literature as a rich source for listening and speaking activities", from the Proceedings of the 2007 Taiwan TESOL Conference. She is currently working on a research project about using technology-enhanced literature circles with EFL students.

Karen E. Lillie is an assistant professor of TESOL at the State University of New York at Fredonia, where she works with graduate students. She holds a Ph.D in Applied Linguistics. Her specialization is in language policy and forensic linguistics. Her research interests include language and the justice system, language rights for linguistic minorities, immigration, critical approaches to language policy, dropout rates and ELs' education, and language ideologies. Her publications include *Policy in Practice: The Implementation of Structured English Immersion in Arizona* (2010), through The Civil Rights Project at UCLA; *Separate and Not Equal: The Implementation of Structured English Immersion in Arizona's Classrooms* (Special Issue, 2012), published with *Teachers College Record*; and two chapters in the book *Language Policy Processes and Consequences: Arizona Case Studies*, via Multilingual Matters in 2014. She is on the Advisory Committee for the Language Policy Research Network (LPREN) and is Editorial Associate for the *Journal of Language, Identity, and Education*. Formerly she was the EL Coordinator for the school district where she taught ELs in 9th–12th grade in Arizona.

Rita MacDonald is an academic English language researcher at the WIDA Consortium, Wisconsin Center for Education Research, University of Wisconsin-Madison. Her research and publications include models of teacher collaboration, integrated content-language instruction, the implementation of systemic functional linguistics in K–12 content classrooms, and formative language assessment for English learners.

Ian G. Malcolm is emeritus professor, and former professor of applied linguistics at Edith Cowan University. He received his B.A. (Hons), Dip. Ed, and Ph.D from the University of Western Australia. His publications include *English and the Aboriginal Child* (co-author, 1982), *Linguistics in* *the Service of Society* (editor, 1991) and *The Habitat of Australia's Aboriginal Languages* (co-editor, 2007).

Sophie McIntosh is a Ph.D candidate at the School of Education, University of Wollongong. She has worked casually in various Early Childhood settings and received her Bachelor of Teaching (Hons) in 2008. Since graduating, she has predominantly undertaken research assistant work, particularly for projects related to Aboriginal and Torres Strait Islander children in Queensland who are learning English as an Additional Language or Dialect for the Far North Queensland Indigenous Schooling Support Unit, Education Queensland. Her publications include (with R. O'Hanlon and D. Angelo), "The (In)visibility of 'language' within Australian educational documentation: Differentiating language from literacy and exploring particular ramifications for a group of 'hidden' ESL/D Learners" in R. Baldauf, ed, *Future directions in applied linguistics: Local and global perspectives—35th Applied Linguistics Association Australia Congress* (2012).

Stephen Moore is a senior lecturer in the Linguistics Department at Macquarie University. He holds a Ph.D and researches and teaches discourse, language for specific purposes, and assessment. He has published academic papers in *Discourse & Society*, *Text & Talk*, *Critical Discourse Studies*, *English for Specific Purposes*, *World Englishes*, and *TESOL Quarterly*.

Simon Musgrave is a lecturer in the Linguistics Program at Monash University. He received his Ph.D from the University of Melbourne for work on the syntax of Indonesian, and he has co-edited a volume on the syntax of Austronesian languages. Other research interests include language endangerment, African languages in Australia, communication in medical encounters, and linguistics as part of digital humanities. Recent articles have appeared in the *International Journal of Bilingualism* and the *Australian Journal of Linguistics*.

Hiroyuki Nemoto is associate professor of sociolinguistics at Kanazawa University. He received his Ph.D from Monash University in 2006. His research interests lie in the area of sociolinguistics, including intercultural academic interactions at the individual and institutional levels, sociocultural approaches to SLA, language management, language planning, and ESL academic writing. He has written widely, including an article for the *Journal of Asian Pacific Communication*, and his book *The*

Management of Intercultural Academic Interaction: Student Exchanges between Japanese and Australian Universities (2011).

Molly Townes O'Brien is an Associate Professor at the College of Law, Australian National University, where she teaches Evidence, Litigation and Dispute Management and Human Rights in the Australian Context. Molly has served on the law faculties of Emory University, University of Akron and University of Wollongong. Before entering academia, she worked as a judicial clerk and as a public defender. She received her A.B. from Brown University (1982), J.D. from Northeastern University (1986), and LL.M. from Temple University (1997). Her recent publications include (with T. Connolly) "The Challenge of the How: Developing a Process for Legal Educational Program Renewal" in L. Wolff and M. Nicolae, eds, *The First–Year Experience in Law School* (2013), and articles in the *Connecticut Public Interest Law Journal* and the *Monash Law Review*.

Aek Phakiti is senior lecturer in TESOL at the University of Sydney. His research focuses on language testing and assessment and second language acquisition. He has published in *Language Learning, Language Testing* and *Language Assessment Quarterly*, and is an author of several books including *Experimental Research Methods in Language Learning* (2014).

Louisa Willoughby is a lecturer in the Linguistics Program at Monash University. She received her Ph.D from Monash University for work exploring language maintenance and shift among students at one multiethnic high school. Her current research continues to focus on language problems in multilingual societies, particularly in health and education settings. Much of her recent work has revolved around language issues affecting deaf Australians. Her publications include articles in the *Journal of Multilingual and Multicultural Development, Disability & Society, Sign Language Studies*, and *Current Issues in Language Planning*.

Hui Ling Xu is a senior lecturer of Chinese Studies within the Department of International Studies at Macquarie University. She holds a Ph.D and her broad research interests include descriptive linguistics, second language acquisition, teaching Chinese as a foreign language, Chinese heritage language education, and the use of innovative education technology.